Hub Perdue

ALSO BY JOHN A. SIMPSON

*"The Greatest Game Ever Played in Dixie":
The Nashville Vols, Their 1908 Season, and
the Championship Gam*e (McFarland, 2007)

Hub Perdue
Clown Prince of the Mound

JOHN A. SIMPSON

McFarland & Company, Inc., Publishers
Jefferson, North Carolina, and London

LIBRARY OF CONGRESS CATALOGUING-IN-PUBLICATION DATA

Simpson, John A., 1949–
    Hub Perdue, clown prince of the mound / John A. Simpson.
        p.   cm.
    Includes bibliographical references and index.

    ISBN 978-0-7864-7225-3
    softcover : acid free paper ∞

    1. Perdue, Hub, 1882–1968.   2. Baseball players—United States—Biography.   I. Title.
GV865.P465S56 2014
796.357092—dc23
[B]   2013029112

BRITISH LIBRARY CATALOGUING DATA ARE AVAILABLE

© 2014 John A. Simpson. All rights reserved

No part of this book may be reproduced or transmitted in any form or by any means, electronic or mechanical, including photocopying or recording, or by any information storage and retrieval system, without permission in writing from the publisher.

On the cover: Hub Perdue posing with a terrier puppy (Perdue family collection, Gallatin, Tennessee)

Manufactured in the United States of America

McFarland & Company, Inc., Publishers
* Box 611, Jefferson, North Carolina 28640*
*   www.mcfarlandpub.com*

In memory of
Roland L. "Larry" DeLorme
(1933–2010)

My undergraduate advisor, mentor, friend and inspiration

Table of Contents

Acknowledgments   ix
Preface: In Search of the Gallatin Squash   1

1. Down Home in Sumner County   5
2. Dawning of the Deadball Era — Tennessee Style   23
3. 1908   46
4. Breakout and Breakdown   66
5. Tennessee Brave   89
6. With the Cardinals   118
7. Interlude in Louisville   135
8. Second Tour in the Southern Association   146
9. The Mogul   169
10. Twilight on the Diamond   195
11. Citizen Hub   209
12. Clown Prince of the Mound   228

Chapter Notes   243
Bibliography   268
Index   273

Acknowledgments

The research material needed to write the biography of Hub Perdue involved extensive research trips to the South as well as long-distance exchanges with many local scholars and librarians throughout the country. I would like to take this opportunity to thank them.

The Society for American Baseball Research (SABR) is made up of dedicated men and women who volunteer their time and efforts to advance the study of baseball. Over the years, I have come into contact with many individuals who put their own research interests aside to run down items and scan microfilm for me. The Friends of Rickwood, a group of SABR members dedicated to the history of the Southern Association, has been invaluable to my own research. They include David Brewer, Skip Nipper and Clarence Watkins. I always look forward to our annual meeting in Birmingham. Steve Steinberg of Seattle has also been responsive to my queries about the Deadball Era, and his balanced thoughts are always welcome. And I have always valued the knowledge, copyediting skills and gentle critiques that Dan Ross, retired director of the University of Alabama Press, shared over the years. Finally, Rex Hamann of Andover, Minnesota, supplied valuable data on baseball in Minneapolis.

A host of librarians deserve special recognition too. The Tennessee State Library and Archive has been my summer home since 1984, and over the ensuing years I have met, and worked with, some outstanding people. Marylin B. Hughes, recently retired, has been indispensable in keeping me informed about happenings at the TSLA, and was ever-helpful in getting me connected with the right people whenever I had a specific research question. Of course, it never hurts to have a baseball enthusiast on staff, and Susan Gordon fit that role perfectly. I don't know what I would have done all of these years without the assistance of Karina McDaniel in Photographic Services. The photographs that appear in this volume from the TSLA are her work. Finally, I would like to thank Charles Sherrill, Tennessee State Librarian and Archivist. Chuck and

I go back a long way, and I am indebted to him for approving the loan of several important reels of microfilm. Another librarian, Beth Odle of the Nashville Public Library's Nashville Room was always ready with answers to my fine-printed questions about the city's history.

A number of librarians outside of Nashville were also helpful. Trying to obtain microfilm as an independent scholar has become quite a chore these days, and I would like to thank the following four individuals for making the experience less excruciating: Betty Malone, Inter-Library Loan Department, State Historical Society of Missouri, Columbia, Missouri; Dena Hutto, Director of Reference Library and Instruction, Reed College, Portland, Oregon; Katie Sloan, Inter-Library Loan Department, Knight Library, University of Oregon, Eugene, Oregon; and Leslie Christensen, Inter-Library Loan Department, Washington State Library, Olympia, Washington.

Occasionally, I needed materials from far-off places, and many librarians stepped up to the plate to offer assistance. These include Brian Spangle, Historical Collection Administrator, McGrady-Brockman House, Knox County Public Library, Vincennes, Indiana; and Sheila Bumgarner, Charlotte Public Library, Charlotte, NC. Independent researchers also provided coverage of smaller newspapers that were important to my biography of Perdue. These scholars include Adam Pratt, graduate student in the Department of History, LSU, Baton Rouge, Louisiana; and Amanda Rindler, Vincennes University Library, Vincennes, Indiana. One search by an unknown individual was conducted at the New York Public Library.

I would like to thank the following people for their support either during visits or through email requests: Richard King, Reference Librarian, Byron R. Lewis Historical Library, Vincennes University Library, Vincennes, Indiana; Jill Larson, Archivist, Byron R. Lewis Historical Library, Vincennes University Library, Vincennes, Indiana; Allen Haynes, Sumner County Historical Museum, Gallatin, Tennessee; the staff at the Sumner County Archives, Gallatin, Tennessee; and Gaines Foster, T. Harry Williams Professor of History and Dean of the College of Humanities and Social Sciences, LSU, Baton Rouge, Louisiana. Gaines and I first became acquainted as graduate students in 1982 over our mutual interest in the Lost Cause in Southern history, and he sent me in the right direction to find a local researcher on Louisiana baseball.

Photographic services were graciously supplied by the Library of Congress, the Chicago Museum of History, Tennessee State Library and Archive, and Jimmy Perdue Family Collection, Gallatin, Tennessee.

No acknowledgment would be complete without mention of Jimmy Perdue, the grandson of Hub. We first met two years ago, and Jimmy and his wife JoAnn graciously invited me to visit them on multiple occasions. In the process, I gained valuable insights into Perdue family history, examined a scrapbook file of newspaper clippings about Hub, and shared wonderful pictures, some of which are quite rare. They allowed me to work on Hub's original travel trunk from his days in baseball — a beautiful antique wooden piece, and an honor for me. Their generosity is quite extraordinary and they have demonstrated through their actions that Southern hospitality still exists. Getting to know the Perdue family and Wiseman family (from my previous book on the 1908 Nashville Vols) has been a true blessing to me. I appreciate these families, one and all. Finally, I deeply appreciate the generosity of Walter T. Durham, State Historian for Tennessee, for granting me an extended interview. A lifelong resident of Gallatin, Tennessee, Mr. Durham provided invaluable insights into local history.

The map of Sumner County was drawn by Andrew Green, one of my former 9th grade U.S. History students. Andrew graduated high school in June 2012, and his story (along with his twin brother, Brandon) is a blessing onto itself. Born with a medical condition which caused seizures and an intellectual disability, the twins were significantly challenged in reading and writing, and early on they were not even expected to survive into adolescence. But they beat the odds and Andrew went on to master the Computer-Aided Design (CAD) class in his senior year. The result of his learning is evident in the map he prepared for chapter 11.

Finally, I would like to pay tribute to R. L. "Larry" DeLorme, my undergraduate advisor at Western Washington State College, Bellingham, Washington. Professor DeLorme was more than an advisor to me. He was a friend and mentor who encouraged me to pursue an academic career in the field of History. The last time I spoke with him was in the mid–1970s, and he died in 2010. I never had the opportunity to tell him directly what an inspiration he has been in my life, but I want to rectify that situation now. Dr. DeLorme, you were instrumental in my lifelong commitment to the historical profession.

Finally I would like to thank a great copy editor — Shirley Simpson, my wife. She went above and beyond the call of duty.

John A. Simpson, Ph.D
Kelso, Washington

Preface: In Search of the Gallatin Squash

This is not a biography of a Deadball Era superstar. Hub Perdue never shared the spotlight with National League icons like Christy Mathewson, Rube Marquard, or Grover Cleveland Alexander. He was not even on an equal footing with the likes of Slim Sallee, Jeff Tesreau, Bill James or Red Ames, although he battled each of these pitchers (and many others) on multiple occasions. Instead, Hub was a mischievous Southerner with a quick wit and a stubborn and rebellious streak that led to conflicts with management and umpires alike, but his blazing fastball, biting curveball and deceptive spitball caught the attention of Frank Chance, John McGraw and Miller Huggins. And later, the Gallatin Squash established a stunning minor league record that still stands.

Although Hub Perdue was a marginal major leaguer, there is substantial rationale for a book about him. First, there simply aren't many biographies about Southern baseball players in the Deadball Era. Second, while this "son of Sumner County" made it to the Big Show with the Boston Braves and St. Louis Cardinals, he spent almost three-quarters of his career in five minor leagues scattered across the South, and there is a dearth of published material about the Southern minor leagues in the Deadball Era. Third, Hub's amateur experience (1900–1904) and professional experience (1905–1923) span the Deadball Era. (Imagine the changes he witnessed in the game!) Fourth, Hub's career touched the lives of many baseball greats besides the players listed above — men like Cy Young, Johnny Evers, Rabbit Maranville, Honus Wagner, Rogers Hornsby, Dode Paskert, Jake Daubert, Casey Stengel, Zack Wheat, Joe Jackson and Tris Speaker. He also faced the greatest all-around athlete of his era, Jim Thorpe. Fifth, his connection with the players' union places him in a unique crowd of player-activists. He was a consummate student of player contracts and negotiations.

Hub's exceptional sense of humor and his skill as raconteur are reasons enough to find him fascinating and the reader will encounter examples of what can only be called "Hublore" throughout this book.

Steeped in oral tradition, retold and embellished by Perdue as well as newspapermen, friends and acquaintances, these tales focus on Perdue's clownish antics. In his seminal biography of Vince Lombardi, David Maraniss posits: "Myth becomes myth not in the living but in the re-telling."[1] While the annals of Hublore are based in truth they usually lack accuracy regarding time and place. There are approximately one dozen Hublore stories; each one is highly entertaining but awfully challenging to confirm or debunk. Today, Hub's image is etched in half-truths and semi-factual written accounts. He is remembered as one of a small handful of notable tricksters and clowns from the era, along with Nick Altrock, Germany Schaefer, Rabbit Maranville and Steve Evans. According to the great Honus Wagner, these pranksters were invaluable to the game.

My early interest in Perdue stemmed from research for my book "*The Greatest Game Ever Played in Dixie*," about the 1908 Nashville Vols and their championship season in the Southern Association. It is an exciting minor league campaign which appeals to fans and scholars alike. As the number two starter in that team's pitching rotation, Perdue emerged as a star with a promising future in organized baseball. His humorous antics and workhorse reputation captured my imagination, and I wanted to learn more about this Tennessean with the golden arm and silver tongue. Perdue's biography is bittersweet — a life story that fits into the sports genre of "might-have-beens."

Chapter 1 sets the stage with background information about Hub's family and its connection with early Sumner County history. It also explores the beginning of the Deadball Era in a rural community as well as a large metropolitan neighbor. Chapter 2 describes Hub's first two years in professional baseball with Vincennes, and uncovers a "lost season." Chapter 3 summarizes the 1908 championship run in Nashville and Hub's contributions to that storied campaign. Chapter 4 chronicles Hub's breakout season when he should have been drafted, and a follow-up year where he was plagued by injuries and further disappointment. Chapter 5 sketches Hub's years in the National League with Boston, and Chapter 6 wraps up his big league experience with St. Louis. Chapter 7 offers an interlude between the majors and minors when Hub signed with Louisville. One of the most laughable episodes in Hublore occurred here. Chapter 8 describes his second tour in the Southern Association, where he set some amazing league records. Chapter 9 analyzes his brief and disastrous stint as manager of Nashville. Hub returned to the playing field in Texas and North Carolina for a final fling in Chapter 10. In retirement, Hub came back to Sumner County where he became a public servant. Chapter

11 also outlines Hub's reconnection with local baseball. In the conclusion, there is an analysis of Hub's career as well as examples of lingering memories about Hub in the public's consciousness.

A brief comment to the reader. I have made several stylistic decisions to enhance readability and avoid redundancies. First, I sometimes utilize league abbreviations to avoid repetitious use of formal titles. Thus, National League (NL), American League (AL), Southern Association (SA), Texas League (TL), South Atlantic League (SALLY) and Kentucky-Illinois-Tennessee League (KITTY) appear in both their full and shortened forms. Second, regarding the use of statistics, I rely on baseball-reference.com and Retrosheet.org for my season summaries. While these sources are riddled with mistakes made by minor league scorekeepers who employed a wide set of guidelines regarding pitcher-of-record, they are the best we have. This biography will not re-write history despite the fact that minor league record keeping was inconsistent at its best and disgraceful at its worst. The official record is simply what it is — the official record.

So, if you are interested in one strong-armed, fast-talking Southerner's sojourn through every level of baseball afforded to him at the time — from the amateur "cow pasture games" of Middle Tennessee to the National League — then the life story of Hub Perdue is for you. It is a narrative about one man's dream to pitch in the majors — and despite his perseverance the dream ultimately died hard. Stories about more successful athletes of his time do not scratch the surface of our understanding about the trials and tribulations faced by bush leaguers in order to compete in the game they loved. Sometimes ordinary people are capable of amazing feats, and such was the case with Hub Perdue, the Gallatin Squash.

"The legacy of minor league baseball in Dixie is a rich one — full of stories of fine players and teams."

Marshall D. Wright
Author of *The Southern Association in Baseball*

Chapter 1

Down Home in Sumner County

Although he answered to a variety of nicknames — Rub-Dub-Hub, Hurling Hub, the Gallatin Squash, the Tennessee Cyclone, or the Untamed Son of Sumner County — his family, friends and baseball fans simply called him Hub. Herbert Rodney Perdue was one of the most personable and exciting pitching prospects to emerge from the hills of Middle Tennessee in the first two decades of the twentieth century. Perdue exhibited a light-hearted personality but contemporaries often criticized his jocular behavior on the diamond. Yet his two years in college baseball (1900–1901), three years on an organized town team (1903–1904) and nineteen seasons at the professional level (1905–1923) spanned the entire Deadball Era. His life story offers an entertaining glimpse into the shenanigans of a rural Southerner who made it to the Big Show and returned to his native region where he established some amazing minor league records.[1]

The Middle Tennessee community Hub would call home is rich in natural and human history. Regarding the region's physical environment, one observer described it as "one of the most beautiful and picturesque places in the State."[2] The topography is punctuated by rolling hills and valleys, thickly timbered ridges, numerous creeks and caves, several sulphur springs, and open fields where wild bluegrass grows knee-deep. The backbone of what would become Sumner County is known locally as "the ridge." The escarpment runs in an east-west direction and bisects the region almost perfectly into northern and southern halves. Above this natural divide lies the Highland Rim and an extensive grassland known as "the barrens." Below the prominent feature lies the rolling Cumberland River Basin where the soil is "exceedingly fertile." Finally, the Cumberland Mountains frame the area to the east. This lush setting produced an abundance of game animals — deer, elk, and buffalo. More dangerous predators such as bears, wolves and cougars also shared the landscape. The natural habitat and plush hunting ground attracted indigenous peoples — the Shawnees, Cherokees, Creeks and Chickasaws — who each laid claim to the area at different times.[3]

The first white men ventured into the region from North Carolina in the mid–1760s, following an old Indian trace. These first visitors found buffalo herds in staggering numbers, a discovery that encouraged their exploitation by the first "Long Hunters." The most famous early inhabitant, Thomas "Big Foot" Spencer, reportedly lived one winter in the hollow of a rotting sycamore tree near a spring and salt lick. Much oral tradition surrounds the exploits of this 400-lb. giant at Bledsoe's Lick. His domicile attracted the first permanent white settler-farmers, and it later became the community of Castalian Springs. The bountiful environment that Spencer inhabited stimulated what Tennessee State Historian Walter T. Durham calls "the great leap westward."[4]

A flood of settlers began to arrive in Middle Tennessee following the Revolutionary War owing to government land grants awarded to veterans for their military service. Soon, violence erupted on the frontier between these farmers and natives incensed by this invasion of their hunting grounds. Stemming from a need for protection from the warring Indians, the Cumberland Association was formed in Nashville, and shortly thereafter the General Assembly of North Carolina created Sumner County on November 17, 1786. Named in honor of Major General Jethro Sumner, a veteran of the French and Indian War and American Revolution, the county comprised 16 civil districts. Four years later, Sumner County joined Tennessee to become a federal territory, and statehood followed in 1796. Sumner's population steadily increased and the original county lines were redrawn to form Macon, Smith, Wilson, and Trousdale counties. The county has retained its current 625 square mile shape since 1870.[5]

Once peace had been restored on the Tennessee frontier following the Nickajack War, Sumner County as well as the rest of the new state of Tennessee experienced a significant population boom. Three locales in particular, Cairo (1799), Gallatin (1802) and Hartsville (1817), grew into prominent centers of commerce for Sumnerians, and they remained at the core of county politics and business well after the Civil War. The county seat, Gallatin, was named for former western Pennsylvanian congressman and current Secretary of the Treasury in President Jefferson's administration, Albert Gallatin. The town's plots attracted immediate buyers.[6]

Public records indicate that the first Perdues arrived in Sumner County from Franklin County, Virginia, shortly after the War of 1812. Five brothers and veterans of the Virginia state militia — Daniel, Matthew, Luke, Eli and Asa — settled with their families in the 13th and 16th Civil Districts at the point where "the ridge" met the Cumberland River Basin. There, the extended family began the laborious task of clearing the virgin forest and establishing farms.

Hub's great grandfather, Daniel, filed a claim on August 12, 1815, and purchased 174 acres of land on the east side of the west fork of Drake's Creek. Within a short period of time his holdings grew to over 1,500 acres, and the family prospered.[7] He built one of the first distilleries and grist mills in the district and owned 70 slaves who toiled on his expansive estate. So many Perdues lived in this northern district that, by the 1830s, the present community of Sengtown was originally known as Perdue. Daniel Perdue produced 17 children through two marriages, and today there are multiple cemeteries across northern Sumner County containing the five Perdue brothers' progeny—including exclusive family sections at Boiling Springs, Leath Road, Old Brush (Portland), and Lower Bethpage as well as individual plots in Old City Cemetery and Crestview in Gallatin.[8]

One of Daniel's youngest children, Daniel Green Perdue, inherited 110 acres from his deceased father's considerable estate in 1843. The land was located in the 13th Civil District of Sumner County, east of the rural Fountain Head post office and three miles south of Portland, Tennessee. Known to the family as "Green," the young Perdue also succeeded as a yeoman planter in the antebellum years.

Prior to the outbreak of the Civil War, Green owned almost 350 acres of land with a cash value equaling the state average, while livestock, grain and tobacco production far exceeded the state averages. At this time, over 8,000 bondsmen were bound to Sumner County soil and although Green owned only four slaves (two adults) his future prosperity was directly tied to the continuation of the peculiar institution.[9] As the slave culture in Tennessee expanded in the pre–Civil War years owing to the corresponding importance of labor intensive cash crops like cotton and tobacco, several noteworthy plantations were erected in Sumner County, like Cragfont, Rose Mont and Pilot Knob.[10]

As Green's farm continued its transformation from subsistence to commercial agriculture, the overall economy of Sumner County was greatly aided by a revolution in transportation, mainly through the construction of railroad lines, steamboat landings, and laying of McAdamized turnpikes and lesser roadways. This transportation transformation began in 1853 with the completion of the Gallatin Pike a major arterial connecting Gallatin with Nashville to the southwest and Scottsville, Kentucky, to the northeast. Known as the Scottsville Pike (Highway 31E today), the highway ran through several smaller hamlets dotting the Middle Tennessee countryside whose inhabitants benefitted economically from easier access to markets. Tiny communities like Bethpage were doubly impacted by the construction of a series of rail lines like the *Louisville and Nashville* (L & N) which crisscrossed the county beginning in 1858.[11] A wide assortment of dirt roads also spider-webbed across the area, adding to the inter-connectedness of even the most remote communities.

Bethpage, in particular, was destined to play a major role in the life of Hub Perdue, and the tiny community benefitted from its location 14 miles northeast of Gallatin on the Scottsville Pike. Several small cottage industries flourished there beginning in the 1850s. The specific nature of these businesses reflected the strengths of the local economy — a tannery which produced saddles, harnesses, and shoes, two small water-powered grist mills, a horse-driven cider mill, a casket maker, and a furniture and cabinetry shop run by Isaac Ashlock, the local Methodist minister. Several large storage sheds dotted the landscape in the Brushy Fork and Bledsoe Creek neighborhoods. Livestock, wood products, corn and tobacco production dominated the economic life of the community. Thoroughbred horse breeding also played a role in local economics.[12]

Into this swirling cauldron of unbridled economic growth was born Marion Blair Perdue on September 12, 1846, one of nine children of Green and Matilda Mattox Perdue. Named in honor of the famed "Swamp Fox" of Revolutionary War fame, General Francis Marion, young Perdue was fortunate to survive the devastating cholera epidemics in 1849 and 1852 which had killed an estimated 10 percent of the county's population. Marion was also favored with an education at Liberty Academy in Cross Plains, approximately 12 miles distant in what is now Robertson County.[13] As a young man, he taught school for seven winters while living on his father's farm. He did not volunteer to serve in the 30th infantry regiment of the Confederate army like other Perdues in northern Sumner County despite turning 18 in the autumn of 1864. But there is no evidence that the family espoused particularly strong unionist sentiments either, although Sumner County had been generally lukewarm toward secession prior to the first wave of rabid volunteerism following President Lincoln's call for 75,000 troops to squelch the rebellion.

Although Hub could not boast about direct family involvement in the Civil War, he was a vocal southern patriot and referenced pride in his Confederate heritage on several occasions later in his life on the diamond and in the political arena. Indeed, wartime activities from 1861–1865 abounded in his Bethpage neighborhood as did stories about rebel exploits. The war had gone poorly for southern forces in the greater Gallatin area, too. Other than the exciting five-hour cavalry clash which featured John Hunt Morgan's raiders, the Federal army occupied Sumner County beginning in February 1862, with only one brief respite until the end of hostilities three years later. An active guerrilla movement flourished in what amounted to Hub's backyard.[14]

Hub later assimilated his neighbor's "secesh" tendencies and belligerence toward Yankee occupation. When a local farmer and pro–Union sympathizer offered his Bethpage property for a Federal encampment, Clinton McAdam incited a number of his neighbors living along Brushy Fork Creek who led several night raids against the blue-bellies. William Keys and Bob Spradlin went so far as to counter-offer their property as a safe haven for Confederate sympathizers. Throughout the county, Southern bushwackers and foraging Yankees angered and frustrated the citizenry on both sides of the life-and-death dispute. Federal patrols were routinely authorized by General Eleaser A. Paine and set out from Gallatin to scour the Bethpage area for rebels. Paine earned an unsavory reputation for ruthless deals with the guerrillas, often executing prisoners on sight without the benefit of a trial. An uneasy and distrusting relationship resulted between county residents and the occupying forces. These memories of wartime atrocities and hardship carried into the Reconstruction era, and they painted vivid images of suffering for children like Hub. Indeed, these were important lessons that reinforced his white Southernness.[15]

On October 26, 1871, Marion married Zoritha E. Durham (b. May 13, 1843), the daughter of Rodney B. and Polly Durham. Together, they had a child — Cotton ("Cot") Warren (b. October 23, 1872). Then, six years later, Marion sold 200 acres of land he had received from his father and purchased 100 acres in the 10th Civil District near the hamlet of Bethpage to be closer to his wife's family.[16] As Marion and Zoritha's fortunes increased, they added four more children to the brood — Daisy Ashley (b. October 30, 1877), Erma Queen (b. May 19, 1880), Herbert Rodney (b. June 7, 1882), and Virgil Blair (b. November 23, 1885).

Marion made an instant impression in Bethpage where he forged a reputation as a successful livestock dealer and farmer. Shortly, the Perdues' holdings increased four-fold. He was a staunch Democrat, belonged to the Bethpage Masonic Lodge # 321, and faithfully served the Mt. Zion Methodist Church (Bethpage) throughout his life as a steward and Sunday school teacher. The church, originally located adjacent to the Lower Bethpage Cemetery, traced its origins to 1818 and claimed to be one of the earliest Methodist meetinghouses in the Bledsoe Creek valley. A further testament to Marion's prominence in local community affairs was the inclusion of his biography in *Goodspeed's History of Sumner County* published in 1887.[17]

As the Perdues of Bethpage thrived, so did the economy of Sumner County. Much of their combined success owed to the postwar continuation of railroad construction in Middle Tennessee. First, the *Cumberland and Ohio* and then the *Tennessee Central* traversed the county in the 1870s. But one line would have a decided impact on baseballer Hub Perdue — the *Chesapeake and*

Nashville road paralleled the Scottsville Pike and laid its tracks between Gallatin and Scottsville and opened a station in Bethpage in 1886. Eventually, by the time Hub began his second baseball tour in Nashville, the Interurban trolley known as "The Blue Grass Line" provided convenient and quick access from Gallatin to Rock City beginning in 1913 a trip taking less than an hour.[18]

Not much is known about the childhood of Marion's middle son — the one that family members nicknamed Hub. Undoubtedly, he helped with chores on his father's prosperous spread, and the rural lifestyle must have been to his liking because Hub resided in Bethpage/Gallatin for the rest of his life. As an adolescent, he created his own income by hunting squirrels and selling them to a local market for a dime apiece. Not owning a rifle, Hub killed his prey with a most unorthodox weapon — rocks. He later quipped that throwing rocks at these small and fast-moving targets strengthened his arm, eyesight and throwing technique. Hub normally bagged only a couple of squirrels at a time, but once he delivered nine carcasses to a surprised merchant. The clerk asked, "Was it difficult?" likely referring to the large number of dead critters. Hub responded by pointing to one of them and replied, "Yes, it was. I had to throw twice at this little one."[19] The witty storytelling skills of Hub Perdue had begun at an early age. Thus was born the first Hublore tale. Owing to the source of the story — oral tradition — it is impossible to refute.

Gallatin, the nearby community that Hub knew as a young man, was beginning to modernize. By 1900 the city was in the throes of technological advancement — electrification, telephone service, underground water mains appeared, and soon the Electric Theatre opened on the town square. Stately Victorian mansions like Guildwood dotted the community's growing urban landscape, and the Gallatin Hotel featured the most "genteel accommodations" in town. The Commercial Club, modeled after the Nashville social and business association, attracted many aspiring middle class entrepreneurs. Perhaps most appealing to Hub was the Gallatin Athletic Club, which opened in 1905. Gallatin, like the rest of Middle Tennessee, was entering the modern age.[20]

Hub likely attended Central High School in Gallatin in the late 1890s where he was introduced to organized baseball. Unfortunately, neither high school records nor local newspaper accounts survived to offer specifics on his athletic experiences as a schoolboy, but he was already a well known, albeit raw, talent and he fit right in when town baseball took off in 1901.

A fortuitous opportunity presented itself to Hub immediately after high school graduation when several Bethpage residents led by J. B. Hanna, W. F. Moss, Joe Harrell, M. M. Cockreham and E. A. Woodson founded Tullatuckee Normal College. Designed to train prospective teachers, the institution also boasted a baseball team. Hub might not have been interested in higher education or a teaching career, but he was intrigued by the prospect of competing at a higher level of baseball against lofty in-state powerhouses such as Vanderbilt (led by a shortstop from Murfreesboro, Grantland Rice), and the University of the South, or Sewanee. Hub enrolled at Bowling Green Business University (later Western Kentucky University), where he pitched on the baseball team for two seasons.[21]

On December 29, 1900, only six months after his high school graduation, Hub married Mable Polk of Oaktown, Indiana.[22] It is possible the newlyweds first met when Hub was tending to his fledgling college baseball career. Mable was one of seven children born to Horace Shepherd Polk and Martha Polk. The Polk family had moved to the Hoosier State from Kentucky where Horace was born on May 20, 1843. His family was directly related to James K. Polk, the 11th president of the United States. During the Civil War, Horace mustered into the 51st Indiana (Co. H) in August 1862, and his unit saw considerable action during all of the major engagements of the Army of the Ohio. He mustered out in June 1865, and returned to buy a farm in Widner Township, east of Oaktown a few miles south of the western-most Shaker community in the United States.[23]

So the Southern-bred Hub married a Yankee! The 18-year-old couple lived temporarily in Marion Perdue's farmhouse but later moved into another dwelling down the road. Hub and Mable remained a couple for the rest of their lives — almost 60 years.[24] Like his father, Hub signed legal documents such as his marriage license and other contracts with his initials, "H. R.," a common practice of the time.

Hub continued to hone his hard-throwing pitching skills in local "cow pasture games."[25] In late nineteenth century Middle Tennessee, small communities like Gallatin ached for amateur recreational opportunities, and town-versus-town baseball contests met this need. It was not uncommon to find a game on any given Saturday afternoon throughout the region. Final scores were outrageously high, but so was the level of entertainment. Hub's stature as a budding star with a blazing "smoke ball" earned him considerable notoriety. Once, in a weekend game in neighboring South Tunnel, one of Hub's pitches shattered the only bat. The game was subsequently called off. On another occasion, Hub was caught in a rundown between first and second base. Seeing his predicament as futile, he broke for the pitcher's box and slid safely onto the rubber. Tickled by Hub's creativity, the umpire awarded him second base.[26] A second installment of Hublore, and equally as difficult to disprove as the first installment, was born.

Urban Middle Tennesseans, like their rural counterparts, were starving for organized baseball. Indeed, Nashvillians underwent a groundswell of interest in baseball beyond the sandlot variety — the city equivalent of "cow pasture games." Since there had been an absence of a professional team in Rock City for several years, young boys had filled the void with homegrown talent on several different tiers of play — from street and neighborhood teams to small company and large factory teams to amateur leagues which included high school and weaker college talent, and top-flight traveling squads such as the Browns. The latter blended outstanding college talent and former professional players from the defunct Southern League, a diverse blend of talent and experience.

Neighborhood teams and company squads also proliferated in Nashville in 1900. An amateur league cranked up for action in early June with games played at fields in Shelby Bottom, the Normal School (Peabody), Glendale Park, Vanderbilt, University and Athletic Park. Some of the company teams included L & N Railroad, East Nashville Hatchers, Overton and Bush, Tennessee Carriage Company, Cumberland Telephone, Berg and Ellis, Brandon Printers, Methodist Publishing House, Lebeck's, Herman Brothers, Black & Sons, and Public Square. Block and street teams also flourished with access to the best baseball diamonds on Summer Street, Fatherland Street, Waverly Place, Edgefield, West End (Murray's), McLemore Street, Market Street, and Cherry Street. By the end of the summer of 1900, the prestigious Nashville Athletic Club (NAC) vowed to sponsor an independent nine the following season. It is an understatement that the existence of so many teams fostered a genuine egalitarian spirit in the downtown community.[27]

It is fascinating that almost every ability level received equal access to the best facility the city had to offer — Athletic Park. With such an explosion of interest, a group of investors stepped forward in July 1900, to underwrite the cost of extensive renovations to the aging stadium which included improvements to the playing surface and erection of a new grandstand. Expansion and improvements in the city's trolley grid brought the stadium within easy reach of most citizens. Everyone expected a full slate of games at Athletic Park for the remainder of the summer.[28]

In an era before sports journalism or a formal sports section overseen by a sports editor, local athletic stories were sprinkled indiscriminately throughout Nashville's broadsheets — the *American*, *Banner*, and later the *Tennessean*. Still, the *American* led the other dailies in its coverage of local baseball in the early years since its city manager pledged to report all contests "in Nashville or in neighboring towns and villages."[29]

The most popular amateur teams routinely attracted large crowds and illustrated Nashville's thirst for good baseball. A sensational Vanderbilt shortstop, Grantland Rice, played for the Browns. Born in Murfreesboro on 1 November, 1880, Rice and his family relocated to Nashville where Rice attended Tarbox School and, later, Wallace School, an exclusive academy that prepared pupils for entrance into Vanderbilt. Rice spent his youth playing sandlot baseball and football, and when he entered the university, the lanky lad played four years as a tight end on the football team and shortstop on the baseball team. His skills on the diamond attracted a great deal of local recognition as well as his elevation to the captaincy of the Vanderbilt nine.

Colored teams were also permitted to utilize the facility, and not just against other African American teams. In July, African American squads from Nashville, Louisville and Atlanta played in a widely publicized round robin tournament in Athletic Park.[30] They also took on a barnstorming "white" team from Terre Haute, a rare occurrence of inter-racial competition on a Southern baseball field. Not only were Negro athletes permitted to use the best baseball diamond in the city, they also competed against Caucasian squads long before integration and the civil rights movement.[31]

The formation of one amateur nine — Cheek-Neal — serves as an example of the strong bond between entrepreneurial "new men" in Nashville and their sponsorship of amateur baseball. Indeed, one of the early corporate success stories in Nashville belonged to Joel O. Cheek, who, along with cousin Christopher T. Cheek, founded the Nashville Coffee Company in 1892. Their innovation — to roast, grind and market the finished product in tin cans — was a huge success. The Cheeks labeled their blend "Maxwell House" after the elegant Nashville hotel which had agreed to feature their hot beverage in its elegant dining room. In 1904, Cheek entered into partnership with James W. Neal and the company expanded rapidly to establish roasting plants in six cities, including Chicago and Los Angeles. Of course, it did not hurt their national sales campaign when President Theodore Roosevelt allegedly commented on the aromatic blend on a visit to The Hermitage (Andrew Jackson's mansion outside Nashville).[32] "Good to the last drop," proclaimed the 26th president; thus a slogan was born and later printed on each tin. The homegrown corporation demonstrated its civic pride when it elected to finance an amateur baseball team, one that quickly developed into a Nashville powerhouse.

The baseball success of teams like Cheek-Neal, NAC and the Browns inspired Hub to consider opportunities beyond "cow pasture games." Town baseball was raging throughout Middle Tennessee, including Gallatin, and it piqued Hub's interest. Teams formed in smaller locales like Bethany, Brownsville, McEwan, Spring Hill, Martin, Greenfield, Trenton, Monteagle, Tiptonville, Bell Buckle, Bridgeport, Leeville, Gladeville, Covington, McKenzie, Sparta, Camden, Springfield, Winchester, Tullahoma, Union City, and Brentwood, as well as larger communities like Gallatin, Lebanon, Clarksville, Jackson, McMinnville and Carthage.

Formal organization of town baseball in Gallatin actually began while Hub was still in Bowling Green, and his involvement likely began as a purely recreational pursuit. Yet, at age 20, he aspired to use his natural but undeveloped talent of throwing a baseball to secure a professional contract to supplement his income, especially after the birth of his son (Polk) and daughter (Kathryn) in 1902 and 1909 respectively. But few athletes made the quantum leap from "cow pasture games" to the ranks of pro baseball in a single move. Hub's raw skills required further development in order to demonstrate to baseball authorities that he was truly worthy of "fast company."

In the summer of 1901, P. L. Anderson recruited an amateur roster in Gallatin and advertised that his nines would take on any opponent in the greater Middle Tennessee region. The manager loaned his nickname, "Butch," to the new team. The Butchers scheduled one weekend game per week and played home games at the old fairgrounds near the C & N rail line. Several road contests were added to the slate in the inaugural season which ran from late May to mid–September.[33]

The first recorded game of the Gallatin Butchers resulted in a 5–4 defeat in nearby Lebanon.[34] Shortly thereafter, the *Gallatin Examiner* commented on the importance of the baseball team to the local community in a front page article.

> For some years the American people have gone base ball wild and this season is no exception — in fact, greater interest is now being taken all over the country in the national game than ever before in the history of this great outdoor sport. Not only is the attention of the public directed to the professional teams, but a real enthusiasm is manifested in all amateur games throughout the United States.

"Gallatin," concluded the *Examiner*, "has been no exception."[35] Public funding for the local nine proved inventive; the revenue from annual appearances of traveling circuses generated some cash, while the proceeds from W. W. Fidler's Mastodon Fusee Minstrels was similarly earmarked exclusively for the Butchers.[36]

It is unknown whether Anderson or Player-manager Willy Guild approached Hub (or vice versa) but a dialog was opened about the possibility of him pitching for the Butchers in the summer of 1902. Guild, a lad with deep family roots in the local community, had played infield for four years at Princeton and captained Vanderbilt for a fifth (apparently there were no collegiate eligibility restrictions in the late 1890s). Guild would affiliate with the hometown team for a decade and moonlight as coach of the Commodores while completing a law degree at Vanderbilt.[37] Guild was attracted to the hurler with undisciplined habits who had already earned a reputation around Gallatin for throwing a baseball with unbridled velocity — Hub Perdue.

In Hub's freshman season, the Butchers met with limited success against their opponents from Springfield, Carthage, Lebanon and Nashville. The

Nashville Tigers, Browns, and Haurys (sponsored by saloonkeeper Chris Haury) dominated Gallatin, and the Lebanon roster earned a solid reputation as "a crack team."[38] The first account of Hub in uniform for the Butchers appeared on August 13, 1902, when he was pummeled by Lebanon in the first game of a doubleheader, 13–1. The *Examiner* criticized Gallatin's weak effort "due entirely to the want of practice."[39] It is probable that Hub had been with the team since the start of the season, but local newspaper coverage of baseball was limited to a few line scores. In fact, the box score did not appear in a Gallatin newspaper until mid–September.[40]

The drubbings the Butchers received in 1902 paid dividends a year later when Perdue's club experienced considerable success. Civic pride had embraced the team's needs and one fund raiser netted sufficient monies to purchase "new suits" to begin the campaign.[41] In late June, 25 faithful fans traveled by rail with the Butchers to Franklin, Kentucky, to root on the locals. At home, it was not uncommon for the Butchers to host a weekend crowd of 500 people at the Fairgrounds.[42] Most important, they repeatedly handled their leading rival and former nemesis, Lebanon, to the absolute glee of Gallatin boosters. In a doubleheader sweep on August 28, both Gallatin and Lebanon fielded completely different lineups for both games, which illustrated the egalitarian nature of town baseball at the turn of the century as well as the popularity and desire of young men to seek membership in the town's club. By late summer, Gallatin was challenging the strongest nine in the region, Nashville's Cumberland Telephone.[43] And Hub was attracting attention down in Rock City as a hard-throwing twirler who could singlehandedly dominate a game when in control of his pitches. Indeed, Newt Fisher announced that his professionals would take on the Butchers in Gallatin after the season. By the following summer, Anderson and Guild had built the Butchers into a regional powerhouse which boasted three pitchers with legitimate professional aspirations — Hub Perdue, Bill Chenault and southpaw Willie Frakes.

As Hub was honing his skills with the Butchers and emerging from the shadows of amateur baseball, there were larger forces simultaneously pushing for the reintroduction of professional baseball in the South. A brief background on the formation of this new Southern Association is necessary in order to appreciate Hub's later nine-year stint in that circuit more fully. Moreover, specific details surrounding the creation of the SA are scattered and have never been fully documented in one place. The new league's organization, with a franchise located so near to Sumner County, kindled the ambitions in many local athletes like Hub, Bill and Willie who dreamed of pursuing a career in professional baseball.

Sources consistently recognize the role of three former player-managers from the defunct Southern League for spearheading the concept of a new baseball conference — Abner Powell of New Orleans, Newt Fisher of Nashville, and Charlie Frank of Memphis.[44] In actuality, the notion of forming a new Southern conference had begun as a series of discussions between two unrelated groups. On June 10, 1900, the *American* reported an upcoming meeting to be held in Louisville orchestrated by M. J. Russell, "a railroad man," and other interested individuals hoping to resurrect the old circuit and begin play on July 1. The article revealed that discussions had been under way "for some time" between several unidentified parties, but it is unknown whether the Powell-Fisher-Frank triumvirate were involved.[45] The Louisville meeting never materialized anyway.

In the meantime, local interest bloomed in Nashville.[46] Haury, the amateur baseball sponsor whose saloon was located across the street from Athletic Park, announced the creation of the Nashville Base Ball Club. Harry was considered "one of the pioneers in local [Nashville] base ball history," and the *American* noted that the beer magnate fielded a team which included several former Southern League stars as well as prominent local college players.[47] The "Haurys" took an extended three-week road trip in the South during the summer of 1900, and hosted several Tennessee town teams in the refurbished Athletic Park as well as a colored team from Louisville. Apparently, the implications of *Plessy v. Ferguson* and legalized segregation had not yet reached Nashville's baseball diamond in this first year of the new century. The Haurys' barnstorming efforts and attractive home slate were met with wide approval in a city thirsting for the return of organized baseball. Rumors surrounding the possibility of a new regional professional circuit were greeted with equal enthusiasm.

There is a smattering of evidence pointing to a series of informal gatherings between Powell, Fisher and Frank throughout the summer of 1900 in Atlanta and Memphis prior to the well-documented plenary session in Birmingham. The Tennessee influence at these pre-organizational talks was substantial. Both Fisher (Nashville) and Frank (Memphis) proposed awarding franchises to six Southern cities with proven track records that had supported baseball in the past — Nashville, Memphis, New Orleans, Birmingham, Chattanooga, and Atlanta. Additional telegrams were sent to prospective owners in Shreveport, Little Rock, Montgomery, Mobile and Selma.[48]

The role of Charlie Frank in the formation of the new Southern cannot be underestimated. Frank began his professional career with the Mobile Blackbirds in 1892, but most recently had managed the successful amateur Memphis Red Stockings. His team, which wore blue uniforms, played before large crowds in Red Elm Park and drew top opponents from as far away as St. Louis and Chicago. Several benefit games were held to compensate Frank as well as raise money for worthy charities. These exhibitions illustrated his popularity with Memphians.⁴⁹ "There has been an awakening in the South [to the worth] of base ball and the real pleasure and healthy pastime it affords," noted the *Memphis Commercial-Appeal*.⁵⁰

The Birmingham meeting was held at the Morris Hotel on October 20, 1900, and it went off without a hitch. Those in attendance included Charlie Frank (Memphis), Abner Powell (New Orleans), Newt Fisher (Nashville), Reed W. Kent (Chattanooga), W. J. Bowles (Birmingham), and George Reed (Shreveport). The goals of these leaders were clearly laid out: awarding franchises, selecting ownership, and drafting a set of bylaws.⁵¹ At precisely the same time, Ban Johnson was in the process of turning his American League dream into a second major league reality. "The prospects for base ball are brighter than they ever were in the South," boasted Frank. "From private correspondence, I know that the promoters of the game in other Southern cities take the same view."⁵² For Frank, the man and the moment had met.

Another primary objective of the Founding Fathers was to make their new Southern Association more financially solvent than its predecessor, which had been founded with little regard to capital management in a Memphis saloon in late 1884. Specifically, they hoped to avoid the infamous Southern League cognomen of the past, "the Fourth of July League."

Frank had warned earlier about the grievous mistakes that had brought down the old Southern League — faulty finances. "Past seasons have taught the lessons," lectured Frank. "We will not endeavor to organize a league on thin air this time."⁵³ Thus, the organizers advocated an initial down payment of $1,000 per franchise to be paid by January 1, 1901, and creating an annual "sinking fund" of $500 thereafter that all franchises would deposit in order to generate operating capital for the league. Furthermore, each team was expected to send 10 percent of all gate receipts to the league office. Then, the Big Three submitted three additional economic reforms that proved crucial to the league's ultimate success: (1) a monthly salary cap of $1,200 (increased to $1,500 in 1908); (2) a roster limit of 12 players (increased to 14 in 1906); (3) a 120-game slate (increased to 135 in 1904).⁵⁴ The foresight of the Big Three in fiscal management laid an essential foundation for the immediate economic success of the SA. Frank also intimated that Southern railways and various local hotels were already cooperating with him to furnish reduced rates to teams for travel purposes. Before adjourning, the team owners formed a Board of Directors and selected Kent to serve as the first president of the Southern Association.⁵⁵

News of the results of the Birmingham declaration set off a flurry of excitement in Nashville where "fandom is baseball hungry." One reporter predicted that the large crowds that had attended amateur contests the previous summer would provide a solid foundation to help professional baseball thrive.

The eight-team league promised to be exceptionally competitive, and it is probable that word of Hub's fiery smoke ball had caught the attention of Nashville manager, Newt Fisher. Indeed, Fisher announced plans give a number of local athletes a tryout![56] Grantland Rice and Hub Perdue were strong candidates for his short list. Among names of established players from elsewhere being bantered about were Johnny Dobbs, Ed "Batty" Abbaticchio and Julius Augustus "Doc" Wiseman.

The league owners set two important dates on the Southern Association calendar in December (later changed to October) and March (later changed to February) in order to evaluate the most recently concluded season and plan for the upcoming campaign, respectively. During these semi-annual affairs, the moguls also debated new policies and rule changes, hammered out the league schedule, hired umpires and discussed related business issues of common concern (such as sabbatarianism, rowdyism and alcohol). Then they adjourned to celebrate at a sumptuous banquet and beerfest. In the inaugural session, held at the Clarendon Hotel in Memphis on March 2, 1901, a figure destined to play an important role in future league administration made his first appearance, Judge Williams Marmaduke Kavanaugh of Little Rock.[57]

The anticipation of opening day in Rock City offered Nashvillians a much-needed respite from a sensational libel trial that had dominated the three local broadsheets. The case potentially threatened the existence of Sumner A. Cunningham's *Confederate Veteran,* a monthly magazine with the largest circulation in the South and published by the Methodist Publishing House in Nashville.[58]

Twenty-five players reported to compete for 12 roster spots on the first day of practice, April 2, but Perdue was not among those present. Doc Wiseman made an immediate impression at the first workout when he "made several exceptionally good [catches] when he went up the dump [right field incline] and captured the sphere when it looked impossible for one to get near it."[59] Heavy rains repeatedly plagued the month-long "ante-season," a normal weather occurrence in springtime Nashville. Local colleges provided the primary competition—Vanderbilt, Sewanee and Cumberland. "Bugs" flocked to Athletic Park, where attendance at exhibitions was surprisingly high, especially during games that featured big league opponents like St. Louis and Cincinnati. The latter listed a popular Nashvillian on its pitching roster—George "Noodles" Hahn.[60] Indeed, many of Hahn's National League appearances in the box were covered in the Nashville press in the first decade of the 1900s.

Known as the Fishermen, the Nashville nine opened the season with a series sweep in Chattanooga. Then both teams boarded a train for Rock City to meet in the Nashville home opener on May 6. At 2 P.M. on game day, the players boarded open-aired tally-ho carriages in front of the Duncan Hotel and paraded around Public Square and down several downtown side streets led by a band playing martial music. In a brief ceremony at Athletic Park, Mayor James Marshall Head delivered appropriate welcoming remarks. The first contest of Nashville's 61-year affiliation with the Southern was promptly "called" at 4 P.M.[61]

Nashville jumped out to an early lead in the league standings. These were different times — this Deadball Era! In July, the amateur Chickasaws club of Memphis challenged Frank's professionals to a game. Likewise, the Jackson (TN) town team, which promoted itself as the best independent team in the South, tendered Mike Finn's Little Rock club an identical proposal. While Memphis ignored the challenge, the Arkansas team did not. Little Rock dispensed with the upstarts, but in doing so they missed a scheduled date with Memphis. Manager Frank immediately protested and the league awarded Memphis a forfeit victory, a loss that would prove costly for the Finnites at the end of the season.[62]

Despite the fact that Southern Association moguls had gone to great lengths to launch their new venture on a strong financial footing, a scandal rocked the league at mid-season, and threatened not only the integrity of the league but hinted at impending bankruptcy for several franchises. In early July, President Kent informed team owners that they needed to pony up an additional $500 apiece, setting off a public wave of speculation that something was financially amiss. Two weeks later, Kent accused the owner of the Birmingham team with fiscal malfeasance and club president Mills of embezzlement. Mills threatened to shoot Kent on sight owing to the personal insult, and the league prexy suddenly went silent. After the *American* broke the story to Nashvillians, the Board of Directors responded by suspending Kent from all duties for alleged "faulty book keeping." Then the *Chattanooga Daily Times* made a shocking revelation — Kent had disappeared with the league treasury! The announcement was a stunning embarrassment for the Southern; it generated serious questions in the press about the financial honesty and integrity of the league's top brass. Nashville investors, reputedly the most prominent "New Men" in the city, were similarly rocked by the news. The Directors hastily selected the owner slandered by Kent — Boles of Birmingham — to finish out the year on an interim basis.[63] It was a public relations ploy to restore faith in the shattered league.

On the field, the inaugural season entered the dog days of summer with the race tightly contested between Little Rock, Nashville and Memphis. On Labor Day, Fisher's squad held a commanding six-game lead over second-place Little Rock, but the "rag" or "banner" or "flag" was hardly sewn up. In fact, the season champion would not be determined until the final games in electrifying fashion.⁶⁴ In the finale between the contenders, the faltering Nashville nine was visiting surging Little Rock on September 18 for a crucial doubleheader that would determine first place. The Arkansas fans were in a riotous mood and turned their belligerence on umpire John E. Johnston when he walked into the stadium with the visiting Nashville Fishermen. With Little Rock trailing by a run in the bottom of the first inning, the umpire called out Little Rock's Dick Crozier in a close play at the plate, setting off a brouhaha. Finn's players exploded off the bench and surrounded the beleaguered arbiter. A rock thrown from the stands by an irate fan struck Johnston in the face and first baseman Joe Wright pummeled the dazed game official to the ground. Policemen rushed the field, arrested the umpire for disorderly conduct and hauled him off to jail with a hostile crowd in hot pursuit. Meanwhile, the Little Rock team refused to take the field in protest, and the twin bill was canceled.⁶⁵ Owner Kavanaugh must have been appalled by the poor sportsmanship and rowdyism exhibited on the field as well as in the grandstands, a subject he would later address with vigor in a more powerful role as league president. Ultimately, Nashville copped the league championship one week later.⁶⁶

The conclusion of the season did not bring an end to controversy, however. President Boles was put to the test at the October league meeting when Little Rock disputed several losses owing to allegations that Nashville had used an unrostered player, Guy Sample. Indeed, Sample had "jumped" from Shreveport to the Fishermen and he won league pitching honors with 25 victories. He was clearly the ace of the Southern. The Sample case illustrated the public's general disapproval of anyone who broke a signed contract. But Nashville returned the volley and charged Little Rock manager Finn with shenanigans as he canceled four head-to-head engagements with Nashville in the last month when the race was neck-and-neck. Of course, the Little Rockers had already been penalized one defeat for the forfeiture event with Jackson. The owners and managers sided with Nashville and left the league crown with Fisher, but the incident reflected an early labor-management problem that was not clearly defined — how to deal with the Reserve Clause and players who flagrantly disregarded it. In an unrelated matter, Powell was so disgusted with his club's disappointing fourth-place finish that he released his entire New Orleans roster at season's end with the exception of one player.⁶⁷ In its final action, the Board turned to a familiar face in an effort to restore public confidence in the league's management. John B. Nicklin of Chattanooga not only exhibited high moral standards, he also possessed impressive baseball credentials as president of the old Southern League from 1893 to 1897.⁶⁸ The Board picked the owner of the Little Rock franchise, Williams Marmaduke Kavanaugh, to serve as vice president. Southern Association officials were fully prepared to police their own regulations, and they eagerly accepted added clout when the circuit joined the National Association of Professional Baseball Leagues, an umbrella organization designed to oversee the management of the minor leagues.

The fledgling circuit had much to celebrate in 1901. They had completed an entire slate of 135 games for the first time in Southern baseball history. It was a testament to the financial stability of the owners and their unwillingness to wither when faced with fraudulent activities. Future prospects appeared bright as the league entered its sophomore season with the addition of Atlanta. Within two years, Frank would replace the disgruntled Powell in New Orleans, where he established a dynasty noted for competitiveness and an above average talent pool.

In Nashville, the 1901 season was deemed a complete success by every indicator — the franchise was financially secure, the team performed well on the field, and the community was infused with a sense of civic pride. And Nashville rooters were jubilant when their team wrestled the league crown from Little Rock. A special post-season treat was extended to the fans when Cincinnati visited for a three-game exhibition in early October. Noodles Hahn, the local favorite, twirled the final game for the major leaguers to cap a fairy tale ending to the 1901 campaign.[69]

While Hub plied his trade in "cow pasture games," more serious family events had struck his household. First, Virgil, Hub's 16-year-old brother, suddenly died (d. April 30, 1902). Two years later, Hub lost both his mother (d. December 17, 1904) and a son during childbirth. An infant daughter, Josephine, passed away at the tender age of one in 1906. They are all laid to rest in the Perdue section of the Lower Bethpage Cemetery. After a short period of mourning, Marion remarried Emma (Nancy) Cochran on April 3, 1905.[70] Thus, life and death were no strangers to the Perdues of Bethpage in the early twentieth century.

There is no denying that Hub Perdue was a product of his Tennessee upbringing. Steeped in the experiences of the early nineteenth century frontier, his ancestors played a significant role in carving an existence out of a harsh environment — surviving dangers posed by hostile Native Americans, epidemics, and everyday hardships associated with clearing the land. Indeed, the Perdue clan contributed to the growth of the northern part of Sumner County and helped move the region from subsistence to commercial agriculture, especially in cotton and tobacco culture and raising livestock. By mid-century, Hub's grandfather was an important figure, a powerful economic and political force in the county. Marriage ties to the Durhams, another prominent family in the region, added to his political clout. Strong feelings toward the Confederate tradition and a sensitivity over Southern defeat in the Civil War were deeply woven into his family's folk fabric, and the cult of the Lost Cause remained a meaningful ideal within Hub, who prided himself on his Southern heritage.[71] Hub remained firmly rooted and committed to his Sumner County homeland for the rest of his life.

Despite the fact that Hub was married with children in his early twenties, the call of the baseball diamond still lured him. The "cow pasture games" had afforded him a stage where he could exercise his awesome potential as a pitcher. The timely birth of the Southern Association cannot be underemphasized in his growing fascination with the possibilities of a career in baseball. Once Hub experienced the intoxicating roar of adoring fans, he wanted more. For the rest of his life, he followed the sounds of the crowd whether in the ball yard or in the political arena. After all, everyone who knew the extrovert agreed that he was a natural showman. Mastering the gift of gab from an early age, Hub employed the lessons of self-promotion and self-aggrandizement, and his outlandish embellishments about events in his life contributed mightily to the growing body of Hublore narratives. "Hub was a legend in his own time," concluded Elmer T. Hinton, "and was one of baseball's most interesting personalities of his generation."[72]

As will be seen, the young man and the growing sport of professional baseball in Tennessee were inextricably woven together. The game was about to come face-to-face with an original clown prince of the mound.

Chapter 2

Dawning of the Deadball Era — Tennessee Style

By the end of the Butcher's highly successful season in 1904, the Gallatin pitching triumvirate of Perdue, Chenault and Frakes had caused quite a stir in minor league circuits throughout the region. Anderson and Guild lobbied successfully to place their three aces with Paducah in the second-year KITTY — Kentucky-Illinois-Tennessee League.[1] As minor leagues were blossoming in the early Deadball Era, the competition for talent was keen. Starting in the low minors, Hub was quickly discovered by a major league club, drafted and sent back to Nashville to mature and face a higher level of competition. Hub's journey, which began in a small river town in Indiana, ultimately led him to the Big Show.

Few differences existed between the brand of baseball played in rural or urban settings. The fields were rough and normally conformed to the configuration of surrounding streets. Regarding equipment, leather gloves were small and bats were enormous cudgels that required a split-hand grip to swing or chop; the players wore woolen flannels that were constantly dirty; contests were played with only one or two baseballs that were scuffed, cut and defaced with tobacco or licorice spittle and often misshapen by the end of the game. On defense, corner infielders often played shallow to prevent bunts while middle infielders exhibited great dexterity and quickness in executing double plays; outfielders positioned themselves shallow to tease batters into swinging for the fences (which were normally too distant to reach on the fly). On offense, the game operated under the rules of "scientific baseball" where teams played for one run and manufactured scores through bunting, stealing and hit-and-run plays. Pitchers delivered the spheroid with a variety of motions — overhand, underhand and sidearm. They also possessed a wide assortment of pitches like the fastball (smoke ball), curve (hook), screwball (fadeaway), knuckleball (floater) and the latest rage — the spitball. Overall, the game required intelligent, alert and aggressive ballplayers. The style of play during the Deadball Era, rough and tumble, suited Perdue's personality and his physical strengths, a blazing fastball and hard, biting curve ball. Soon he was introduced to the "moist ball," which became his signature pitch.[2]

The colorful purple prose of Victorian Age sportswriters also lent charm to the Deadball Era, and many of the terms listed below were utilized to describe Hub and his surroundings at one time or another. Some examples were: sphere or pill (ball); bag, sack or pillow (base); dish (home plate); willow or stick (bat); hurler, twirler, spinner or slab man (pitcher); sackers (basemen); bingle (single); four-bagger (home run); scribes (sports writers); flag, rag or banner (pennant); mogul (owner or manager); dope (inside information); detail (scoreboard); slab or box (mound); garden (outfield); kranks or bugs (fans); nines (baseball team); whip or soup bone (throwing arm); wickets or pins (legs).[3] Hub would make a unique contribution to this genre of literature through his clownish behavior addressed in Hublore stories.

When the three Gallatin lads — Perdue, Chenault and Frakes — reported to Paducah to begin their professional careers in May 1905, the Class D KITTY circuit maintained poor records. In fact, baseball sources today do not even have rostered players listed for that squad owing to the fact that league officials never submitted statistics for publication at the end of the year. Still, Frakes was considered a top signee and drew $100 per month in salary. Hub, "the crack pitcher of the Butchers," was tendered a lesser contract, $75 per month. "It is said by experts," reported the *Paducah Sun*, "that [Hub] pitches the best drop ball in the South."[4] But, Indians manager Harry Lloyd released Hub prior to Opening Day. Then, in a feat of self-promotion, Hub donned the uniform of South Kentucky College in Hopkinsville on May 6 and tossed a one-hit masterpiece with 21 strikeouts over visiting Madisonville.[5] "The magnificent pitcher" caught the attention of the professional Hopkinsville Browns and Hub immediately re-signed.[6]

Nicknamed for the team's owner, Charles Brown, the Hoptown franchise exhibited weak financial support since its charter membership in the league. On the field, the Browns dropped into the cellar almost immediately while Paducah and Vincennes distanced themselves from the rest of the pack. It did not take Hub long to establish himself as a premier pitcher with the Browns. In his first professional appearance, he limited the Henderson Hens to one hit.[7] Manager [and battery mate] Lou Rutledge was duly impressed. In early June, the Gallatian was labeled "a phenom" with a "tantalizing up-shoot" and "baffling spit ball."[8] When he led the bottom-feeder Browns past both Paducah and Vincennes several times, his successes against the league's elites did not go unnoticed.[9] In one face-off with Vincennes, the Alices scored in a most unconventional manner: "The Vincennes scores were both made in the first inning on a lost ball," reported the *Hopkinsville Kentuckian*, "which could not be found under a bunch of weeds beneath the right field fence."[10] Rutledge rewarded Hub's diamond triumphs and selected him to open the prestigious Decoration Day (later Memorial Day) doubleheader, a sign of his rising status and importance on the Browns staff.

Rumors about the Browns' weak finances caused a stir in mid–June when the team nearly failed to meet its payroll obligation owing to poor attendance. The club operated for another month without incident and, in the meantime, Hub continued to dazzle his opponents. One highlight of the summer occurred when teammate Charlie Bomar (from Wartrace, Tennessee) tossed a 21-inning victory against Princeton on June 27. Two weeks later, Hub pulled his team out of the cellar with a two-hit victory over Vincennes.[11]

On July 4, the three Sumner County prospects returned home to pitch for the Butchers against the highly touted Nashville YMCA.[12] Apparently, players were free to bounce between professional and amateur ranks in 1905 in stark contrast to today's rules which prohibit such a practice. At the moment, Frakes, a wildly popular fellow who exhibited "gentlemanly qualities" both on and off the field, boasted one of the best records (12–3) in the KITTY.

Back in Hopkinsville the franchise struggled for economic survival. However, even Hub's heroics in the box upon his return were insufficient to save the franchise. On July 18, the league president-secretary and owner of the Vincennes Alices, Clifton C. Gosnell, declared that Hopkinsville and Henderson had been dropped from the KITTY.[13] The truncated conference would play a split season, said the mogul, who also suggested a post-season playoff between the winners of each half.[14]

Gosnell's announcement devastated the bluegrass community of Hopkinsville. "The attempt to break up the league was the talk of the town yesterday and base ball ardor was never stronger," defended the *Hopkinsville Kentuckian*. The newspaper supported the Browns owners, saying they had met payroll AND the team had posted a winning record, 19–14. "It is now the IT League," stated the newspaper cryptically, "with the emphasis on the I."[15] The baseball facility was promptly sold to a snuff company, dealing a death blow to local baseball enthusiasts.

In his ten weeks of active duty with Hopkinsville, Hub notched an 11–5 record. Therefore, his services were in high demand especially in light of the tight race being waged between the Indians and Alices for the league's banner. Indeed, Paducah had tendered a generous offer to purchase Hub's contract several weeks before Hopkinsville folded. Likewise, the scavengers in Vincennes hovered over the unemployed Browns with an eye toward landing Perdue and Bomar for the remainder of the truncated season.

On July 21, Hub signed with Vincennes, a decision that might have been influenced by its close proximity to the residence of his in-laws in Oaktown. The Alices were ecstatic over the acquisition of Hub, a "very fast man" and "one of the best pitchers in the league." The *Vincennes Capital* predicted that Perdue would win a minimum of two-thirds of his games in his new surroundings.[16] "The Alices have probably fared better than any of the other clubs as a result of the disbanding of the Henderson and Hopkinsville teams," asserted the *Vincennes Morning Commercial*.[17] Paducah officials made a last-ditch effort to dissuade Hub from joining the Indiana club. Their efforts fell upon deaf ears, however, and Hub became an Aliceman. Together with future Nashville teammate Johnny Duggan, a resident of nearby Franklin, Indiana, Hub formed a powerful one-two punch for the Vincennes club.

Hub's new manager was Eddie Kolb. A native of Cincinnati, Kolb grew up playing sandlot baseball and later joined an amateur team called the Ivanhoes. In his adolescent years he assisted Harry Weldon in scoring professional games for the *Cincinnati Enquirer*. While working in a hotel cigar shop in 1899, he befriended Cleveland coach Joe Quinn, who was in the midst of a woeful season during which his National League Spiders won only 20 games. Kolb connived Quinn into using him as a pitcher in the last game of the season against Cincinnati, where he was victimized for 19 runs and earned the distinction as the final losing pitcher in a 134-loss season, a major league record. Lacking in major league skills, Kolb never lost his enthusiasm for the game. He entered the coaching ranks in 1902, and in his first four seasons at the helm (including two in Vincennes) produced championships. The natural leader rarely inserted himself into the lineup, but he did make himself available in the box as needed for the Alices.[18]

Hub lost his first start in Vincennes at League Park on July 25 to first-half champion Paducah.[19] Still, the Gallatin native was masterful in defeat. He mesmerized Indians batters, who nicknamed him "Rube," and not one opponent reached base until two outs in the seventh inning. A double and a single accounted for the lone score which spoiled Hub's debut, a disappointing three-hit loss, 1–0.[20]

Although Hub's second appearance in the box several days later was not nearly as spectacular, it offered a glimpse into his mental toughness which pleased both teammates and local fans alike. Nursing a two-run lead in the second inning, Cairo twirler "Thunderbolt" Lane lost control of an in-shoot and Aliceman batter George Wilkerson spun completely around to avoid the pitch. Unfortunately, the ball struck the big first sacker "a frightful blow" in the back of the head near the base of his skull and he slumped to the ground unconscious. He lay there for five minutes without moving while two physicians who were in attendance frantically attempted to revive him. He regained consciousness, and the woozy "Wilk" was led to a buggy and driven home.

An inning later, catcher L. Q. Matteson was struck on his throwing hand by another errant offering by Lane. Nursing a swollen thumb, the tough "Matty" remained in the game but Kolb shifted him to second base.[21]

Hub had seen enough. In the top of the sixth inning, Cairo's "Kitty" Gerard stepped up to the dish and dug in. Hub did not hesitate. He planted a fastball on the side of the left fielder's head, "sending [him] into dreamland." Gerard, too, collapsed to the ground and lay there for several minutes before regaining his composure. He was pulled from the game and Hub coasted to a victory in a sloppy contest where both defenses combined for eight errors.[22] More important than his victory, Hub had sent a message to his teammates that he would defend them from wildly aggressive hurlers.

Hub was sensational over the last month of the season. Paducah clung to a thin lead in the standings but the dynamic duo of Perdue and Duggan kept the Alices within striking distance. Cairo and Princeton were, for all practical purposes, non-factors. Hub entered the box eight times in August and manager Kolb used him almost exclusively against the Indians. Highlights included a 13-inning loss to Cairo where Hub's throwing error accounted for the winning run, and a one-hitter at Princeton.[23] The *Cairo Bulletin* reported that Hub had developed a "sleep ball" guaranteed to put the batter into a trance."[24] A change-of-pace? It is also likely that Hub was experimenting with the latest new craze, the spitball.

Perhaps the most memorable game of the summer took place on August 3 when Hub was locked in a sensational pitchers' duel in Paducah with his good friend, Frakes. Both teams had put forth excellent defense and the slab men were practically untouchable. While Frakes bested his Gallatin chum (2–0), Hub provided unexpected fireworks in the field where he completed a spectacular triple play. The rare gem was set in motion when an Indians batter popped out to catcher Matteson behind home plate and near the grandstand. With two runners aboard at the corners, the heady backstopper whirled around and fired the ball to the first baseman to register a double play on the inattentive base runner. In all of the commotion, the runner on third base lit out for home, whereupon first baseman Wilkerson delivered the sphere to Hub, who was alertly covering the dish. Hub applied the tag to complete the first triple play in the KITTY that season.[25] The game had ominous overtones for Frakes and Perdue, however, as a tragic event would soon reveal.

In another personal achievement two weeks later, Hub defeated Paducah, 2–1, in a thrilling 16-inning contest where he allowed only two hits after the ninth frame.[26] Just as important, the Alices had taken a three-game advantage over the Indians, but their victory was overshadowed by a stunning announcement. President Gosnell informed reporters that the KITTY regular season would shut down the following day owing to the spread of a yellow fever epidemic which had broken out in New Orleans. He intimated that there were other considerations for disbanding the league. Princeton owners had opted to quit because of poor attendance (lack of revenue), and the *Vincennes Capitol* opined that Cairo had decided to leave because they could not win the league title.[27]

The anticipated playoff between first half champion Paducah and second half champion Vincennes would proceed as planned, however. The opening game in the championship series was slated for August 18. Each team would host six games (three doubleheaders) between August 18 and 27 and, if necessary, a deciding contest would be held at a neutral site, Evansville.[28] The 13-game spectacle promised more head-to-head battles between Perdue and Frakes.

Frakes was not in good health, however. He last appeared in the box on August 7 against Cairo, and by the time the league closed ten days later he had already returned to Gallatin suffering from "boils." Although he was unavailable for the upcoming tilt versus Vincennes, he curiously volunteered to hurl several contests for the hometown Butchers.[29]

Hub and Duggan carried the pitching load for the Alices while Dick Brahic filled in for Frakes' Indians. All three hurlers became familiar adversaries over the next ten days. In the second playoff game on August 20, Hub drubbed Brahic in a masterful two-hitter, 11–1. "Bullets" Perdue was "invincible" while his teammates struck for 13 base hits and Indians infielders contributed eight errors.[30] But Hub's joy in winning the game was short-lived. Shocking news had reached Vincennes that Frakes was dead![31]

The *Gallatin News* broke the details. Frakes had taken violently ill shortly after returning to his Dry Creek Road home from a Butchers road trip to Shelbyville. Within hours he was dead. The published cause of death was listed as intestinal blockage. But could Frakes have succumbed to the dreaded "yellow jack" that had shut down the KITTY? The entire community in Gallatin was stunned. Frakes "did more to popularize the national game in Gallatin than any other player," eulogized the local newspaper on its front page.[32]

The Alices swept the first six playoff games in Vincennes, but one dispatch claimed that Hub was so distraught over the death of his pal that he would not accompany the team on the road. Instead, he would return to Gallatin. But Hub did travel to Paducah with his teammates. With a heavy heart, he entered the box on August 24 but the game ended in the first Indians victory, 2–1.[33]

Two days later, Hub hurled what turned out to be the championship game. Familiar adversaries, Brahic and Hub locked in a classic 13-inning encounter where both men combined for 20 strike outs. Three Indians batsmen struck for doubles, but Hub repeatedly wiggled off the hook despite the fact that his infielders played poor defense. Helping his own cause, the Gallatian drew a base on balls and scored the first run of the game in the top of the 13th inning.[34] In the immediate aftermath of the game, the mentally spent Perdue wired President Gosnell at the mogul's expense: "'bout all in."[35]

A meaningless ninth game was played the next day to increase weekend gate receipts. Paducah won by a score of 1–0, and historians have erroneously identified it as the 13th, and final, game for the championship. In point of fact, the Alices needed only eight games to determine the crown, and Hub had wrapped it up the previous day. Vincennes perched atop the 1905 Kentucky-Illinois-Tennessee League not only based on the head-to-head postseason series, but also owing to their two-game advantage in the final league standings. Both teams disbanded immediately after the final out, and the 1905 campaign for the KITTY officially came to a close.

When the Alices returned home after capturing the league flag, they were met at the Vincennes train depot by a throng of loyal rooters. Led by the First Regiment Band, the conquering heroes were paraded through the city streets in open-air carriages and delivered to John Gatton's downtown restaurant for a banquet. Afterwards, the crowd of revelers took the trolley on Fairgrounds Avenue to Lincoln Park where they danced and drank the night away.[36] Quite satisfied with his contribution to Vincennes' championship, Perdue returned to his home in Bethpage wearing his signature red overcoat.

Although Hub's first professional season was over, a personal baseball tribute to his fallen friend, Frakes, was not. In Gallatin, the community banded together to organize a benefit game with the proceeds earmarked for the young ballplayer's widow. Over 20 fans paid 25-cents admission (the price of a major league ticket) to participate in the fundraiser at the Fairgrounds. In a typical iron man exhibition to honor his departed friend, Hub pitched both ends of a doubleheader against Nashville's top amateur team. Cheek-Neal and the Butchers had split four head-to-head encounters during the summer and each claimed the unofficial title of amateur state champion. Thus the matchup held added significance. In the opener, Hub allowed only five hits, struck out 13, and coasted to a 5–1 victory. He dropped the second contest on two unearned runs in a sloppy affair that produced 13 errors. In the deciding game three held the next day, Hub handcuffed the Nashvillians, 6–1.[37] Hub was now heir to Frakes' local fame.

As a reward for their masterful slab work in Vincennes, Perdue and Duggan were invited by first-year manager Mike Finn to Nashville for a tryout in mid–September. But the franchise was in financial disarray so Finn offered a contract only to the Hoosier hurler. The Vincennes Alices, on the other hand, were so highly impressed with Hub's rookie year that they reserved him for the 1906 campaign.[38] After all, he had pitched well in Hopkinsville (11–5) and Vincennes (8–4) for a combined 19–9 record, and proved a workhorse in slinging over 250 innings. These statistics comprise Hub's lost season of 1905; they are heretofore unrecorded in any baseball data bank, reference book or official MLB source.

In 1906, three new teams joined the KITTY from Illinois — Jacksonville, Danville and Mattoon-Charleston — and bitter competition between the three surviving franchises — Paducah, Cairo and Vincennes — intensified. Despite the fact that every team had established formal nicknames, the local journalists in each community created negative cognomens for their rivals to heighten a sense of competitive banter. Thus, the Jacksonville Jacks became "Lunatics," Danville Old Soldiers "Veterans" and Mattoon-Charleston Canaries "Hyphens." In Vincennes, the most derisive slurs were reserved for the Paducah Indians (Igerrotes) and Cairo Giants (River Rats).[39] Not to be outdone, most out-of-town newspapers called the Vincennes Alices the "Girls." So, even at the lowest classification of professional baseball — Class D — there existed spirited broadsheet competition between small towns. Sometimes the verbal exchanges grew quite heated. In Vincennes, three dailies preferred to call their local nines "the Champs."

Hub reported to the Alices with eager anticipation to start his second campaign. To prepare for the regular season, he pitched exhibitions against Evansville, Terre Haute and Indiana University, and set a pattern for strikeouts that he would replicate throughout the upcoming year in notching six to ten whiffs per game.[40] His reputation as a power pitcher with a hard, biting curve ball was spreading, and opponents conferred his first nickname in baseball, "Rub, Dub, Hub."[41]

The Vincennes club secured three important dates on the new schedule before the first pitch had even been thrown. The Alices would host all three of the coveted holiday doubleheaders — Decoration (Memorial) Day versus Cairo, the Fourth of July with Danville, and Labor Day against Paducah. Perhaps President Gosnell had provided owner Gosnell with preferential treatment. This coup had as much to do with favoritism on the field as with business perks. Conversely, Cairo and Paducah were slated to host only one holiday event apiece.

Vincennes welcomed Danville on Opening Day, May 3, 1906. A special pre-game ceremony was planned which followed a typical itinerary not only throughout the KITTY, but in minor league circuits nationwide. Two hours before game time, the First Regiment Band spearheaded a parade of players, local politicians, and business dignitaries in open carriages along Main Street and Fairgrounds Avenue to the ball yard. Children frolicked behind the procession. Trolley cars ran every four minutes from the city's center to League Park in anticipation of a large crowd. Upon their arrival at the field, both teams lined the base paths and a short speech was delivered by the mayor. Many businesses closed a half-hour before the game was "called," and a crowd estimated at over 1,000 filled the grandstand. One reporter observed that "many society women from the city" attended, a symbol of civility.[42]

Kolb selected "'bout all in" Perdue to open the new campaign, a reference to Hub's telegram to Gosnell at the conclusion of the 1905 season.[43] The first Alicemen game was a resounding success. Hub baffled the Old Soldiers with the new pitch that was sweeping the land. "Perdue's spit ball worked in fine style," observed the *Vincennes Daily Sun*.[44] He also stroked a base hit, "something rare for him," a notorious weak hitter. Hub's two-hitter was detailed in an article appearing on the front page of the newspaper, which lent further credence to the importance of these contests in small-town America.[45]

Hub cut down every league opponent at least once in the month of May and led the staff with a 7–1 record. These

Hub in Vincennes uniform (*Vincennes Daily Sun*, May 3, 1906).

victories included a pair of two-hitters and two three-hitters where he routinely struck out more than eight batters. Hub worked well with catcher Mattison and both were recognized as club "comedians." Yet Hub's fantastic month came at a price when a reporter revealed that he suffered from a sore arm, the first report of the arm issues that would plague him for the remainder of his career.[46] He overcame this ailment one week later to hurl the signature game of the month on Decoration Day (May 30), an 18–2 drubbing of Cairo.[47] Hub was never afraid to pitch while stiff and sore, testimony to his mental toughness.

Kolb added two important building blocks to the Vincennes slab crew when he picked up Bob Farrell from Lancaster in the Ohio & Pennsylvania League, and Hub's good friend, the versatile Chenault.[48] Discarded by Paducah, Chenault was a great asset as a utility player who could catch, pitch and play outfield. The reunited Gallatians rose rapidly to the top of the league's pitching charts. On June 29, Chenault proved his worth when he overwhelmed Cairo in both ends of a doubleheader; he allowed only ten hits and no runs scored.⁴⁹ Along with Hub and southpaw Hubert Whitley, the additions of Chenault and Farrell insured that Vincennes would contend for the league crown. In a pinch, Kolb even elected to toss several games himself.

Several idiosyncrasies came to light in Vincennes that became lifelong habits for Hub. First, never known for his skill with a bat, Hub wielded an oversized 42" cudgel that became a personal trademark. Strangely, he struck for four base hits on June 6 in Danville, a day before his twenty-fourth birthday, divulging a second eccentricity; in each of Hub's nineteen seasons he took the slab one or two days on either side of his birthday, June 7. Third, he chose to wear a red overcoat and later a crimson long-sleeve undershirt beneath his jersey. He maintained this flamboyant look for the remainder of his career regardless of official team colors, which suggests his psychological need to be noticed. Indeed, Hub flourished as the center of attention. These three pieces of trivia—the club-like bat, the "birthday game" and the red apparel—were incorporated into Hublore and first displayed in Vincennes.⁵⁰

Between Decoration Day and July 9, Hub won nine out of 11 starts, the only defeats coming in two one-run road losses in Danville and Cairo, the latter resulting from a balk.⁵¹ During the streak, he faced Paducah's ace, Brahic, in several memorable confrontations. By mid–July, Hub boasted an eye-popping 16–4 mark, and a few major league teams were beginning to take notice—Chicago [Cubs], St. Louis [Cardinals], and Washington [Senators]. Telegrams from teams in the Three I also announced their interest in the Hub sweepstakes. But Gosnell refused to consider any offers for his ace until the KITTY flag was firmly secured by Vincennes.⁵²

Hub's jocular personality was also emerging in Vincennes. He was proficient in "kicking" (baiting) umpires, which he took to a higher level using humor. Once, umpire Bill "Peek-a-boo" Veatch ejected Hub from a game for wearing street clothes on the bench, a clear violation of league rules, but not before the incensed hurler had created a "hollering scene."⁵³ Terms like "jolly," "comic" and "comedian" were typically applied by Vincennes sports editors to describe the Gallatin slab man.⁵⁴ Incidentally, arbiters in the KITTY worked alone and announced balls and strikes from the field, where they were frequently struck by line drives.

Paducah fell off the ferocious pace set by the Kolbites, and the Alicemen shared first place with Cairo for nearly two months. By the Fourth of July, the Indiana club asserted itself atop the standings and never relinquished the lead again. Conversely, tumultuous events unfolded in Cairo and contributed to their on-field collapse. First, owner Maurice J. Farnbaker reportedly disbanded the team, citing poor attendance and player indifference. A retraction followed but then manager Dan McCarthy fired half of the team without pay. The Giants slumped and finished in the middle of the pack. This crisis points to the tenuous nature of professional baseball in small communities like Cairo at the turn of the century, especially when teams failed to live up to expectations of owners and boosters.[55] In mid-summer, the Alices put together a 16–4 run, and opened a double-digit lead over Jacksonville. The league banner was in sight and most of Vincennes contracted pennant fever.

Hub saved his most dominating and nail-biting performances for Paducah, the arch rival of Vincennes. Squaring off against Brahic at Wallace Park on July 12, he registered a disappointing four-hit loss, 2–0. Upset by the outcome, he begged Kolb to return to the box for the second tilt, a request Hub made on numerous occasions under identical circumstances in later years. He never tolerated defeat when it was avoidable. Kolb agreed and the plucky slab man notched another four-hitter, but this time he earned a 15-inning victory. By day's end, Hub had hurled 24 innings in a twin bill that exceeded four hours. " 'Rub, Dub, Hub' ... proved himself beyond a doubt the premier pitcher of the Kitty," congratulated the *Paducah Evening Sun.* "He set the pace for all pitchers, whether big or little leaguers."[56] Only utility infielder Frank Quigley had any success against "invincible" Hub; he banged out two of his team's eight hits and scored two of its three runs. Perhaps July 12, 1906, was Hub Perdue's greatest day ever on a baseball diamond.

Then Hub dropped his fifth decision of the year against Jacksonville and one report stated he was suffering from "chills." He disappeared from the bench to his in-laws' farm in Oaktown where he convalesced for several days.[57] Was Hub really ill or had he been out celebrating his 24-inning iron man outing against Paducah with John Barleycorn and Bud Weiser? No matter. Upon his return to the box, Hub promptly went on a five-game win streak which included a trio of three-hitters and pushed his season mark to 21–5. In Chicago, Cubs manager Frank Chance was beginning to take serious notice of the young Tennessee spitballer.[58]

In early August, the Alices opened up a 14-game lead over its nearest rival, Jacksonville. At this time a colorful social commentary appeared in newspapers around the KITTY describing alleged scandalous behavior at Ladies Day events in Vincennes. Local prostitutes, so the story ran, were taking advantage of reduced ticket prices at League Park to attend games and flaunt themselves at potential customers in the grandstands. Rival towns relished this juicy gossip and commented about the questionable social values on display in the Vincennes ball yard. Paducah and Cairo scribes suggested that ticket window clerks in Vincennes should refrain from selling ducats to "scarlet women," and policemen needed to actively escort "women of shady reputation" from the grounds.[59] The snippet coincided with Hub's most overpowering performance of the season, a one-hit shutout over Danville where only two Vets reached first base and 11 batters whiffed.

Although Vincennes had all but wrapped up the league crown, the pitching staff showed signs of overwork and the offense was sputtering. Indeed, the entire club had seemingly lost its focus while sporting such a monstrous lead, and Hub's lack of concentration led the way. Between August 8 and September 3, the Gallatin hurler went 2–4 with three no-decisions. The swoon enabled Jacksonville to cut Vincennes' league lead in half, but not enough to cause any real concern. There is no doubt that Hub's drop in performance was caused, in part, by distractions caused by rumors about his impending selection by a major league outfit. His spate of inconsistency first appeared in Danville where he set a KITTY record with 14 strike outs, but he let a 6–3 lead in the ninth frame slip away, which resulted in an 11-inning no-decision.[60] A week later, Hub was protecting a 4–2 lead over Brahic in Paducah, where he swatted two safeties and scored twice, when disaster struck again in the bottom of the ninth. Quigley, the master of Hub, stole home and flustered the Tennessean, who followed immediately with an ill-timed balk which tied the score. The game was suspended owing to darkness after 12 innings.[61]

The next day, Chenault was driven from the box in the third inning after a freakish accident when he was struck by a line drive on his throwing elbow. Kolb summoned Hub in relief since the other pitchers were bedridden. The fatigued hurler promptly coughed up seven runs and absorbed another loss. Still, the August blip hardly concerned anyone associated with the frontrunners even after losing four straight to last-place Mattoon, which trailed the pack by 23 games. To deal with the depleted pitching staff, Kolb assigned himself to the box as well as first baseman Wilkerson, a player with absolutely no pitching experience. Even so, Vincennes soon reestablished its double-digit lead over Jacksonville after a number of head-to-head beatings of the second-place Jacks.[62]

Big news! A story broke on August 21 that Chance had purchased the rights to both Perdue and Chenault from Gosnell for $800.[63] The Vincennes mogul also sold Hub's batterymate, Mattison, to Evansville to complete the sale of talented Alicemen. Some suggested that the drafted Tennesseans might accompany the Cubs for the last two weeks of their magical season, a roster Chance was building into one of the greatest teams of all time.[64] In his first outing since being sold to Chicago, a rejuvenated Hub outmuscled Jacksonville with Chenault calling signals behind the dish. The future Cubbies were responsible for several runs and Hub ran the bases "like a greyhound."[65] It must have bruised the future major leaguer's ego somewhat to drop a 7–6 road contest in Mattoon following his next outing in front of a sparse crowd of 65 fans.[66]

The season was winding down as the Labor Day doubleheader loomed against Paducah on September 3. In the first game, Chenault fired a nifty three-hit shutout to wrap up the league crown for Vincennes. Hub equaled the three-hitter in the second affair, but his game lasted 12 innings and ended in a 0–0 tie. The visiting Indians had been held to six hits and no runs for the entire afternoon.[67] Hub wrapped up the season in Cairo where he carried a no-hitter into the eighth inning, but settled for a two-hit shutout for his 25th, and final, victory of the season. Ironically, Hub also slapped his team's final base hit of the regular season as his storybook season drew to a close.[68]

The Hoosier club finished a remarkable 1906 season at 77–49 (.611), led by Hub's superb work in the box. The Tennessean notched a 25–8–3 record in 321 innings and struck out 260 batters. His WHIP (walks plus hits per innings pitched) was a remarkable 0.75, and Hub's control was impeccable; he surrendered fewer than one base on balls per 12 innings pitched. In the course of the season, Hub fired one one-hitter, two two-hitters, seven three-hitters, and one four-hitter. Together, Chenault and Perdue led the Alices to the league title with a convincing nine-game cushion over second-place Jacksonville. Offensively, Hub would never again reach such a lofty plateau — a .216 average with 29 hits and one stolen base. The team's championship photo appeared in the 1907 *Spalding's Official Guide to Base Ball* with chubby-faced Hub wearing his red coat.[69]

Not everyone reacted with jubilation at the close of the 1906 season. A tragic episode occurred in Mattoon when John O. Backus, a twenty-eight-year-old employee with the city's traction system and manager of the Canaries, committed suicide following his involvement in an accident where two trolleys collided at a busy switch. One conductor was killed and several passengers were injured. Backus had been traveling the line to the Mattoon ballyard.[70]

In mid–September, Kolb took some of the Alices on a barnstorming tour through Illinois and Indiana. The Duggan brothers — Johnny and Elmer — invited the Kolbites to swing through their hometown, Franklin, Indiana, for a contest. While the trip was advertised as a victory lap for the club to earn a little bonus money, none of Vincennes' four starting pitchers — Perdue, Chenault, Whitley or Farrell — participated. Thus Kolb substituted "four punk pitchers." The tour became an instant embarrassment when several town teams defeated the professionals, so Kolb canceled the remainder of the post-season excursion.[71]

In early March 1907, Hub arrived in West Baden, Indiana, wearing his distinctive red jacket. The resort community 65 miles northwest of Louisville was home to a hot springs and the Chicago Cubs' spring training facility. The players "enjoyed taking the waters" between workouts, and Hub struck up an immediate friendship with pitcher Mordecai Brown. "Three Finger" showed Hub his mangled right hand, the result of a farm-machinery accident as a youth that had cut off his index finger and deformed several other digits. Hub admired Brown's physical courage and was doubly impressed with Brown's friendliness and willingness to share secrets about their craft in the big leagues. "If I thought it would make me a pitcher like Brown," Hub told reporter Charles Dryden in the *Chicago Daily Tribune*, "I'd stand for the feed chopper in a minute."[72]

Hub shared his rookie, or "Colt," status with two other players destined to play an important role in his professional career — shortstop Bill Sweeney and catcher J. Warren "Doc" Seabough. In camp, Hub endeared himself to his veteran colleagues with his "clownish" antics. Once, he provided a comic play-by-play rendition of an unsavory event — a staged fight between a captured badger and a bulldog.

Hub also received attention as a man with "an appetite like a piano mover." It was the practice of team trainer Jack McCormack to dole out $1 for each player's daily food allowance while on the road. McCormack would sit at a table, shuffle a stack of crisp dollar bills like they were a deck of cards and distribute the cash as if he were dealing a hand of poker. Once, Hub used

Hub in spring training, 1907, with the Chicago Cubs. Manager Frank Chance is standing in the background (courtesy of Chicago Daily News Negatives Collection, Chicago History Museum, # SDN-005533).

his allotment on a bowl of "thin soup," and the hungry rookie went back to McCormack and asked to be dealt in once more. Hub impressed the Chicagoans when he devoured a large black sea bass while on a brief road swing to Mobile. Several teammates joked that Hub should shy clear of the city's wharf where a docked freighter was presently unloading 20,000 bunches of bananas from Latin America. Later, after Hub had been released to the minors, McCormack swiped a restaurant menu while the Cubs were visiting Pittsburgh, and mailed it to "Hungry Hub."[73]

The Cubs left West Baden and traveled south to play a series of exhibitions in New Orleans. Over the week, Hub appeared several times for the pitcher-starved Pelicans, and manager Charlie Frank liked what he saw.[74] Chance held a different opinion. In Hub's first trip to the box, Cubs sluggers torched him for six runs on seven hits in only three innings. To add insult to injury, Johnny Evers stole home on the inattentive rookie.[75] In a second appearance, the defending National League champion Cubs scattered Hub's pitches all over the ball yard. Interestingly, Hub's true name was listed under an alias, Long, in these exhibitions. "Say, man," marveled the Gallatian, "they never did hit them at me that way in the Kitty league."[76] Welcome to the majors, Hub! His lone victory for the Cubs occurred against the Mobile Sea Gulls, a Southern Association entrant.

The Cubs broke camp in the Crescent City at the end of March and headed north, where they had three exhibitions slated in Nashville. Chance had already decided to release Hub and the Chicago mogul wanted to showcase him in front of hometown fans. Donning his trademark red flannel undershirt on the 27th, the Tennessean went six strong innings and left the game with the score tied, 2–2. Several hundred fans had traveled from Gallatin to root for their favorite son to "deliver the goods." Afterwards, Chance tendered an offer to first-year skipper Johnny Dobbs to purchase Perdue's contract, and a deal was quickly consummated.[77] Hub was pleased because he could commute to Nashville by rail from his Sumner County home, a luxury very few professional athletes enjoyed during this time period. For their part, "the Cubs are sorry to part with their chief joker," lamented Dryden in the *Chicago Daily Tribune*.[78] Hub, in turn, boasted to his big league chums that they had not seen the last of him.

A native of Chattanooga, Dobbs had his hands full with the players assigned to him. A 32-year old utility infielder with five years of major league experience, Dobbs had been hired to replace Finn, who had left Nashville for Little Rock. Dobbs was the newest member in a colorful assortment of skippers in the Southern: "Tobacco" Billy Smith (Atlanta), Charlie Babb (Memphis), Charlie Frank (New Orleans), "Irish" Mike Finn (Little Rock), Harry "Dad" Vaughn (Birmingham), Tom Fisher (Shreveport), and John "Liz" Malarkey

(Montgomery).[79] The rookie Dobbs was long on enthusiasm but inexperienced in the managerial ranks, and his fledgling team put him to the test.[80]

The Nashville roster in 1907 was a mixture of grizzled veterans, career minor leaguers and a sprinkling of raw rookies new to the Southern. Regarding the former, some of the central figures included major league castoffs like catcher John "Scrappy Jack" Hardy and hurler Stanley "Yank" Yerkes. Minor league lifers included Doc Wiseman, first baseman Pete Lister, hurler Bill Sorrells, and moody infielder Mike "Dude" McCormick. Tennessee represented the dash of young rookie hopefuls with Perdue and power-hitting third baseman, Pryor "Mac" McElveen.[81] A marginal pitcher with an unimpressive three-year resume in the majors, Yerkes was long on advice and short on work ethic, and a leading thorn in Dobbs' side. Similarly, Sorrells, a minor leaguer who bounced around the Southern Association, Texas League, and Cotton States League for 11 seasons, had never landed in one spot for very long. He would cause significant tension on the Nashville bench in the upcoming campaign despite leading the team with 41 appearances.

Other than Nashville's six-year veteran in right field (Wiseman), most of the rest of the squad suffered from an identity crisis when it came to public recognition. Three daily newspapers were about to change all of that. In May, Luke Lea hired Vanderbilt graduate Grantland Rice as the city's first sports editor at his new *Nashville Tennessean*. In Rice, he found the rare combination of dedicated sportsman, insightful reporter and classical writer. The new sports scribe was struck by Nashville's shallow talent pool but reserved criticism of fellow Tennessean Perdue. Rice's hiring inspired Nashville's other two broadsheets to hire sports desk chiefs too. Within a year, the *Nashville Banner* and *Nashville American* selected Richard Hunter Yancey, Jr., and William James Ewing, Jr., respectively. Altogether, this triumvirate elevated the up-and-coming profession of sports journalism, especially in baseball.[82] At first, the Nashville editors did not know what nickname to use for their professional nine. The *Banner* referred to them as "Boosters" while the *American* used "Hustlers." The *Tennessean* preferred the standard practice of the day in selecting team nicknames by referencing the manager's last name, thus the "Dobbers."

Outside of amateur baseball circles, Hub was a relatively unknown figure in Nashville. Indeed, the *American* misspelled his name — "Purdue" — for the first month of the new season. The *Banner* introduced Hub to enthusiastic fandom as "a right-handed, spit ball artist."[83] Dobbs was ecstatic over the Cubs castoff; he claimed Hub could control his spitball from three different release points — overhand, underhand, and sidearm. Hub was equally enthused about his opportunities in Nashville, acknowledging that he was not quite ready for the majors. "I haven't shaken all of the hayseed out of my hair yet," admitted the Gallatian in the *Chicago Daily Tribune*.[84]

Dobbs did not hesitate to use his most recent acquisition. Inserting Hub in the starting rotation which already featured Duggan, Yerkes and Sorrells, the manager called upon the Gallatin native to throw several innings of relief against John McGraw and his visiting New York Giants on April 2. The youngster was roughed up for four runs, and must have been in awe — it marked his first face off with the legendary Christy Mathewson.[85]

The Industrial Revolution directly impacted Nashville baseball in Hub's inaugural season in the Southern. The club's owners installed two arc lamps and placed them atop the grandstand so that patrons could keep track of the number of outs. League president Kavanaugh had also directed all teams to post current scores from around the league, provided by electric ticker, on slate boards attached to the outfield fence. Several "details" were also set up in the downtown theatre district, outside the three newspaper offices and at select businesses. The Hippodrome skate rink, for example, was a popular location frequented by baseball loyalists. The club called games at 3:30 P.M. to afford factory workers the opportunity to attend. And Nashville's bourgeoning traction network made it possible for people living several miles away to utilize the trolleys to reach Athletic Park.[86] Finally, Dobbs agreed to telephone final line scores when the team was on the road, and local detailers promptly scribbled these results on their chalk boards. Most of these arrangements reflected the new economic order of rapid communication and mass transportation as well as the emerging spirit of progressivism which emphasized organization and preparation. Baseball was one of the major beneficiaries of economic and social reform in Nashville. Once, when Dobbs' contingent was out of town, the club owners rented Athletic Park to a traveling circus which set up its rings on the infield grass.[87] Not all improvisation reflected the new spirit of modernization.

Hub's first month in the Southern was a rough adjustment. In early May, he owned a paltry 3–3 record when he entered the box at West End Park in Little Rock. His presence excited the Finnites, who relished the opportunity to face "a big league cast-off."[88] Hub did not finish the fourth inning, and he was fortunate to escape with no decision. More important, the affair marked a disturbing weakness that became a trend — if Hub was not "on" at the beginning of his outings he usually fell victim to multiple first inning tallies.

Hub justified his slow start with Nashville to the official scorekeeper and sports editor of the *Banner,* Yancey, confiding that he was "a warm weather pitcher,"[89] an excuse that would be tendered frequently throughout his career. At the *American,* Ewing hinted at a more plausible reason: "Perdue's poor showing to date is probably due to his [overweight] physical condition."[90] Had Hub contracted pork chop fever? He twirled a gem in Memphis less than a week later but then disappeared from the slab for a month.

Nashville trolley on Buchanan Street with poster advertising Vols game on June 28, 1907 (courtesy of Tennessee State Library and Archive, Nashville).

Dobbs utilized Hub between slab appearances as the third base coach, a duty he first undertook in Vincennes. The boisterous Tennessean quickly became a fan favorite; his chatty and humorous jibes entertained Nashvillians who quickly became accustomed to his on-field antics and distinctive "Gallatin accent."[91] But something was physically wrong with Hub when the team checked into the stylish St. Charles Hotel in New Orleans. Shortly, Yancey and Ewing were reporting that the affable slab man was confined to his room with a case of mumps. His jaw, claimed the latter, hung down over his chin like bags of corn meal and he had no discernible neck. As the team pushed on to Shreveport, Hub was left at the hotel with instructions to make his way home as soon as possible.[92]

Lying on his sickbed in the St. Charles, Hub was visited by several members of the Atlanta squad who had just arrived for a three-game tilt with New Orleans. Jim "The Human Giraffe" Fox and Louis "The Cuban" Castro did not realize Hub was sick so they played a prank. When the Atlantans realized that the normally fun-loving Hub was not receptive to their joke but quite ill with a contagious disease, they bolted from the room. The players raced down to the lobby, demanded different accommodations on the other side of the hotel, and pleaded with manager Smith to vacate their entire team from the building as a precaution. As Hub recuperated, Dobbs added Clarence Nelson to the pitcher-starved roster, but his presence hardly impacted the club's fortunes, which were in the midst of a month-long swoon.[93]

By mid–June there were disheartened rumblings that disharmony was spreading among several players on the Nashville bench. At this critical juncture in the season, Dobbs brought back Hub, but the decision was premature. His first four appearances following his five-week hiatus all resulted in one-sided losses in which the Dobbers were outscored, 23–3. The club also lost its top hitter, catcher Jack Hardy, to an injury following a violent collision at home plate. The team was reeling out of control and slid deeper in the second division of the league standings.[94]

The Nashville ship momentarily corrected itself when Hub pitched a dandy shutout over Montgomery in late June. "To see Mr. Perdue back on the shift in such elegant form pleases the fanatics [fans] immensely," cheered Rice in his first-ever acknowledgement of Hub in print. "Ever since the fatal mumps overtook Hub and laid him low in May he has been a blighted being."[95] Over the next six weeks, Hub won seven games and singlehandedly kept the club out of the league basement. In the midst of the streak, Ewing noted that Hub exhibited "good speed, plenty of curves, a good spitter, and perfect control."[96] He also revealed that Hub frequently got down on himself if he fell behind early in contests. In one of the victories over Ted "Old Man" Breitenstein of New Orleans, Hub pitched with added edginess — he suffered from a nagging toothache. Realizing Hub's reputation for inconsistency, Rice bestowed the first of his many nicknames on the Gallatin product — "the untamed son of Sumner County."[97]

Dobbs was desperately searching for answers when he brought in new players like Grant Shopp and Art Nichols in mid–July, but these fixes were too late. By early August, the Boosters-Hustlers-Dobbers were, once again, dropping in the standings and battling player defeatism. The acquisition of shortstop Lew Carr from Shreveport spelled an impending explosion from within the ranks of the team. The keystone duties had belonged to McCormick, but the Jersey City product exhibited an erratic glove. No one questioned his offensive credentials or base running skills. But McCormick displayed a contentious attitude toward teammates and a volatile and negative relationship with hometown fans. The disgruntled shortstop was a catalyst for "knockers" (complainers) on the roster and a leading roadblock to Dobbs' leadership.

Hub offered his own brand of disenchantment. Feeling aggrieved that he had lost salary when the Cubs sold him to Nashville, he petitioned the National Commission to claim that, since the major league season ran a month longer than the Southern Association, he was entitled to an extra $200 from the Nashville organization. The arbitration board denied his request, pointing out that Hub's current club had generously agreed to pay his monthly salary at the big league rate.[98] This instance was the first, but certainly not the last time Hub would challenge management over money issues.

The wheels completely fell off the Nashville wagon when the Dobbers traveled to Birmingham to open a three-game series at the Slag Pile. There, pitcher Sorrells, a McCormick ally, was severely roughed up in the first game of a doubleheader and refused to take the box to finish his work. Dobbs had also inserted Carr to start at shortstop. Undoubtedly, McCormick was steamed and Sorrells put on "the baby act" to support his deposed pal. McCormick did not appear in Nashville flannels again in 1907. Feigning homesickness, Dude packed his bag and headed back to Waterbury in the Connecticut League.

Then came the fallout. Disaffection spread when outfielder Ed Pearsons left the team unannounced.[99] The departure of McCormick and Pearsons played havoc with Nashville's already shaky defense. Playing out of position, McElveen and Wiseman both attempted to fill in, without much success.

Hub's lone highlight of the 1907 season occurred when he twirled both ends of a doubleheader just as he had done in Vincennes. His iron man effort against Montgomery on August 6 resulted in a split decision, and he uncharacteristically drove in the winning run in game one in the top of the ninth inning. Feeling elated over the come-from-behind outcome, he asked Dobbs if he could go for the sweep. The second tilt, however, marked the beginning of a prolonged personal slide as Hub lost seven out of his final eight appearances and missed the opportunity for a winning season record. In these seven defeats, Hub's teammates plated only five runs.

One of Hub's losses during his team's collapse in the dog days of summer was a gut-wrenching loss to Charlie Shields in Memphis on September 1. There, a standing-room only crowd had jammed into Red Elm Park for a Sunday matinee.[100] Over the years an intense commercial rivalry had developed between Tennessee's two largest metropolises, Memphis and Nashville, and this spirit of competition spilled onto the baseball diamond as well. "Nashville fans would rather beat Memphis," proclaimed Yancey in the *Banner,* "than any other team on the whole circuit."[101]

In a fine display of craftsmanship, Hub allowed only two Memphis base runners to reach first base in the first seven innings, on a base on balls and a single, and both were thrown out attempting to steal second base. Thus, Hub had faced the minimum 21 batters as he walked to the box in the bottom of the eighth inning. An error by right fielder Wiseman led to an unearned run, but Doc redeemed himself a few plays later by throwing out a base runner at the plate to close the frame. Although the game resulted in Hub's fifth straight loss (1–0), his stirling three-hitter produced enough ammunition to bring the Tennessean back to Nashville in 1908 for another look.[102]

For all intents and purposes Nashville had given up by Labor Day, and the club fell into the cellar, never to dig themselves out. Players' frustrations spilled over on the bench when a fistfight broke out between Hardy and Yerkes a couple of days later after the pitcher made a caustic comment about the catcher's perceived lack of effort in retrieving a passed ball. The incensed backstopper wiped his muddy hands on the jersey of the opinionated pitcher and the brawl was on.[103] Sorrells was suspended for a couple of games, but bad feelings and low morale persisted. Once a stellar athlete himself, Rice opined that the team was rife with sulkers and loafers who put forth a listless brand of baseball. Simply stated, the Dobbers lacked "ginger."[104]

On the last day of the 1907 season, Hub faced New Orleans in the first game of a meaningless home doubleheader. The crack of bats striking balls echoed around the sparsely filled grandstand in Athletic Park. In an uninspiring demonstration of pitching, fielding and hitting, Nashville could not keep the visitors in check as they pounded out a lopsided victory. In the second contest, Sorrells surprised everyone with a rare win, having lost 12 of his previous 14 appearances. Rice labeled the twin bill "a farce."[105]

Rice spared no one in his critical post-season analysis of the Nashville Base Ball Club. He charged that the entire organization, from top to bottom, required a complete overhaul. Indeed, the observant sports editor had provided his outline for success weeks earlier in his *Sportsgram* column. "It's going to take an awful lot of money, time, attention and wise baseball judgment now to set things right again," opined the prophetic scribe.[106] Rice's brutally honest analysis of individual personnel did not sidestep the painfully obvious — Hub had drastically under-performed. The Tennessee twirler was too erratic; "he looked like a major leaguer one day and very bad the next," concluded Rice.[107]

In retrospect, Nashville had floundered since the McCormick Affair in mid–June when the club was mired in one of its losing streaks and ripped by dissension. Too few of the rostered veterans offered much as a positive role model for rookie Perdue, who was young, impressionable, and quite mischievous. Surrounded by mediocre athletes, the hard-throwing right-hander posted a pedestrian 11–15 record. No one could offer a valid explanation, but Hub had turned into a streak pitcher. From June 29 until August 6, Hub's record was 7–1, but only 1–7 thereafter. It is true that his teammates provided very little offensive support, averaging only 2.8 runs in Hub's 29 starts and only five runs in his last seven losses. Only once, on July 26, did his offense actually provide him with a comfortable double-digit lead. On 14 occasions, Nashville scored zero, one or two runs for the Gallatin native. These were stark numbers even by Deadball Era standards.

Several general tendencies were exposed in Hub's first three seasons in professional baseball. First, there were ample opportunities for a pitcher with a lively arm in the KITTY. The league almost exclusively scheduled doubleheaders (owing to travel costs), which placed a lot of physical stress on pitching staffs. Still, Hub was guaranteed a lot of work. Second, Hub witnessed firsthand the instability of team ownership in these early years. In Hopkinsville the franchise folded; in Vincennes, Gosnell threatened to relocate his successful team to Terre Haute; in Nashville, apathetic owners placed a substandard product on the field. And field managers coped little better. Kolb was a beacon of fresh air in Vincennes, but then again, his teams won championships. In Nashville, Dobbs did not fare as well. Throughout his career, Hub would see the best and worst of front office types and field generals.

Hub developed positive traits and bad habits in Vincennes and Nashville that would affect him throughout the remainder of his career. First, if he showed signs of trouble in the box it usually appeared in the first frame or in the sixth or seventh innings. This pattern suggests that he did not warm up properly and that he faded late in contests. The issue was likely connected with his constant struggle with weight. Being out of shape not only affected his slab work, it also adversely impacted his performance in the batter's box and on the base paths. From the outset, Hub was a poor hitter and plodding base runner. He made it no secret that he would not expend any more energy than was absolutely necessary. Second, Hub behaved in a contradictory manner on the baseball diamond. While he was argumentative with umpires regarding balls and strikes or decisions made in the field, he unleashed a marvelously entertaining personality on the bench. Fellow teammates reveled in Hub's clownish antics because he broke up stress and tension over a long and grueling season. Third, Hub was blessed with an amazing and powerful arm, but it is highly doubtful that he took proper care of it. It is extremely significant, in conclusion, that he threw the spitball from the earliest days of that controversial pitch. While other hurlers in the major leagues and Southern Association discovered and popularized the "moist ball," Hub, a rookie in baseball's hinterland and lowest professional classification, was flinging it with remarkable success. Late in life, Hub denied ever throwing the spitter. He was not telling the truth.

Other habits were also becoming apparent in Vincennes and Nashville. In the Indiana river town, Hub bore down against tough opponents like Paducah, but he slacked off against weaklings like Mattoon. Similarly, in Nashville he was highly competitive versus Memphis, but disappeared against Shreveport. Did Hub lose focus easily? Did he rise to big challenges but fall when the competition was mediocre? Why did his managers continue to show confidence in him? After all, Hub normally appeared in all three high-profile holiday doubleheaders on Decoration (Memorial) Day, the Fourth of July and Labor Day. Then there is the matter of the birthday game. In Hub's 19 seasons, he started 16 times between June 5 and June 9, and on two other occasions he was injured. It is not surprising for a slab man in the starting rotation to be present on or near June 7, but not on limited rest. Did Hub lobby his managers to appear on this personally significant date? These birthday engagements were not necessarily well-contested (6–8–2). But the matter suggests that Hub geared up mentally for certain games, motivated either by the opponent or the special occasion. Indeed, when Hub was in the right frame of mind he was practically untouchable, but when he was off he was awful. This inconsistency was clearly evident in 1905 and it carried through to 1923. Finally, Hub showed his competitive spirit most definitely whenever he dropped a heartbreaker in the first game of a doubleheader. On many occasions over the course of his career, he lobbied successfully to toss the second game as well. Such perseverance not only established Hub's reputation early on as an iron man, but often it also resulted in a victory.

All in all, Hub's up-and-down performances in 1907, questionable work ethic and association with "rounders" left his future in the Southern open to doubt heading into the off-season.

Chapter 3

1908

Someone in Nashville had listened to Rice's biting criticisms of the '07 baseball team. Before New Year's Eve, the club sported new ownership and field manager, and ambitious plans were made to refurbish Athletic Park. Rice did his part to generate public interest in creating new player nicknames, orchestrating a public referendum to select a more fitting cognomen for the new nine, and renaming the ball yard to meet the needs of his unique poetic writing style. These changes were closely followed by local sports readers, but none received more scrutiny than the hiring of Bill Bernhard to replace Dobbs who had resigned and eventually returned to manage Chattanooga in the new SALLY circuit.[1] A seasoned former big league hurler with Philadelphia and Cleveland, "Strawberry Bill" brought an impressive resumé to Nashville. Bernhard worked closely with his best friend, Indians manager Napoleon Lajoie, to "farm" talented prospects or injured (but veteran) players to Nashville. Hub stood to benefit from the new skipper's firm leadership and vast knowledge of pitching mechanics, but only if he chose to become more serious and disciplined about his craft. Perhaps, Hub might reach new heights, rekindle old prospects with the Majors, and contribute to his third championship in four seasons. With Bernhard's arrival, the slackers were put on immediate notice—the shenanigans of '07 would not be tolerated under his command. Was Hub listening?

Rice was adept at hanging quirky monikers on ball players in an effort to generate public interest in the product—Southern Association baseball. Rice instinctively liked Perdue—both men were Tennesseans by birth and practically the same age. Rice once referred to Perdue as "... our old college chum from Sumner County," perhaps an indication that they had once competed against each other at the collegiate level.[2] The slender scribe was taken by Hub's husky frame—5' 10" and close to 200 lbs. The hurler carried a good portion of his weight below the waist, and Rice could not help but notice that his shape resembled a pear or hubbard squash. Working from the assumption that Hub was his christened name, Rice nicknamed him "Hurling Hub." His tongue-in-cheek sobriquet, "The Gallatin Squash," came much later.[3]

The poetic Rice was adept at attaching labels to Southern Association teams and stadiums which added special flavor when he promoted the upcoming season. In operation since 1885, Athletic Park had crumbled into an archaic facility in desperate need of repair or demolition. The location of the stadium, however, was the envy of many southern franchises for its ideal proximity to established big businesses as well as a new residential district, North Nashville. A group of entrepreneurs stepped forward to purchase the franchise. The new corporation included James B. Carr (president of B. H. Stief Jewelry Co.), Thomas James Tyne (lawyer and state legislator), J. T. Connor (real estate), James A. Bowling (contractor), Robert L. Bolling (lawyer), Rufus E. Fort (physician), William G. Hirsig (automobile and tire dealer), and Ferdinand E. Kuhn (shoe merchant). Well known attorney S. A. Champion agreed to supply legal services. These new owners envisioned an ambitious project to totally renovate the downtrodden ball yard along the lines of recently completed facilities in Atlanta (Ponce de Leon Park) and New Orleans (Athletic Park).[4] Mayor James S. Brown, a self-proclaimed baseball fanatic, encouraged the investors to provide a stable financial base for their new venture. These men of wealth took Brown's advise and coughed up a staggering sum by Southern standards, $50,000. Kuhn was selected to head the Board of Directors.[5]

President Kuhn and the Board accepted a new stadium design submitted by J.A.G. Sloan Company of Chicago. Sloan's design called for a complete overhaul; the reconfiguration moved home plate slightly toward third base, erected a covered grandstand and uncovered bleachers down both base lines, installed "opera" (box) seats for affluent customers, built a state-of-the-art clubhouse with plumbing and lockers, framed a covered shed atop the grandstand roof behind home plate for Nashville's sports scribes, hung a hand-operated chalk scoreboard from the right field wall, and improved the playing surface and drainage system (which lay 22' below street level and only one-quarter mile from the spring floodwaters of the Cumberland River). These progressive times also demanded greater attention to public safety in construction materials as well as considerations of city beautification. While some of these regulations were addressed, Nashville's new baseball temple would more typically resemble the familiar nineteenth century all-wood models found in junior circuits throughout the country, and not the current trend in fireproof structures made from concrete and steel in large urban venues.[6]

One of the charms of minor league parks, then and now, is their peculiar field layouts, and Nashville's planners were forced to work around a couple of physical irregularities and unique natural obstacles. The pancake-shaped infield was especially close to the spectators with third base only twenty-six feet away from the stands, and first base only forty-two-feet away. The fans' proximity to the field was cozy, but the left field line was quite spacious:

center field: 421'

left field: 334' right field: 262'

    The tight right field corner and cavernous power alleys conformed to street patterns outside the stadium, and the layout inside posed difficulties particularly for visiting outfielders. The right field wall a left-handed power hitter's dream, but defending it became a nightmare and not simply because of the short porch. Indeed, this "garden" was the ball yard's hallmark oddity and baseball stadium historian Philip Lowry called it "the craziest right field in history."[7] The irregular contour of the land itself caused an additional problem. Beginning at 225' down the right field line the ground sloped upward at a 45 degree angle for approximately twelve feet and then leveled off at a ten-foot terrace. From this point, the angled slope resumed all the way to the outfield wall. In all, the playing surface ascended approximately twenty-five-feet. Nashville's right field was soon known as "the Dump" in part because the city's smoldering landfill lay just beyond the wall but largely because it was extremely tricky to defend because of the uneven terrain. Montgomery outfielder Casey Stengel once joked that he laid down a perfect bunt along the right field line for a home run.[8] Pitchers did not find the close confines nearly so amusing, however; in later years they wryly nicknamed it "suffer hell." A gradual, but much more playable incline also existed in left field. However, a man-made obstacle protruded from the left field corner in foul territory — a sulphur spring house. Finally, a sewer/drainage ditch traversed outermost center field adding another odiferous quality to the field.

    Wiseman had patrolled the Dump with pinpoint precision since the birth of the Southern Association in 1901.[9] Rice deeply admired the career minor leaguer's work ethic, defensive skills, handsome boyish looks, and longevity in a Nashville uniform. "Any time an athlete sticks to a minor league town over three seasons," said the sportswriter, "you can put it down as a safe bet that he is delivering the stuff from year to year."[10] Admiring fans had bestowed a less commonly known nickname on Wiseman because he had successfully mastered the idiosyncrasies of the Dump. "The Goat" routinely positioned himself at the base of the first incline. On long fly balls, he turned his back on home plate, methodically raced uphill, picked up the flight of the sphere, and made the catch. Occasionally Wiseman threw out runners at first base on hard hit grounders to right field. Such defensive prowess earned Wiseman mention in Edward Michael Ashenback's 1911 book, *Humor Among the Minors.*[11]

Rice, eager for the season to get underway, decided that Nashville's new arena also needed a new name befitting its fresh new facade. He believed an elegant name would elevate the building to a higher level of social acceptability while making a positive architectural contribution to the city's changing urban landscape in much the way Poncey did for Atlanta and the Slag Pile failed to do for Birmingham. After careful consideration, the scribe suggested "Sulphur Dell." He hoped the choice would make a pastoral connection with the unique physical feature which had dominated the grounds since primordial times — the sulphur spring. Equally important, Rice believed that "dell" provided more rhyming possibilities for his lyrical urges. His first poem, entitled "In Sulphur Dell," appeared on the *Tennessean's* sports page on January 14.[12]

> There as a sound of revelry by day
>   In Sulphur Dell with axes swinging free —
> And every fan there passed, yelled "Hip-Hooray —
>   Lay on McDuff, and give one punch for me."
>   And from afar the echo rolled in glee —
> "The Nashville grandstand's being torn away."
>
> Sweet are the songs which Madame Calve sings
>   But not so sweet as that of falling axe
> In Sulphur Dell where every echo rings
>   With timbers falling under mighty whacks
>   Keep up the good work — break your blooming backs;
> Keep up the good work — break your blooming necks
> We'll give a cheer each time the axlet swings.[13]

Rice also hoped to bestow a bucolic name on the field in order to add rural flavor to its distinctly urban setting.

As the stadium neared completion and players began drifting back into Nashville for the "ante season," Rice tackled one final chore — settling on a team moniker. On the eve of the league's winter meeting at President Kavanaugh's residence in Little Rock, Rice opened this public discussion by reminding readers that the Nashville nines had played under three nicknames in '07 — the Hustlers, Boosters and Dobbers. Rice quipped in *Sportograms* that "it took an awful lot of nerve to call them 'Hustlers' especially after the first of August."[14] The idea of finding a more suitable and lasting nickname inspired Rice and his two colleagues to put their heads together and sponsor a contest.

Actually, Ewing had originally invited Rice to join him in picking a team name in hopes of standardizing baseball accounts in the city's three newspapers. Yancey concurred but suggested "the tagging" should be left to the "vox populi." "The cognomen of a baseball team usually is one of its most important assets," argued Yancey, "and a nickname that is attractive helps the popularity of the club."[15] The sports editor of the *Banner* further appealed to his colleagues in other Southern Association cities to stick with the formal nickname chosen by the member teams. He pointed out that Montgomery, Little Rock, and Memphis had each used more than one sobriquet in '07.[16] He conveniently neglected to mention that Nashville had used three.

On February 15, the *Tennessean*, *Banner*, and *American* simultaneously announced a contest to select the new club's name.[17] The sportswriters narrowed the choices for the public to consider. The self-appointed screeners mulled over a list of several nominees — Hermits, Politicians, Presidents, Beavers, Tigers, Sulphurites, and Hickorys. Meanwhile, Rice stressed the importance of selecting a name "that would stick," like Pelicans (New Orleans) and Barons (Birmingham). The scribes settled on three finalists: Volunteers, Rocks and Lime Rocks. Rice's favorite choice, the Vols, referenced the spirit of volunteerism which had swept over the state in every war beginning with the War of 1812. "Volunteers is the appellation that makes the Tennessee heart swell with pride," agreed Yancey, "[because] the name suggests courage, and should prove a talisman of victory."[18] Rice, a master of baseball slang, instructed the bug colony [fans] to mail their choice to manager Bernhard before the deadline on February 28. The contest excited the public and more than 1,000 ballots were cast. On the 29th, the three dailies concurrently declared the overwhelming winner beneath front page headlines — Vols copped top honors with over 950 votes.[19] Rice had been instrumental in hanging nicknames that stuck — on stadium, team, and Hub Perdue.

Hub was anxious to get the new season underway. While he wintered in Gallatin as a bank clerk, a funny story appeared in the Nashville newspaper. It seems there were only two employees working the till, and one of them had gone to lunch. Eating his noontime meal in a local restaurant, the first teller was shocked to see Hub walking through the door. "Did you lock the safe, Hub," he frantically inquired? "Naw, but I did put a chair under the [safe] handle."[20] Always a jester, Hub's future *did not* lay in banking.

Bernhard penciled in Perdue as the Vols final starter — a tenuous slot which implied his shaky status in the rotation. During his first outing, the sixth game of the season, Hub limited the powerful Montgomery lineup to only three hits. He mixed his blazing fastball with a sharp curveball, and changed speeds effectively. Not known for his batting, the Tennessean surprised the crowd and dropped down a bunt single to continue an important rally and eventual victory. In his second appearance against the same Senators, Perdue surrendered fourteen base hits in only six innings.[21] Such inconsistent results supported his bogus claim that he was a warm weather pitcher. Another Hublore entry.

In early June, Perdue brashly complained to Bernhard that he wasn't getting enough slab work despite his poor 2–4 showing. So, the manager decided to test his disgruntled hurler and slated him to face perennial powerhouse New Orleans several days later. Hurling Hub made good on his word, scattering seven hits in eight frames before being yanked with the score knotted at 2–2.²² Over the next two weeks, Perdue went on a tear winning five straight including a three-hit shutout over Atlanta where he struck out nine Crackers. As further evidence of his farm boy toughness, he plunked opposing pitcher, southpaw Grant Schopp. Bernhard's confidence in his young protégé started to rise, and, shortly, the chirpy Perdue was selected to third base coach between pitching appearances.

A jubilant Perdue sought out Rice at the *Tennessean's* sports desk near the end of his winning streak. Rice asked the affable Volunteer slab artist to what he attributed his recent success. Giving up cigarettes had bettered his physical endurance, Perdue began. "As long as I was hitting those nails, I was never in good shape to work." He also praised Bernhard who had set aside three days each week to offer instruction "on the mechanics of delivery." Perdue added that his teammates held Bernhard in high esteem. "A fellow that wouldn't work for Bernhard wouldn't be willing to work for anybody," confided Hub.²³ In Bernhard, Hub had found the mentor he most desperately needed.

Indeed, by the Fourth of July, Bernhard was molding the club into his image of a winner. He had released two disgruntled pitchers (Yerkes and Sorrells), and after McCormick took "french leave" for the second year in a row, the troubled infielder was blackballed from organized baseball by the National Commission. He sought out and received rookie first baseman "Gentleman Jake" Daubert and veteran outfielder Harry "Deerfoot" Bay from Cleveland to solidify the defense. And he purchased the contracts for Walter East (second base) and Johnny Siegle (center field) to complement his big league additions. Finally, he moved Willis "Kid" Butler and McElveen to their natural positions — shortstop and third base respectively. Yes, Bernhard's Vols were beginning to exhibit different attitudes.

One of Hub's most memorable performances in his 19-year career occurred less than one week later. The Volunteers were in Mobile on July 9 for a series with the competitive Sea Gulls in cavernous Monroe Park. Bernhard had recently settled on a pitching rotation that offered the club its greatest chance of success, and it featured Hub's promotion to #1. Looking to the future, Hub would twirl almost every series opener for the remainder of the season. In Oyster City, Hub was locked in a scoreless pitchers' duel with Lucien "Clarence" Torrey; indeed, both hurlers appeared to gain strength as the contest wore on. Neither team mustered much offense. Torrey kept the bases empty between the 9th and 14th, and only two Vols ever reached third base. Costly base running mistakes cost Hub a victory in each of the final two frames. Owing to darkness, Umpire W. B. Carpenter ended the three-hour marathon after 17 innings without a single run crossing the plate.

Pitchers Perdue and Torrey were hailed as iron men for their masterful slab work. Hamilton Love, a clerk by profession and beat writer for the Vols in *The Sporting News*, surmised that Perdue "has done more than any one man to hold up the [Nashville] team."[24] Rice proclaimed it "the greatest game of baseball that has ever been witnessed."[25] But Yancey said it best when he concluded that the Perdue-Torrey matchup had been the greatest game ever played in Dixie, an encomium Rice resurrected to describe the league championship game on the final day of the 1908 season.[26] Regardless of these superlatives, Hub's no-decision on July 9 went down as the second-longest game in Volunteers history, and the longest scoreless feature *ever* in the Southern Association.[27]

In a script that could not have been imagined in Hollywood for its dramatic effect, Hub took the mound four days later in Little Rock. Charles Ebbets had journeyed from Brooklyn to scout two Vols on his payroll plus take a look at Travelers rookie sensation Tris Speaker. Hub failed to field his position, and his two throwing errors in the third gave the home squad an early lead. Then Hurling Hub buckled down and threw ten scoreless frames. After 13 innings, the umpire terminated the game with the score wedged, 3–3. Crestfallen, Hub trudged off the field. He had thrown 30 innings in the span of four days without earning a decision. In 59 innings, the fast baller had surrendered only three earned runs.[28]

Hub was chagrined to learn that Ebbets had not been impressed by his gritty slab resumé. The Superbas owner confided in Bernhard that he deemed Ralph "The Human Ripcord" Savidge, the Memphis knuckleballer, the best pitching prospect in the Southern, and not Hub. Furthermore, Ebbets was very impressed with Speaker.

In Hubesque fashion, Perdue had inadvertently contributed to the growing prowess of Speaker while, at the same time, lowering his own stock. In a story recounted nearly 40 years later to the Old Timers Baseball Association of Nashville (OTBA) and reported by Raymond Johnson in the *Tennessean*, Hub recalled his longest swat in 1908 — a blast that was never recorded as a base hit. With two Vols aboard, Hub cracked a hard line drive to center field, but while he sauntered toward first base he decided to jibe Travelers benchwarmers on the way. Meanwhile, Speaker picked up Hub's screamer and fired the ball to first base to put out the trash-talker. The official scorecard read "8–3." The foolish antic served to reinforce Ebbets' positive evaluation of Savidge and negative opinion of Hub.[29] It did not, however, prevent Hub from outlasting Memphis in an 11-inning, one-run victory during his next appearance on the slab, his third extra-inning tilt in four starts.

Hot and humid weather took its toll on the Nashville workhorse, and every pitcher on the staff was nursing a sore arm. On July 30, the visiting Memphis Turtles were on the receiving end of a no-hitter through six innings when Bernhard suddenly pulled Hub after he surrendered a pair of runs. Afterwards, Hub allegedly contracted a fever. The Nashville manager sent his prize hurler home to recuperate, but rumors circulated that Hub was upset over being yanked. Returning on the next morning's train, Hub admitted to Rice that he felt "under appreciated." He also complained of a sore shoulder.[30] In his next start against cellar dwelling Birmingham, Hub's attitude continued to suffer as he appeared indifferent on the slab "and fielded like an elephant," according to Yancey.[31] Barons left fielder Noah Henline lit up Hub for four hits and scored the Barons' first three runs. Then the visitors from Alabama pureed the mush-armed Perdue, and hecklers in the Sulphur Dell grandstands clamored for Bernhard to "take out the cheese."[32] Fatigued, Hurling Hub did not pitch again for over two weeks. Meanwhile, Bernhard recalled Carl Vedder Sitton from Jacksonville in the SALLY to replace him.[33] Sitton and Savidge had been teammates on the 1907 Jays, and together they perfected a devastating spitball and knuckleball, respectively.

Hub returned to action in Montgomery but it was a disaster. Blustery wind blew billowing clouds of dust across the infield, and both teams took advantage of the inclement weather to register 12 runs in the fifth. The umpire stopped the farce several times, and 24 safeties were recorded against Hub and his counterpart, Herb Juul. Ewing lampooned the contest as "a merry-go-round."[34] Perhaps a more apropos return to the box occurred two days later when Hub made a rare relief appearance against Birmingham and held the Slagmen to one base runner in six scoreless innings, but earned no decision.

Bernhard was not convinced that Hub's shoulder had mended sufficiently to return to full-time duty, so he demoted his ace to the bullpen. But events sometimes outweigh the most thoughtful plans of managers. The truth is that injuries had decimated Nashville's pitching corps. When Hub performed brilliantly in closing out Birmingham in the first game of a doubleheader on August 22, he pestered Bernhard to start the second game. The skipper agreed out of necessity, but the results were disastrous. Hub lasted less than two innings and suffered through a six-run onslaught at the hands of the Barons. His replacement on the slab was an unlikely candidate — first baseman Daubert.[35]

Although Hub had been taken out of action, he was destined to play another role in the Birmingham twin bill. The sun was setting in the fifth, and two innings later twilight had settled over the field. Barons shortstop Tom Downey ignited some loose papers in the pitching box, a hint to the umpire that it might be wise to discontinue the game. Not to be shown up, umpire Tom Brown fined Downey $5 for his antics. Minutes later, Hub appeared in the third base coach's box clutching a lit candle. Unamused, Brown tossed him out of the game. Once decorum had been restored, the umpire ended the contest on his own terms an inning later.[36] The flickering candle story entered the annals of Hublore.

As the Southern circuit entered the final month of the season, a playoff atmosphere enveloped the city of Nashville as its team battled neck-and-neck with New Orleans and Memphis for first place. On August 30, President Kavanaugh traveled to Red Elm Park to watch a key encounter between the Vols and Turtles. An intense interstate rivalry had been heating up all season between the Tennessee teams, and this particular matchup promised to be extra special. Hub was coaching third base when Bernhard summoned him to the box in the eighth to relieve Duggan with the score jammed at 1–1. Hub pitched the final six innings, but the Vols blew two scoring opportunities when shortstop Willis "Kid" Butler committed a base running mistake and added a fielding gaffe. The umpire suspended the 14-inning affair, and Hub had been connected with yet another extra inning no-decision.[37]

The following day, August 31, was an important date for minor leaguers who held big league aspirations because it marked the occasion when major league clubs announced which prospects they planned to draft as well as release from their contracts. This process directly affected half of Nashville's personnel. The Big Show axe fell on veteran pitchers Winford "Win" Kellum and Duggan, outfielder Bay, and catcher Hardy. On the up side, Brooklyn tendered a contract to third baseman McElveen, and Cleveland made offers to first baseman Daubert and pitching sensation Sitton. Concerning Perdue there was only disappointing silence.[38]

A new champion would be crowned in the Southern based on how the three contenders played in the final weeks. Nashville opened the September slate with four consecutive doubleheaders owing to the league's inefficient policy which allowed managers to decide when cancelled games should, or should not, be made up. This scheduling gauntlet took place every September and it placed tremendous pressure on pitchers and players alike on every contender, not just Nashville. Tensions spilled into a bench brawl reminiscent of the Hardy-Yerkes brouhaha on the Nashville sideline in 1907. It occurred during the first game of a doubleheader in New Orleans. The fracas erupted when Kellum called McElveen a "fathead" and screamed that the third sacker "did not know his business" after committing a fielding error and showing no remorse afterwards. Punches were exchanged and the unlikely pugilists were quickly separated by teammates. The squabble did not end there, however. Later that evening, Kellum jumped McElveen in a hallway at the St. Charles

Hotel and the fisticuffs resumed. Both men sported facial bruises and injured pride as the team boarded a train bound for Mobile the next morning.[39]

Although out of contention for the league banner, the Sea Gulls were a dangerous opponent — a middle-of-the-pack squad with nothing to lose. And the Vols would play them seven times in the final two weeks. Hub, a true gamer who understood the importance of every late-season contest, took the slab in the opener in the Gulf Coast city. The Tennessean set aside his personal feelings in not being drafted, scattered six hits and struck out seven. But opposing pitcher Gordon "The Featherweight Phenom" Hickman matched his efforts. The scoreboard showed nothing but zeroes in the bottom of the ninth when the normally reliable right fielder, Wiseman, turned into the defensive goat by misplaying a leadoff single which rolled between his legs. Rattled, Hub issued a base on balls and a clutch single to end the game in heartbreaking fashion, 1–0.[40]

Shaken by the gut-wrenching defeat, Hub pleaded with Bernhard for permission to start the second game of the twin bill — the second request of its kind in less than two weeks. Bernhard mysteriously consented again. Nashville's offense manufactured an early two-run cushion, and Hub dominated with a four-hit shutout. Seabough, who had been part of the Cubs' rookie class in 1907 with Hub, had been picked up by the Vols in the off-season, and the Springfield (MO) native became Hub's personal catcher for the next three years. Known for his defensive agility, the backstopper performed his duties in both games without an error and made 14 putouts.[41] On the Mobile side, a young rookie acquired from Shreveport played in his first Southern Association contest — future Hall of Fame outfielder Zack Wheat.

Hub's 17 frames versus Mobile were impressive in their statistical breakdown; only one run and ten hits allowed with 14 strikeouts. Hub's accomplishment stood out as one of the major highlights for his team; moreover, it marked a turning point in the Vols' gradually improving fortunes. Newspaper accounts were describing the three-way race in terms of percentage points three weeks prior to the conclusion of the season, and daily coverage from three sources had whipped Nashville's baseball citizenry into a frenzy.[42] Earning a split in the four-game series with the Sea Gulls, the Vols were in high spirits at the Mobile train depot. There, battery mates Perdue and Seabough entertained travelers with "a number of farewell songs" including a rendition of the wildly popular vaudeville tune, "Take Me Out to the Ball Game."[43]

As dawn broke on the morning following the Labor Day doubleheader with the Turtles, the Vols' sprint to the league title began. That afternoon's finale witnessed new benchmarks for Nashville in pitching, batting, and fielding which they'd repeat on a consistent basis over the next two weeks. Bernhard juggled his batting order and pitching rotation in anticipation of the all-important encounter with the Turtles, and he selected Hub to twirl.

Hub faced a familiar foe in Savidge, the knuckleballer who had stolen his thunder with Ebbets and was recently drafted by Cincinnati. Working for the first time since his 17-inning stint five days earlier, the undrafted and highly motivated Hub hurled what eyewitnesses described as his most overpowering performance of the year. Ewing stated that he had never seen the Tennessean throw so hard, and Rice added that Hub pitched "the best game of his rural life"—a four-hit shutout (10–0) with seven strike outs.[44] Meanwhile, the Vols reached a lofty offensive plateau; they stroked 15 hits, including two home runs by Daubert, a power surge practically unheard-of in Southern circles.

Nashville's offensive juggernaut now combined with three notable pitching performances to completely demolish the reeling Little Rock club, now Speaker-less. First, the slab hero, Duggan, fired a no-hitter in which only two Arkansans reached base. "They couldn't have hit him with a gatling gun," quipped Rice.[45] The following day, the Vols buried their opponent, 20–1, and Sitton pitched a one-hit gem. Finally, Hub provided the topping with an 11–1 pasting to conclude the third one-sided massacre. The Vols had outscored the punchless Travelers (32–2), outhit them (51–9), and totally flustered their hitters. "The race has reached the sizzling point," cheered Rice gleefully.[46]

Hub started only once more in 1908—the final home appearance of Mobile immediately prior to the club's winner-take-all showdown with New Orleans. Memphis had already been mathematically eliminated from the race by the time Hub took the box to face an old adversary. But the diminutive Hickman left his control at the Duncan Hotel. He quickly fell behind by five runs, and plunked Bay on his bad knee. When the Phenom tossed his third wild pitch in as many frames, Lee Garvin stripped off his catcher's gear in frustration and removed himself from the firing line. Meanwhile, Hub picked apart his hapless opponent "with his old-time smoke" and approached the matinee as if it were a scoreless tie. Rice summarized the lopsided 10–1 route, and amended his earliest moniker for Hub, referring to him now as "The Pride of Sumner County."[47] No longer was Hurling Hub considered "untamed."

Hub had put the Vols in position to compete for the league championship in a winner-take-all, season-ending series versus the New Orleans Pelicans. During the recent 13-game home stand, the Vols offensive had established total domination over their foes. The club averaged 13.8 hits and 7.5 runs per contest, and batted .382 as a team, most un–Deadball-like figures. Stellar performances from the hurlers also figured prominently in the recent successes, with Hub setting the tone at Mobile. His iron man lesson in sheer determination surely inspired teammates who were locked in the throes of a tight pennant race. While the offense provided tremendous run support, Hub and Duggan posted identical 4–1 records in the decisive final month.[48]

Championship weekend, 1908. The tables were set for a marvelous head-to-head showdown between the Vols and Pels. Only two teams in the circuit remained from the original eight, and their winning percentages were separated by the thinnest of margins—.007. A publicist's dream! Both managers liked their odds of taking two out of three games from their worthy opponent to cop the league crown. Bernhard was encouraged by the manner in which his squad had competed against the Pelicans to begin the streak. "Athletic Park to-day, to-morrow, and Saturday will harbor within its four corners the most numerous, the wildest, and the craziest assortment of frenzied humanity ever gathered together in any baseball lot in Dixie Land," predicted Yancey.[49] The climax to the 1908 Southern Association series had arrived. The three tiffs promised high drama, excitement, and raw emotion.

The Nashville–New Orleans series was important not only to the principal cities involved. Neighboring communities in Middle Tennessee were sharing in the excitement. Chalk scoreboards were set up outside telegraph and newspaper offices on several town squares to inform followers of the inning-by-inning progress of each game. For example, in Hub's hometown the *Examiner* mounted a detail, and by game time the entire east side of Public Square was blocked off to traffic by a sea of humanity. Fellow Gallatians commented with pride about the contributions made by their homegrown hero, Hub Perdue.[50] "Interest is at a fever pitch all over the South," concluded Yancey.[51] Well, at least in Middle Tennessee.

Large numbers of visitors were arriving at Nashville's stately Union Station from the surrounding countryside, and choked the city's trolley lines two hours before game time. But not everyone was in town to see the game. The Tennessee State Fair, slated to open on September 21, contributed to the festive atmosphere as well as the weekend population boom. And a high-profile Democratic gubernatorial debate between incumbent Malcolm Patterson and challenger Edward Ward Carmack at the Ryman Auditorium also attracted its fair share of patrons. Politics, baseball and the state fair — each event added substantially to the city's congestion.

The mood at Sulphur Dell was electric for the first game. A capacity crowd of 5,000 anxiously buzzed in anticipation of the first pitch, and their excitement infected the Vols. Rice thought that the hometown boys looked nervous in warm-ups in contrast to the cool looseness projected by the team on the other side of the diamond. As game time approached, the temperature climbed to 86 degrees. Called for 3:30 P.M., the lateness was intended to allow workers from the commercial district an opportunity to attend the game. Umpire W. B. Carpenter, considered by many baseball people to be the best

Baseball "detail" in front of *Nashville Tennessean* and *Nashville American* (courtesy of Tennessee State Library and Archive, Nashville, Tennessee).

strike-and-ball arbiter in the league, flipped the ball to Nashville's surprise starter, Big Bill Bernhard. The championship series was under way.[52] Hub watched the gripping game from his vantage point in the third base coach's box.

As Bernhard's boys struggled with shaky nerves and porous defense through the early innings, the Pelicans performed efficiently. "Playing scientific ball and working like a well oiled machine" was the way Rice described them.

An appreciative Nashville crowd applauded several splendid defensive plays turned in by the visitors. Rice described "the fast and snappy 5–1 drubbing as "a clean cut, non-debatable victory for New Orleans.[53]

Now Nashville trailed New Orleans by 1.5 games with two meetings left. The question on everyone's mind was why Bernhard had not thrown southpaw Kellum, the former major leaguer and "Pelican-killer" with three victories over New Orleans in the regular season. No answer was forthcoming to the second guessers. Diehard Vols fans understood that the club must overcome its defensive lapse, rediscover its offense, and pitch at a higher caliber if they expected to raise the championship banner in Nashville. Bernhard selected Duggan to hurl the must win second game.[54]

It was Manager Frank's turn to fall victim to public scrutiny when he overlooked star twirler Ted Breitenstein, and instead chose William "Silver Bullet" (or "Whoa Bill") Phillips to oppose Duggan. Frank had great confidence in Phillips' 40 year-old arm, but Rice and Ewing were perplexed that the 17-game winner, Breitenstein, had not received the nod instead.[55]

Another sellout crowd filed into Sulphur Dell on September 18 hoping that the 1908 season would not come to an end for their beloved Vols. For the second straight day, mid-afternoon temperatures climbed to the mid–80s with blue sky overhead. As the contest proceeded, Duggan breezed through the Pelican's lineup; on the other hand, the Silver Bullet was tagged for several clutch extra-base hits, including a solo home run by Daubert which cleared the right field fence and sealed the 6–2 victory for Nashville. With confidence restored in the hometown nine, Rice boasted that the Pelicans had as much chance of winning "the rag ... as Taft had of carrying Texas."[56] One sensed that momentum had shifted to Nashville. So whom would Bernhard and Frank select for the title game?

President Kavanaugh announced that he would attend the championship game on September 19. Anticipating an overflow crowd, club president Kuhn requested the loan of 3,000 stadium chairs from Vanderbilt University to be placed along the outfield wall. George A. Dickel, the whiskey magnate from Tullahoma, donated a winner's purse of $100 should the Vols capture the crown, and fans offered to take up collections in the grandstands. The game promised to be one of historic proportions; never before had the championship game of the Southern Association been decided in head-to-head competition on the last day of the season.

Bernhard announced another surprise — he slated Sitton, not Hub, to fling the championship match on September 19. There was wisdom behind his choice. Hub had thrown more recently than Sitton and he was 0–2–1 versus the Pelicans. By contrast Pels batters had been mesmerized by Sitton's spitball. To no one's surprise, Frank called upon his ace, "Old Man" Breitenstein, to deliver the goods in game three.

The contrast between Sitton and Breitenstein was not lost on Sam J. Stockard, a visiting columnist from Memphis. Indeed, the journalist sketched an engaging, symbolic interpretation of the impending pitcher's clash. He spotted the obvious — a generational gap between the hurlers. "It is youth against age: enthusiasm and confident determination and consciousness of superiority against frazzled-out stars.... Youth triumphs over age. It will be so today if youth backs up youth, and does not forget the main fact — that they are, and of right ought to be, masters of the diamond at Sulphur Dell this afternoon. Determination and grit will win today's battle," concluded Stoddard. Rice interjected that "Sitton was fit to pitch the game of his life."[57] Thus, the dissimilarities between Breitenstein-Sitton were set — age vs. youth, veteran vs. rookie, lefty vs. righty, favorite vs. underdog.

At noon, most businesses in the commercial district closed and downtown streets emptied. A spontaneous throng of people, from captains of industry to hourly wage laborers, lit out for Sulphur Dell in an unorganized, egalitarian march with a shared common goal: to witness Nashville's third championship in eight years. Some employees refused to work during the game in the few stores and factories that chose to remain open. Nashvillians had contracted pennant fever.

The Sulphur Dell ticket booths opened at 1 P.M. on the balmy afternoon of September 19, where a large throng of enthusiastic fans had been waiting impatiently since mid-morning to purchase their precious ducats. Police officers were caught in the middle of the madcap rush, and they were unable to preserve any sense of orderliness. In less than an hour every seat had been sold despite the fact that the game would not begin until 3:30 P.M. A standing-room-only crowd eight people deep lined up behind a roped-off area that encircled the entire outfield, which necessitated special ground rules. Many bugs expected the game to produce multiple runs and ground rule doubles as routine pop flies might land amidst the crowd standing on the playing surface. An extra squad of constables patrolled the jammed garden to prevent excitable patrons from acting irresponsibly. A crowd of African Americans sat in the bleachers, a testimony to the interracial popularity of the Vols and their susceptibility to pennant fever.[58]

Important local dignitaries attended. President Kuhn sat beside Mayor James S. Brown, who threw out the game ball from his box seat to signal the beginning of the contest. The mayor boldly claimed to be the Vols' #1 fan. Super booster Alf Williams made the identical claim from his place in the band. A makeshift detail was erected on Capitol Hill, and a man using a pair of binoculars supplied updates by zeroing in on Sulphur Dell nearly a half-mile away. Government officials, including Governor Patterson, left their offices and congregated on the north lawn to cheer for their Vols.[59] The only notable absentee from the festive gathering was President Kavanaugh, who canceled his trip to Nashville owing to illness.[60]

Sulphur Dell rocked with screaming fans as captains McElveen and George Rohe met the umpire at home plate and exchanged lineup cards. When the Vols burst from their bench onto the field to assume their positions, a collective roar from over 10,000 throats filled the air. Game time! Outfielder Roy Montgomery stepped up to the plate and Sitton prepared to deliver his first moist pitch. Yancey, the official scorekeeper, noticed that the moment produced a "sudden silence so intense that a blind man might have thought the park was empty."[61] Then "the Spitball King" sent the sphere over for a strike and the crowd exploded in relief. The much anticipated game was finally under way.

The game quickly settled into a battle of wits between the two hurlers. There was little room for error. The Pelicans mounted two serious threats throughout the afternoon, and McElveen snuffed out both rallies. The first alarm sounded in the second inning. Bob Tarlton, a first baseman recently acquired by the Birds and a five-year star in the Cotton States League, led off the frame by beating out a slow roller to Butler at shortstop. Next, Charlie Dexter grounded out to Daubert but advanced Tarlton into scoring position. "Diamond Joe" Rickert followed with a swinging bunt down the third base line. Tarlton immediately broke for third base as McElveen charged in. Recognizing he had no chance to gun down the fleet Rickert at first base, he barehanded the ball and feigned a throw to Daubert. At this moment, the rookie base runner made a most egregious mistake when he rounded third base too far. McElveen spun around in a flash, lunged at Tarleton, who was retreating to the sack, and applied the tag for the second out. Mac single-handedly thwarted the first Pelican scoring opportunity.[62]

The Tennessee third baseman was directly involved in a second sensational defensive play three innings later. Gus Dundon led off the fifth, a light-hitting batter and an unlikely person to initiate a rally. However, the Pelicans' middle infielder tied into one of Sitton's floaters and blistered "a red hot liner" in the direction of the hot corner. McElveen instinctively leaped toward shortstop, and with every ounce of strength he stretched out parallel to the ground and pawed the frozen rope out of the air with one hand. The crowd roared its approval for the acrobatic play. Nashville's three scribes agreed that Mac's snare had robbed the swift leadoff batter of a sure extra-base hit (with no outs) and therefore nipped a potential rally in the bud.[63] The next two New Orleans batters made routine outs. It was now apparent, at the midway point in the game, that a single run might make the difference between victory and defeat.

"The bloody seventh" is what Yancey dubbed the bottom of the pivotal inning, but it began rather inauspiciously for the Vols.[64] After Daubert popped out to Dexter at shortstop and Butler hit an unassisted grounder to Tarleton at first, the Vols offense came to life. An unlikely offensive spark plug, hefty catcher Ed Hurlburt, began the two-out rally with "a crashing single to right field." Then Sitton made weak contact with a pitch that trickled between Tarleton and Dundon for a scratch single. Bay observed from the batter's box that Tarleton held Sitton on at first base and Rohe was positioned deep over at third. Taking advantage of this defensive alignment, Deerfoot pushed a perfect bunt down the third base line. The bases were now loaded with Vols. Nearly half a century later, Bay recounted that his surprise bunt to load the bases to keep the rally alive in the 1908 championship game was his fondest memory in his long baseball career.[65]

The crowd sensed the defining moment of the game had arrived and mounted a frenzied "huzzah" in the grandstand as Wiseman approached the dish.[66] Everything hinged on his at-bat. Nerves were tight on both benches. Some ladies in the crowd held their hands in a prayerful position and others covered their worried faces. Men screamed themselves hoarse. Children jumped up and down excitedly with thoughts of what might occur next.

Then came Breitenstein's offering. The ball seemed to float in slow motion and all eyes shifted to Wiseman as he initiated his swing. Crack! The spheroid jumped off his bat. The sizzling line drive barely eluded the outstretched grasp of Dundon and bounced several times before resting in Bris Lord's glove in straightaway center field. Hurlburt, the last man added to the Vols roster in late August, broke for home plate "like an ice wagon" to record the first run of the game. Sitton, an excellent athlete with good foot speed, sprinted around third base. Did the third base coach try to hold him up? Was it Hub? No matter. The aggressive base runner was determined to score and break the game wide open. In the meantime, Lord pivoted and fired an accurate throw toward home. Blocking the plate with his left leg and bracing his body for a collision, catcher Harry Matthews received the ball just as Sitton launched a headfirst slide, which was more of an uncontrolled fall. The star spitballer hit his head hard on the catcher's outstretched knee and bounced off the rubber dish, but not before Matthews applied the tag. "Out!" shouted umpire Carpenter, "side's retired." Sitton, overly eager to score, had committed a base running mistake. Still, the Sulphur Dell faithful were delirious with excitement. The Vols commanded a 1-0 lead with six outs to go.[67]

Exuberance changed to dismay in an instant. As the dust settled, Sitton lay prone across the plate as teammates rushed to his aide. The Vols carried their fallen, semiconscious pitcher to the bench. The fans lapsed into an eerie silence. Bernhard shouted for Hub to warm up — and quick. But Sitton revived after several moments and insisted on finishing the game. The crowd welcomed Sitton's courage with cheers.

His adrenaline still flowing, Sitton took the slab in the ninth to face the heart of the powerful New Orleans lineup — Rohe, Lord and Tarleton. Yet the spitballer was supremely confident; he had not allowed a single base runner since the fourth. When Tarleton whiffed for the final out to preserve Sitton's three-hitter, pandemonium broke loose on the field and in the stands. He had delivered the 1908 championship to Nashville by the slenderest of margins — .002 — a league record that withstood the test of time for over three decades.[68]

The city was giddy with glee. As Vols emerged from the players' entrance, they were escorted by enthusiastic revelers to several nearby restaurants where they were treated to supper. Afterwards, the teammates reconvened at Hardy's cigar shop on the corner of Fourth and Union to replay the events of that afternoon. A brass band was procured and a spontaneous parade formed with the players lined up in marching formation through downtown streets. Sidewalk spectators became hilarious as many straw hats were punched out and rims placed around the necks of favorite players. That evening, Governor

The 1908 champion Nashville Vols. Hub is reclined in front row, left (*Nashville Banner*).

Patterson issued a statement: "We should all be proud of the victory," he said. "With the finest heroes ... and now the best baseball team in the South, Tennessee ought to be reasonably satisfied."[69] Ewing had mingled through the streets with the champions, and noted that "great satisfaction" did, indeed, linger into the wee hours of the morning.[70]

Writing on the *Tennessean's* editorial page the next day, Grantland Rice put the championship contest to verse:

> The tumult and the shouting dies —
>   The captains and the teams depart —
> No more they'll hit or sacrifice
>   Or round the bases quickly dart;
> We finished first — the One Best Bet —
> Where is the Fan that will forget?[71]

Perhaps Rice had already recognized the dramatic similarity between Hub's supreme test of endurance in Mobile, which Yancey had called "the greatest game ever played in Dixie," and the recently concluded championship game. For those who know about the Vols and their sensational 1908 season, perhaps both events should share the encomium. Owing to Rice's literary gifts, "the greatest game ever played in Dixie" was elevated to epic status in Nashville, and the title game remained firmly entrenched in public memory into the 1930s and 1940s, and revisited in a newspaper story in the 1960s. Thereafter, "the greatest game" faded into obscurity.

Many friends, neighbors, and acquaintances of Hub were justifiably proud of his indispensable contributions to the Vols' magical success. The native son of Sumner County received a thunderous welcome at the Gallatin train depot late in the evening following the great victory at Sulphur Dell. The celebratory crowd of several hundred admirers paraded Hurling Hub around Public Square while a makeshift band played "See the Conquering Hero Comes."[72] Never had the small Middle Tennessee community witnessed such a joyous celebration for a sports figure. And Hub deserved the reception.

Hurling Hub had built quite a pitching resumé in 1908. His endurance and perseverance in spite of a tired and aching arm in August and September, along with 16 victories in 34 starts, qualified him for honors along with Wiseman, McElveen, and Daubert as the Vols' most valuable player.[73] His four no-decisions could easily have gone the other way and turned Hub into a 20-game winner, a benchmark for excellence among pitchers of any era. His 4–1 record in September, when the pennant was on the line, was further evidence that he placed his team in an opportune position to cop the rag. Two iron man performances also demonstrated to teammates and fans alike his gritty demeanor.

Hub's 17-inning affair on July 9 was bittersweet, however; on one hand, it marked his coming of age as a twirler. On the other hand, while it cannot be documented medically, it is highly probable that his 30-inning workload in five days were the root cause of recurring arm trouble (elbow and shoulder) that plagued Hurling Hub for the remainder of his career. Late in his life, Hub confided that he had pitched for several more seasons with an ailing soupbone before seeking medical attention.[74] By that time, it was too late to repair the damage.

Further evidence from the championship series points to Hub's emergence as a character who could be counted on. The fact that Bernhard called upon Hub to warm up when Sitton was injured in the collision at home plate speaks volumes about the manager's confidence in his maturing ace. The selection of Hub as third base coach, a practice first seen in Vincennes, is further testimony to his rising status as a team leader through example.

Bill Bernhard was the best thing that ever happened to Hub Perdue on a baseball diamond. Hub boasted a live arm, but he had also developed an unflattering reputation, prior to Bernhard's arrival, as a heavy smoker and frequenter of saloons and pool parlors. He also fit in with grousing pitchers. Despite all of these flaws, Bernhard had taken a special interest in Hub, and there is no doubt that 1908 marked the defining moment in Hub's coming-of-age as a professional baseball player.

Greater individual accolades would come Hub's way in the next dozen seasons, but in 1908 he still needed to refine his skills and progress from a hard thrower into a pitcher with major league potential. Bernhard had spent countless sessions directing and perfecting Hub's mechanics as well as instructing his Tennessee pupil on the mental aspects of setting up batters.

Hub's future appeared bright despite his disappointment in not being drafted by Ebbets. With another year under Bernhard's tutelage, Hub would build upon his gains in the upcoming 1909 campaign and produce some of the most impressive numbers of his entire career.

Chapter 4

Breakout and Breakdown

During the off-season, Hub Perdue had ample opportunity to reflect on his recent development as a pitcher, savor the team's lofty accomplishment, contemplate his future and take a well deserved rest. Not only had he thrown a lot of innings, but the way in which they were bunched in iron man frays had fatigued his shoulder and elbow. He was painfully aware that several key components from the roster had now moved on to faster company — corner infielders Daubert and McElveen as well as Sitton. Only time would tell whether suitable replacements could be found. Hub realized that more would be expected from him in 1909 and he was prepared to deliver the goods and earn a spot with a major league outfit. "Hub Perdue is a good bet for a better year," predicted Rice, "as the classic Slab Son of Sumner has been coming forward every season. With the same improvement shown, Hurling Hub should take his place with the premiers of the [Southern] circuit."[1] Indeed, Hub would prove Rice to be a prophet. Hub entered the 1909 with high expectations for a breakout season, but he would also have to deal with painful realities posed by a break-down.

While Hub wintered, the city of Nashville was in the throes of the vibrant progressive movement. The high-profile trial and guilty verdict of Duncan Cooper, the "wet" editor accused of assassinating the "dry" gubernatorial candidate Edward Ward Carmack on the streets of Nashville, dominated the front pages. Everyone in "the Athens of the South" had an opinion about the inflammatory case and the equally volatile subject of prohibition. Related headlines discussed the impending passage of a bill which would create statewide prohibition more than ten years ahead of the national model. Into this municipal caldron of controversy stepped Hillary Howse, "a colorful city boss who was destined to dominate Nashville's politics for almost three decades."[2] Howse, a career politician, was Hub's kind of guy, "a gregarious fellow" with a beefy build who liked bright-colored vests, not to mention an unabashed "wet."[3] These turbulent times in the political arena must have been intoxicating to Hub, and very likely planted a seed for his later involvement in public affairs.

Just prior to the Vols assembling for spring training to lay the groundwork for defending their title, Hub floated a rumor that he intended to take a hike to the independent (outlaw) California League. Maybe he wanted to accompany his hometown pal, Chenault, on a West Coast adventure; Bill had recently signed with Portland of the Northwestern League. Or perhaps he was still smarting from Ebbets' snub. Whatever his reason, Hub announced his desire to join the Fresno Raisin Growers, a club that offered $600 per month in salary. Bernhard, who had wintered in Nashville and earned extra money officiating in the city's thriving indoor baseball league, was aghast. The news floored Nashville baseball loyalists, too. The manager told reporters the Fresno tender was legitimate; Hub was not guilty of fabricating the story, but he was using it to negotiate in public. This was the first time Hub employed this type of chicanery to gain an advantage at the bargaining table. It would not be the last time. The day before spring camp was scheduled to commence, Bernhard traveled to Gallatin to speak face-to-face with his disgruntled ace.[4]

The inclement weather worked in Bernhard's favor so that he could extend his talks with Hub. The Cumberland River was in its annual flood stage, and Sulphur Dell lay beneath several inches of water. Therefore, Bernhard postponed the first practice several times. Even a stray goat that had nibbled on the outfield grass throughout the winter months disappeared from the grounds owing to the rising flood waters. As Hub boarded a train at the Gallatin depot a local fan yelled at him, "Hey there, Hub, you 'lurn-ed' fool. Don't you know that Fresno is a long ways from that smokehouse filled with good things to eat which you have up at Bethpage?" He simply nodded in response.[5]

Another sticking point had stalled Bernhard's contract discussions with Hub. Since the end of his first season with Nashville, the team owners had been concerned over Hub's business connection with a pool hall in Gallatin. Such establishments were typically hangouts of gamblers, and players who patronized them were frowned upon by baseball magnates everywhere. Verner Moore Jones, the new sports editor at the *Banner,* mused that Hub's winter training as a bank shot artist "has given him additional strength to his already stout shoulder and biceps muscles."[6] Ewing reported, erroneously, that Hub had already sold his interest in the parlor "lock, stock, and barrel."[7] Wiseman and East, two returning stars, joked that Hub was best prepared of the returnees "to run Bernhard's 'marathon' runs around the outer edge of Sulphur Dell because he's spent the better part of the winter circling a pool table."[8] Bernhard's visit to Gallatin, therefore, had this second purpose: he wanted to investigate first-hand the degree of Hub's involvement in the questionable venture. There was sufficient innuendo in both newspaper accounts to suggest that Hub was also woefully out of shape.

Hub ended speculation that he would jump to Fresno when he signed a Nashville contract prior to the first practice. On March 18, he appeared in the first intra-squad game featuring the Vets and the Colts when he locked up for nine innings in the box against Bernhard — a lengthy and questionable duration in light of the arm trouble experienced by both hurlers at the tail end of the previous year. Soon, Hub was complaining about a sore shoulder and he temporarily moved to shortstop.[9]

Bernhard made drastic improvements to the exhibition schedule, which no longer featured unproductive match-ups with Vanderbilt and amateur clubs like NAC and the YMCA. Instead, the Vols were slated to meet the Philadelphia A's, Chicago Cubs, Boston Red Sox, Brooklyn Superbas, and minor leaguers from Evansville and St. Paul. These engagements, played between March 26 and April 12, remained miraculously intact since the weather cooperated, and Bernhard rescheduled only one date with a local amateur nine. Nashville fared poorly against the major leaguers, won only two encounters with minor league affiliates, and dropped an embarrassing game to NAC, 17–16.

Bernhard selected Hub to face his former employer, the Chicago Cubs, on March 30. During the warmups, Hub and Kellum joined several Cubs players in the latest pre-game exercise and they thoroughly captivated the crowd. The players stood in a circle and tossed a baseball randomly to each other, forcing everyone to keep alert, an early form of the hot potato drill. "Hub added extra comedy touches," noted Jones in the *Banner*.[10] Once the game commenced, Hub scattered two hits and allowed only one run in five innings, but afterwards his impressive outing was marred by a stiff shoulder.[11] He told Rice after the game that he would never again complain to Bernhard about lack of work like he had done last summer. "I came pretty near pitching my shoulder off after I had put in a bid to work more games.... About two games a week, or a game every fourth day, is the pick I would make, if it was up to me," urged Hub.[12] One newspaper subscriber was noticeably irked by the excessive amount of publicity Hub was receiving in the national media. "They are talking 'Perdue' from Buffalo to New Orleans. He's a regular Teddy Roosevelt," concluded the peeved patron.[13]

Hub worked a second game against Brooklyn, but he was roughed up from the start. Facing Ebbets' contingent made up of former Nashville teammates Daubert, McElveen and George Hunter caused some degree of zest in the Tennessean. McElveen planted one of Hub's offerings into deep left field for a home run. The sphere landed amidst "a colony of chickens" and someone chuckled that Mac had hit "a fowl." Hub struggled on the cold afternoon and left after five innings with recurring stiffness in his shoulder, reported as a "charlie horse."[14]

Rice, Ewing, and Jones printed their predictions for the upcoming campaign, and they agreed with other scribes around the circuit that Atlanta and New Orleans would challenge the Vols for league supremacy. Rice interviewed Bernhard, who replied coyly, "Nobody could tell at 4 o'clock on the last September day of the race who was going to win it last season. So, what chance has anyone to get away with a guess six months in advance of that date?"[15] One thing was certain — no one would take Nashville for granted this time around.

Opening Day for the reigning league champion was an extra special occasion in the Southern Association. Several days before the festive date (April 15), the three dailies outlined the itinerary for the public. The line of march would assemble in Public Square at 1 P.M., weave its way through the downtown business district, and proceed to the ballpark where there would be an elaborate flag-raising ceremony. The Industrial School band announced the procession of automobiles with players from Nashville and visiting Montgomery, Mayor Brown, President Kavanaugh, and club directors Kuhn and Chambers (of the Senators). Invitees also included super-fan Alf Williams and a young African American "mascot" and unofficial bat boy-equipment manager-groundskeeper nicknamed "Rubber"— a racial reference to his dark skin color to be sure. A ragtag collection of newspaper boys brought up the tail end of the brigade. The office of Governor Malcolm Patterson disclosed that the state's chief executive also planned to be on hand for the ceremony.[16]

The event went off as scheduled. Once the procession arrived at Sulphur Dell, both teams lined up along the first base path. Then, Kavanaugh and Kuhn made brief comments to the crowd. The *American,* the cleanest Nashville newspaper in terms of print quality, captured the championship flag-raising moment with a historic photograph. Williams hoisted the banner on a special pole erected in the right field corner with the assistance of a young girl wearing a white dress, a familiar turn-of-the-century symbol of purity at public ceremonies in the white South. Mayor Brown assumed his customary role and threw out the ceremonial first pitch to new Vols captain East, and the formalities came to a close.[17] The start of the 1909 campaign was only minutes away.

Bernhard's first lineup card reflected two significant changes in personnel with the return of Jim Robertson (from Scranton in the New York State League) at first base and newcomer Harry Noyes (from Hartford in the Connecticut State League) at third base. Filling the holes in the corner infield positions caused by the departures of Daubert and McElveen raised immediate questions about the new defense. Equally important, how would the duo fill the void in offensive firepower? Their resumés provided some doubt. The rest of the Vols defense was unchanged with returning veterans Butler and East handling middle infield duties. And the Vols boasted the fastest outfield in the Southern with Wiseman, Siegle and Bay. Bernhard planned to split the catching duties between Seabough and newcomer Charlie Tonneman. Several new pitchers vied for a roster spot, but it was generally understood that Perdue, Duggan, Bernhard and Kellum would handle most of the slab load. In a piece of team trivia, the *American* and *Banner* took note of the unusually large number of Vols players who were married — ten.[18] Perhaps this revelation would translate into a more mature roster.

A large crowd caught the morning train from Gallatin to witness the opening day gala. But they were sorely disappointed when Bernhard did not select Hub to twirl the game, an honor normally reserved for the team's best pitcher. Instead, the manager opted for his top prospect, southpaw Tom Gilroy (from Lawrence in the New England League). Still, the 4,500 fans were treated to a 4–3 victory.[19] Hub's appearance the next day satisfied his loyal rooters, however. "At every strike out," observed Rice, "the Gallatin contingent arose *en masse* and howled with the battle call of the Sumner clan."[20] Hub looked "unusually strong" in his first outing, changed speeds effectively and struck out eight Senators to notch his first victory in the young season.

In the first month, Hub shattered the perception that he was a slow starter with six straight lopsided victories. "Sumner's Son of the Smoke and the Spit," punned Jones, an unabashed reference to Hub's masterful control and blend of the fastball and spitball.[21] During one of these appearances, Hub limited preseason favorite Atlanta to three hits, and he stole his second career base to the absolute astonishment of the Dellians. Throughout his string of early successes, he consistently baffled opposing batters, racked up impressive numbers of strikeouts, and allowed a total of only three runs in five contests.[22] If this continued, Hub was poised for a breakout season.

Around Nashville there were explosive events transpiring in the spring of 1909 that diverted the attention of the citizens away from baseball, however. First, a guilty verdict had been handed down in the Carmack murder trial at the end of March. The turmoil generated by the shooting did not end there; rather, it expanded into a broader public debate over statewide prohibition. Tensions boiled over when Governor Patterson commuted Cooper's sentence. Also, the year witnessed an important milestone in Nashville's ex–Confederate community with the erection of two monuments spearheaded by Cunningham and his Nashville-based *Confederate Veteran* magazine. First, the Sam Davis statue was dedicated on Capitol Hill, and several months later the monument to the Private Confederate Soldier was unveiled in Centennial Park. These

Lost Cause commemorations paid homage to a dying, yet sacred, element within white society — the rapidly dwindling ex–Confederate population. The Carmack (prohibition) case and the flurry of Confederate iconography, although unrelated, offered perspective into the social tensions that were pulling at conservative, progressive and traditional values in Nashville at precisely the same time the Vols were charging onto the field at Sulphur Dell.[23] In a very real sense, the Nashville Base Ball Club provided a respite from societal angst which had divided the community along the lines of "wet" and "dry" and "black" and "white." Prohibition, ex–Confederates and baseball did not stand in isolation from one another; instead they shared the stage, and all were interwoven into the folk fabric of the times.

Hub had surprised himself with his fast start in 1909. In an introspective moment, the hurler asserted that the new year would be different from the past. "I'm going to see if I can't give some of these leading pitchers [in the Southern] a run this summer," said Hub in a serious tone. "I got off to a bad start [last season] and didn't get going right until the middle of the race.... If I can keep my arm right I'd like to bet somebody that I win twice as many games as I lose. I'm about due to have a good season in this league," he concluded.[24] Setting goals are always important for athletic achievement, and Hub placed his motivational bar high in 1909.

Rice concurred with Hub's keys to self-improvement. He knew that Hub had a history of starting slowly and finishing in a flurry. He opined that the Tennessean's current streak owed more to mental preparation than physical skill. "Not only is Hub's arm in better shape than heretofore," pointed out the scribe, "but he knows more baseball and more about pitching than at any previous stage of his career." Rice also commented on Hub's past tendency to surrender late-inning runs, and observed a difference in the pitcher's behavior that would conserve energy. "Hub is taking his time now — watching the game better — resting when there's an opening ... and mixing up his speeds ... to better effect. Bernhard has had Hub in tow and as a result of his coaching, the Gallatonian Gad-fly is stinging them right and left."[25] Bernhard and Hub made a good team.

Hurling Hub was not only learning how to mix his assortment of pitches, he had also mastered the technique of throwing inside-outside and up-and-down to keep the batters off-balance. "The first offering is usually a high, fast one around the windpipe," observed Rice, and the second pitch "a sharp curveball over the outside corner of the pan."[26] If the batter crowded the plate, Hub did not hesitate to deliver a beanball. By using his "noodle," Hub had transitioned from a thrower into a pitcher who commanded all corners of the strike zone. Had the Tennessee twirler with the wavy pompadour and large forehead the right stuff to move on to the next level?

Bernhard did not hesitate to use Hub in relief roles just as he had done throughout the previous summer. Against Birmingham, he entered in relief and set down the seven Barons he faced to preserve a rare win for Gilroy. Rice put Hub's heroics to verse:

> And when the first one whistled by
> With speed to fell an ox,
> Not a rooter in the place could doubt
> 'Twas Perdue in the box.[27]

Hub's confidence was at an all-time high, and he conducted himself with an increased swagger on the field. When he blew away the Barons, "the noted marksman calmly carved another notch in his gun-handle [and] he started for the clubhouse in all the sombre, lonely grandeur that unexcelled fame always brings."[28] Hub, the gunslinger?

Friends and fans in Gallatin were overjoyed at the twirler's early accomplishments. The *Banner* leaked a story about a surprise public celebration being planned at the Sumner County seat to honor Hub. Following his fifth consecutive victory, a contingent of several hundred people assembled on the Public Square and heard stirring speeches from noted citizens and baseball followers alike. Then the crowd met Hub at the depot and escorted him to his residence and place of business on East Main Street, where they were treated to remarks "that any orator might be proud of."[29] There is no doubt Hub was the focal point of hero-worshipping Gallatians. Claude "Blinky" Horn, the iconic Nashville journalist, later acknowledged that the locals always knew when Hub would depart for Nashville. On days when Hurling Hub was slated to pitch, adoring fans would give him a rousing send-off as well as a welcome greeting upon his return later that same afternoon.[30]

Hub's ego was on a collision course with reality, and it occurred on May 10. Facing Birmingham for the third time, Hub was victimized by four Barons runs in the top of the first inning, a 15-minute "shooting gallery." Then he settled into a comfortable routine and put up goose eggs on the scoreboard for the rest of the contest. But, opposing pitcher Moxie Manuel made the first inning tallies stand up.[31] Jones, an accomplished poet in his own right, parodied Hub's first defeat with a play on *Casey at the Bat:*

> Somewhere in this favored land the sun was shining bright.
> Somewhere bands were playing and somewhere hearts were light;
> Somewhere men were laughing and children smiling too,
> But there was no joy in Gallatin when they hammered Hub Perdue.[32]

The loss launched Hub into a tailspin and he lost five out of his next seven starts.

Two interesting criticisms of Hub appeared in print during the swoon that partially explained his weakness at the plate and in the box. First, Rice observed Hub's bad habit while at bat. "Some day, while at bat, Hub is going to hang that left hoof of his in the water barrel," jibed Rice. "He couldn't reach a ball over the far side of the plate with a fishing pole, much less the regulation forty-two inch bat."[33] Stepping in the bucket was never advantageous for a batter. Jones offered a mental assessment of Hub's slab work following a 17-hit drubbing in Mobile: "One of Hub's leading troubles seems to be that he possesses the artistic temperament and that's something powerful tough to handle.... That peevishness at times overtakes the afflicted ... and the artistic germ may have been working overtime [today]."[34] In other words, Hub sulked. During the debacle, Hub looked to the bench for sympathy. Every Sea Gulls batsman except ex–Vols catcher Hardy hit safely in the contest, and Hub expected Bernhard to relieve him in the box. "All the relief I could find," said the downtrodden pitcher afterwards, "was the whole gang doubled up laughing, and Bill [Bernhard] leading the way."[35] His teammates continued to razz the pouting hurler on the bench after the inning ended. Apparently, Hub's notorious sense of humor had temporarily escaped him.

In the middle of Hub's downturn, the Vols lost their command of first place, and they rotated the top honor with Little Rock, Mobile and Atlanta into the summer. Nashville struggled with western division opponents, and worst of all against their #1 rival, last-place Memphis. With Hub in a slump and Bernhard, Duggan and Kellum all nursing sore arms, the Vols made two roster moves to relieve the slab crisis. After releasing the ineffective Gilroy, Bernhard purchased Bill Viebahn from Atlanta and Charlie Case from Springfield in the Three-I League. Both pitchers picked up the slack and eventually appeared in almost 60 games for the Vols.[36]

Meanwhile, Bernhard searched for answers to restart his ineffective ace. He decided to employ a new technique where he would pull Hub at the first sign of trouble at any point from the sixth inning onward.[37] The manager understood that his team needed Hub more rested in the late season. "A ball club needs some reserve strength to fall back on when the showdown comes [in September]," he commented philosophically.[38] Bernhard's strategy for Hub remained in tact for the remainder of their joint tenure in Nashville, and it usually produced satisfactory results.

By the traditional midway point in the Southern Association season, the Fourth of July, Hub had accumulated an impressive 11–5 record. Thus he amended his earlier statement on the number of appearances he needed to stay crisp in the box. "I'd like to work every three days in place of every six," said the Tennessean.[39] Despite his current fortunes, Hub was still nursing a wound; he was seen wearing an ankle brace for an undisclosed injury. Jones chuckled that Hub might put the brace to better use by wrapping it around his elbow, a veiled comment that he was still suffering from soreness.[40]

Hub usually managed to keep his sense of humor intact. He always relished engaging fans in interactive banter whether he was pitching or coaching at third base. Once, Hub was pitching a fairly routine game in Mobile when Sea Gulls fans tried to rile him, but he responded in kind with witty remarks that entertained everyone. "The idea of trying to get the best of Hub in a talkfest [is impossible]," concluded Ewing.[41] On another occasion at Sulphur Dell, Hub and Seabough were singled out for their special abilities to rev up the hometown crowd. The *Banner* noted that the battery mates had elevated the art of base coaching to new levels. Each man was able to "stir things up" in a different manner, too. Seabough specialized in arousing enthusiasm in the grandstands where middle class patrons sat, while Hub's specialty resided in the bleachers with the working classes.[42] There was no denying Ewing's observation: "The bugs are crazy about Hub Perdue."[43]

One of the most humorous episodes of the season occurred in mid–August when Hub was defending a 9–0 lead over Montgomery. Rice recounted the hilarious event in detail. While batting, Hub "swung idly at a curve ball from [Herb] Juul and missed the pellet, pinking him in the groin. Hub writhed in mortal agony for a minute or two, and, after straightening out ... limped down to first. [Umpire "Vinegar Dan"] Pfenninger had, of course, called it a strike, and Hub was waved back to bat, but he kept running down the first base line. 'Get on back, Hub,' broke in Viebahn, 'you struck at the ball.' But, Hub still kept on toward the bag." He remained at first base for several minutes, undoubtedly to compose himself, and returned to the batter's box only after Bernhard ordered him to do so. "I guess you fellers think you're pretty funny," Hub scolded his frolicking teammates. Hub got the last laugh later when he lashed his third base hit of the season.[44]

Atlanta arrived in Nashville for an important series on July 15–17. The Crackers had methodically risen in the standings after a slow start, and they presently perched atop the league. Duggan and Case had dispatched the visitors in the first two encounters, much to the satisfaction of the local rooters. Since Hub had handcuffed Tobacco Billy's squad on a pair of shutouts at the beginning of the season, Bernhard called upon his Tennessee protégé to do it again. It was apparent from his first pitch that he had returned to form. "The minute Hub stepped into the box any keen-eyed observer could see ... the cry of anguish from Gallatin of late over a nearly shattered idol had stirred up all the smoke in his system," waxed Rice. "His fast ball whistled over the pan like a shell from a thirteen-inch gun and when it cracked into Tonneman's glove it roared like a barrel of crockery pushed down the cellar stairs."[45] Hub scattered four hits in his third shutout over the top-rated Crackers.

The Atlanta series marked the beginning of a 14-game winning streak by Nashville, including four phenomenal series sweeps on the road. These were desperate times for the Vols if they were to catch the fast-paced Georgians. It frustrated Bernhard's bunch, however, to see the Crackers practically match them win for win. By early August, the race had boiled down to these two teams, and they were separated by only one game (.004). A monumental head-to-head series loomed ahead at Poncey which for all practical purposes would decide the league champion.[46]

Everyone who followed Southern Association baseball realized the importance of the five encounters over three days between the Crackers and Vols which started on August 11. With three shutouts over the Crackers already to his credit, Hub was slated the pitch in the opening salvo. Hub had recovered from his brief losing skid in May and dropped only three games in July and August, a remarkable 12–3–1 record that would extend through Labor Day. In one contest during his hot streak, he set down 16 Little Rock Travelers in a row. In another affair, Hub carried a perfect game through six innings in New Orleans. On a third occasion, he twirled a masterful three-hitter where he "had grease on the ball and handled it to perfection."[47] At the moment, however, the focus was on Atlanta with their razor-thin advantage in the standings over Nashville.

After the Vols dropped the first game of a doubleheader, Hub prepared for the second tilt in front of a boisterous Atlanta crowd. The scoreboard read 2–2 in the top of the ninth when East drove in Wiseman for the go-ahead run on a controversial play. Atlanta's manager, an argumentative fellow, protested vehemently to umpire Carpenter without effect. Wiseman's tally held up and decided the outcome. The arbiter required a police escort back to his hotel but not before Hub plunked his slab opponent on his "funny bone" with a hanging curve ball.[48]

The Atlanta series did not go well for Nashville; only Hub's victory helped to avoid a clean sweep by the Crackers. In desperation, Bernhard called upon Hub to stem their momentum in the finale on only one day's rest. Locked in a pitcher's duel with Brown Rogers, the ex–Cumberland University star, Hub's teammates resorted to scientific baseball to manufacture a run off a bunt single, sacrifice, and single. The crowd was treated to a finely contested ten-inning tie but the no-decision dealt the Vols' chances of catching the Crackers a severe blow.[49] In hindsight, one shaky weekend in the Georgia capitol had cost the Vols dearly.

The next ten days were crucial as the Vols returned to the secure confines of Sulphur Dell. There, the Vols' split two series bouts with Birmingham and Montgomery, but the Crackers swept the same two opponents. A month before the end of the campaign, Nashville's sports scribes declared that the Vols pennant hopes had been dashed. "Now that popular excitement over another hoped for pennant has subsided," lamented Jones, "the local public is seemingly accepting like good sports the apparently inevitable defeat."[50] Hereafter, there was a noticeable drop-off in baseball coverage as Rice, Ewing and Jones shifted their attention to the upcoming college football season.

On August 31, normally the best pitcher in the Southern Association would be given serious consideration on major league draft day, and Hub led all the hurlers with 23 victories. He seemed a lock for some pitcher-starved club in the Big Show. But the date came and went without his selection![51] It was a mystifying slight. Hub struggled to come to grips with his personal disappointment and ended the month on a whimper at 1–2–1. Two consecutive big league rejections stung.

On September 9, Hub rebounded briefly against Little Rock ace Jim Buchanan in what headlines called the "BEST BALL GAME OF THE SEASON AT THE DELL." Through 11 innings both teams battled with sensational defensive plays and stellar pitching by Hub and Buck.[52] The no-decision was an appropriate ending to the Vols' futile six-week chase of the Crackers and Hub's two-year chase of the elusive majors.

Following the game, Hub invited Siegle and Wiseman to his Sumner County home for "a regular old-fashioned country dinner," so said Ewing. But Rice had a different twist to the story. The trio had gone to Gallatin to engage in a "gay and giddy social whirl" and likely tied one on. When they returned to Nashville following their weekend getaway, none were in physical condition to play. Bernhard, smarting from his team's elimination from first place, was unamused. Hub did not pitch for a week and Wiseman sat out the remainder of the season with a reported "charlie horse," a muscle-grabbing ailment frequently used by managers to cover up a wide range of player indiscretions. Wiseman had only missed two games in the last three seasons and just completed his ninth year with the club.[53]

Bernhard's bunch had won eight more games than in the championship season, but they could not keep up with the blistering pace set by Atlanta (87 victories). The Vols finished in second place, five and one-half games behind the Crackers. In the immediate aftermath of the season, the three dailies were quick to jump on several perceived weaknesses of the club. Robertson and Noyes were not suitable replacements for Daubert and McElveen, and the oft-injured Duggan and Kellum had to go. Furthermore, the dependable Wiseman was in a snit. Unhappy over his late-season banishment to the bench, he asked for his release and announced that he would take his talents to the California League. Perhaps the popular right fielder had been speaking to Hub about the advantages to heading West. Time would tell if he and Bernhard would reconcile. Wiseman stayed in town and attended the Tennessee State Fair, which was his post-season custom.[54]

Despite reports to the contrary, Hub had not disassociated himself from the pool hall business in Gallatin. Rather, he had simply turned over its operation to Bill Bluff while he played baseball.[55] Over the winter, Hub often frequented his establishment where local fans sought him out. His hot stove sessions and entertaining embellishments from the annals of Hublore were widely attended, much to the continued annoyance of Nashville's owners. The Directors feared the parlor was a gathering place for gamblers, and Hub's association with them would damage the wholesome reputation of baseball. Yet the dilemma posed by Hub was a delicate one because the team coveted their ace and desired to retain him more than any other player. The 23-game winner recognized who held the advantage, and he fueled speculation that he might accompany Wiseman to the West Coast. Hub enjoyed such posturing when it came to contract negotiations.

At the winter meetings of the Southern Association, owners and managers made significant changes to league operations beginning in 1910. First, they dropped the Little Rock franchise over protests from President Kavanaugh, himself a Little Rock resident and part-owner of the team, in favor of Chattanooga. The decision was largely financial — the league would save travel expenses by tightening the geographic perimeter of the conference. Second, they adopted a season slate which reversed the location of the home-away series. The schedule, which had favored Nashville in 1908 and 1909, now worked against them. The Vols' last home date, the Labor Day doubleheader, would be succeeded by road visits to Montgomery, Mobile, Birmingham and New Orleans. Third, the owners approved a stringent salary cap that, if strictly adhered to, would generate greater profits but also hamstring managers from signing top-caliber players.[56] Fourth, Kavanaugh announced that his circuit would not use the latest invention, a "cork-centered ball" produced by Spalding. In fact, umpire Harry "Steamboat" Johnson later confided that the Southern had always purchased its spheroids from P. Goldsmith Sons, a baseball equipment store in Cincinnati "ever since the old National [League] was a 12-team circuit."[57]

In the off-season, Bernhard was faced with reconstructing the entire Vols infield. Captain East had gone with former Atlanta manager Smith to Buffalo in the Eastern League, and Bernhard released Robertson and Noyes. To fill their spots, he picked up aging second baseman Tim Flood from Little Rock, and first baseman Ted Vinson from the KITTY. Both infielders were in the twilight of their careers, but they were also inexpensive acquisitions. Bernhard landed a young shortstop, Mike Lynch, to replace Butler, who had been drafted by the Indians and turned over to the Toledo Mud Hens. To round out the infield, Bernhard plucked a promising power hitter, third baseman Herman Bronkie, from Waterbury in the Connecticut State League. Thus, the Vols infield, which had transitioned with two new players in 1909, was now totally revamped from its championship season. The tight salary cap largely dictated these personnel choices, and Bernhard faithfully adhered to the new regulation. Finally, the Nashville mogul shipped the oft-injured Duggan to Indianapolis in early February in return for a promising young southpaw, Henry Keupper, and landed reserve catcher-outfielder Pete Erloff from Pittsburg in the Western Association.[58]

Bernhard was satisfied with his pitching staff going into 1910 anchored by Perdue, Case, Viebahn and newcomer Henry Keupper. Yet by late February none of the hurlers had signed their Nashville contracts. While boiling out in Hot Springs, Hub voiced his disapproval of the restrictive salary cap imposed on all Southern Association clubs. He was supported by Rice, who worried that meager salaries discouraged major league cast-offs from drifting to the Southern. Even Bernhard expressed his annoyance with the new statute, stating that it had handcuffed him from landing top quality players. Without directly saying so, Bernhard was preparing Nashville fans for yet another letdown; indeed, most baseball authorities were picking the Vols to drop into the second division.[59]

An assortment of veterans and rookies drifted into training camp in mid–March, but Hub remained in Arkansas. He enjoyed the hot springs, saying the bath waters made him feel like the eighth inning in a mid–August afternoon at Sulphur Dell. Rice quipped that the portly pitcher had "boiled out seven pounds of blubber" when he finally signed a late agreement along with the other remaining hold out, the disgruntled Wiseman, who also heard "the call of the contract."[60] Still in Bernhard's dog house, the veteran right fielder did not play for almost two weeks.

On his first day in camp, Hub entertained his teammates with some trick bicycle moves on the only dry patch of ground in the Sulphur Dell outfield. On a more serious note, Jones noted that Hub could not throw without pain and was currently receiving medical attention. The scribe criticized the hurler for failing to follow prescribed arm exercises and an off-season regimen of physical exercise to maintain his weight.[61]

An intriguing slate of major league opponents faced off against Nashville for the second straight year. Connie Mack returned with his Philadelphia A's, followed by the Cubs, Superbas, Naps, Tigers and Red Sox. The exhibitions concluded against Tobacco Billy's Buffalo Bisons, and the barnstorming Cuban All Stars.[62] A stellar performance by Viebahn against the A's resulted in the Vols' first victory over a major league opponent since 1908, which provided a false sense of optimism for the upcoming campaign.

Bernhard decided to use Hub sparingly in the pre-season and limit him to five innings per outing. He naturally picked the former Chicago prospect to open against Chance's Cubs, and Hub limited the big leaguers to two hits and left with the score tied, 1–1. Over the next ten days, he surrendered no runs to Brooklyn and threw a perfect five frames against Cleveland. Despite his lingering complaint about a sore arm, Hub appeared ready to pick up where he'd left off in 1909, and Rice predicted Hub would be playing "under the Big Tent in 1911." Yet in his final exhibition appearance, Buffalo roughed up Hub with a grand slam home run in the first frame and nine runs in all.[63] The Bisons game was a harbinger for Hub.

Over at the *American,* a new person sat behind the sports desk — Allen Johnson. A poetic rival to Rice and Jones, *Johnson's Junk* was a decided improvement over Ewing's stiff and sterile (matter-of-fact) reporting style. As a way of introducing himself to the Nashville readership, he used a medium familiar to Nashville sports fans — poetry.

> We don't know whereof we're writing
> When we're doping baseball — but
> We just keep right on reciting,
> With the same old chesty strut;
> Verner Jones opines and mumbles;
> Grantland Rice just hums and rumbles;
> Yours truly stalls and stumbles —
> Every baseball scribe's a mutt.[64]

Johnson's keen sense of humor and self-deprecating style fit well with Nashville's other sports scribes.

Disquieting rumblings persisted in the press that Hub's arm was not right, and he threw erratically in his first start in Memphis. Then he settled down and notched four road wins in a row, including a classic 13-inning pitchers' duel in Atlanta.[65] But there were other warning signs. The Vols defense performed poorly with sloppy infield work compounded by frequent mental errors. "It isn't any easy matter to grab off four infielders from different points of the compass," mused Rice later in the season, "and mould them into a compact machine."[66] They never did gel.

A funny story emerged from the Atlanta trip which contributed to the growing collection of Hublore. A Crackers fan jokingly shouted to Viebahn from the grandstands after he had swung wildly at two offerings in the batter's box. The rub? The heckler had facetiously misidentified the big Dutchman as "Perdue." The insinuation so nettled Viebahn that he smacked a single and later a double. "I can stand for some things," said Viebahn afterwards, "but the idea of being put in the same class with Hub Perdue as a batter made me as mad as a hornet!"[67] Hub enjoyed the comic notoriety.

Shortly after Hub's first appearance in the box, the temperatures across the South plummeted and a snow storm shut down the league for several days. "With blustery breezes blowing and with conditions better [suited] for snowballing than baseballing," Rice thought that the frigid respite might allow the descending Vols to regroup. When the league resumed action, both Memphis and fledgling Chattanooga were winning the fictional "battle of Tennessee" as Nashville cascaded into the second tier. On the Vols' first road trip to Chattanooga, Hub sought out a Negro masseur, Doc White, renowned for his treatment of sore muscles, thus beginning a relationship that lasted for several years.[68]

At the beginning of a month-long road trip, Hub held a commanding three-run lead over the Turtles in Red Elm Park when he was overcome by a sharp pain in his right elbow and he asked Bernhard to be relieved. "A physician was summoned from the stands," noted Rice, "to hold an autopsy over the mangled remains of the badly hung soupbone."[69] The doctor determined that Hub suffered a detached tendon above his elbow, and he recommended several weeks of total rest.

Returning from Memphis, the Vols transferred to a train at Union Station bound for Chattanooga, but Bernhard left Hub behind in Nashville. Hurling Hub did not take the demotion well. He "was seen this morning on the street nursing besides his sore wing a very emphatic grouch over the break in affairs that has rendered him useless for duty."[70] With Hub on the shelf, the depleted Vols pitching corps was forced to rely on Bernhard and Keupper to pick up the slack. Hub missed two starts against the Lookouts and Barons.

On the last day of the extended road trip, Bernhard took a chance and pitched Hub in Montgomery. Despite his ailment, the Tennessean threw a solid game against Senators ace Forrest Thomas. Trailing by one run in the eighth inning, Hub stroked a one-out Texas Leaguer over the outstretched reach of first baseman Ed Gremminger, and now he represented the tying run. Hub lost focus in the moment as the next batter, Bay, sent a popup in back of third base. Leading off from first base, Hub stood totally mesmerized by Bay's high loft. Shortstop Joe Pepe corralled the sphere and threw it across the diamond to Gremminger to complete the unexpected double play, squelch the Vols rally, and end the inning. Nashville eventually lost the contest (2–0) but Hub's mistake pointed to another personal weakness, his lack of concentration in critical situations.[71]

Back in Nashville the next day, Hub was sent to the hospital to have an X-ray taken of his elbow. The result showed badly inflamed ligaments. Bernhard decided to shut down his ailing ace indefinitely, and Hub started only once in the next 25 days. To pass the time, Hub coached third base and watched over Bronkie's brown and white dog which he tied to the team's bench between innings. Bernhard assumed Hub's slab work and experimented with the team's porous infield by moving Seabough from behind the dish to defend a position he had never played before, first base. The manager was desperate; he could no longer tolerate Vinson's 24 errors at first base and Flood's poor execution around the keystone sack caused by a hand injury that forced him to perform one-handed in the field and at bat. By the end of May, the underperformers were replaced by Hamilton Patterson (second base) and Bill "Blab" Schwartz (first base). During Hub's absence from the lineup, the Vols languished in fifth place but remained within striking distance of the surprise league leader, Chattanooga.[72]

When the doctors cleared Hub for active duty on June 21, the Vols were in desperate need of a victory. The upstarts in Chattanooga had pasted Nashville on six previous engagements. Dissatisfaction was spreading among the rooters in Sulphur Dell, and their frustrations had filtered into the local newspapers in the form of angry letters to the sports editors. A sampling of missives "knocked" many of the players and some even questioned Bernhard's handling of the team. Few Vols players were spared the wrath of fandom, including Hub, who appeared a mere "shadow of his former self" against the surging Lookouts.[73]

The thin pitching staff had been stretched to the limit, and Bernhard had pressed Hub back into service out of necessity, whether or not he was healthy. The team had reached a critical juncture in the season. An attractive July home stand offered the best and perhaps last opportunity to get over the hump and climb back into the race. Hub "returned from Elba" to twirl the first of his seven games that month, a three-hit loss to Atlanta. But Rice pointed out that the Vols were in the midst of an offensive drought, "scoring only in every other battle."[74] Between May 21 and July 19, the Vols had produced only ten runs in five of Hub's seven slab appearances. It was amazing that he was able to mount a 5–2 record during this time period thanks to four consecutive shut outs. Perhaps the Tennessee Deadballer was back in form.[75]

Yes, Hub held up his end of the bargain in July. In back-to-back 1–0 squeakers over Birmingham and Montgomery, he tallied 17 strikeouts on only two days' rest. In the latter event against the Senators, he struck out the side to end the game and was dubbed "the luminous star of the contest."[76] "With the dark clouds as a backdrop," noted Jones, "Hub threw open the throttle and his delivery was hardly visible to the naked eye."[77] An equally impressive performance occurred in his third consecutive shutout when he did not allow a single Mobile Sea Gull to reach first base until two outs in the seventh inning when Julius Watson slapped a scratch single on a full count. Only one other opponent reached base and Hub faced 29 batters altogether in a stirring display of power pitching.[78] When he earned his fourth straight shut out four days later, Jones boasted than no one in the league was currently pitching any better than Hub, with the possible exception of Harry Coveleski.[79]

Hub continued to soar, but the overall stock of the Vols dropped by the end of July. Although Bernhard's team boasted the second-best home record in the circuit they were last in the league on the road. New Orleans distanced themselves from the pack, and Nashville soon trailed by 14 games. The Vols had fallen out of the hunt.

Hub posted his fifth consecutive slab win in Mobile and solidified his reputation as #1 in the rotation the next day when the Vols moved on to New Orleans. The Crescent City contest had already assumed a playoff atmosphere when Perdue entered the game in relief. With one out and the bases loaded in the bottom of the ninth inning and the Vols clinging to a slender one-run lead, Hub faced the heart of the Pelican's batting order, John Weimer and cleanup hitter Joe Jackson. The latter, a rookie outfielder, was a runaway favorite to win the 1910 Southern Association batting title. The crowd worked itself into a frenzy, precisely the kind of atmosphere in which Hub thrived. With pinpoint precision, Perdue struck out both sluggers to preserve the victory.[80]

As spectacular as the month of July had been for Hub, the next month was a nightmare. Indeed, for 40 days between July 28 and Labor Day, Hub tossed only one victory in 11 tries and his team nose-dived in the standings. To demonstrate the depth of Hub's despair, he dropped three face-offs against Atlanta, a team he recently bested. Paradoxically, his lone victory came in a most unlikely place — Andrews Field in Chattanooga.[81] After a tough loss in Atlanta a week later, Rice endeared the hometown hurler to Nashvillians with a brand new nickname — "the Sage of Squashville."[82] Clearly, the poetic scribe was close to bestowing the famous moniker that would forevermore be associated with Hub Perdue — "the Gallatin Squash." But not yet.

A number of personnel issues combined in mid–August to explain the utter collapse of the Vols. First, Siegle contracted typhoid fever and did not return to center field until the last week of the season. For his replacement, Bernhard selected the agreeable but slow-footed Seabough. Bay nursed two broken ribs, and all of a sudden the most dependable outfield in the circuit had become the most suspect. The infield defense had improved since the departure of Vinson and Flood, but the team remained anemic at the plate.

Hub lost sight of the strike zone at precisely this moment when his colleagues lost their batting eye. In back-to-back losses in Chattanooga and Memphis, the unpredictable hurler was victimized by 13 and 14 hits respectively and 17 combined runs. Against the Turtles, Bay registered the only Nashville hit, and an ensuing double play provided pitcher Al Klawitter with the rare feat of facing only 27 batters for the entire game.[83] Hub dropped his next two outings by identical scores, 1–0. "Hub Perdue, thou hast our sympathies in large lumps," quipped Johnson in the *American*. "It is heart-rending how the mighty have fallen."[84] Hub had become an enigma. Then came an unexplained surprise!

On September 1 the Brooklyn Superbas drafted Hub despite his current 1–7 losing skid and mediocre 12–13 record. Commenting on Ebbets' draft day choice, Rice offered insightful commentary: "Will Hub stick [with Brooklyn]?" the scribe pondered. "Depends upon how much he hustles.... So far as the physical stuff is concerned, Hub has no superiors anywhere.... It is more a question of disposition.... As it is, he has his chance if he cares to take advantage of it."[85] Back in his playing days, Rice had epitomized on-field hustle and a never-say-die attitude, and he harbored mixed feelings about Hub's work ethic. His observation was not a glowing endorsement, and the realization might have stung Hub. Still, Hub was overjoyed by Ebbets' selection. In his first appearance since draft day, the Gallatian pitched a nifty four-hitter at the brand new Rickwood Field in Birmingham, but the Barons took top honors by inflicting still another 1–0 defeat.[86]

Hurling Hub Perdue completed his first four-year tour of duty with Nashville on September 10. In characteristic fashion, he edged Mobile (1–0) in the first round of a twin bill. He also received permission to start game two, his fifth iron man assignment in six years, but he was pounded for six runs in two innings and then pulled. The split decision marked Hub's final playing appearance in Sulphur Dell until 1916.[87]

The 1910 edition of the Southern Association went to New Orleans with 87 wins. Fourth-place Chattanooga captured the Tennessee championship by besting fifth-place Nashville and seventh-place Memphis. The standings had been tight in the middle — fewer than five games had separated fourth from seventh place.[88] Still, the Vols had fallen from grace and the local media and owners were unhappy with the 21-loss increase from the previous year. Was there change in the air?

Bernhard twirled the final game of the season in Sulphur Dell on September 17, a meaningless 6–3 victory over the champion Pelicans on the same day that a new luxury accommodation opened in downtown Nashville, the Hermitage Hotel.[89] It marked the 23rd time the manager appeared on the slab, far too much service for his aging arm.

On the following Monday, the Board of Directors met and announced a stunning decision to fire Bernhard. Their resolution caught the Nashville baseball community completely off guard. Some Board members, who had forgotten the rough treatment shown to Dobbs, erroneously believed that Bernhard had inherited a talented team rather than developing one in 1908.

The notion that Bernhard largely fell into a good situation was ludicrous. First, he sliced off the dead wood — Yerkes, Sorrells, Nichols and McCormick. Then he brought in Daubert and Bay owing to his major league connection, and added Sitton, Siegle and East. He put Butler and McElveen in their natural positions and gave them an opportunity to play every day. Some of the shortsighted Directors who praised Johnny Dobbs in 1910 were the same ones who had clamored for his removal three years earlier.[90] Simply stated, the Directors had been spoiled by unexpected success in 1908. The fact that Bernhard's Vols dropped 21 more games than the previous season was reason enough for a small minority of people to agree with the decision to terminate the popular manager.

Rice and Johnson bemoaned Bernhard's removal as a huge mistake. Johnson recognized that Bernhard had been the only manager in the Southern to comply openly and honestly with the rigid salary cap set forth by the league owners. "The few clubs that stuck to the agreement," concluded Rice, "were always the goats. The directorate made a large, juicy mistake in turning loose a corking good manager."[91] It took Memphis owners only one day to fire Charlie Babb and hire Bernhard to manage the Turtles.[92] Picturing Bernhard in the hated rival's uniform the next season would be difficult. Within a week, the Nashville Directors chose Bill Schwartz to manage the Vols in 1911.[93]

Owing to the public's outcry, the Board felt an obligation to explain its decision to release Bernhard, but it did not resolve the swirling controversy. Instead, it increased the general disenchantment with the manner in which the club was being governed. Apparently, the Board had authorized Bernhard during the season to spend more liberally on available talent, a clear breach of the rules they themselves had established, but the manager had steadfastly refused. The newspapers blew the whistle on shady business dealings of other franchises and stood by Bernhard as a man of integrity. "All things come to those who wait and Manager Bill is a good sport," said Jones. "Other managers with half the trouble have been fretting, fuming and grabbing ... and violating salary limits and other rules."[94] Some of the owners were peeved because Bernhard did not wheel and deal in the same illegal fashion as other club managers in the circuit.[95] The Board's decision was all the more ironic in light of the fact that Cleveland had been rumored to be interested in hiring Bernhard away from Nashville to replace Lajoie.

There is one other way to interpret Bernhard's termination. Clearly, Bernhard reflected a quiet and instructive style of leadership the players found approachable. Yet this was hardly the norm in the Southern Association where blusterous, bullying, intimidating managers like Smith in Atlanta, Frank in New Orleans, Babb in Memphis, and even Dobbs in Chattanooga had set the temperamental standard for on-field managerial behavior. Though colleagues were confrontational and argumentative by nature, Bernhard's personality was much more low-key, and his players respected and admired him precisely because he was not outspoken or flamboyant. Bernhard's managerial style would be the mold used by Hub to judge his future field generals, ten in all. Most of them did not measure up.

Compelling evidence suggests that Hub played an indirect role in the firing of Bernhard. Shortly before the season ended, a disturbing story appeared in Nashville speculating that Brooklyn had no intention of opening a roster spot for Hub in 1911. In fact, Ebbets had allegedly written a letter to Kuhn inquiring into whether Nashville would be interested in having their ace returned. If not, he would probably release Hub to either Rochester or Atlanta. Neither Kuhn nor Bernhard wanted to see Hub competing against them in the Southern. Had Brooklyn's mogul been overzealous in drafting him? A weaker argument suggests that the draft had merely been a ruse to keep Hub from bolting to the PCL or the independent California League. Or had Ebbets simply erred in evaluating the contradictory data from Hub's breakout and breakdown years? The Brooklyn magnate did not offer an explanation.

The issue muddied when Birmingham's manager, Carlton Molesworth, made an attractive offer to purchase Hub's contract. Frantically, Bernhard telephoned the Boston Nationals, the cellar dwellers who were desperate for quality pitchers. He leaked information to the Dovey Brothers that the Superbas were about to drop Hub, and they should be ready to pounce. The plan worked. In late October the Doves plucked Hub off the waiver wire and Bernhard averted the possibility of facing him in a Crackers or Barons uniform. The cloakroom shenanigans did not speak very highly of Brooklyn or Nashville, two teams with completely different motivations regarding where Hub should land in the future.[96] Bernhard had not been able to save himself, but he did save Hub. Were the Directors upset with his interference on Hub's behalf?

Hub and Bernhard were not the only casualties of change immediately following the season. Only hours after Bernhard's release, the *Tennessean* purchased the *American* in a stunning move of media consolidation. The corporate buyout meant that Rice would supplant Johnson as sports editor.[97] On December 10, Rice's daily column suddenly disappeared from the sports page. A heavy work schedule had taken its toll on Rice's young family and he coveted a more active role covering national sports stories. To resolve both problems, Rice accepted a position for less money and less responsibility with the *New York Evening Mail*. He was replaced at the *Tennessean* by Spick Hall. From his new perch in the Big Apple, Rice continued to monitor Hub's career with the Braves, especially when he faced John McGraw's New York Giants and, later, Wilbert Robinson's Brooklyn Robins.[98]

The final breath of change occurred in the Vols' front office. The decision to release Bernhard had shaken the Board and created dissension. In the subsequent fallout, Kuhn resigned as President in favor of automobile magnate W. G. Hirsig prior to the winter league meeting.[99] Had Kuhn objected to

Bernhard's termination? After all, the president and manager had been close. Kuhn never did offer a public explanation for his resignation. Then another disconcerting rumor surfaced that the team was up for sale. So the Vols' 1911 season would be interesting on many levels with a new chief administrator, new field manager and new reporters. Only three players from the championship season opened camp in 1911—Wiseman, Bay and Seabough. Within a year, they would all be gone, too.

Hub's breakout and breakdown require separate analysis because the respective campaigns were so completely different in outcome. Hub stood atop the Southern Association world in 1909. He topped the league with 23 wins, rarely missed a scheduled start and led the Vols pitching stable with 37 appearances.[100] Part of his increased workload resulted from the new administrative decree of President Kavanaugh concerning the prompt manner in which rainouts would be made up. No longer could clubs skirt cancelled games with no intention of making them up, decisions that were often based solely on self-serving needs. This manipulation of the schedule had played into the hands of Nashville in 1908 to the detriment of Memphis. Kavanaugh declared that missed games must be automatically rescheduled on the first available meeting in the form of doubleheaders. Managers across the circuit attempted to circumvent Kavanaugh's reform by playing only seven innings in the second tilt, and late in the season some teams tried to limit both games to seven frames. Kavanaugh's intent was clear; he wanted to avoid the usual buildup of many twin bills late in the season, a situation that most managers tried to avoid because of depleted pitching corps. But Kavanaugh's reform, a good one in principal, had resulted in a number of doubleheaders as early as April, which adversely affected pitchers' arms in August owing to the overwork.[101] Increasing the number of roster spots by two players, a plan supported by the managers and players but opposed by owners, would have alleviated much of this problem.

Hub's breakout in 1909 was also attributed, in large part, to Bernhard continually schooling him in pitching mechanics. Bernhard spent countless hours honing Hub's delivery and teaching the finer points in how to set up batters by working the corners of the strike zone. There is no doubt that Hub's growth in 1909 merited major league attention. And this is where the big mystery begins. Why was Hub bypassed in the 1909 draft? Perhaps Bernhard's relationship with Cleveland had soured since Lajoie's demotion, and Sitton had not panned out in his rookie year. Ebbets was Hub's best bet, but the Brooklyn mogul was more impressed with Speaker and less impressed with Hub's showboating theatrics in Little Rock which he witnessed firsthand. The Superbas had also been burned recently by the other Nashville hurling prospect who had blown out his arm, Duggan. Ultimately, Hub's joking personality might have broken an unspoken rule, too. Although he had amassed impressive individual statistics that qualified others for a tryout in the Big Show, was he viewed as a potential team distraction? Finally, one wonders exactly how much of Hub's lingering elbow/shoulder issue was a matter of public knowledge.[102] For whatever reason, Hub's ticket to join "fast company" was not punched and he returned to the Vols for a fourth season.

It is, perhaps, more perplexing to explain why Hub was drafted in 1910. Had Ebbets made a secret agreement with Bernhard and Kuhn a year in advance to draft the Nashville ace regardless of his performance? If so, the selection was half-hearted at best, for Ebbets dropped Hub shortly after the World Series. He had been a Superba for less than six weeks. He would not have the opportunity to play alongside other Southern Association graduates like Daubert, McElveen and Wheat.

So how did the 1910 season help as well as hinder Hub's chances for big league notoriety? Hub certainly hoped that his sixth full season in the minors would lead to greater things. But the Vols were wracked by personnel troubles. Bernhard had shopped for a completely new infield, a backup catcher, three new hurlers and one outfield replacement. As a result, the club remained competitive only until early summer, and a large measure of blame fell on the abysmal offense. Discounting his first and last losses during his 2–11 slide, Hub's Vols mustered only seven runs behind him for an average of .9 runs per game between July 28 and September 10. Even by Deadball Era standards, these paltry numbers would not guarantee success for even the greatest pitchers of the day.

The weather turned bitterly cold at the onset of 1910 but Hub pitched a fast brand of baseball, and he led the club after winning four of five starts. Then he exacerbated the shoulder injury, missed periodic starts and fell into a nose-dive at the end of the season.[103] The significance of Hub's decline in productivity is more fully appreciated when compared to Bernhard; the skipper's statistics nearly matched those of his ailing ace. In a larger sense, Hub's drop-off mirrored that of the entire team; he slipped to 13–16 while the club fell to fifth place, 29 games off the pace.

Certain trends about Hub remained constant in his last two years with Nashville. First, he continued to show a streaky nature in the won-lost column. His rapid beginning in 1909 (6–0) and 1910 (4–1) contributed to impressive stretch runs of 12–2 and 7–1 respectively. But both seasons were punctuated by disappointing losing skids of 2–6 and 2–11, respectively. Between these highs and lows, Hub often dug himself into a rut by neither winning nor losing more than a couple of contests at a time. Second, Hub's first tour in the Southern exhibited a glaring weakness first laid bare in Vincennes — when troubles appeared in the first and seventh innings it often signaled his downfall. Third, Hub remained out of shape physically. Although Rice had not yet sprung his nickname on the Gallatin native, it was hardly flattering to compare Hub's body shape to a hubbard squash. On the eve of his departure to Boston, a moment that should have been reserved for celebration, it was revealing that reporters questioned his work ethic. This perception of a lazy and out-of-shape Hub stuck to his public persona like flypaper.

Hub's first tour in the Southern Association (1907–1910) was instructive and modestly successful. He accumulated a 62–55 record and fared best against Alabama clubs where he held mastery over Birmingham (13–9) and Mobile (8–5). Indeed, the Barons, Sea Gulls and Montgomery Senators/Climbers accounted for exactly half of his total victories. Conversely, he struggled against New Orleans and reserved his most heated competitions for Memphis.[104]

Hub certainly kept in high spirits for the most part during his time with Nashville. Whether he was seen riding a bicycle down the Sulphur Dell base path or catering to the needs of a teammate's dog on the team bench or arguing with fans or acting as a cheerleader or holding a candlelight vigil in the coach's box or being struck in the crotch by an opponent's fastball, there is no question that his teammates turned to him for comic relief to cut the tension and stress. For clownish behavior there was no one second to Hub Perdue.

The 1911 season would be a different year for the Nashville Vols. Many familiar faces were gone. And it was time for Hub to join the exodus and move on to the Boston Doves, the worst team in the National League.

Chapter 5

Tennessee Brave

Hub was elated when he received word that the Boston Doves had drafted him even though his recent performance in Nashville had been less than spectacular. His growth under Bernhard's tutelage had been steady and impressive as the power pitcher added spot location to his blazing fastball. Yet there was cause for concern regarding his nagging sore arm which first surfaced in 1908 and might jeopardize his big league career. Furthermore, the Boston club was in turmoil with different owners and field managers during Hub's three-and-a-half-year tenure in Beantown, none of whom befriended him or contributed to his improvement as a hurler despite the fact that he rose to #1 on the pitching staff. In Boston, Hub's good nature frequently contributed to Hublore stories but also interfered with slab results. While he showed glimpses of greatness against elite teams, his overall performance was quite pedestrian. By mid–1914, both "the Gallatin Squash" and the "Miracle Braves" were headed in opposite directions. Indeed, Hub's biggest contribution to Boston was made *in absentia*.

Ebbets made a point of keeping a close eye on talent in the Southern Association where he had already mined such nuggets as Daubert and Wheat. And he held Nashville's Bernhard in very high esteem. Despite Hub's inconsistencies in 1910, Bernhard steadfastly recommended his ace to the Brooklyn mogul, who finally agreed to draft him. Less than one month later, Ebbets released the Tennessean without explanation, and the pitching-starved Doves picked him up for the waiver price of $1,500. So eager was Hub to begin his major league career that he broke with personal tradition and became the first Bostonian to sign his 1911 contract.[1]

When Hub arrived in Boston, South End Grounds III was in decrepit condition. Built on the original site of South End Grounds II, which was destroyed in the catastrophic Great Roxbury Fire of 1894, the wooden palisades resembled a medieval castle with its conical shaped towers at either end of the grandstands. Located at Columbus and Walpole streets, the stadium enjoyed excellent access to trolley lines. Railroad tracks paralleled the third base line, and a roundhouse was situated just beyond the outfield wall. Its field configuration was spacious — 394' to center field and the power alleys but pull hitters found success straight down the lines (left field, 250'/right field, 255'). A 20-foot high wall in right field and a shorter six-foot porch in left field only modestly discouraged out-of-the-park home runs. The old ball yard held 11,000 fans, but outfield areas were occasionally roped off to accommodate overflow crowds. An incline in right field, similar to Sulphur Dell, required an added degree of athleticism by defenders in that sector.[2]

The Boston Nationals, who had purchased Hub, were known locally as the Doves. They received their nickname from the Dovey brothers, George and John, who had purchased the team following the 1907 season.[3] One of their first moves was to fire manager Fred Tenney, the third-year skipper of the former Beaneaters. Although the deposed player-manager owned a significant amount of stock in the Boston franchise, the Doveys traded him to the New York Giants — in today's world, a tremendous conflict of interest.

The Boston franchise had developed an unflattering reputation for penny-pinching on player salaries and finishing in or close to last in the National League. In other words, the club was known for fiscal mismanagement and on-field mediocrity. When Ebbets released Hub, the beleaguered Doves were up for sale again. A partnership led by William Hepburn Russell (a New York lawyer), Louis and George Page (Boston publishers), and Frederic J. Murphy (a Boston insurance magnate), stepped forward and offered $100,000 for the unsuccessful team. The Dovey Brothers accepted the generous offer and the new owners renamed their nines the "Rustlers" in honor of their primary new owner. Murphy served as team secretary.[4]

The recent past did not offer much in the way of optimism for the 1911 Rustlers. The new club president immediately bought out interim manager Fred Lake's contract and re-instated Tenney as field general. Beginning his professional career in Boston in 1894, Tenney possessed extensive major league credentials. A catcher-first baseman, Tenney was widely recognized as the originator of the 3–6–3 double play, and the versatile Bostonian had perfected the modern style of defensive positioning at first base — "deep and well off the bag."[5] Then Russell dangled an offer Tenney could not refuse; in exchange for purchasing his shares of team stock, the Massachusetts native agreed to manage the club for two years. Strapped for cash and nearing retirement, Tenney accepted the proposal. By all accounts, Tenney and Perdue developed an amiable, if unproductive, working relationship.

One of four Southerners on the Rustlers roster, Hub likely felt a little out of place in New England. He was accompanied by another Tennessee rookie, William Patrick "Rebel" McTigue, a 21-year-old southpaw with a

Hub Perdue (left) and Bill McTigue, two Tennessee rookie pitchers with the Boston Nationals, 1911 (Jimmy Perdue Family Papers, Gallatin, Tennessee).

penchant for wildness and ultimately assigned to the bullpen. Did the pair form a friendship?[6] The remainder of the Boston players were comprised of has-beens, misfits, and a sprinkling of new talent. Leading the aged brigade was Tenney at first base and two important mid-season acquisitions: 35-year-old catcher Johnny Kling and legendary pitcher Denton "Cy" Young, in the final year of his storied career. The middle infield was patrolled by Hub's rookie season acquaintance with the Cubs, Bill Sweeney (second base) and error-prone defender Buck Herzog (shortstop). An ineffective pitching staff was anchored by veterans Charles "Buster" Brown and Al Mattern, and the newcomers Perdue, McTigue and another promising southpaw, George "Lefty" Tyler.

Tenney invited 32 players to spring training, which opened on March 9 in Augusta, Georgia. In the first session, Hub was flung into an intra-squad exhibition in which the "Regulars" roughed him up for eight runs. But he established his reputation immediately. "Perdue, the comedian of the party, needs such [warm] weather in order to get off a little of the surplus tissue that he acquired during the winter," observed T. H. Murnane in the *Boston Daily Globe*.[7] Thus, from the first moment Hub toed a major league pitching rubber, he was known as a comic cut-up and someone who required warm weather in order to produce positive results. Fittingly, he arrived in camp overweight. These three impressions shadowed Hub for the next 12 years. The Tennessean saw limited action in Augusta owing to "a kink in his deltoid muscle," a worrisome comment which strongly suggested that Hub was suffering from arm trouble upon his arrival in the National League.[8]

At 28 years of age, the rookie from the South did not have long to dwell on his relocation to the cold climes of Beantown. His first appearance in a major league uniform occurred on April 19, and despite his nursing the effects of a tender elbow, he was inserted by Tenney in the ninth inning of the second game of a doubleheader against Philadelphia. Legendary Phillies hurler Grover Cleveland Alexander made a lasting impression on the nervous Tennessean, and his lone inning of relief went uneventfully.[9] Having successfully passed the test, Hub made his first start two days later against Brooklyn. While Hub did not finish the sixth inning, he notched his first big league victory despite being tagged by his former Nashville teammate, Daubert, for a triple, two singles, two runs scored, and a stolen base.[10] Hub contributed a single and one RBI in his first Rustlers start. He appeared in several short relief stints in early May, but he was the recipient of rough treatment. Dick Hoblitzel, the slugging first baseman for Cincinnati and a man destined to play a key role in Hub's final professional season, was particularly effective.[11]

Something was drastically wrong with Hub's soupbone. The pain in his elbow became so intense that Tenney benched his Southern-born recruit. At first, Hub underwent "electric treatment" therapy for the tender joint. When his arm did not respond favorably, the club authorized an X-ray which determined he had a chipped bone (floater) that was irritating tissue around the elbow and causing tendon inflammation. Surgery was necessary to remove the splinter, and he rehabbed for over a month.[12]

While Hub recouped, the Rustlers languished in the cellar, and in one stretch the club dropped 14 straight games. Russell unceremoniously relieved Tenney of his "captaincy" after his trade for Kling, but even the aging catcher could not reverse the team's downward spiral. By the time Hub returned to the slab on June 23, Boston had won only 14 games and had fallen 22 games off the pace.[13] Even his reappearance offered no relief to the pitching woes. For example, in mid–July, Hub was involved in two slugfests at South End Grounds over a four-day span, a loss to St. Louis (13–6) and a victory over Chicago (17–12).[14] Placed together, these encounters (in which he gave up 25 runs) suggest that Hub's elbow had not sufficiently healed. In his next ten appearances, Hub neither won nor lost more than one game at a time. As the Tennessean continued to flounder in late innings, Kling opted to use him more sparingly in relief roles.[15] The Rustlers were well on the way to earning a reputation as "the deadball era's worst pitching staff." Not even the mid–August acquisition of Cy Young could salvage any degree of respectability for the beleaguered Boston slab men.[16]

In the midst of the dog days of August, Murnane facetiously referred to the Rustlers in print as "the Hopes." On August 12, Hub tossed a four-hitter against Brooklyn but barely outlasted the Cubs, 12–8 (despite surrendering seven runs in the final frame) to offer a glimmer of optimism. But later in the month, the Reds mauled him for seven runs in the first two innings and two days later the same opponent snatched a come-from-behind victory after Hub was tabbed for two runs in the final frame.[17]

Hub showed inexplicable promise against the National League champion New York Giants. His first appearance against McGraw's club in the Polo Grounds occurred on June 30 and was heralded as a resounding success. Hub kept the powerful Giants batters guessing on the way to earning his second victory, 7–4.[18] Later, in front of the largest home crowd of the season, 10,600, on September 12, Hub limited the Giants to three runs in the first game of a heralded twin bill before departing without earning a decision. In the second contest, the aging Young and Christy Mathewson faced off in a game advertised as a titanic tilt between legendary pitchers. But the future Hall of Famers failed to live up to the hype and both hurlers were sent packing by the third inning. The outcome was anti-climactic.[19]

Hub wrapped up his rookie season with a thud on October 3 when he dropped his fifth consecutive decision. He lasted only one inning against the Phillies in tiny Baker Bowl where he fell victim to three runs on five hits.

Fewer than five hundred fans sat through the chilly finale.[20] As the season folded, newspaper speculation resurfaced about the severity of Hub's damaged wing, and suspicions were confirmed less than two weeks later beneath the sports headline: "Perdue Operated Upon." Apparently, the first surgery on Hub's elbow had been inconclusive and it was necessary to "scrape a growth of bone [calcium deposits?] above his elbow." It is amazing that he underwent two surgeries in the same season. Even more surprising, the team doctor conducted the second "minor surgery" in Hub's room at the Hotel Oxford.[21]

If Hub evaluated his first session in the majors realistically, he probably did not expect to return in 1912. He posted a 6–10 record with an inflated 4.98 ERA on a team that finished dead last and trailed the first-place Giants by 54 games. No Rustlers hurler generated more than eight victories, and the club occupied the bottom rung in attendance. Hub was prone not only to falling behind early and/or failing to hold onto late-inning leads, he was also susceptible to giving up the long ball, ranking sixth in the National League despite only 19 starts. His WHIP (walks plus hits per innings pitched) was a robust 1.61.[22]

In the off-season, Boston underwent its third change in ownership in two years when Russell died unexpectedly. Spearheading an interested group of investors were John Montgomery Ward and James E. Gaffney. Ward, a former major leaguer and principle organizer of the Brotherhood of Professional Baseball Players, currently practiced law in New York City. Gaffney, a construction magnate whose firm had excavated Penn Station and Grand Central Station in Manhattan, held membership in Tammany Hall, the notorious political machine. The duo practically doubled Russell's original purchase price to the Dovey Brothers, and their generous offer was accepted without reservation.[23] Ward was installed as club president and Gaffney served as secretary for their new venture. Owing to Tammany's use of an Indian chief as its symbolic logo, Gaffney changed his team's nickname to "Braves," a moniker that has withstood the test of time even after franchise relocations to Milwaukee (1953) and Atlanta (1966).

Gaffney immediately turned his attention to improving the physical plant and reshaping the rough playing surface at South End Grounds. His renovations included enlarging the grandstands and tearing down the left field bleachers with ambitious plans to move the wall back 100 feet (eventually 25 feet). No more cheap home runs in this ball yard![24]

While Hub spent the off-season listening to the changes taking place in Boston, Ward officially terminated Tenney as manager and replaced him with Kling, Hub's battery mate for more than half of his starts in 1911. The new skipper undoubtedly knew Hub's strengths and weaknesses better than anyone else. For this reason, the hurler probably viewed Kling's promotion with some sense of trepidation.²⁵ For a second straight year, Hub was one of the first players to sign his contract, and Kling ordered his plump hurler to report to Hot Springs two weeks prior to the opening of spring training in order to "boil out."²⁶

By the 1880s, the small community of Hot Springs had grown into a popular destination built around 47 natural thermal springs. The goal of ball players was to melt away excess pounds in the 143-degree waters. In the early twentieth century, the resort was frequented by professional baseball clubs, and some outfits even held spring training there. For example, the Boston Nationals had sent a small contingent of athletes to Hot Springs on an annual basis for years. Many players took residence in the opulent Hotel Eastman, a "mammoth and elegant" lodging built in 1890. The 500-room luxury hotel connected to its own bathhouse consisting of 40 porcelain-lined tubs. Visiting ball players were treated like royalty, and they reciprocated by engaging in exhibitions while there. In 1912, the American and National Leaguers met in two unofficial all-star games at Whittington Park, and Hub appeared in both scrimmages. His first visit to the retreat as a major leaguer had been a delightful experience.²⁷

Kling opened the Braves' new spring training session in Augusta, and chubby Hub stood on shaky ground. With only one partial season of big league experience, he still had a great deal to prove. He hoped, his surgically repaired arm had healed in the off-season. He rejoined returning hurlers Tyler, Brown, McTigue, and experienced newcomers Otto Hess and Walter "Hickory" Dickson — a mediocre list that forebode a repeat of the previous season's collapse. While Kling put his charges through their paces at Warren Park, President Ward paraded newspapermen around town in his shiny new automobile.²⁸ Kling used Hub sparingly in exhibitions, but he threw one nifty four-hit complete game in Baltimore after the Braves had broken camp and traveled north toward Massachusetts.²⁹

In hindsight, Kling and Perdue were destined for a rocky relationship. Kling had entered professional baseball in 1896 and "was generally considered the best defensive catcher of the Deadball Era's first decade."³⁰ After five years in the minors, Kling broke into fast company in Chicago. Known as "a modest and clean-cut family man" who neither drank nor smoked, his on-field behavior was paradoxically punctuated by incessant jabbering at umpires and players alike. Yes, Kling came by his nickname naturally — "Noisy." The stern Kling and the light-hearted Hub were on a collision course owing to their different personalities.

The second Boston mogul in as many years was left with too few options when he selected Hub to open the season at home against Philadelphia on April 11. Mayor John F. Fitzgerald was on hand to throw out the ceremonial first ball, and a crowd in excess of 10,000 welcomed the Braves in their colorful new uniforms. Hub was "very wild" at first, but he settled down and bested Alexander, the pitcher he later acknowledged to be his idol, by a score of 7–4.[31] Four days later, Hub handcuffed the visiting world champion Giants with Mathewson on the slab. The game was scoreless for six innings and Hub allowed only two safeties in the final five frames to wrap up a 3–0 victory.[32] Without question, these back-to-back successes over Alexander and Mathewson were among the greatest achievements and most exciting moments in Hub's entire career. Less than one week later, Hub continued his mastery over the Phillies on the road where he struck out Gavvy Cravath three times and Mike Doolan twice in a victory.[33] It seemed that Hurling Hub had finally elevated his game to major league standards.

Hub's rare sprint out of the gate in April (4–0) was followed by five consecutive road losses in Chicago, St. Louis, Cincinnati, Pittsburgh and Philadelphia.[34] Despite the early wins over the Phillies and Giants, he performed poorly against both lineups, and eventually dropped four out of six and two out of three contests to them, respectively, over the remainder of the campaign. Winless in six tries for the entire month of May, Hub's slab fortunes declined along with that of his team. He did not break into the win column again until June 11 when, in the tenth inning against visiting St. Louis, he singled and scored the winning run.[35] To his credit, however, Hub showed remarkable resilience throughout his roller coaster season. Indeed, he missed only three starts in the first half of the season, and two of those owed to disciplinary infractions.[36]

Following his sixth consecutive loss on June 1, Hub engaged in two highly publicized flair-ups with team officials. President Ward had taken a strong, hands-on approach in dealing with Braves players, and he was particularly critical of Hub's recent pitching slide. The former players' union organizer had several specific recommendations for his faltering ace. First, he suggested that the Tennessean should throw more waste pitches when he held a favorable count with two strikes. Hub thought the owner was meddling and ignored the advice, chiding that it was outdated. Not to be dismissed so easily, Ward persisted; he also opined that Hub needed to take his batting more seriously and swing sooner in the count. Hub disregarded this recommendation too. Soon, newspaper accounts were reporting that Hub was on the verge of being sent to the Giants, a transaction Hub coveted and a rumor that he likely planted himself. Hub liked the gregarious McGraw and truly enjoyed the atmosphere of the Polo Grounds. Although the speculation quietly disap-

Opposite: Warming up on Opening Day, 1912 (Jimmy Perdue Family Papers, Gallatin, Tennessee).

5. Tennessee Brave

peared, Hub did not start another contest for ten days.[37] The Tennessean was in a particularly foul mood on June 21 after losing a heartbreaking contest to Rube Marquard, who notched his 16th consecutive victory at the expense of Hub's seventh loss in nine tries.[38] The stage was set for a colossal meltdown.

The explosion occurred on June 25 when Hub and Kling locked in a public confrontation on the Braves bench, a scene reminiscent of the fisticuffs on the Nashville bench between Hardy and Yerkes in 1907 and Kellum and McElveen in 1908. The ruckus began in the third inning after Hub fell behind Brooklyn, 7–0. Kling ranted that his ace was not putting forth any effort and called him "a quitter" in front of the entire team. Believing he had been shown disrespect, Hub replied that the manager had overworked him while more highly paid pitchers loafed on the bench. For good measure, Hub called Kling "a fat head." But the angry exchange did not stop there. Hub went on to criticize Boston's owners and Kling for trading promising outfield slugger Roy "Doc" Miller to the Phillies for ten-year veteran John Titus, who was nearing the end of his major league career. Smarting over the pasting Brooklyn was administering to him, Hub also lashed out at his teammates, claiming that the anemic Braves offense required four base hits in order to produce a single run. Hub later complained to newspaperman Elmer Hinton that Kling had overworked him and thrust him into nine games over an 18-game stretch, a calculation that became deeply embedded in Hublore.[39] The rhubarb received a huge amount of attention in the Boston press, and Kling suspended Hub indefinitely without pay.[40]

The altercation spilled into the Boston clubhouse where Hub shredded his uniform, packed his bag, said farewell to teammates, informed reporters that he would never play for the Braves again and stormed out. In the days following the incident, Kling began shopping Hub to several interested teams. Strangely enough, Ebbets tendered an immediate offer to purchase Hub's contract, but President Ward declined the offer. A second potential deal with the Phillies for pitcher Earl "The Steam Engine in Boots" Moore also fell through. Hub's status was in limbo as the Braves left town for a western road trip, and the nettled ace stayed behind to watch the Red Sox-Yankees series. Shortly after the Fourth of July, Hub and President Ward made peace, and he was ordered to rejoin the team in St. Louis.[41]

Hub took advantage of this delicate moment to make a most outrageous demand for a raise in salary. It was a striking request in light of the recent turmoil with Kling and his mediocre pitching record to date (6–7–1). Why did he announce this preposterous proposition now? There are several possible explanations. First, Hub had emerged as the legitimate #1 pitcher in the Braves stable, and he might have felt the time was right to press the issue for more money. Second, Boston management might have been overly concerned about the threat of a third major league currently being proposed by John T. Power. Certainly, Ward did not want to lose his best pitcher to these upstarts. Third, Hub still harbored resentment over his treatment by Kling and his tender might have been a veiled attempt by him to force a trade, not a far-fetched notion as the Giants were reportedly still interested in obtaining his services six weeks after the incident. It was simply shocking on a number of levels that Ward actually acquiesced and signed Hub to a new three-year deal one month later.[42]

Hub returned to the box on July 8 and held the Cardinals' bats in check over ten innings to squeak out a 2–1 victory.[43] But Hub's outings over the next 60 days were hardly noteworthy. He added a three-game winning streak in mid–August and subtracted from it during a three-game losing skid in early September. Still, *Sporting Life* concluded that Hub was the best pitcher on the Boston staff. "With a winning team," claimed the national weekly, "Hub Perdue would soon be touted as one of the wonders of the big leagues. He is a cool fellow and works best when in trouble."[44] Which was often!

During the western road trip, an interesting story was printed about how Hub had acquired an article of clothing from Cy Young at the end of the previous year — a long-sleeved undershirt. Hub employed a tailor to patch and alter the threadbare garment, and he wore the treasured item beneath his game jersey for good luck. The superstitious Hub hoped that some of Cy's success would rub off on him.[45]

A fascinating and overlooked aspect of Hub's life was revealed in September when he was elected to represent the Boston Nationals on the Board of Directors of the newly formed Fraternity of Professional Baseball Players of America. The union was the by-product of a controversy resulting from the temporary suspension of Ty Cobb earlier in the season for punching an abusive fan who, as it turned out, was handicapped. The issue hand concerned the vulnerability of players on the field and their perceived lack of protection from abusive and obnoxious fans. Hub had been the recipient of catcalls himself and likely sympathized with the Georgia Peach. So did 296 others, including Mathewson and Doolan. His former Nashville teammate and consummate advocate for unionization, Daubert, was chosen the secretary of the new group, and Sweeney, the Braves' team captain, became its vice president.[46] Clearly, Hub was not the empty-headed Southern baffoon that some people suspected.

Hub's most sensational contest of the year took place on September 2 when Boston hosted New York for the traditional Labor Day doubleheader. In game one, Hub locked up with Marquard in "a real screecher," an extra-inning battle in front of the largest home crowd of the season (15,000). Marquard gave way to Mathewson in the ninth with the score bunched at 2–2, but Hub remained in the contest for the Braves. With two outs and two Giants on base in the 12th, Hub wanted to intentionally walk Larry Doyle to set up a force-out situation. Doyle was a dangerous hitter who fared well against Hub throughout the year, but Hub was told, "no." The Giants' second baseman promptly launched Hub's first offering over the right field wall, a blow which eventually won the game.[47] The Perdue/Marquard-Mathewson face-off marked still another in a growing list of well-pitched games by Hub against McGraw's charges. Coincidentally, the day also marked the arrival of Walter "Rabbit" Maranville, a promising homegrown shortstop, to plug the glaring weakness in the Braves middle infield. Indeed, the club had utilized five different players at the pivotal position, a further example of their defensive dysfunction.

Hub improved markedly in several important categories in 1912, but it was probably a season he'd just as soon forget. He led the team with 13 wins and trailed only Tyler and Hess in innings pitched (249) and games started (30), despite missing over 20 days for disciplinary and injury reasons. Opposing batters lit up Hub for 11 home runs to lead the National League, and he served up the fourth-highest number of base hits and earned runs. He dominated only one club—the St. Louis Cardinals (4–2)—and really struggled against the Chicago Cubs (0–4). His woeful batting was still cause for general concern (.138), and once he missed a home run because he neglected to touch one of the bases. And he did not produce a single RBI! Hub's failure to take care of details in either box—the batter's or pitcher's—was beginning to count against him.

There were subtle signs of optimism in Boston, but there was plenty of room for improvement. Hub had signed a three-year contract extension, locking him up through 1915, but he still boasted a losing record. And while the club improved by eight games in the win column, they still trailed the champion Giants by 52. The Braves finished in the National League cellar as the cross town Red Sox captured the American League title, led by the dynamic Tris Speaker. After the season, Hub remained in Boston to watch the first games of the World Series between the Red Sox and Giants. One week later, he was back in Gallatin, where he pitched for the Butchers against Acorn Brand in the Rock City League. Hub struck out 21 batters in the two-hitter against the amateur opponent.[48] Apparently, professionals were allowed to participate in amateur contests without penalty.

Hub was turning into something of a local celebrity in Boston. In January 1913, the *Boston Daily Globe* commissioned him to write several articles about his observations from a ball player's perspective. The pieces were likely ghost-written by Murnane. Considering the most sensational defensive play he ever witnessed, he recounted McElveen's deception in the 1908 championship game in Nashville. "This was the most important incident in the greatest game of baseball I ever saw," recalled Hub. "I cannot imagine a much more exciting game than that one."⁴⁹ Hub's article included two nicknames which appeared in print for the first time; it identified his former third baseman as "Mac," and referenced himself as "the Gallatin Squash."⁵⁰

The Nashville press picked up on Hub's new moniker, too. On January 2, Hub and his wife were spending a holiday at the Tulane Hotel when Hub dropped in on Jack Nye at the *Banner's* sports desk. "Hurling Hub Perdue, the Pride of Sumner, the Gallatin Squash and holder of several other honorary titles by reason of his prominence in the baseball world..." said Nye about the local celebrity.⁵¹ "The Gallatin Squash" was born.

One of Hub's selections forecast thoughts about his own future in baseball. "When I get through with the Big Show and they start me back to the minors," Hub contemplated, "I want them to buy me a ticket to Nashville, as it is my wish to wind up my days of usefulness on the Sulphur Dell diamond."⁵² Clearly, Hub conveyed a heartfelt loyalty toward the Vols. He also understood that his days in a Boston uniform would not last forever.

As the 1913 campaign loomed ahead, the on-field and head office leadership of the Braves fell into disarray for the third straight year. Indeed, the team's ownership had begun to unravel shortly after the dust settled in 1912. First, club President Ward abdicated most of his administrative responsibilities to Gaffney, who immediately removed Kling as manager. The catcher remained on the team until early May, and he might have influenced the thinking of his successor on the nuances and peculiarities of players on the Braves roster.

George Tweedy Stallings was no stranger to a baseball diamond when he was hired by Gaffney to lead the Braves in 1913. While his experience in the majors was limited to only 20 at-bats, he amassed a six-year playing career in the minors.⁵³ Debuting as player-manager for his hometown Augusta Electricians in the old Southern League in 1893, Stallings added managerial stints totaling 13 years in Kansas City, Nashville, Detroit, Buffalo, and Newark. The New York Highlanders hired Stallings in 1909, and he stayed in the majors until 1920. Known for his dapper attire, "Gentleman George" directed the game from the bench in street clothes just like his more famous contemporary, Connie Mack. And, like Mack, Stallings was all business in the dugout; he possessed neither patience nor a sense of humor, especially when it came to sloppy play, physical errors, and mental mistakes. His manner was often gruff and verbally abusive toward his players. Nothing sent him into a fiery tirade quicker than wild pitches and bases on balls. George Whitted later commented that Stallings "admired brains first of all, and hated stupidity and wild pitchers."⁵⁴ When he first saw the Braves personnel in spring training, Stallings reportedly commented, "I have never seen any club in the big leagues look quite so bad."[55] The no-nonsense attitude of the new Braves field general would directly impact the future of the Gallatin Squash.

Hub had been overjoyed when he first heard the news about the hiring of Stallings. It meant he would no longer be subject to Kling's rants. Although Stallings was Hub's third manager in as many years, Hub viewed the change as a decided improvement. In the *Tennessean,* he suggested that the latest mogul must make it a top priority to improve the Braves' paltry offense.[56] It is probable that Hub also welcomed the opportunity to play for a fellow Southerner, a distinction he had not experienced since his first year in Nashville under John Dobbs.

Stallings made many roster changes which were destined to pay big dividends for the Braves. First, he added two young pitchers, William "Seattle Bill" James and Dick "Baldy" Rudolph. Next he shored up the defense by making everyday players out of shortstop Maranville, first baseman Ralph "Hap" Myers, and catcher Bill Rariden. He signed a flock of new outfielders — Les Mann, Joe Connolly, and Bris Lord — to defend the mammoth garden at South End Grounds.[57] To all outward appearances, Stallings was concerned first and foremost with building up the Braves defense; he introduced a large number of rostered players in search of a winning combination. As a result, Stallings is often credited with pioneering the platoon system.[58] In a move first attempted by Kling, Stallings had also made a concrete offer to package both Perdue and Sweeney to McGraw at the winter meetings.[59] Is it possible that the union activities of the team clown and team captain did not sit well with the new skipper? Indeed, Hub had counseled Maranville on the finer points of salary negotiations, which resulted in a hefty pay raise for Rabbit in 1913.[60] No matter. Trade talks fell through when Stallings demanded one of McGraw's star outfielders.

The Braves moved spring training in 1913 to Athens, Georgia, in order to be closer to Stallings' plantation. Hub, "whose shoulder is still a trifle lame," saw limited slab action in March. One photograph caught the team trainer wrapping Hub's wrist in an effort to keep it in a locked position to take stress off of his elbow.[61] Stallings used Hub sparingly in exhibitions, but he did make two brief appearances in Atlanta, and one each against Bill Clymer's Buffalo Bisons and Clark Griffith's Washington Senators.[62] Limited duty, indeed!

Opening Day, 1913. Hub had anxiously awaited the new season for a variety of reasons. Starting on the road, Stallings handed the ball to Hub to hurl the inaugural contest against the defending National League champion Giants. McGraw selected Jeff Tesreau to do the slab work, and over 20,000 fans jammed into the Polo Grounds or sat on Coogan's Bluff in anticipation of a one-sided slaughter. But Hub shocked the aggregate; he pulled off a two-hit shutout to stun Giants players and their rooters. "Meek, humble and subdued were those beloved Giants," quipped James C. O'Leary, Jr.[63] The New York press called "the Gallatin Squash" sensational.[64]

A week of inclement weather blanketed the East, and when it cleared Stallings gave Hub a rare opportunity not only to fling the home opener in Boston but to face Christy Mathewson and those same New York Giants. Post-season playoff excitement permeated the damp atmosphere as 8,000 fans jammed through the turnstiles. The game was deadlocked at 2–2 after regulation, and both managers had utilized scientific baseball as well as more modern strategies to gain an advantage. For example, McGraw employed a double steal and the first and third delayed double steal in failed attempts to manufacture a run. And Stallings sent 17 different batters to the plate, including four pinch-hitters. The entertaining opener was so hotly contested that Sweeney was booted by the umpire. Doyle continued his batting mastery over Hub with four safeties including a double and home run. Boston miraculously scored twice in the bottom of the ninth, but by the time McTigue was gunned down at home plate to end the extra-inning affair in favor of the visitors, Hub

Hub in Boston overcoat on Opening Day, 1913 (courtesy of Bain Collection, Prints and Photographs Division, Library of Congress, Washington, D. C.).

had long since departed.⁶⁵ Both of his masterpieces against the Giants were harbingers for Hub.

Hub's twin gems against the Giants received plenty of attention around the league. "Boston, the despised Braves," stated the *Philadelphia Evening Star*, "the lowly team that not only trounced the so-called Giants but humiliated the National League champions by shutting them out," arrived in the City of Brotherly Love to play the Phillies.⁶⁶ The scribe explained "the wonderful pitching of Hub Perdue" as the product of "several simple little tricks"— the unleashing of a spitball that batters had rarely seen in the senior circuit and a new pitching delivery "more baffling than a Chinese puzzle." "If Purdue (sic) can thoroughly master the spitter, he will be a wonderful pitcher this year," concluded the article, "for nobody has a better fast ball or better control."⁶⁷ Incidentally, the day after his Boston home opener, National League President Thomas Lynch fined the "cunning" Perdue $10 for "discoloring the ball."⁶⁸

The next two months witnessed the return to a more familiar pattern for Hub. He lost his birthday game in St. Louis on June 9 by a lopsided 12–6 score for a measly 2–5–2 record. One week later, Hub tossed a victory over last-place Cincinnati to put an end to his misfortune and set him on track to win eight out of ten games. While in Cincinnati, Stallings made his second attempt to trade Hub, this time for the Reds' outstanding outfielder, Bob Bescher, who was leading the league in stolen bases and bases on balls.⁶⁹ Like Stallings' previous offer to McGraw, this deal also fell through, but it was no secret that the Boston manager was actively searching to improve his outfield, and his leading pitcher was the trade bait.

The hallmark game of Hub's season took place on June 16 in Pittsburgh, and it was easily considered his finest endeavor. Locked in a pitchers' duel with Marty O'Toole, both pitchers allowed only three hits and the Braves scored the game's lone run on an late-inning RBI single by John Titus, "old reliable," the player Hub had previously disparaged as being over the hill. Later, Hub shamelessly claimed that this was "one of the few games" in the majors when he put forth 100 percent effort. ⁷⁰ He was genuinely motivated to defeat the bonus baby, O'Toole, and O'Leary penned it "one of the prettiest games all season."⁷¹

Ten days later, Hub orchestrated another drubbing of the Giants at the Polo Grounds in an "air tight pitching battle" with Marquard. O'Leary's headline read: "HUB PERDUE, GIANT KILLER." The Gallatin Squash was rather pleased with himself as the stadium emptied. After taking "a flagon of aqua pura from the fount," Hub sought out the Boston scribe and recited the following poem:

> 'Tis true, we dropped a game a day to Philly;
> Although we gave the Quakers quite a rub:
> But please observe that we are not so silly
> As to get walloped twice by any club.

One can only speculate whether Hub was drinking water or something stronger![72]

After "the prettiest game" and "the Giant killer game," Hub hurled "the wildest game" in Philadelphia on July 7. The Braves and Phillies combined to pound out 33 hits and 26 runs in the first game of a doubleheader. In one spectacular blast, Titus bounced the ball "off the bull sign" on the center field wall to win a $50 prize. In the ninth, the Braves plated five insurance runs but the Phillies touched Hub for seven tallies themselves. Hub outlasted five Phillies hurlers and won the 15–11 slugfest.[73]

Hub notched his fifth consecutive win on July 14. Locked in yet another close competition with a Pittsburgh hurler, Charles "Babe" Adams, neither team was afforded many scoring opportunities. Hub sprinkled three bingles over seven innings and struck out six Bucs while whiffing three times himself. Honus Wagner collected the lone RBI but it was not enough to overcome Boston, which won 2–1.[74] Commenting on the Dutchman's prowess with the willow, Hub calculated wistfully that it would take him 403 seasons to overtake the future Hall of Famer in total base hits.[75]

The Bastille Day contest was also significant because of an incident that became one of the most widely publicized episodes in Hublore. Prior to Hub taking his first at-bat against Adams, Stallings pulled his starting pitcher aside and, like Ward had tried earlier, advised him to take his batting more seriously and "mix 'em up." In his first plate appearance, Hub struck out batting right-handed. On his second trip to the dish, he switched to the left side and, likewise, struck out. In his third attempt, the jester took two strikes from the right side, changed over, and took a called third strike from the left side. Unamused, Stallings fumed over Hub's cavalier attitude in the batter's box. "When I got back to the bench," Hub recalled, "George demanded to know what in the h___ I thought I was doing." "Obeying instructions," Hub replied, "but I don't believe George sees the joke yet."[76] While it is impossible to pinpoint the exact moment when Perdue fell out of favor with Stallings, it is conceivable that the seeds were sown in Pittsburgh.[77] The tale became a cornerstone of Hublore.[78]

Hub lost his next start in Chicago and then missed two weeks in the rotation. Upon his return to the box, he resumed his familiar streaky pattern (6–7–3) for the remainder of the season although he sneaked in five straight wins between August 21 and September 6.[79] In one moment of frustration, he was tossed in the first inning of a game in Pittsburgh for arguing a call at first base and shoving the umpire.[80] It was the only time in 19 years that Hub was ever ejected, a remarkable feat in light of his adversarial and wise-cracking attitude toward arbiters in general.

The one-inning stint versus the Pirates set off a spate of brief and awful appearances in the box; Cubs (one inning, three runs), Cardinals (three innings, four runs), Dodgers (one inning, four runs), Reds (one inning, five runs, four innings, six runs).[81] By Hub's own admission, Cubs slugger Henry "Heinie" Zimmerman had been his primary nemesis all season.[82] Hub also experienced a rare pleasure when he squared off at Redland Field against his first mentor in the majors, Mordecai Brown. And there was one exciting moment during his skid when an electric storm unleashed its fury while Hub held a commanding lead over the Reds — a flashing bolt of lightning struck a flagpole across the street from South End Grounds, abruptly ending the game and Hub's chance for a much-needed victory.[83]

Looking back over the season, Hub pitched in front of the three largest home crowds when he twirled against the Giants on Opening Day (8,000) and the Phillies on June 21 (16,500) and September 6 (13,000). In addition, he had opened the National League season in the Polo Grounds before the largest road gate for the Braves — 20,000. The Labor Day weekend affair underscored Hub's up-and-down tendencies in 1913. In the September matchup, Hub tossed a complete game against the powerful Phils lineup of Paskert, Lobert, Magee, Cravath and Luderus for his fifth straight win. Only one bingle out of three safeties made it out of the infield; the others were scratch hits barely beyond the grasp of Maranville at shortstop. Hub's victory resulted in two important league milestones — it derailed the Phillies' hopes of catching the Giants, and inched the Braves into fifth place ahead of the Dodgers.[84]

By late in the season, Stallings had discovered Bernhard's secret by employing a quick hook with Hub. For instance, the hurler was victimized in Philly on September 25 for four first-inning hits which resulted in four runs. Hub did not return to the slab in the second frame.[85] Likewise, his season ended with a whimper a few days later at home against the champion Giants when McGraw rested his starters for the upcoming World Series. Hub, the starter, witnessed the Braves' sensational comeback from the bench.[86] Still, Hub had made a lasting impression on McGraw and its manifestation would take a most interesting twist shortly.

In 1913, the Boston Braves had risen to fifth place and Hub claimed several personal bests. First, he recorded his first winning season in the National League at 16–13, sharing most team wins with Tyler. Plus, Hub continued to whittle away at his ERA, bringing it down to 3.26, an improvement of .54 over the previous season, and his WHIP dropped from 1.40 to 1.13. In another benchmark, he pitched more than 200 innings for the second consecutive

Hub wearing his trademark (red) long-sleeved undershirt, with glove resting on terrier puppy (Jimmy Perdue Family Papers, Gallatin, Tennessee).

year. Perhaps most impressive was his domination over the Giants, 3–0 with three no-decisions. He also tossed a single-season career-high three shutouts. Reporters routinely refer to him as a Giant-killer, an important measuring stick for NL pitchers of the Deadball Era.[87] Still, it was unsettling that Stallings had twice tried to trade his ace.

Statistically speaking, it appeared the Gallatin Squash was learning from past mistakes. He could not shake several recurring trends, however. In his 32 starts, he allowed first-inning runs on 14 occasions, and many of these tallies were multiple in nature. In other words, Hub often dug himself and his team into an early hole from which they were often unable to recover. Furthermore, he was second among the Braves hurlers in starts (32), but recorded the fewest complete games (16) on the four-man starting rotation of a staff that led the league in that category. Finally, and just as significant, Hub still faded in the late innings; arm soreness and late-season fatigue were largely to blame.[88]

Despite his well-documented flaws, Hub was widely regarded as the ace of the Braves pitching staff. He helped Boston achieve a level of respectability that had previously eluded them in the highly competitive National League. Compared to the previous season, the 1913 edition improved by 17 wins, closed the gap in Games Behind by over 20, and finished in fifth place. Perhaps as a reward, the team owners had agreed to present Hub with a lucrative three-year contract extension in August 1912.[89] Hub's future in Boston appeared financially secure but looks could be deceiving. Stallings had shown little patience as he experimented broadly with the team's personnel. Over the course of the season, he had inserted 46 players, including 13 pitchers, into the lineup.[90]

Hub felt satisfied when he returned to Bethpage for the off-season. There, an interesting story never incorporated into Hublore unfolded. Shortly after his final appearance against New York, McGraw received permission from Stallings to invite Hub on a barnstorming world tour being put together with Chicago White Sox owner Charles Comiskey. Hub's triumphs over the Giants had intrigued the "Little Napoleon."[91] Furthermore, the sports editor at the *New York Evening Mail* and McGraw's confidant, Grantland Rice, had lobbied for his fellow Tennessean's inclusion on the select team. At first glance, his nomination might have seemed odd in light of the stodgy and aggressive personalities of the two organizers. Neither promoter was known as a humorous fellow. Still, a list of notorious cut-ups and imbibers had already signed on with "the tourists," most notably Germany Schaefer and Steve Evans.

McGraw had an ulterior motive for tendering an invitation to the Tennessean on the world tour — he wanted to learn about his pitching secrets which had been so devastating against his National League champions. Later on, Hub confided to the Giants manager that he believed his success with the spitball owed to a special brand of chewing tobacco, the Pat Burnley twist. Manufactured by the Willard Tobacco Company in Hartsville, Tennessee, since 1896, its spittle gave his fingers just the right amount of lubrication to make the ball behave in unexpected ways. Upon learning about Hub's disclosure, McGraw ordered all of his pitchers to use Hub's brand of tobacco.[92]

Hub told McGraw he would give him an answer about the trip before the World Series began, and an itinerary typed on onion skin paper is still among the artifacts in Hub's travel trunk. For whatever reason, Hub opted not to join the party.[93] Instead, he stayed at home and patiently awaited the 1914 season.

Physical conditioning was not part of Hub's repertoire in the off-season. Rather, he chose to split time between the Bethpage Farmers and Merchants Bank, where he cashiered alongside his brother, Cot (or "Heavy," as Hub nicknamed him), and farmed his father's land. Although he remained busy in the winter months, he always arrived at spring training pudgy and out of shape. Thus, Stallings contacted Hub and ordered him to accompany captain Sweeney to Hot Springs three weeks prior to spring training in Macon in order to "boil out." The directive was well deserved because Hub reported to the Deadball Era's leading resort 18 pounds overweight.[94]

Stallings might have had an ulterior motive for sending Hub and Sweeney away so soon — to get his two stars away from the national media while a blockbuster trade was in the works. Indeed, the baseball rumor mill was swirling again and Hub's name was frequently mentioned in the mix. Supposedly, the Cardinals, Cubs and Giants were bidding for his services along with two teams in the new Federal League, Joe Tinker's Chicago Whales and Henry "Doc" Gessler's Pittsburgh Stogies.[95] Indeed, Stallings had attempted to trade Hub to the Giants at the winter meeting, but McGraw still would not part with any of his prized outfielders.[96] Then came a blockbuster announcement — the Braves had picked up the temperamental Johnny Evers from the Cubs for cash. Hub and Sweeney reportedly completed the compensation package.[97]

The hypersensitive Evers was bitter over a perceived snub by Chicago owner Charles W. Murphy, and he refused to report to Boston at first, claiming that the two-for-one trade was unfairly weighted in favor of the Cubs. In reality, the diminutive second baseman feared that bonus money owed to him by Murphy might be lost in the transaction. Evers threatened to jump to the Federal League instead. And Hub and Sweeney were caught totally by surprise. President Gaffney supported Stallings' decision to ship the team's joker and captain for the no-nonsense Evers.[98] Beneath a photograph of the three principal parties in *Baseball Magazine,* William A. Phelon and editor F. C. Lane described the proposed Perdue-Sweeney swap for Evers as the biggest trade of the decade.[99]

Details of the proposed deal were being hammered out over the next several days, and Hub and Sweeney were still flabbergasted. Should they follow Stallings' original directive and leave for Hot Springs and then report to Macon, or should they head directly to Tampa, the winter home of the Cubs?

Amidst all of the uncertainty, Hub commented, "I don't know where I'm going, but I'm on my way — provided the way suits me."[100] Hub repeated his interest in the Giants, and intimated that he might even accept "exile to St. Louis." He was fond of managers McGraw and Huggins, albeit for different reasons. Hub let it be known that he would also welcome new scenery in Chicago, the team that had first drafted him in 1906.[101] Regarding the entire episode, Hub maintained that he was "perplexed."[102] Indeed, the negotiations were turning into a media circus.

Amidst this speculative atmosphere, Hub and Sweeney departed for Hot Springs, where a new twist to the drama unfolded with Hub placed squarely on center stage. While he bathed in the steaming waters, Hub was approached by an unidentified agent who offered him a substantial increase in salary to jump to the Federal League. Hub later claimed that he fended off this offer, and proclaimed that he would honor the remaining two years on his Boston contract. Then he packed and headed for Macon, where he informed Stallings of the audacious advance.[103] In the meantime, National League President John K. Tener brokered a deal where Chicago and Boston simply swapped second basemen, Evers for Sweeney. Tener decided that Hub must remain a Brave.[104] Undoubtedly, Stallings was upset, as he had failed to move his ace for a fourth time.

Once Hub arrived in Macon, Stallings peppered him for specific details regarding his contact with the Federal League official. The situation heated up when Doc Gessler, the manager of the Pittsburgh Stogies, registered at the Braves' hotel under an alias. Gessler, an eight-year veteran who once patrolled the outfield for several major league clubs, was rumored to be an old aquaintance of Perdue's dating back to 1907. The rookie manager was a rarity in professional baseball because he actually possessed a medical degree and operated a practice in Indiana, Pennsylvania.[105] Now, Doc hoped to lure the #1 hurler of the Boston Braves to his Federal League.

Stallings took immediate action. Writing in the *Boston Daily Globe*, O'Leary reported that the Braves mogul had secured an injunction from a member of the Georgia Supreme Court to protect his contracted players from such collusion. The State of Georgia, as it turned out, had drafted one of the most stringent statutes in the nation regarding labor agreements, no doubt to protect the system of sharecropping which had flourished there since Reconstruction times.[106] Meanwhile, following a four-inning exhibition against Newark of the International League on March 20, Hub was invited to Gessler's room "for a social call."[107]

Hub later confessed that he was nervous about meeting privately with Gessler, so he enticed reserve outfielder and ex–Vanderbilt player Wilson Collins to accompany him as a witness to the gathering. The choice of Collins made sense. He was a fellow Tennessean and Hub needed someone he could trust. The meeting went off as scheduled but the players were in Gessler's room for only a few minutes when there was a sharp knock on the door. It was Stallings and a deputy sheriff. Quickly, Gessler pushed his Southern guests into an adjoining bathroom to hide. When he opened the room door, the infuriated manager burst in with the deputy in hot pursuit. Stallings fumed that he knew Hub was in the room but he did not have a warrant to search the premises. The three men left for the lobby to discuss the severity of violating an injunction and tampering with Georgia state law. Shortly thereafter, Gessler checked out of the hotel without any further contact with Hub.[108] A crisis had been averted. Or had it?

Hub denied any complicity with Gessler and his Stogies, but the episode did not sit well with Stallings. Hub was not as innocent as he portrayed, thought the suspicious manager. As the Braves' union representative, Hub was always angling for the best possible contracts for himself and teammates. Two years remained on Hub's lucrative contract, but Stallings redoubled his

Hub Perdue (right) and Johnny Evers in Boston, 1914 (Jimmy Perdue Family Papers, Gallatin, Tennessee).

efforts to make a trade on the eve of opening day. Perhaps the fifth time would be the charm. There were simply too many practical reasons to cut ties with Hub.

Behind-the-scenes bargaining continued with Hub on the chopping block when Stallings installed Evers as team captain. Now the Braves players would be subjected to the same hot-tempered treatment on the field as on the bench. Stallings' message was loud and clear: there would be no room on his roster for loafers, jokers or slackers.[109] "Gentleman George" had big plans for Boston in 1914 and they did not include Hub Perdue.[110]

Despite the serious overtones and speculation surrounding him, a degree of levity enveloped Hub in the waning days of spring training. Fred Mitchell, a former big leaguer who had been hired by Stallings to work with the pitchers, recalled a humorous incident about Hub. As the Braves broke camp and headed north toward Boston, the team stopped in the nation's capitol for an exhibition against the Washington Senators. In the contest, Hub was nailed by an inside pitch thrown by a young hurler, Carl Cashion, that hit him squarely in the stomach. The sound of the ball hitting Hub's mid-section, chuckled Mitchell, resonated throughout the grandstands like "a brass drum." The following spring, the exact same scenario played out only this time the fireballer, Walter Johnson, dusted Hub.[111]

Coming off his best season in the majors, Hub was selected as one of 90 big leaguers to be depicted on the B 18 Blanket Series marketed by the Egyptienne Straights Cigarette Company. The flannel fabric, measuring 5.25 inches square, was wrapped around the tobacco, and many people sewed the colorful collectibles together to make blankets, throws, or pillow covers. Most players appeared in two different color schemes, and Hub appeared in the "very rare" red infield edition which is highly valued by collectors today. It shows Hub striking a pitcher's pose on a red background and framed by blue base paths and brown outer trim. Not all players were honored in this manner, and Hub's inclusion signified his value to the Braves organization as well as his importance to the commercial world of baseball memorabilia.[112]

To no one's surprise, Stallings chose Lefty Tyler to open the 1914 season, a snub which irritated Hub. The manager's decision foreshadowed several flair-ups between Hub and Stallings which soon turned public. Hub aggravated the tense relationship by starting off slowly in the box. In his first appearance he lost an exciting game in Philadelphia's Baker Bowl (5–3) in which Paskert drove his very first offering over the wall for a home run. Hub responded in a most unexpected fashion and smashed a triple with his oversized cudgel that drove in a pair of runs. Still, Stallings yanked him in the sixth.[113] "It became clear the effect that the laborious dash around the bases had had on Perdue," noted O'Leary. "When he walked out to the middle of the diamond he was puffing and panting and seemed tired out from his three-sack trip."[114] Once again, out of shape and falling behind early in the game — these trademark weaknesses haunted Hub.

By early May, he had posted an uninspired 0–4 record, with no complete games and an ERA that ballooned over 5.00. When Hub blew an opportunity to defeat the Giants in the Polo Grounds on May 11, Stallings had no choice — he benched his struggling star for almost a month.[115] In fairness to Hub, it should be noted that the Braves had gotten off to a slow start, too. They lost many one-run contests and even dropped an exhibition to a soap company team.[116] Most experts recognized that the club's main weakness lay in the outfield, and Stallings desperately sought to plug this hole.

Once he returned to the rotation, Hub's outings in June were hardly noteworthy (2–1–2), with the lone exception being back-to-back appearances in Pittsburgh.[117] Both contests required long relief efforts to preserve Boston victories. "Hub did not appear to be extending himself," criticized O'Leary. The reporter twisted Hub's own words and chided him with a variation of his worn-out excuse: "The weather was a little too warm for Perdue!"[118] These games were not without controversy as irate Bucs batters accused Hub of "doctoring" the baseballs. Umpire Bill Klem "rejected a crate of eight baseballs" and had them shipped to President Tener for his inspection.[119] While no disciplinary action resulted from the charges, the incident was likely the last straw for Stallings. On June 18, Hub engaged in a one-run encounter with St. Louis in what appeared on the surface to be an inconsequential affair in spite of 30 players seeing action. In reality, Stallings was showcasing his Tennessee Brave to Miller Huggins.

On June 24, Hub threw his final game in Boston flannels, a 4–0 loss to Marquard's Giants. Four days later, the Boston manager shipped Hub and his abysmal 2–5–2 record (only two complete games) to St. Louis for versatile utility man George "Possum" Whitted and outfielder Ted Cather. There would be no miracle for Hub in 1914.[120] Stallings later parroted another oft-used excuse by Hub that he was a "warm weather pitcher" who never adapted to the cold New England clime. It was more plausible, in the words of the renowned sports editor of the *Nashville Banner* and later Hub acquaintance, Fred Russell, that Hub had joked his way right off of the Boston roster.[121]

How should Hub's three and a half years in Boston be assessed? On the positive side, he averaged 187 innings per season in the box. Only Tyler threw more frames in the same time period. While the workhorse label was not uncommon for power pitchers in the Deadball Era, the definition fit the Gallatin Squash. "In his day [Hub] was a high-class moundsman," noted *The Sporting News*, "never a star, but capable of lots of work."[122] During his time in Boston, Hub's ERA dropped significantly by over 1.70. He took the ball twice on Opening Day, and inexplicably fared best against the league's toughest opponent, the New York Giants. He battled against a number of mound legends and future Hall of Famers — Alexander, Mathewson, Brown and Marquard — on multiple occasions. Hub also matched up well against other solid performers like Jeff Tesreau, Red Ames, and Slim Sallee. He matched wits with many top hitters like Honus Wagner, Jake Daubert, Gavvy Cravath, Hans Lobert, Larry Doyle, Dode Paskert, Zack Wheat and Heinie Zimmerman. Finally, Hub teamed in Boston, however briefly, with several noteworthy future Hall of Fame players — Rabbit Maranville, Cy Young and Johnny Evers, and eventually Rogers Hornsby and Miller Huggins in St. Louis.

One of the lesser-known aspects of Hub's career in Boston centered on his involvement with the Baseball Players Fraternity. Hub had always been a cagey customer when negotiating his own contract and he never hesitated to use ploys such as holdouts or threats to play elsewhere in order to squeeze the most favorable terms from management. His involvement with Dave Fultz's group further signified that Hub was savvy in a business sense and recognized the value of collective bargaining in order to achieve the best possible contracts. When it came down to dollars and cents, Hub was far from the southern goober he liked to parlay in public, and one can only speculate on whether a connection existed between his affiliation with the union and the multiple attempts made by management to trade him.

Evaluating Hub's physical ailments in Boston is less mystifying. Everyone from owners to managers to players seemed in agreement that Hub was notoriously slow at the beginning of the season. His "bread-and-butter" pitches — a blazing fastball and biting curve — had seriously irritated his elbow and shoulder prior to arriving in Boston, and he pitched through the pain despite two corrective surgeries. And his increased reliance on the spitball did not alleviate the situation. There is little argument that when his control was on, Hub overpowered opposing batters. But when he was off, they struck his pitches unmercifully. One wonders whether Tommy John surgery and/or a rotator cuff procedure might have restored his talented arm. Hub frustrated fans, scribes and managers alike with a pattern of inconsistency they could not explain, twirling low-hit affairs only to be followed by multi-run debacles. It caused some to question his preparation and motivation. The true culprit was a dead arm.

A careful examination of photographic evidence reveals another problem — Hub's faulty pitching mechanics. Hub is often pictured leaning back while planting his left heel at the moment he released the ball to the plate. This technical flaw caused his pitches to elevate in the strike zone and make them much more attractive to power hitters. Second, while he normally hurled the ball from the 3/4 arm slot position, which was not uncommon in the

Deadball Era, his fingers were rarely on top of the spheroid, which caused his pitches to float or drift around the strike zone. Third, by dipping his right shoulder, the angle of Hub's release point constantly changed, too, and led to erratic deliveries and inconsistent location. These errors contributed to wildness as well as inconsistent results from start to start. In conclusion, the modifications Hub made in his delivery might have been intentional in order to compensate for and/or disguise the root problem — the pain bursting from his elbow and shoulder.

As Hub entered the final month of the season wearing Cardinals flannels, his former teammates slipped into first place on September 8 and never looked back. They didn't simply edge out their opponents either; they crushed the second-place Giants by 10.5 games to win the National League crown. In the World Series, the Braves humbled the heavily favored Philadelphia Athletics to win the world championship. The "Miracle Braves" completed their storybook season without Hub.

The renowned Boston sportswriter, Harold Kaese, claims that the 1914 Braves were the weakest, luckiest and gamest team ever to win the league title and championship crown.[123] It pained Hub to miss these "miraculous" events, and he voiced conflicting opinions about Stallings. The Tennessean used diplomatic language, conceding that his former boss was a good manager and a fine fellow. But Hub recognized a significant personality difference between himself and Gentleman George. "He ain't my style," drawled Hub. "He is too all-fired strenuous in his language for me.... Why, he don't know what he is doing when a game is being played. He just jumps around that bench like a grasshopper and says anything and everything.... And, man, he can talk something awful. I never saw a man who had quite such a flow of language."[124] Clearly, Stallings offended Hub through his rough vocabulary and aggressive in-game behavior.

The personality differences between Hub and Stallings exposed an underlying issue of personal pride and Southern honor as well. In December 1914, Stallings wrote three feature articles in the *Boston Daily Globe* (similar to the pieces drafted by Hub a year earlier) in which he recounted the steps he had taken to deliver Boston its first league title and championship crown.[125] The third installment was devoted almost exclusively to a volatile exchange that led to the final estrangement between manager and pitcher and Hub's ultimate trade to the Cardinals. The manager explained to the readers how he typically worked his pitchers on game day. "I have a regular system," he explained, "where I pick two pitchers for every game and call them No. 1 and No. 2.... As soon as the contest starts No. 2 pitcher is supposed to hike out to the warm-up pen and take just enough work to be ready to go into the box in case the [starter] cracks." While on an early-season road trip, Stallings selected

Bill James to start and told Hub he'd be first relief. James cracked in the first inning and when Stallings saw Hub slouching at the other end of the bench instead of warming up, he became incensed. "Why, you big, lumbering, lazy chump," screamed the manager at his ace. "Do you think the No. 2 assignment entitles you to a ringside seat here on the bench?" Stallings lost his composure and launched a few extra expletives that visibly shook Hub. As it turned out, James settled down and Hub was not needed. After the game the Gallatin Squash contemplated "licking" his manager in the clubhouse, but Stallings told his rankled pitcher to settle down and ignore his biting comments — they were offered in the heat of battle. Hub thought Stallings' explanation was disingenuous and he never did forgive him.[126]

One of the most time-worn stories in Hublore describes a base running gaffe by Hub that dated to his last months in Boston. In one version, Hub lashed a home run, but he missed first base and the umpire called him out. The humorless George Stallings reputedly fumed over the fundamental mistake. In another version of the same event, Hub was driven in from second base but missed third base. When Stallings allegedly questioned Hub on the bench, the weak-hitting Gallatin Squash replied, "I had not visited third base for months and I could not locate the sack."

Later, Hub added a little Tennessee flavor to the original account by insisting that the future manager of the Vols, Larry Gilbert, had driven him in with a triple. This third version was clearly directed at a Nashville audience who knew Gilbert and Hub. Fred Russell, the dean of Southern sportswriters, Grantland Rice protégé and Hub Perdue confidante, later wrote in *I'll Try Anything Twice* that Hub had gone hitless for three months prior to the incident and had stroked a double in this instance.[127] All sorts of questions arise from the multiple telling of the same event. Did it occur in Boston? Was Stallings the principle protagonist? Did Gilbert really play a role? Was Hub's snafu the result of a double, triple or botched home run? There is no evidence in the *Boston Daily Globe* to substantiate the story although Gilbert and Hub were both credited with hitting a triple in 1914.[128]

Hub could be philosophical and, at the same time, quixotic in his final assessment of his former skipper. "George Stallings is the greatest manager that ever stepped in shoe leather and that goes for McGraw and Mack," Hub opined. "The only mistake Stallings ever made was when he released me."[129] But in an honest reflection, Hub admitted that he had rubbed Stallings the wrong way. "Stallings doesn't like any fooling around and I always like to have a little fun," reminisced Hub after reporting to St. Louis.[130] Responding to a minority of public opinion that believed the Braves had not been miraculous but merely "lucky" in 1914, Perdue replied, "I want to say that he [Stallings] can make a ballplayer out of a wooden Indian. Down in Gallatin

... we have a police [officer] who has one leg made of wood.... I honestly believe that Stallings could ... make him the best base-runner in the National League.... He is a superman."[131] Still, there was no doubt that Hub sought revenge against his former manager and team. Once, when asked what he had learned from his playing days in Boston, Hub answered in a bittersweet tone, "I got smart!"[132] Hub understood he had blown the opportunity of a lifetime.

In St. Louis, Hub was afforded a second chance to make good in the Big Show. Only time would tell if he could build stronger and more positive relationships with new skipper Miller Huggins and team owner Helene Robison Britton. Or was it too late? Had the mischievous Gallatin Squash entered the twilight of his career in major league flannels?

Chapter 6

With the Cardinals

If there was another National League team that mirrored Boston's lack of success in the first decade of the twentieth century, it was the St. Louis Cardinals. But Hub welcomed the change because the Gateway to the West was much closer to his Sumner County home and its weather more closely approximated that of Middle Tennessee. He also looked forward to playing for a less bellicose manager and owner in Huggins and Helene Robison Britton. Hub joined a young and rising pitching staff featuring Bill Doak, Slim Sallee, and Pol Perritt. An international event which led directly to the outbreak of the Great War in Europe took place the very day of Hub's trade, and it rightly overshadowed sports news for the next four years, but it did not diminish the future battles in store between Hub and the Giants and Braves and the fact that the Federal League persisted in wooing him. Key contributions to Hublore poured in from St. Louis with two of the more famous stories involving the father/son relationship and the memory of the Civil War. As his talents started to ebb, Hub found solace in a new role in the bullpen and spot starts versus the other weaklings of the National League, Cincinnati and Pittsburgh. Regarding Hub's major league career, the end was in sight.

At the time of Hub's trade to St. Louis, Huggins, or "Hug," had guided the Cardinals into fourth place, a shocking position for the normally low-flying club, and they trailed the Giants by only six games while leading the Braves by five. On the surface, the trade seems to had favored Perdue. Indeed, Hub was now a member of a storied professional program that dated back to 1882 although it had not tasted success for many years, and fans viewed Hub as their new savior on the slab.

For much of the current season, Huggins' Cardinals had competed with McGraw's Giants for supremacy of the National League, and they reflected their pugnacious skipper's temperament. Huggins and his hometown chum, Doc Wiseman, had both been standout players in city leagues, high school and college. They were also protégés of William Howard Taft at the University of Cincinnati's School of Law. Wiseman and Huggins were similar in stature and fielding skills, but the former was relegated to a career in the Southern Association while the latter rapidly advanced to the National League. Huggins quickly earned a reputation "as a gutsy second baseman and effective switch-hitting leadoff" batter. His first managerial post was in St. Louis, where he replaced Roger Bresnahan and inherited a 1913 team that lapsed 49 games behind the league champions and matched the Braves for ineptitude.[1]

Helene Robison Britton had inherited a controlling interest in the Cardinals in 1911, and she took an active interest in the everyday operations of the club along with her husband, Schuyler, who served as team president.[2] The first woman to own a major league franchise, Mrs. Britton was "soft-spoken, intelligent, and strong-willed."[3] The magnate renamed her wooden structure Robison Field, located at Natural Bridge and Vandeventer Avenues. Originally built in 1893 and remodeled twice after devastating fires, the spacious grandstands contained 21,000 seats. A shoot-the-chute thrill ride was erected near the left field foul pole for the enjoyment of the fans and the derision of baseball purists who claimed the amusement detracted from the primary purpose of the facility. The ball yard was in poor condition, but it was a friendly environment for pitchers with measurements of 380' (left field), 435' (center field), and 290' (right field). The lopsided premodern dimensions and large foul territory favored power pitchers. And the St. Louis stable housed several strong arms, including Hub Perdue.[4]

On June 28, Archduke Franz Ferdinand, heir to the Austro-Hungarian thrown, was assassinated in Serbia, and the date coincided with Hub's trade to the Cardinals.[5] Although potential deals with the Cubs or Giants never materialized, Hub was far from disappointed when he landed in St. Louis. "Boston is too cold for a Southern gentleman," postulated the Gallatin Squash later in the season. "I like my weather hot. The hotter it gets the better I like it, and they can't knock St. Louis by telling me it is next door to where Mr. Devil lives."[6] Perdue also appreciated the close proxmity of St. Louis to this middle Tennessee home.

According to Sid C. Keener, the young sports editor of the *St. Louis Times* and future Director of the National Baseball Hall of Fame, Huggins had been trying to swap for Hub since the previous summer. He made a second overture to Stallings at the winter meetings, but the Boston mogul was asking for too much — Albert "Cozy" Dolan — and negotiations fell through. When Hug's right-handers faltered in the first half of 1914, he made the famous two-for-one offer which Stallings accepted. Writing in his column, *On the Side Line,* Keener claimed that the trade came as quite a surprise in St. Louis.[7] Huggins hoped that the addition of Hub would translate into lots of innings pitched. "Perdue is French for 'lost,'" noted the *St. Louis Daily Globe-Demo-*

crat. "We hope the trade does not mean that the Cardinals are lost."[8] Time would tell.

Sports writers disagreed on the physical shape of the Gallatin Squash when he arrived in St. Louis. "The Bostonians will be dumbfounded when they obtain a glimpse of Hub Perdue minus the bay window which formerly gave the Gallatin wonder the appearance of a Tammany politician," teased the *St. Louis Star*.[9] *St. Louis Post-Dispatch* sports writer W. J. O'Connor voiced a different opinion. "Hub is a bit fat," quipped the scribe. Analyzing the two-for-one trade , L. C. Davis joked in his *Sport Salad* column that "pound for pound [the Cardinals] got pretty near an even break."[10] The sports crowd in St. Louis looked forward to the arrival of the Braves at Robison Field and a much-anticipated showdown with the Gallatin Squash.

Hub was visibly nervous in his first contest wearing a St. Louis uniform, and for good reason; fans and journalists alike interpreted his arrival as a measuring stick for their Cardinals against the defending champion Giants. Making his home debut on July 9, Hub faced a familiar adversary in the box — Jeff Tesreau and the Giants. It was a rather noteworthy beginning because the heralded Gallatin Squash served up a home run to Bob Bescher on only the second pitch. After the Redbirds spotted Hub three runs in the same frame, the game settled into a rhythm. Hub went seven innings before Huggins pulled him in favor of Sallee, who flung six more frames. Hub's new club ultimately outlasted the visitors from Gotham, but he did not receive credit for the win. He accepted full responsibility for his ineffectiveness and evaluated this first outing as "bum pitching."[11]

His second stint on the slab was equally dramatic as Hub squared off against his former teammates from Boston. Hub's former mound buddy, Lefty Tyler, out-pitched him, and the contest appeared lost until the Cards battled back in the bottom of the ninth to score twice and steal the game, 3–2.[12] Hub notched a satisfying victory despite being victimized for 12 hits. Incidentally, less than six weeks after moving to the Cardinals, the Braves took temporary residence in Fenway Park and shared the facility with the Red Sox for the remainder of the season while they awaited the completion of their own new ballpark, Braves Field.[13]

Hub quickly won over the fan base in St. Louis with his folksy mannerisms, down-home drawl and winning ways in the box. Although he gave up 41 hits in his first four starts, Hub was credited with three victories and one no-decision which the Cardinals eventually won. He was mixing a "zippy fast ball" with "a tantalizing slow ball" to disrupt the timing of the batters, and even though he dealt with a lot of base runners, Hub clamped down "airtight in emergencies." For instance, at Ebbets Field, Hub surrendered a mammoth home run to Daubert, but the Cardinals offense rallied for five runs to support him. Hub responded by shutting down the Dodgers in order over the final three frames. Many observers in St. Louis began believing that Hub was the difference-maker who would lead the Cardinals out of the second division and into contention for the NL flag. O'Connor quipped, tongue-in-cheek, that Hub was certainly "big enough" to plug any hole in the Cardinals defense. The only criticism of the Gallatin Squash was the usual complaint that he loafed on bunt coverage.[14]

Hub reveled in these press clippings and proclaimed boldly that his goal was to win ten straight games. St. Louis owned a seven-game winning streak at the time, but Hub's brash announcement was ill-timed as the Cardinals arrived in Philadelphia to face the much-improved Phillies. Once again, Hub faced his idol in the box, Grover Alexander, who was in the early stages of a phenomenal season. The "father of baseball umpires," Bill Klem, officiated. When the game ended Hub was on the downside of a 3–0 score.[15] Still, Hub was quite satisfied; he knocked a rare base hit against Alexander and celebrated the occasion with teammates on an off-day excursion to the Atlantic City boardwalk.

The Braves reversed their earlier loss to Hub at the end of July on the same day events burst in Europe and thrust the continent into total war. In his first slab appearance in Beantown since the trade, Hub tossed a marvelous six-hitter, but three safeties by Les Mann and two more by Rabbit Maranville sealed his defeat, 2–0. Plus, Dick Rudolph limited St. Louis batters to only two singles. At one point, Hub got the crowd buzzing when he tucked a fastball underneath Rabbit's chin and nearly cork-screwed the pint-sized shortstop into the ground.[16] There was no doubt that Hub's errant throw was purposeful. In both of his outings versus the Braves, Hub desperately wanted to demonstrate to everyone that his trade had been good for his new employer. And revenge can be a powerful motivating factor!

Hub further endeared himself to St. Louis fans and sports writers with his colorful antics. After just two weeks on the Cardinals roster, Keener reported, Hub had replaced the departed Steve Evans as the team's resident comedian. His extra-long bat was a focal point of curiosity; some rooters said it resembled a fungo stick while others thought it resembled a redwood tree. It was not uncommon for a group of players to huddle around the Gallatin Squash in a hotel lobby when the team was on the road to be entertained with funny yarns, especially the "mix 'em up" tale.[17] Baseball aficionados respected the way he worked the strike zone — up, down, inside, outside — with pitches seldom grooved.

Two National League nines were making a surprisingly strong statement in mid-summer: the Braves, who had climbed out of the cellar and were beginning their steady ascent to the top, and the Cardinals, who were likewise challenging the Giants for first place. For Boston and St. Louis to be so near the top of the league standings was uncharted territory for both franchises. But whereas the Stallings' bunch continued its ascent, Hug's team hit a snag in the first two weeks of August.

Hub always finagled his managers into pitching him against the Giants. He considered McGraw's team the benchmark of baseball excellence and he relished toeing the slab in the Polo Grounds. Yet a game on August 10 turned disastrously for the Cardinals when Cozy Dolan misplayed a fly ball in left field. Dolan claimed the sun had temporarily blinded him. The error led to a Giants rally capped by a Larry Doyle home run. The problem? The afternoon was heavily overcast. Dolan's questionable effort nearly incited a brawl on the Cardinals bench, where Hub proceeded to "blow up like a toy balloon pricked with a pin." The ensuing loss was the ninth for the Cardinals on the recent road trip and Hub's most embarrassing defeat as a Redbird.[18] L. C. Davis captured the moment in a limerick entitled "Old Brother Hubbard:"

> The Giants all rubbered,
> When old brother Hubbard
> Was slated to hurl the pill;
> And when they got through
> With Hubbard Perdue,
> He seemed to be very ill.[19]

Hub's contrary pattern had returned. From the last week of July until the end of the season, he neither won nor lost more than two games in a row. As Hub struggled to last more than five innings, Huggins began to utilize him more and more frequently out of the bullpen, a decision that would carry over into Hub's slab time in 1915.

As the Great War entered American homes via the daily newspaper, so too did it influence baseball coverage, at least metaphorically. Mirroring the gloomy war reports from the Western Front as the Germans were unleashing the Schlieffen Plan, O'Connor noted that Hub hung on to beat Brooklyn despite a pair of hits by his Dodgers nemeses, Zack Wheat and Casey Stengel. "Deadly sharpshooting by Hub Perdue held the enemy in check," noted the scribe, "until Field Commander Huggins deemed it wise to start heavy firing."[20] The Cardinals seemed poised to make a legitimate run at the faltering Giants at the end of August when the red-hot Braves paid a visit to Robison Field.

As the Cardinals had rolled over the Dodgers all season, so too had the Braves dominated the Cardinals. O'Connor surmised that the National League was exhibiting "parity" for the most part, but the Braves still bulldozed right through the Cardinals. Hub threw well in his final matchup of the year against Boston but his counterpart, "Hummingbird" Tyler, tossed a one-hit shutout

Slugging Hub Perdue with his famous long bat the day he defeated the Brooklyn Dodgers (courtesy of Bain Collection, Prints and Photographs Division, Library of Congress, Washington, D. C.).

to complete the Braves' sweep over the Cardinals.[21] The outcome might have been different had two Cardinals base runners not been tossed out at the plate in the 1–0 affair. Cardinals observers feared their pennant hopes were slowly beginning to slip away.

There was room for optimism, however, as the Cardinals were slated to play 14 games (home and away) in early September against the weakest opponents in the standings, Pittsburgh and Cincinnati. While newspapers in St. Louis were prematurely adding victories to the Cardinals' win column, the Pirates and Reds had different ideas. In the first series, Pittsburgh shocked St. Louis in a four-game sweep that effectively dampened the Cardinals' aspiration to catch the Giants. Hub snapped the seven-game losing streak in Cincinnati with the aid of 17 Cardinals hits, a rare offensive outburst. A touch of levity occurred in the seventh, when Hub hit a weak grounder to Heinie Groh and he stopped running to first base "to conserve energy." The second baseman held onto the spheroid and forced the "obese" Hub to resume his trek down the base path, and Hub did so — walking! Groh completed the putout but the Cincinnati faithful were unimpressed. After all, they were on the short end of a 12–2 tally.[22] The Cardinals had other matters on their minds, however.

The Giants were no longer their target since the Braves had staked a miraculous claim to first place.

Late in the month a revised goal presented itself to the St. Louis club; they were mathematically within reach of overtaking the second-place Giants. Hub did not help to realize this new objective when he failed to match Alexander's masterful two-hit shutout in Philadelphia, his 23rd win of the season. Old Pete faced only 28 Cardinals and struck out 11.[23] But then Hub stepped up to beat the Giants in the Polo Grounds on September 24 to pull the Cardinals to within one game of second place.[24] They never got any closer. The resurgent Pirates and Reds finished the campaign as spoilers and the Cardinals were forced to settle for third place.

The top story in major league baseball in 1914 was the "Miracle Braves," but there was no doubt that the equally unexpected improvement of St. Louis had also surprised league experts. One sports writer believed that the Cardinals had played so ferociously down the stretch because of an incentive clause in the players' contracts stating that they would receive a 25 percent bonus on their base salary if the team finished in second place and 20 percent if they made it to third. "It is wonderful what five per cent will do to animate a team," chuckled Heywood Broun in the *New York Tribune*.[25] Hub was satisfied with the surprising finish of St. Louis despite his exclusion from the World Series of 1914. "It is worth the [lost] money to be out of the reach of Stallings' sharp tongue," admitted the Gallatin Squash.[26] But in a more pensive moment years later, Hub stated with genuine sorrow, "I was traded right out of the World Series."[27]

When the lights dimmed on the 1914 season, the Cardinals' owner, manager, and players alike celebrated their lofty accomplishments. The Cardinals finished in third place, the team's highest finish in the Deadball Era. Their final record, 81–72, was an improvement of 30 games in the win column over the previous year, a greater differential than that achieved by the Braves. There were encouraging signs for the future as Cardinals pitchers combined to lead the National League with a 2.38 ERA; Doak and Sallee had been nothing short of spectacular. Hub's record of 8–8, while unremarkably pedestrian, paled in comparison to his drop in ERA from 5.82 in Boston to 2.82 in St. Louis.[28] Hub also topped 200 innings on the slab for the third consecutive season. He continued his dominance over Brooklyn (4–0) and Cincinnati (3–0) and stood toe-to-toe with the Giants in several memorable games. Only the Phillies held "the buffalo sign" over Hub, in what was becoming an annual circumstance.

Hub made no secret of the fact that he appreciated playing in St. Louis. He preferred its warm climate, enjoyed its fans, respected his manager, Hug, and fit in well with his teammates. Yes, Hub was a happy Cardinal — "a whole lot better satisfied," he said.²⁹ By all indicators, Hub looked forward to another season in the west.

New signs of Hub's deteriorating arm strength were beginning to emerge, however. Whereas he had routinely shown difficulty late in the season throughout his career, he was now showing evidence of severe weakness in early-to-mid August. As Bernhard and Stallings had resorted to a quick trigger in removing him in late innings, Huggins did too, but the Cardinals' skipper added even more extensive time in the bullpen, a formula he would stick with the next season.

Sandwiched between the end of the season and the start of the World Series, St. Louis fans were treated to the annual city championship series between the NL Cardinals and the AL Browns. On paper, the Cardinals held a decided advantage in pitching and hitting, but the upstart Brownies put up stiff resistance and copped the crown by winning four out of five games. Huggins split the pitching duties between two or three hurlers so as not to overwork anyone. Hub drew assignments in the second and fifth games, both losses. He split time with a youngster named Dick Niehaus, a rising reliever who would modestly impact Hub's future in St. Louis. The contests were reasonably well attended, and the winners' share ($127) and the losers' cut ($71) served as a nice bonus.³⁰

Throughout the recent campaign there had been a lot of concern voiced in St. Louis newspapers about the possible loss of rostered Cardinals and Browns players to the local entrant in the Federal League. Indeed, manager Fielder Jones of the St. Louis Terriers had expressed interest in several unidentified local pitching stars. Was Perdue really being wooed by Jones as one rumor suggested? It is likely that Hub encouraged this gossip since he had enjoyed the earlier hoopla with Gessler's Pittsburgh Stogies. Such intrigue might also serve as a handy bargaining chip when renegotiating his contract for 1916.

Prior to Hub's reporting to spring training in 1915 for what turned out to be his final year in the majors, Marion Perdue allegedly sat down with his big league son and had a serious talk about money. The elder Perdue expressed disappointment in how Hub had always managed to squander his big league paycheck during the season. So he proposed a wager: if Hub were to come home at the end of 1915 with any amount of money whatsoever, he would match it.³¹ Time would tell whether Hub accepted his father's challenge.

Hub reported to spring training in San Antonio a shadow of his former self. "Heah Ah is: look muh ovah!" announced the Gallatin Squash to his shocked teammates. Hub had trimmed off 30 pounds in the off-season, and O'Connor noted that he had accomplished this drastic weight reduction "without the use of a knife."³² Hub intimated that he was motivated to drop the excess poundage in order to compete for the #1 right-handed role since the Cardinals had traded Perritt to the Giants in February. Still, Hub pitched only ten innings in three exhibitions in spring training against Fort Worth, Newark and Cleveland. And he was completely absent from the box in the annual pre-season kickoff tournament against the Browns.[33] Was Huggins protecting Hub from cold weather? A sore arm? Or had the skipper settled on a rotation consisting of Sallee, Doak, Dan Griner and Lee Meadows?

During an intra-squad game shortly before the opening of the 1915 season, "the Miracle Man" mystified his teammates with his dazzling spitter. The local press incorrectly credited Huggins with "conceiving the idea of developing Perdue into a moist-ball specialist."[34] In reality, Hub had been loading his pitches for a decade.

The strength of the Cardinals' 1915 roster lay, arguably, in its fastball/spitball pitchers. Left-hander Harry "Slim" Sallee had anchored the staff since 1908. Facing his wicked "crossfire" delivery, where he stood on the extreme edge of the rubber and released the ball as he fell off toward the first base line, right-handed batters fared poorly against the 6' 3" standout.[35] Accompanying Sallee was a talented spitballer, Bill Doak, who had cracked the rotation late the previous year. Perhaps best known for developing an improved fielding glove (which was successfully marketed by Rawlings Sporting Goods Company of St. Louis into the 1960s), Doak turned into the surprise pitcher of the National League in 1914 when he led all pitchers with a 1.72 ERA.[36] Together, Sallee and Doak had accounted for 37 wins in 62 starts and 538 innings pitched. They were the cornerstones of the Cardinals pitching staff, and Hub would compete against Griner and "Rifle Jim" Middleton for a starting assignment.

Once the regular season was under way, the Cardinals started off slowly and Hub did not take the box until the seventh game, on the road in Cincinnati. Something was drastically out of place. Hub was no longer the go-to-guy; Huggins had decided to leave him in the same role he had filled at the end of the previous season — a spot starter against weak lineups (Reds and Pirates) and increased bullpen duty. The *St. Louis Globe-Democrat* mentioned that President Britton was making overtures to shop the old warhorse to the Reds and Dodgers.[37] "Old Hub," lamented J. B. Sheridan, "no arm, no speed, no curve, but control and knowledge of what to do with it" following his first victory of the young season, a shutout over the Pirates.[38] By mid–July, Hub had made nine out of 12 appearances on the road. Was Huggins sheltering Hub from rancorous St. Louis fans and scribes?

The swirling rumor mill and lack of slab work did not affect Hub's legendary appetite for good food, however. Roy Stockton wrote a Sunday feature in the *St. Louis Globe-Democrat* about the well-known kitchen and boarding house of Mother Dorn, a fabulous cook who had been preparing meals for Cardinals players for 16 years. Her brick establishment was located on Natural Bridge Road and she was famous for preparing delicacies such as apple pie, fried chicken and sirloin steak. A loyal Cardinals rooter, Mother Dorn refused to cook for the rival Brownies unless the Redbirds were out of town. Featured prominently in Stockton's selection on "the culinary artist" were three Cardinals with ravenous appetites — Perdue, Doak and Griner.[39]

Hub's renowned sense of humor remained fully intact in the last year of his contract. One on-field incident illustrated Hub's temper and devotion to the region of his birth. "Y'know there's still some feelings between the Northerners and Southerners about the Civil War," noted *The Sporting News.* "Remember old Hub Perdue, who used to heave 'em over for the Cardinals? He came from the sunny South and was a rabid admirer of Robert E. Lee. One day Hub smashed a line drive that skimmed past first base foul by inches. Perdue didn't know it was foul, and ran as hard as he could. Umpire Art Fletcher, from Illinois, couldn't stop him, so he yelled, 'Let the rebel run. He got the running habit from his old man, who ran from 1861–65.' [Fletcher's comment] nearly started the war all over again."[40] Clearly, southern patriotism and a sensitivity to the outcome of the Civil War still abided in Hub's Tennessee character. This story is another selection of Hublore. But the story is also a simile—Hub's baseball world was turning upside down in 1915 just as Confederate hopes had been dashed 50 years earlier.

On a different level, the war news from Europe was consuming the front pages of American newspapers, including the horrific sinking of the passenger liner *Lusitania* by a German U-boat in early May. At the same time, Hub's career was beginning to plunge too. Serious warning signs first surfaced on May 12 during an eastern road swing through Boston. Hub was clinging to a slender 1–0 lead when Larry Gilbert spearheaded a five-run counterattack in the fifth to scuttle the Cardinals. Hub "surprised the crowd" by stroking a single and later scoring all the way from second base, but Bostonians were hardly shocked by the outcome of the game.[41] Four days later, three Phillies sluggers — Gavvy Cravath, Bert Niehoff and Beals Becker — each launched home runs off Hub — all in the same inning![42]

Hub's disastrous loss to the Phillies dropped the Cardinals into the cellar, and St. Louis scribes were looking for a scapegoat. "Perdue is not a spring pitcher," jabbed the *Globe-Democrat.* "Some unkind folks might say that he was never a summer pitcher ... and these are cruel words."[43] He disappeared from the box for ten days, and when he returned he threw two innings of game-winning relief at the Polo Grounds to earn his first victory in almost a month. The next day he started against Marquard but lost a lopsided contest, 11–4, when he gave up 19 hits.[44] Hub had probably talked his way into the back-to-back encounters.

During the one-sided beating by the Giants, Hub was at the center of a spirited rhubarb. In the bottom of the first, McGraw accused Hub of committing a balk and argued vociferously with umpire Malcolm Eason. The temperamental McGraw not only lost the squabble, but the ump also booted him from the field. The Giants bench erupted in anger and launched into a vicious tirade at Eason. The besieged arbiter halted the game several times and slowly eliminated Giants players from the dugout. By the end of the game, only the original nine starters and two base coaches remained on the bench, the rest being "sent to Devil's Island." Hub was greeted in the eighth by five consecutive singles and five runs before departing from the box.[45]

Huggins had seen enough of Hub's inconsistency, and he removed the struggling hurler from the starting rotation. The Gallatin Squash would be utilized almost exclusively out of the bullpen for the remainder of the disappointing campaign. After a birthday game defeat to Cincinnati in early June, Hub did not start another contest for six weeks. Huggins offered his puréed Squash a little redemption when McGraw's crew visited Robison Field on August 4. Trailing 9–2, the Cardinals staged a ferocious comeback and tabulated seven runs in the seventh to take the lead. Huggins felt comfortable and called on Hub to shut down the powerful New Yorkers. Too bad. With two outs, Larry Doyle stroked a home run, and two follow-up singles resulted in a tie game. Huggins pulled the plug on Hub to end the "farce comedy."[46]

A four-game home sweep of the defending world champion Braves in mid–June infused the Cardinals with a glimmer of hope; they still might be able to salvage their season. During this brief interlude of public optimism, Hub reached the ultimate depth of despair on June 24 in Chicago. The first-place Cubs held a thin 1.5-game edge over St. Louis when the series began, and another sweep by the resurgent Redbirds would catapult them into the league lead. Expectations for the series ran at fever pitch in Mound City; beating arch-rival Chicago was always a high priority for Cardinals rooters. But the mood quickly deflated when Sallee lost the opener of the series on June 23. The second contest seesawed back and forth with both teams utilizing multiple pitchers in an attempt to stem the offensive onslaught. By the eighth, the Cardinals grabbed a 13–10 lead and Huggins chose Hub to close out the Cubs. Then disaster struck. With one out, Fred "Cy" Williams singled, Jimmy Archer doubled, Howard "Polly" McLarry singled and Heinie Zimmerman, always a tough out for Hub, doubled. All of the damage from the four Cubbies took place with two strikes. The destruction netted three runs to tie the slugfest, and Huggins pulled his struggling reliever and put in Doak. Zimmerman advanced to third base on an infield ground out, and then, to add further insult, he stole home on the inattentive Doak to register the eventual winning run. Immediately following the game, the police flooded onto the infield to prevent a near-riot between jubilant fans and frustrated Cardinals players.[47]

Hub was crushed. After the game he sat alone in a corner of the Hotel Sherman lobby, visibly "disgusted with himself." In another corner, Cardinals players were huddled together recreating the shocking letdown. "Ah can't count th' games Ah've lost on that hill that hurt me as much as this one," Hub lamented to his catcher, Frank Snyder.[48] And a scathing reception awaited Hub back in St. Louis.

As expected, reporters and rabid fans were angered by the losses to their bitter rivals in Chicago. Writing in the *St. Louis Star,* Billy Murphy laid the blame squarely on Hub and Hug. The sports scribe leveled severe accusations at Hub. First, Hub was "laying down" on the team, and Murphy believed he knew why. "You know that no pitcher goes into a game and wins it unless his control is conclusive. But, how many of them pitch the Game of Life with the slightest idea of the value and importance of control?... They [Cardinals fans] point out that practice, work, sobriety, good sleep, fresh air and careful living have not always been sought by this gentleman [Hub]."[49] Murphy's harangue about Hub's questionable habits was laying the groundwork for his dismissal, and the sports writer jabbed that there had been nothing exceptional about Hub's record since his arrival in St. Louis (11–15). Murphy even cast doubt on Hub's major league credentials. He criticized Hug, too, for perceived blind loyalty toward his beleaguered pitcher, and his failure to recognize Hub's glaring weaknesses. "You [Hug] are a damp firecracker" when evaluating pitchers, said the bellicose scribe. Murphy believed Huggins possessed a stubborn streak when it came to Perdue, and he recommended that the manager replace Hub with Dick Niehaus, a young but seldom used hurler. It was easy to sympathize with Murphy's lack of patience with Hub; the reliever had blown five leads, and each one had ended in a loss.[50]

Murphy found an ally in O'Connor in the *St. Louis Post-Dispatch,* who charged that Huggins had mishandled Hub in the Chicago affair. Tempers were wearing thin in the press, and the contrasting success of the Federal League Terriers did not make the Cardinals' current predicament any more palatable. "Huggins should imitate Fielder Jones [manager of the Terriers]," stated O'Connor emphatically. "The manager of the Cardinals seems too lenient in his treatment of pitchers."[51] The only way to escape this groundswell of public criticism focused on Hub was for Huggins to work him far away from condemning eyes.

The visceral commentaries of Murphy and O'Connor had expanded to include Huggins because they saw him as a difficult (and uncooperative) personality in interviews. Indeed, the skipper was an aloof and introspective person. Everyone admitted that Huggins understood baseball strategy, but the scribes could not abide in his fierce loyalty toward underachieving players like Hub. In their seminal study, *1921: The Yankees, the Giants and the Battle for Baseball Supremacy in New York*, co-authors Lyle Spatz and Steve Steinberg note that Huggins was criticized by the New York press for precisely the same reason — hanging on too long with Yankees slab men who found themselves in trouble.[52] And this later gripe came during a pennant-winning season! Murphy had simply established himself in the forefront of a long line of sports writers who were frustrated by Hug's managerial style and non-communicative approach with the press. From a player's standpoint, his brand of leadership might have been interpreted more sympathetically, as a sign of support.

Hub was not totally without defenders after his collapse of June 24. Sid Keener stood up for the Gallatin Squash in the *St. Louis Times*, stating that fans and fellow journalists were wrong to label Hub a "quitter." Their criticisms simply did not take into account Hub's intensity and competitive spirit. "AH'M NOT QUITIN'," stated Hub emphatically to Keener.[53] Still, Huggins did not reinsert Hub in the box for almost three weeks and thereafter he usually limited him to short relief stints mainly on the road. Hoping to seize on an opportunity, the St. Paul Saints of the American Association submitted a bid to purchase Hub's contract.[54] Huggins would not desert the Gallatin Squash, however, and the proposed deal never materialized.

Upon his return on July 13, Hub flung four solid innings of relief against Boston to earn his fourth win of the season, but he followed up with three horrendous outings in Philadelphia where he secured only two outs.[55] In his fourth relief appearance in as many days, he entered a tie game in the ninth against the Giants. To everyone's surprise, Hub pitched seven strong innings of long relief and allowed only three hits before fading in the 16th frame.[56] Hub always managed to save a little extra for the Polo Grounds crowd but his checkered performances out of the bullpen were now beginning to match his inconsistencies as a starter.

Hub's rough comeback trail continued in a rare start on July 22 in Brooklyn, where he sported new spikes. In an efficient display of pitching reminiscent of the former Gallatin Squash, he held the Dodgers batters spellbound as he weaved an impressive four-hitter and grabbed an 11–1 win.[57] One wonders whether Ebbets' snub of Hub back in 1909 had somehow motivated him to clamp down whenever he competed against Brooklyn.

Hub's return as a starter was short-lived, however. He lasted only two innings on the slab in his next outing, and Hug's experiment came to an abrupt end. The diminutive manager exiled Hub to the bullpen where he threw only eight innings over the next month. Incidentally, on this extended eastern road trip, the Cardinals held an honorary distinction of opening the new Braves Field on August 11, but Hub did not appear in the festivities.

6. With the Cardinals

Hub warming up alongside St. Louis manager Miller Huggins (Jimmy Perdue Family Papers, Gallatin, Tennessee).

Then, just as it appeared Hub's career was all washed up, he surpassed everyone's expectations one final time in his favorite venue. On August 23, Hub entered in relief of Leon "Red" Ames in the Polo Grounds and saved game one of a doubleheader, 5–4. When Hank "Lefty" Robinson needed a spell in game two, Huggins brought in the Gallatin Squash in the third, trailing Mathewson, 3–0. Hub not only shut down the Giants but he swatted a single and scored the winning run to notch the victory. A doubleheader sweep of McGraw's Giants and both contests credited to Hub's nine innings of relief![58] The "Giant-killer" had done it one last time, and it was no less spectacular owing to the Giants' struggles in 1915. This achievement was not only a satisfying highlight of Hub's tenure with the Cardinals, it was the capstone to his five years in the National League. Seldom were curtain calls sweeter. But such last-minute bravado was too late to resurrect Hub's big league career, which was now in free-fall.

Hub played out the remainder of his string with the Cardinals in typical roller coaster fashion. Four days after his domination over the Giants, he lasted only three innings in Brooklyn. Then, in Philly, Hub had been watching from the bullpen as his hero painted the corners of the plate all afternoon when Huggins summoned him to relieve the bespectacled Lee Meadows. Perhaps Huggins was showing respect to his former ace when he allowed him one last opportunity to square off against the mighty Grover Alexander. The results did not go well for Hub, however. He registered two outs but offered up a single and drilled Dode Paskert with an errant pitch. As the winning runner stood on second base, a familiar adversary from Hub's past stepped into the batter's box. With one strike, another former Bostonian, Possum Witted, banged one of Hub's spitters deep toward the left field corner. Bob Bescher, now a Cardinal, raced toward the spheroid, which bounced off the top of the wall, struck the outfielder in the chest, and landed in the bleachers as the winning run scored.[59] Shades of Jose Canseco! Less than a week later, Huggins placed Hub in the exact same situation in Cincinnati. With the bases loaded in the bottom of the final frame, outfielder Wade Killifer promptly drove Hub's first offering into deep center field to push across the winning run for the Reds. Victimized by two walk-off hits in his last three outings,[60] Hub was done.

The final start of Hub's major league career occurred on September 1 in Pittsburgh. Hub registered only four outs against the Pirates and gave up four runs on six hits and a wild pitch.[61] A bitter postscript took place on September 18 when the visiting Braves arrived in Mound City for a doubleheader. The Cardinals' rookie shortstop, Rogers Hornsby, opened the floodgates with an error in the top of the first, and Hub reported from the bullpen to put out the fire (or else pour gasoline on it). Surprisingly, he smothered the Braves' rally in the first, but he was totally torched in the next frame and mercifully removed by Hug. Trailing by 11 runs in the bottom of the second, Bescher took exception to several inside offerings by Dick Rudolph. At this precise moment in the Cardinals' disappointing season, raw feelings overflowed in their dugout. When Bescher took offense to yet a second "bean ball," he charged the mound. Both benches emptied and it took a large police contingent and several expulsions from the game to restore order. Boston pinned a colossal 20–1 hurt on the hapless Cards, the most runs scored in a National League contest in 1915.[62] The decisiveness of the score also served as an appropriate metaphor for the Gallatin Squash's impending exit from the Big Show. Hub toed a big league slab for the final time on September 30, 1915. The third Cardinals pitcher of the game, he took the box in the tenth with the score tied against the Pirates. He did not last long and suffered the loss. Hub Perdue was abused by major league batters for the final time.[63]

In the immediate post-season, the Cardinals squared off against the Browns in their traditional city series, but the National Leaguers lacked motivation. Both squads had finished in sixth place in their respective leagues, and the American Leaguers won the title for the second year in a row, taking four games out of six. "Steamboat" Johnson, later a renowned arbiter in the Southern Association with a distinguished 37-year career behind the dish, participated in this extravaganza.⁶⁴ Johnson had earned a reputation for colorful on-field antics and a booming *basso profundo* voice when announcing batters to the crowd. Hub made no appearances and had likely returned to Tennessee.⁶⁵ He would see Steamboat again.

Hub was frustrated by this lack of success and demotion to the bullpen in 1915. His record dropped to 6–12 and his ERA ballooned to 4.21, almost 1.5 runs higher than his closest teammate. He relieved more games (18) than he started (13), and led the National League in relief losses (five), a figure that does not incorporate all his blown leads. In 115⅓ innings pitched, his lowest as a major leaguer, he surrendered 141 hits, including seven home runs.⁶⁶

Hub had spent 15 months in St. Louis, and by most indicators, he enjoyed the experience. There is no question that his elbow-shoulder malady dampened his results, and Huggins recognized the problem when he adopted the Bernhard-Stallings approach, pulling Hub in the late innings and assigning him late in the season to the bullpen. Whereas Hub had once struggled to finish the late innings, now he struggled to get through the month of August. The timetable for his seasonal decline would eventually move back to early July.

Hub returned to Tennessee penniless, but he remembered the lecture about saving money and the wager put forth by his father prior to the season. So before he went home, Hub paid a visit to the First & People's National Bank on Public Square in Gallatin and took out a loan. The exact amount has grown over the years depending on the source; $200, $1,500 or $2,000.⁶⁷ The lesser amount is the most sensible sum — the most outrageous figure surpassed his contracted wage for the entire season. When Marion saw the cash that Hub had brought home he was pleased at his son's newfound thriftiness, and he promptly equaled the amount as promised. Then Hub returned to the bank, repaid the borrowed sum and pocketed the rest.⁶⁸ This humorous anecdote is a classic cornerstone in the Hublore legend. But is it true?

The details of the wager are accurate but the time and place are fictional. Placing the story in Hub's final season in the majors makes for a great culminating laugh. But there is no primary source documentation to support the event ever taking place in the St. Louis years. There is, however, a facsimile recorded prior to Hub's rookie tryout with the Cubs in 1907. Had Hub been a spendthrift in Vincennes? Was Marion trying to teach his soon-to-be big league son about saving money? No matter. The father-and-son discussion and bet was documented in newspapers in 1907, *not* 1915!⁶⁹ Placing the story in its true historical context — at the beginning of Hub's career (not at the end) and in the minors (not the majors) — is a less glamorous setting. Still, the myth persists in Hublore as one of the major tales despite its error of time and place.

Hub had spent 11 seasons in professional baseball, an impressive stretch of time for a pitcher of any era, and his longevity is all the more remarkable in light of his nursing an injured arm. Although the downturn in his statistics pointed toward retirement, Hub was not convinced. In November, the Cardinals attempted to send Hub to the San Francisco Seals as compensation for a drafted player. Hub turned down the offer, stating publicly that he could not accept the severe cut in salary.[70] The Golden City was simply too far away from home and he did not know the players in the PCL. Plus, the culture of northern California was quite different from Middle Tennessee. Anyway, the springtime weather conditions in SF—fog, wind and rain along with cool temperatures—mirrored the blustery conditions of Boston. Coming to the end of his lucrative three-year contract, Hub was released by the Cardinals at the winter meetings.[71] One week later, the Gallatin Squash notified the *St. Louis Globe-Democrat* that he had decided to invest in a cafe on Gallatin's Public Square, "one of the show places of the town," and revealed that he was "through with baseball."[72] But was he?

At Christmastime, Hub was mulling over his options when his name surfaced in regard to one final swap. Apparently, Stallings felt guilty over the trade that had sent Hub to St. Louis; it was clear that the Braves had profited the most from the exchange. So Stallings generously shipped a bale of cotton from his Georgia plantation, The Meadows, to President Britton as a Christmas present. The Boston mogul vehemently denied that the gift was intended to soothe his guilty conscience, but it made for a good story in the press.[73] Surely, Hub was not amused; it intimated that he had been exchanged for two bench players and a bale of cotton to be named later. This is one of the amusing selections of Hublore not manufactured by the grand embellisher himself.

Everyone in the baseball business had written off Hub for the 1916 season, except no one had convinced the Gallatin Squash that he should quit the game he loved so deeply. But the unavoidable question was quite simple: what would he do next?

Chapter 7

Interlude in Louisville

Big league dreams die hard, and Hub still believed he could compete on the baseball diamond. But he did not want to travel to the West Coast, unfamiliar territory, to ply his trade. In mid–March, the Louisville Colonels were gathering in Columbia (TN) in preparation for spring training, and Hub decided to pay a visit to Bill Clymer's camp. Although he had previously voiced strong objections about returning to the brush, Hub had no control over the situation; if he wanted to continue competing, it would be in the lower circuit. Clymer offered Hub a limited tryout. If it panned out, his American Association team was prepared to offer Perdue a contract to pitch in 1916.[1] At age 34, Hub was the old man on a much younger and more inexperienced Louisville pitching staff which included future big leaguer Adolfo "The Cuban" Luque and successful minor league hurlers "Rifle Jim" Middleton and "Jerky Jake" Northrop. Perhaps Clymer wanted Hub to mentor his stable of young hurlers. The time Hub spent in Louisville provided one of the most outrageously funny narratives never included in Hublore. The Louisville interlude also served as a brief respite between his big league days and his triumphant return to more familiar surroundings in the Southern Association.

Clymer was the Colonels' rookie manager and he possessed impressive minor league credentials. Beginning his playing career in 1891, "Derby Bill's" true calling was in the managerial ranks where he would orchestrate teams for 28 seasons beginning in 1903, mostly in the American Association, International League and New York-Penn League. He emulated the fashion style of Connie Mack and always appeared on the Louisville bench wearing a suit. "For the first time in years," commented the *Louisville Courier-Journal,* 'Louisville has a team leader who possesses brains, generalship and an abundance of aggressiveness."[2] It was likely that Clymer remembered Hub from 1913 when the Gallatin Squash was at the peak of his game and he'd shut down Clymer's Buffalo Bisons in an exhibition.

The city of Louisville possessed a rich baseball history dating back to the formation of the American Association in 1882, a river town league formed to rival the National League that was eventually incorporated into it.[3] The Colonels had played in their current stadium, Eclipse Park, located at 7th and Kentucky streets, since 1902. The team was owned by Otho H. Wathen, son of the famed Kentucky whiskey magnate and distiller, J. B. Wathen.[4] Independently wealthy, Wathen was an active owner, and he frequently traveled with the Colonels on the road. Known as the *Gateway to Dixieland*, the greater Louisville area also excelled in thoroughbred horse racing. Fine whiskey and fast ponies fit in well with Hub's personal interests. Indeed, Tom W. Cooke later reported in the *Louisville Courier-Journal* that Hub was quite the horse racing aficionado and often visited the local race track at Douglas Park.[5]

The Colonels broke camp in Columbia on April 1 with Hub in tow, and they headed north to Nashville to play three exhibitions versus the Vols. Hub, always considered a big draw in Sulphur Dell, was slated to pitch in one of the contests, and a large delegation arrived from Gallatin to watch their local hero perform. The five-inning affair lasted only 50 minutes; a soaking rain terminated the action, but Hub overpowered the opposition, allowing only two hits.[6] In another preseason scrimmage, Hub crushed the Class D Frankfort Old Taylors of the Ohio State League, 16–0, on a four-hitter. Squeezed between Hub's two successful appearances, the Colonels had slated the Pittsburgh Pirates and Chicago Cubs at Eclipse Field, but snow and gusty winds caused cancellations. Joe Tinker's club managed to thrash Hub on one bitterly cold contest of limited duration. Derby Bill was satisfied with Hub's three outings, and the dapper manager tendered him a contract. But the manager's decision must have been a close call; Hub was absent from the traditional team photograph which adorned Louisville's sports page on Opening Day.[7]

The results of a preseason poll of American Association team owners projected Minneapolis, Indianapolis, Louisville and Kansas City in the top tier for 1916, a prediction later validated by the final standings but in a slightly different order.

Joe Cantillon brought his Minneapolis club to Louisville to open the season. "Pongo Joe" had been at the helm of the Millers since 1910, and they were perennial favorites to win the league title. Hub appeared in only one game against the Millers, four innings of shutdown relief in which he sealed a lopsided victory and allowed only two hits. Cantillon would not forget Hub's mastery in the box.[8]

Hub wasted little time in establishing his reputation for clownish behavior. Early on, he tried to engage Luque in a trick bet that he [Hub] would bat over .000 for the season. The Cuban, who referred to Hub in broken English as "Ha," did not take the bait.[9] Cooke also confirmed in his *Diamond*

Sparks column that Hub was emerging as a fan favorite in Louisville.¹⁰ As the team waited at the train depot to begin its first extended road trip of the season, Hub was in rare form. One player in the crowd stated that Grover Cleveland Alexander had tossed 50 games last season, and Hub drawled, "Why that's nothing. While I was with George Stallings' gang in Boston I pitched over 100 full games [in] every one of the two and a half years I was [with him]."

The shocked player challenged Hub, claiming that the official record did not support his assertion. Hub responded, "When I wasn't in a regular scheduled contest Stallings had me in the 'bull pen' warming up, and he never issued orders for me to stop getting 'het up' until the real game was over." Everyone in the depot laughed. "The Gallatin Squash enjoys the enviable reputation of being one of the most humorous players in professional baseball," chuckled the *Courier-Journal.*¹¹

After a loss on opening day, the Colonels peeled off 12 straight victories, and by June 1, Hub had raced to a 4–2–1 record. But Hub's success was misleading. He had largely drawn opponents destined for the second division — St. Paul, Milwaukee, Columbus and Toledo. Incidentally, most games were taking two hours or longer to play, well above the Deadball Era standard of 90 minutes, an interesting phenomenon probably connected to the growing number of relief pitchers used per contest.

On his birthday game, Hub faced Roger Bresnahan's Toledo club on the road. "The Duke" had purchased a majority interest in the team and brought it back from Cleveland, where Charles Somers had relocated it in 1914 to protect the city from Federal League expansion. Bresnahan changed Toledo's cognomen owing to his concern that the Mud Hens name had been jinxed by a losing image and did not excite fear in the minds of opponents. Furthermore, he believed a new label would signal a fresh start for the club and "Iron Men" projected a much more masculine tone than that of a dirty chicken. Someone piqued that the team should be known as the "Bresna*hens*," but the new skipper's choice won out.¹² Despite the name change, Hub fared well against the anemic Iron Men throughout the season.¹³

A fierce competition was under way between the league's four quality teams — Louisville, Minneapolis, Indianapolis and Kansas City. By mid–June, Louisville held a slender lead, and Hub made contributions to the club's success until his old injury reappeared. On June 12, as he was coasting to his sixth victory in St. Paul's Lexington Park, he complained about a stiff shoulder. When the Colonels returned to Minneapolis the next day, Clymer ordered an X-ray on his ace. It was feared that he had suffered a torn ligament, but the official diagnosis later determined that it was a shoulder strain. Clymer sent Hub home to Tennessee to recuperate for two weeks.¹⁴ In actuality, Hub would be absent for over one month. In the meantime, Cooke noted that a gloom descended over the club caused by Hub's "temporary retirement," since his "cheery personality" had kept the club loose.[15] Hub's ill-timed injury combined with a broken leg sustained by Bert Daniels a week later. The stellar left fielder and No. 2 man in the batting order would be sorely missed. The absence of Perdue and Daniels was unfortunate for the Colonels as they slipped behind the surging Indians and Blues.

While Hub was convalescing in Gallatin, one of his hometown acquaintances was making headlines with the Vols. Ten years Hub's junior, Tom Rogers was born in Sparta, Tennessee, but he lived with an aunt in Gallatin.[16] Nicknamed "Shotgun" for his powerful yet erratic control, Rogers struck third baseman and former Vols teammate Johnny Dodge on the temple with a fastball in Mobile on June 18. Dodge collapsed at the plate and remained unconscious for several minutes. Carried to the locker room, he passed out again and was taken to the local hospital. Tragically, Dodge passed away from a brain hemorrhage the next day. It was later revealed that Rogers and Dodge, fellow Tennesseans, had been close friends.[17]

The beaning of Dodge overshadowed the public's perception of baseball in the Southern Association for the entire season. Rogers miraculously rebounded to throw a perfect game against Chattanooga less than three weeks later, and the Lookouts batters were undoubtedly skittish about stepping into the batter's box against Shotgun. The amazing part about the perfecto was that Chattanooga hurler Jim "Lefty" Allen flung a one-hitter at Nashville. Rogers scripted 24 victories in 1916, led the Vols to their first title since 1908, and captured the attention of the St. Louis Browns. Despite his notoriety and talent, Rogers was haunted by the memory of his fallen friend for the rest of his life.[18]

Returning to the scene of his most recent injury on July 14, Hub did not look sharp on the slab. His checkered performance against the Saints could be summarized by the number two — two innings pitched, two runs scored on two hits and two bases on balls. "Perdue's pitching arm was far from right," concluded Cooke.[19] Indeed, Hub neither won nor lost more than two games in a row for the remainder of the season, a familiar pattern once his arm flared up.

Hub targeted the Brewers, led by Jim Thorpe, to pad his slab stats. Indeed, Milwaukee had fallen into the AA cellar and dropped 20 games off the pace. Just two days after Hub's shaky return action in St. Paul, he handled Milwaukee on a four hit shutout. Hub's deliveries were "moving" so unpredictably that Brewers batters complained to the umpire that Hub was "putting something on the ball." There might have been some merit to the allegations. A week later, the visiting Kansas City Blues repeated the accusation of Hub "'doctoring' the pellet" because the spheroid was "breaking in such a mystifying manner."[20] No disciplinary measures came from these allegations but they were highly suspicious. Had Hub learned how to deface the ball or had he mastered a new pitch like the forkball?

"Cunnel Perdue" remained a fan favorite in Louisville. His happy-go-lucky personality and visibility in the third base coach's box along with his trademark red undershirt and large cudgel—"said to be the longest [bat] in captivity," endeared him to local fandom.[21] As the Colonels prepared for an extended road trip, the equipment manager asked Hub to leave his "long bludgeon" at home since it was "a couple of feet longer than the club's bat bag." Hub fretted, tongue-in-cheek, that his batting average would suffer owing to the absence of his favorite stick.[22] A check of official league statistics published monthly throughout the year documents that Hub's batting average was so low that his name never appeared in the lists.

In the first two weeks of August, the Kansas City Blues caught fire and Louisville and Indianapolis suddenly found themselves playing catchup. Trailing the Blues by two games on August 20, Louisville traveled to Kansas City for a crucial five-game tilt. The unbelievable occurred when the Colonels swept the Blues behind the stellar pitching of Middleton and two castoffs from the New York Giants—Ralph "Sailor" Stroud and Emilio Palermo. Hub tossed the final game but he was not the pitcher of record. No worries. Louisville had regained first place for the first time in two months.[23]

The Colonels were full of confidence when they traveled to Columbus to play the seventh-place Senators. One reason for jubilation in the Louisville clubhouse was knowing that the final month of the season favored them with an extended home slate. Yet the Columbus club proved uncooperative and defeated Louisville in four of six games. Hub pitched one of the losses when he surrendered back-to-back triples to the first two batters he faced. A bases-loaded, plate-to-first double play initiated by Hub got the Colonels off the hook, but the Senators made their two opening round tallies stand up.[24] Hub was miffed at the outcome, a lost opportunity. Fortunately, the Kansas City nine was beginning a prolonged losing streak and they became non-factors in early September.

The Louisville club concluded its long road trip in Indianapolis at a time when both teams were deadlocked atop the AA heap. Then, at this crucial juncture in the season with the league crown swinging in the balance, Hub disappeared. Thankfully, Middleton and Northrup held up and the Colonels swept the Indians to take a razor-thin lead in the standings.[25]

Where was the Gallatin Squash? The reason for his mysterious absence was explained, but not convincingly, by Tom Cooke twelve days later in the *Courier-Journal*. It seems that, as the Colonels boarded a northbound train bound for Indy, Hub had jumped aboard a southbound train to Nashville. Writing in a sidebar, the scribe mentioned that Hub looked tanned and ten pounds lighter "since he made a flying visit to his dear old Gallatin home." Cooke concluded that the pitcher seemed "cured of an attack of nostalgia," but he offered no other explanation other than homesickness.[26] It was highly irregular (and unacceptable) that Hub would abandon his team during the important head-to-head encounter with the Indians. Was Hub hurt or was he still smarting from the 2–1 loss in Columbus? Hub was prone to snits when he lost games he thought he should have won.

Twelve days elapsed between Hub's disappearance and his reappearance on September 7. His next two appearances resulted in no-decisions, which fortunately turned into Louisville victories. It was likely that Hub's unscheduled defection had irked Clymer.[27] A third McGraw spinoff, Alexander "Rube" Schauer, a Russian immigrant, had relieved some of the strain on the Colonels' pitching corps—a timely addition.

Louisville blew an opportune series with Toledo over the Labor Day weekend, and the slip-up resulted in tightening the race as it came down to the wire. Then the Colonels stiffened and won four key series against Minneapolis, St. Paul, Milwaukee and Kansas City to solidify their position. But they could not shake the pesky Indianapolis Indians.

Hub's only contribution during the Colonels' surge from September 6 to September 20 was a string of blazé performances—three winless outings until September 15, when he earned his sixth victory over those hapless cellar dwellers, the Brewers.[28] The Indians hung a couple of games in back of the Colonels during the win streak while Kansas City went into a swoon and fell ten games behind. The waning days of the AA had turned into a two-team race between Louisville and Indianapolis.

Ten home games remained on the Colonels schedule against Columbus, Indianapolis and Toledo. After a clean sweep of the Senators, Clymer's club opened a comfortable five-game lead over the Indians. During this time, Hub had seen no action in the box and it became apparent that the manager had either lost confidence in his hurler or else he was punishing him for going AWOL. Another possible explanation? Hub was hurt.

Indianapolis failed to make substantial gains during its brief visit to Eclipse Park, and Louisville needed to win only one game against Bresnahan's Iron Men to clinch the pennant. In a surprise move, Clymer picked Hub to fling the first encounter. Hub always had a flair for the dramatic and never shied away from meaningful games. This time he did not let down his manager, teammates or fans—he crafted a four-hitter and the 6–4 victory wrapped up the league title.[29] Incidentally, it marked Hub's fourth team championship in 12 seasons.

7. Interlude in Louisville

The Colonels won an impressive 101 games, and Hub was responsible for 14 of them, but discounting his quick start in April and May, he neither won nor lost more than two games in a row. Taking a page from Hug's play book, Clymer used Hub twice as often on the road, and ten of his victories came at the hands of the two weakest teams in the circuit — Milwaukee (6–0) and Toledo (4–0). On the positive side, Hub won 14 games (second on the staff), threw 222 innings (second), produced a respectable 1.10 WHIP (third), and lost four games by one run.[30] On the negative side, he was injured twice and missed six weeks of the season, and his two week unauthorized departure at a crucial point in the campaign was unsupportable. Thus, Hub's overall contributions to the Colonels was a mixed bag.[31]

On October 4, Louisville met Omaha, the winners of the Western League, in the start a seven-game set referred to as "the world series of the minor leagues." Hub was not thrilled with the extended season and let it be known at the Colonels' championship banquet that he planned "to return to the shade of his own vine and fig tree and there [in Gallatin]."[32] But when the team's train left the Louisville station for Omaha, Hub was on board.

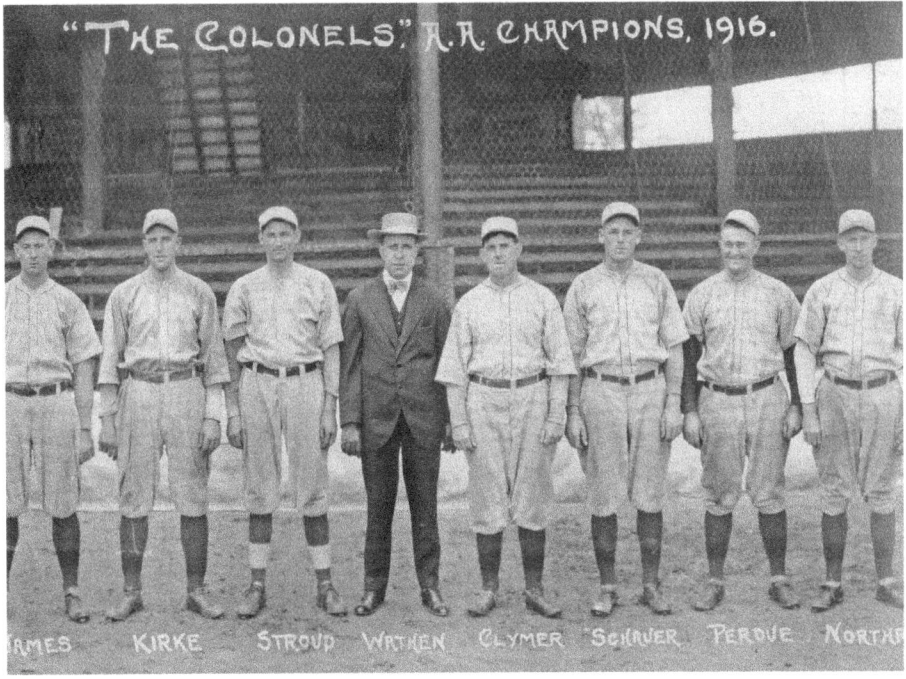

Smiling Hub Perdue and the 1916 American Association champion Louisville Colonels (Jimmy Perdue Family Papers, Gallatin, Tennessee).

Louisville and Omaha appeared evenly matched as the first game ended in a 12-inning tie. Omaha won the second encounter handily, but the Colonels swept the next four games to cop the unofficial title of minor league champs. Hub squared off against a former big league adversary from Pittsburgh in the fourth game, Marty O'Toole, and he notched a convincing 11–3 win. As the Gallatin Squash laid plans to head home to his Tennessee farm, he did not depart from Louisville without causing a stir. "If the tabaccy crop ain't good, maybe I'll come back next springtime."[33] Not exactly a solid endorsement for his return to the Colonels.

The next spring, the Colonels opened training in Athens, Tennessee, with a roster lightened by the loss of its two most productive pitchers from the 1916 squad; Middleton and Northrup now hurled for the rivals in Indianapolis. Hub was elevated to the status of Louisville's mound leader by default, followed by Luque and Stroud. The Colonels scheduled several exhibitions with Tennessee's three entrants in the Southern Association — Chattanooga, Nashville and Memphis. Meanwhile, Hub voiced his usual contempt for physical exercise and training camp in general: "I think I'll run foh (sic) office again," Hub chimed. "I would like to be Mayor of the South and stop all this hard work on spring training trips."[34] The Gallatin Squash approached his 13th spring training with indifference, but for a while the press jokingly referred to him as "the Mayor," a moniker that did not stick.

Clymer utilized the Gallatin Squash only once before opening day, four innings of shutout relief against Tris Speaker's big league contingent from Cleveland. The game hinged on one dramatic defensive play in the eighth when Hub forced Speaker to ground out weakly to first baseman Jay Kirke with the bases loaded to stifle an Indians rally. One reporter observed that Hub "had his big curve working to perfection."[35] But, Hub worried about a lack of control on his breaking ball which he released toward the batter's chin. Once, lamented the Tennessean, he had broken an opponent's jaw on a bender that did not break (Gerard in Vincennes?). Why was Clymer refusing to use Hub in other exhibitions? It is reasonable to assume that Derby Bill still harbored bad feelings stemming from Hub's behavior the previous year? Did Hub's unapproved leave jeopardize his chances with the Colonels now?

Prior to the team's departure from Athens, a humorous story broke with Hub as the central figure. While the team sat in the lobby of the Georgian Hotel waiting out a rainstorm, Hub noticed a peculiarity in the front window of a carpet and millinery store across the street. One of the signs advertising "mattings" was missing one letter, a "T." The sign read "Ma tings." Hub immediately recognized its humor value, and he hatched a scheme to play a practical joke on some of his unsuspecting teammates. Gathering a small group around him, Hub whispered, "Fellas, if I can borrow a dress and wig

7. Interlude in Louisville

we can have about seven pecks of ol' fashioned country town fun.... Shove yeh chairs closer and give me yeh ears feh a minute or two."

Hub pointed to the sign across the way and explained his plan to the small group. "I'll frame with the proprietor to let me sneak up to the millinery department and pose as 'Ma Tings,' a Chinese fortune teller. Then, you fellas visit me and tell the rest of these yaps what I told yet 'bout yer hitting in games last year. It's a cinch they will fall for the joke because I'll be chattering about things that actually occurred."

The conspirators rounded up the props and set the charade in motion. A short time later, "a rather stout-looking woman walked across the hotel lobby and out the ladies entrance, leisurely strolled across the street," and disappeared inside the aforementioned building. "A few moments later, Joe McCarthy ... turned to his unsuspecting teammates in the lobby and said in a loud voice, 'Boys, I'll bet that 'Ma Tings' means that there is a Chinese woman fortune teller ... [over there]. Count this Irishman [in] giving her a chance to 'wise him up' as to what Fate has in store for him.'"

Playing along, Roxey Roach encouraged McCarthy in a loud voice to have his palm read by Ma Tings and report back to the group. McCarthy agreed and he, too, walked across the street and entered the building. Re-emerging fifteen minutes later, McCarthy returned in an animated state. Not being part of the gag, Clymer asked his second baseman why he was so excited. "Gee whiz, Bill," McCarthy replied. "There is a Chinese woman fortune teller over yonder that told me something about every game I was in last year. She took my breath when she came to bat with an account of that Omaha series, and actually told me the number of bingles I got and all about the arguments we had with the 'Omahogs.'" The mystery soothsayer provided a thorough rundown of his previous season averages in batting, fielding and base running, said McCarthy.

Kirke soaked up the story. Perhaps "the lady chink" could tell his future, too, so he led an assemblage of a half-dozen players who rushed to meet Ma Tings. Kirke returned to the Georgian a short time later with a satisfied look on his face. The palmist had told the first baseman that he would hit .325 in the upcoming season. Johnny Corriden, "Topsey" Platte and Ralph Comstock received similar reports, and each one expected a telegram shortly to be called up to "the big top." And Ma Tings had only charged the players $3 apiece to share her clairvoyant observations.

"At the height of the [players'] rejoicing," Ma Tings reappeared in the hotel lobby counting a pile of greenbacks. "'What ah you idiots raving about? You sure are a dumb lot,' drawled the counterfeit sorceress." The crowd, recognizing Hub's voice, stood speechless. Removing his wig, the Gallatin Squash let out "a merry laugh" and promptly exited the lobby. As the dumbfounded players retreated to their rooms, Kirke muttered epitaphs. "I always believed that dadblasted [sic] Perdue was crooked," he lamented.[36] The Ma Tings narrative belongs in the annals of Hublore as a feature entry, but it was never popularized by the Gallatin Squash himself. Instead, it was embedded deeply in the sports pages of the *Louisville Courier-Journal*.[37]

As the Colonels prepared to break camp in Athens, the league owners took a straw poll and overwhelmingly selected Louisville to repeat as league champs. But the country was not in a festive mood. The day after the Ma Tings episode, President Woodrow Wilson somberly addressed a joint session of Congress asking for a declaration of war in response to Imperial Germany's resumption of unrestricted submarine warfare two months earlier. The forthcoming combat would overshadow everything in American life for the next 14 months, including baseball.

Booster's Day, 1917, was a big event in Louisville. Slated for the first Saturday home game, the occasion was marked by a parade including marching bands, local dignitaries, and players. Similar to Hub's championship ceremonies in Vincennes and Nashville, the procession weaved its way through the downtown district and upon entering Eclipse Park, the marchers walked to the center field wall to hoist the 1916 pennant. Old Glory flapped in the breeze atop an adjoining flag pole. The band struck up several martial airs, and everyone joined in the singing of *The Star-Spangled Banner*, *My Country, 'Tis of Thee* and *America the Beautiful*. Hoisting the baseball banner took secondary importance to the more pressing need to express national patriotism collectively, and rightly so.[38]

Clymer picked Hub to fling the prestigious Booster's Day game against Toledo. The Gallatin Squash responded with another command performance against Bresnahan's Iron Men. He allowed only one hit after the fourth inning and bested young Clarence "Dazzy" Vance in the box. He especially delighted in shutting down former St. Louis outfielder and team comedian, Steve Evans, who was "guyin'" Hub from the bench throughout the game.[39] Hub did not look nearly as sharp in his second appearance against Kansas City ten days later. The Blues drove him from the box in the third with the Colonels commanding a 6–3 lead.[40]

On May 2, Hub pitched his last game in the Gateway to the South. In the contest, he overpowered St. Paul for seven innings, allowing just three hits. But he totally broke down when the Saints struck for three runs in the eighth and ninth innings. Just days before the running of the fabled Kentucky Derby, Clymer surprised everyone in the press when he released Hub. The Colonels had recently acquired Fred Beebe from Cleveland as well as two familiar American Association hurlers, Dixie Davis and Alex Main. These pitchers would combine to hurl 72 victories in 1917. The Gallatin Squash was simply expendable.

Hub had expressed interest in returning to the Southern Association, too. Indeed, reports immediately surfaced after his release that Hub was about to sign with Norman "Kid" Elberfeld's Chattanooga Lookouts, a team that had scrimmaged the Colonels several times in spring training.[41] But the move was fraught with question marks. Foremost, how would Hub's personality mesh with Elberfeld's legendary temper? After all, "The Tabasco Kid" did not arrive at his nickname because he enjoyed Mexican food. Rather, Kid and Gentleman George shared an identical coaching style and mercurial temperament. Only time would tell if Hub would fit in.

The Louisville interlude had pumped new life back into Hub's floundering baseball career. He had made a solid contribution to the Colonels in 1916, but Hub's heart lay further south in Tennessee.[42] The Gallatin Squash was coming home.

Chapter 8

Second Tour in the Southern Association

The American Association was an unfamiliar landscape, and Hub had voiced a preference to play closer to home in a league he knew much better. When Clymer released Hub from the Colonels after only three appearances he remained unemployed for less than a week, signing with the Chattanooga Lookouts on May 9.[1] Chattanooga had a rich baseball tradition and formed an in-state rivalry with Tennessee's other two entrants, Nashville and Memphis. Hub's year with the Lookouts was nondescript, but his successes against New Orleans led to a reunion with John Dobbs, a fifth championship to his credit and a lofty individual accomplishment. His return to Nashville completed Hub's baseball circle until a new injury threatened to cut down his prodigious playing career. Hublore entries proliferated during his return stint to the Southern Association, too. In conclusion, the length of Hub's second tour in the circuit matched his first tour at four years; but whereas the first tour had launched him into the major leagues, the second tour propelled him into the minor league record books and led to a wonderful new opportunity.

Joe Curtis, the sports editor of the *Chattanooga News*, welcomed Hub's return to the Southern. Not only would Hub contribute to a thin Lookouts pitching staff, but simple name recognition of the Gallatin Squash would help to fill the stands with rooters as well. But playing for fiery manager Norman "Kid" Elberfeld, the field general of the Lookouts since 1913, was an interesting proposition, for Hub had established stormy relationships with similar strong-willed managers in the past (Johnny Kling and George Stallings). Now, he added Elberfeld to his resumé of hot-tempered skippers. In a sidebar observation, Hub played under only one manager over his entire career with any pitching experience—Bill Bernhard. Only time would tell how Hub's relationship with Elberfeld would pan out. Certainly, there was cause for concern.

Writing in the *Chicago Evening American,* William F. Kirk accurately captured Elberfeld's personality in lyrics:

> The lads today are quite as fast —
> There's many a fancy stepper;
> But we must dig into the past
> To get the old Red Pepper.
> In some respects he's been excelled,
> But for Go, and Grit, and Gall,
> Our little Norman Elberfeld
> Was Daddy of them all![2]

Elberfeld was notorious for his blistering antics on the field, and he earned a reputation as a manager for recruiting pitchers who mirrored his own aggressive behavior.[3]

The Scenic City of the South was a perfect location for Hub to begin his second tour in the Southern. The city boasted a long baseball history dating back to the Roane Iron Company in the early 1880s — a semi-pro team that traveled throughout the region competing against other town teams.[4] One of the earliest promoters of the game in Chattanooga, hotel magnate John C. Stanton, built a baseball diamond next to his state-of-the-art hotel — the Stanton House — in an attempt to lure a professional team to the city.[5] He succeeded.

Chattanooga was a charter member of the original Southern League in 1885, and the team slated its games for Stanton Field. The franchise folded in the middle of its second season, but the city received another entry in 1889. The entire SL folded in early July, and the circuit acquired an unflattering moniker — the "Fourth of July league."[6] Then, in 1901, a group headed by Mims Hightower filed for charter membership in the newly reorganized Southern Association. The team was ably managed by Lew Whistler, but attendance remained low and the club was transferred after only two years to new owners in Montgomery.[7] "Baseball has died in Chattanooga so many times," noted David Jenkins, "that it's a miracle that it lives at all."[8]

In 1909, Oliver Burnside (O. B.) Andrews assembled a new baseball corporation in Chattanooga with several prominent local businessmen, including Z. C. Patten, Jr.[9] This group of entrepreneurs was awarded a franchise in the South Atlantic League, or SALLY. Richard Yancey, the Nashville transplant at the sports desk of the *Chattanooga Times,* ran a name-the-team contest, and the public selected "Lookouts" over a variety of other nominees. The nickname referenced the conspicuous mountain that dominated the landscape as well as the location of the famous Civil War battle "fought above the clouds." Andrews wooed Dobbs, a resident of nearby Chickamauga, Georgia, out of retirement to manage the team. The nines temporarily used Chamberlain Field, the baseball home of the University of Chattanooga.[10]

Andrews had big plans for his Lookouts. Construction of a new stadium, Andrews Field, began in the 1100 block of East Third Street and O'Neal. Built next to a rail line and susceptible to spring floods from the Tennessee River, the all-wood structure was akin to its contemporaries in Nashville (Athletic Park/Sulphur Dell), Memphis (Red Elm Park/Russwood), Little Rock (Red Elm Park/Kavanaugh Field) and Birmingham (Slagpile/Rickwood). Indeed, like all stadia in the Southern, the Chattanooga facility was eventually rebuilt, reconfigured and renamed. Andrews was rewarded at the end of his first season in the SALLY when he purchased the financially strapped Little Rock Travelers.[11]

Chattanooga was playing a respectable brand of baseball when Hub took the box on May 12 in his Andrews Field debut. The club trailed New Orleans by five games and was perched in the middle of the pack with a .500 record. But not even the slugging exploits of Lookouts right fielder Ham Hyatt could keep the visiting Crackers from dismantling Hub on this holiday occasion — Mother's Day — and the Atlantans chased him from the slab after plating eight runs in six innings. After the game, the fireworks continued when a deputy sheriff arrested the umpire for allowing the game to take place; after all, it was Sunday.[12]

Hub's rocky beginning continued in two slugfests against Nashville and Mobile, but he was not the pitcher of record in either affair. An aging Charles "Gabby" Street tagged one of Hub's offerings for the Vols that bounced off the outfield wall for a double. As the Lookouts settled into their customary spot as a middle-of-the-road club, Hub did not register a win until Memorial Day.[13] This first victory, in Sulphur Dell, was deemed "phenomenal"; the Gallatin Squash always saved a little extra when competing against his former team in front of hometown supporters.[14] Incidentally, a new arbiter greeted Hub behind the plate, but not an unfamiliar face — Ted Breitenstein.

Working on one day's rest, Hub pitched his birthday game in Memphis, but these surroundings, unlike the Dell, were not familiar. The new owner, Russell E. Garner, refurbished Red Elm Park in 1915, a park originally constructed in 1896. The owner renamed his new facility "Russwood," and he hired John D. Martin to run the club, a figure destined for a larger administrative role in league affairs. Garner and Martin changed the cognomen of their team from "Turtles" to "Chickasaws," but the team was popularly known as the "Chicks."[15] On his 35th birthday Hub squandered a 5–1 lead in Russwood and absorbed a disappointing 6–5 loss.[16]

On June 27, as General Pershing's American Expeditionary Force was landing in France, a twister touched down in Chattanooga, destroying the roof of the Andrews Field grandstand and scattering debris all over the field. The next day's game with Memphis was cancelled on account of cyclone damage, but when both teams retook the field on June 29, the Chicks continued the whirlwind with 15 hits and 13 runs against an assortment of inept Lookouts hurlers, including Hub.[17]

As the month of July dawned, Hub had been less than sterling with the Lookouts. He posted a 4–3–3 record, and his offerings were frequently hit hard. Two losses were controversial. In New Orleans, two Pelicans scored off Hub on a play where runner interference was charged, and Elberfeld protested without effect. A week later, Hub entered in relief of southpaw Floyd Kroh in the tenth with the bases crammed with Little Rock Travelers when mayhem broke loose. In a botched squeeze, Hub alertly picked off Ernie Manning at third base, but the Lookouts' backup catcher, Chuck McDaniels, dropped the spheroid in the ensuing rundown and lost the game. Hub's total mastery over the woeful Mobile Bears was his only accomplishment in his first six weeks with Elberfeld's bunch.[18]

Hub started to heat up in July when he was the pitcher of record nine times. In one of his most impressive outings, he pitched "a masterful" three-hitter in the friendly confines of Sulphur Dell in the opening game of the traditional Fourth of July twin bill.[19] He lost twice to New Orleans; one was a heartbreaking 3–2 loss after Larry Gilbert (now in the Southern) swatted a RBI single in the thirteenth inning. In the other, Hub relayed a mishandled ball in the outfield but his errant throw to the plate missed the mark by 20 feet and allowed the hustling Gilbert to jog home for the winning tally.[20] Gilbert always had Hub's number. Thank goodness for Mobile. Hub defeated the Bears twice in July by the same lopsided score, 7–0, and he saved a third encounter in relief of Kroh.

At this time, the newspapers were filled with stories about America's growing involvement in the Great War and a dramatic revolution in Russia, but Chattanooga's sports page offered a respite from world news. Hub's dominant command over the hapless Mobile Bears received a lot of attention. "Great credit is due to 'General' Perdue," lauded the *Chattanooga Daily Times* in martial tones, "who anticipated every move of the enemy and had each point so well reinforced that the enemy were unable to make any advance whatsoever."[21] Military lingo was beginning to infiltrate sports accounts.

As the season entered August, the "battle for Tennessee" heated up along with the weather. Although all three teams were off the pennant pace by double digits, only two games separated fourth-place Memphis from fifth-place Nashville and sixth-place Chattanooga. Throughout the month, Hub was busy — he battled Memphis four times — splitting the action evenly between Andrews Field and Russwood, and winning three times, including a nail-biter over Clarence "Dazzy" Vance.[22] Then the Lookouts lost their batting eye and experienced a 24-inning scoring drought. Yet Hub pitched well at this moment. Not only did he snap the team's losing streak at home with a shutout over the Chicks, but he also provided fireworks at the plate with a long sacrifice fly to left field to drive in "the Tense Tabasco One" for the only run of the afternoon.[23] Elberfeld piled on Hub's already heavy workload in August (4–3) with three appearances of long relief, normally an ingredient for arm trouble.

On August 17, Hub took the slab against Mobile in one of the most memorable games of the summer. The pitiful Alabama squad had already dropped 45 games back, and they caught Hub "in phenomenal form." Conversely, the two Sea Gulls hurlers, Dick Ching and Tom Long, could not contain the Lookouts' onslaught of seven runs in each of the first two frames, and Chattanooga took "the vaudeville farce," 16–0. The *Chattanooga Daily Times* derisively called Mobile "the worst outfit ever to don a Southern Association uniform."[24] Hub feasted on Bears batters all season, reeling off five straight victories against them.

By early September the Atlanta Crackers, now managed by Charlie Frank, were pulling away from Dobbs and the New Orleans Pelicans as Tennessee's three entrants shuffled between fourth and sixth place (where they remained all summer). Seldom had more than three games separated Memphis, Nashville and Chattanooga, but each program had fallen at least 15 games behind the frontrunners by September 1. Thus, the Lookouts, Vols and Chicks were primarily motivated by state pride and final positioning in the standings as the season waned. Hub earned his 13th victory of the season in Sulphur Dell on Labor Day, his second three-hitter over the Vols, which earned him accolades across the Volunteer State.[25]

Hub wrapped up the 1917 campaign on the road in Little Rock's Kavanaugh Field, the former West End Park. The ball yard had been renamed in 1915 shortly after the premature death of Williams Marmaduke Kavanaugh, the highly touted administrator of the Southern since 1903. As the curtain dropped on the diamond, Chattanooga fell 20 games behind Atlanta and finished in sixth place.[26]

When Hub first arrived in Chattanooga, Elberfeld knew that the glory days of the Gallatin Squash were behind him. No longer an overpowering hurler, Hub subdued the batters with cunning, guile and a lot of chicanery. It is remarkable that no public confrontations took place between the intense Tabasco Kid and his jocular ace. The Chattanooga skipper inserted Hub into the rotation almost immediately and he proved his dependability in missing only one start. Clearly, Elberfeld was determined to squeeze every ounce of baseball out of Hub before he expired. And the results were quite impressive.

Hub had had remarkable back-to-back seasons. Consider his statistics as a Lookout: 15 wins (second on the staff), 217 IP (fourth), 1.95 ERA (first),

Hub in his second tour of the Southern Association (Jimmy Perdue Family Papers, Gallatin, Tennessee).

and 1.07 WHIP (second). And Hub finished uncharacteristically strongly. From August 10 to the end of the season, he won seven of eight games, including five shutouts and three victories over Memphis.[27] Had the Gallatin Squash reinvented himself? Certainly, these were the kind of results that attract attention, and New Orleans manager and Chattanooga resident, John Dobbs was one potential suitor. Dobbs was unhappy because his Pelicans fell seven games short of Atlanta, and he was looking to bolster his stable of hurlers.

As the players were returning to their winter homes, the leaders of the Communist revolution in Russia had sent Czar Nicholas into exile in a key development. Meanwhile, Hub was unsure about his own future in Chattanooga because the club's owners were attempting to muzzle their demonstrative manager by insisting that he run the team in uniform the next season from the bench. Elberfeld found these terms unacceptable so he resigned only a week after the season had concluded.[28] The Chattanooga club was further in flux as rumors about potential bankruptcy swirled in the press. Hub was unsure of his status with the Lookouts when Dobbs made overtures and signed him in February 1918.

Local military draft boards were impacting team rosters across the Southern at this time. Dobbs and President A. J. Heinemann had been scurrying to sign talent, and Hub was considered a great acquisition. Hub had benefited too; it was rumored that his New Orleans contract made him the highest paid pitcher in the entire circuit.[29] There were high expectations placed on Hub in the Crescent City for his continued success.

Hub threw only five innings in spring training and, as the Pelicans broke camp in late March, Germany unleashed a major offensive on the Western Front dubbed Operation Michael. General Erich Ludendorff devised the plan in hopes of defeating the British and French forces before American troops arrived in Europe. Initially, the attack was successful as German forces pushed within 55 miles of Paris, and it sent shock waves throughout the Allied world. In this climate of war hysteria, Provost Marshall General Enoch H. Crowder began to vigorously implement the "work or fight" order issued earlier by Secretary of War Newton Baker.[30] These regulations did not apply to Hub, who met the exclusionary requirements of occupation (farming) and age — he was 35 years old (although he qualified for the third registration on September 12, 1918, which extended the minimum age to 45). Still, the call-up impacted many players in the Southern along with 2.8 million other young Americans. Unknown at the time, the mighty German offensive bogged down and ground to a halt in mid-summer, and an armistice went into effect on 11 November.[31]

The presence of General John "Black Jack" Pershing's American Expeditionary Force had stalled the German advance, and while the AEF was notching battlefield victories at Belleau Wood, Chateau-Thierry and Second Marne, Hub entered his 14th campaign in the box. Among the new faces with Hub was catcher Frank "Pop" Kitchens, a transfer from Mobile destined to play a role in Hub's twilight year in Texas. Kitchens, a throwback to an earlier era, disdained wearing shin guards.

The season opened in Mobile for one game to celebrate Patsy Flaherty's managerial debut. Then the series shifted to New Orleans, where the season had been originally slated to begin. The traditional opening day festivities in New Orleans followed the familiar minor league pattern in the South — a parade to the stadium with mounted policemen, the mayor and city councilmen, ten automobiles carrying the Bears and Pelicans players, a contingent of Confederate veterans, several marching bands performing martial music, and a motorcade of 25 cars crammed with "invited guests." Patriotic speeches were delivered with an important plug to purchase Liberty Bonds. League president Robert H. Baugh traveled from Birmingham and tossed out the first ball to officially mark the beginning of the season in Louisiana. An estimated 6,000 fans crammed into Heinemann (or Pelican) Park to watch the hometown Pels come from behind in the bottom of the ninth on a clutch RBI by Pop Kitchens, which gave Hub his first win.[32]

Hub earned a second victory one week later in Ponce de Leon Park — a lopsided 9–1 route of the Crackers in which his teammates pounded 12 hits and stole seven bases. The game was noteworthy to Tennesseans because Hub squared off in the box against Joe Engel, who was destined to make a name for himself as the colorful owner of the Chattanooga Lookouts. The contest also produced an on-field fistfight instigated by Atlanta manager "Cholly" Frank.

Frank was frustrated by the winless start to Atlanta's season in defense of its 1917 crown and fueled by "a long standing feud" with Heinemann regarding alleged monies not paid. The brouhaha required police intervention, and several players were injured. Hub, for one, reported a case of ptomaine poisoning following the skirmish.[33] The affliction kept Hub (and Gilbert) out of the Pelicans lineup for a week. Was the reported illness accurate, was it a journalistic metaphor for something else, or was it covering up possible injuries sustained in the fisticuffs? When Hub returned to the box he gave a "groggy" performance but held on to edge Birmingham for his third consecutive victory despite allowing nine enemy hits and six bases on balls.[34] Indeed, the Barons crammed the sacks in practically every inning and umpire Breitenstein made several controversial calls on the base paths. Still, Hub was emerging as the kingpin on Dobbs' pitching staff.

The pennant race seemed to fly by in a blur, and Hub defeated every opponent in the circuit to earn seven victories by June 1. During his blistering stretch, Hub bested Nashville's 17-year-old rookie phenom, Waite Hoyt, in a tight pitchers' duel (2–1) at Sulphur Dell. Ten days later he earned his sixth win of the season at Russwood, where he unleashed a change-of-pace and "foozling slow ball" [forkball?] that had the Chicks bamboozled.[35] Meanwhile, ominous warnings were starting to appear in Southern newspapers about the possibility that the Southern baseball circuit might close down soon in order to comply with the government's "work or fight" proclamation.

In the meantime, Hub was enjoying his rediscovered pitching success, and it spilled over into rare offensive contributions. In Little Rock he drew a bases-loaded walk to force in the go-ahead run. "Hub jumped around the plate much after the fashion of a chicken and actually teased Ted [Murchison] into giving him a walk," reported the *Times-Picayune*.[36] In Chattanooga, the Gallatin Squash found his batting eye and lashed two hits, scored once and recorded an RBI.[37] The only blemish to Hub's incredible first-half success occurred on his birthday start in Sulphur Dell in a weather-shortened five inning affair.[38] A week later, Hub returned to form and outlasted Mobile for his eighth win of the season although he needed Kitchens' two-run wallop in the bottom of the 9th to seal the deal. The former Bear backstopper went 3-for-4 with three RBI and lacked only a home run to hit for the cycle.[39]

Then, came the alarming announcement that baseball fans had been dreading — the Southern Association would disband on June 28. On closer examination, there were ominous financial considerations that also influenced the decision to shut down operations. Since the beginning of the season most of the Southern franchises had suffered from very low attendance. With declining gate receipts, most teams on the road could not muster enough revenue to pay their travel expenses owing to the standard practice of receiving reimbursement by the host team of 11 cents per ticket sold. Only two franchises, New Orleans and Mobile, had escaped this fiscal dilemma owing to a fortuitous home schedule. In a cost-cutting measure, the league president also announced that only one umpire would be employed per contest until the league formally closed down.[40]

As the truncated season wound down, only Little Rock posed a threat to the Pelicans, who were poised to capture the league crown. As the deadline approached, Hub out-dueled Travelers pitcher Oscar "The Cuban" Tuero, tossed a spellbinding five-hit gem against the Lookouts that took only 66 minutes to play, and shut out the Vols on four hits to clinch the pennant. On the final day of play, Hub dominated Birmingham to earn his 12th victory.[41]

Hub had done the unexpected in 1918; he had put together his third solid season in a row. His overall record (12–2–1) topped the Southern, and he made a major contribution to the Pelicans earning the league title, Hub's sixth team championship. While no official ERA statistics were published until 1917, Hub's 1.08 WHIP (third) and 122 IP (second) ranked highly among Pelican slab men, and he remained consistent with his two previous seasons. Hub had proven his worth to Dobbs and New Orleans.[42]

The day after the Southern shut its doors, Hub was sold to Joe Cantillon's Minneapolis Millers along with battery mate Kitchens and outfielder Ed Edmondson; the American Association was planning to continue operations indefinitely. Hub arrived in Minnesota shortly after the Fourth of July, and he found his new team struggling to stay out of last place. Pongo Joe wasted no time and debuted the Gallatin Squash at Nicollet Park on July 7 against the first-place Kansas City Blues. Hub and opposing pitcher Charles "Babe" Adams (an ex–Pirate) were engaged in an exciting contest, but a one-out single followed by a triple in the ninth sealed Hub's fate, 1–0. He returned to the box three days later in Milwaukee, where he allowed only four Brewers to reach second base and whiffed eight batters. Then Hub started to slip. He won in extra innings versus St. Paul in spite of 14 Saints base runners, and he needed a home run by Carl Cashion in the tenth to secure the outcome. In Milwaukee, he couldn't finish the opening frame owing to a solid progression of Brewers hits — a single, double and home run had put his Millers in a deep hole that took the entire game to overcome. On July 20, Hub lost to Kansas City for the second time, and then the American Association suddenly suspended play. Hub had been a Miller for only two weeks and established a mediocre 2–2–1 record.[43] The Gallatin Squash went home, and at the time of Armistice Day in November 1918, Hub was providing volunteer war relief work at the Nashville YMCA.[44]

The annual February meeting of the owners and managers of the Southern was uncharacteristically late in 1919 owing to the directive of its new president, John D. Martin of Memphis, and the uncertainty of minor league baseball in general.[45] Their agenda was most interesting, a microcosm of issues that permeated the game at every level. The moguls agreed to pay meal allowances of $1.75 per day when teams were on the road, opened their stadiums for use by military teams, instructed all managers to wear the team's uniform, and vehemently condemned the use of the spitball while not voting to ban it officially. That formality occurred shortly.[46]

Hub did not participate in the highly heralded exhibition series between New Orleans and the Cleveland Indians, but he did pitch in Beaumont's Magnolia Park just prior to Opening Day. The meaningless encounter with the Texas League affiliate created a buzz, however, when Hub slipped on a muddy mound in mid-delivery and injured himself.[47] He was absent from the traditional series against Shreveport on the final weekend of the preseason for the unaccredited Louisiana state title. Suspicions arose that his arm was not quite right. "Hub's Arm May Keep Him Out Some Time," reported the *Times-Picayune*. Indeed, the Gallatin Squash did not return to the slab until mid–May.[48] His spot was filled by a promising local semi-professional, Frank "Parson" Lankenau, and Chester "Red" Torkelson, a recent castoff from Cleveland.

Dobbs released Kitchens in order to make room on the roster for the Gallatin Squash, and when Hub returned to the rotation on May 18, the Pelicans were flying high. Hub promptly aided the team's 9–1 streak with three commanding victories of his own. In one of these contests, against Nashville, the normally weak-hitting Hub lashed three safeties. " 'Babe' Perdue has developed into a fence buster," snickered the newspaper.[49] But "the Fightin' Pels" soon went on a losing skid and Hub accompanied them from the box, going 1–4.[50]

Hub's return to form coincided with the return of Tennessee's renowned hero from the Great War, Alvin York. As the Pels boarded a train for the Tennessee capitol, local civic and business leaders in Nashville were busy planning a "York Day" celebration at Sulphur Dell. Postponed twice owing to inclement weather, the promotion was finally held on June 11 in a steady rainstorm. The game receipts from "a monster crowd" were earmarked for York and his new bride to purchase a farm. Governor Albert H. Roberts caught the honorary first pitch from York following the first game exploits of another Tennessee legend, Hub Perdue.[51]

Two of Hub's finest accomplishments of the season took place in mid–June — back-to-back 1–0, five-hit shutouts over Little Rock and Memphis. Hub might have been inspired in the former contest owing to the presence of a talent scout from the Washington Senators "sniffing around," and the latter event coincided with the hoisting of the 1918 championship banner in Heinemann Park, a special celebratory occasion.[52] During June and July, Hub twice strung together four consecutive wins at home. Entering the month of August, he had not dropped a single contest in front of the home crowd.

On July 2, Hub faced Atlanta's Tom Sheehan in the first of four memorable match-ups in the summer of 1919. Taking a no-hitter into the seventh frame at Poncey, Hub's carelessness affected the outcome — his throwing error and a base on balls were quickly followed by a double and triple which resulted in a loss.[53] Hub and Sheehan were evenly matched, and in their second meeting one week later both hurlers struck out six and walked only two batters. But Hub held the upper hand, he punched out Hardin Herndon three times, including once in the fifth with the sacks loaded. "Hub is fat and more or less forty," lampooned the *Times-Picayune*. "His age is uncertain and he won't let anyone look at his teeth."[54] All horsing aside, Hub had earned his seventh straight home victory and he evened the score against Sheehan.

In late July, Hub earned his 13th victory but his blistering pace eased over the final 60 days. Old trends had resurfaced whereby Hub fell victim to early runs, multiple hits and late-inning collapses although there was a sprinkle of dazzling outings. Three days after routing the Vols in Sulphur Dell when he smacked two hits, scored twice, and drove in one run, his team headed for Chattanooga. There, Hub carried a 3–1 lead into the bottom of the eighth when Lookouts batters accused him of throwing an "emery ball." The umpire inspected half a dozen balls and deemed them "paraffined" by the Gallatin Squash. Strangely, Hub was not disciplined; instead, new baseballs were procured, and the Chattanooga onslaught began. When the dust settled, Hub had absorbed a 4–3 loss.[55]

As July drew to a close, Hub revealed an unsettling incident to a reporter. Apparently, a belligerent fan sitting down the right field line had been giving him "guff" while he coached the bases. Hub apologized publicly to some ladies sitting nearby after he had lost his temper and directed several "colorful" epithets at the bellicose rooter. Hub claimed the same individual had been haranguing him most of the season. The bold heckler even stood behind the Pelicans bench to holler vulgar obscenities at him. Clearly upset by such disrespectful treatment, Hub declared, "I won't stand for being publicly reviled."[56]

The following day, July 31, Hub reasserted his iron man credentials and swept the visiting Vols by scores of 4–1 and 2–0 to earn his tenth and 11th straight home victories. In the twin killing, Hurling Hub had thrown 16 innings, allowing only 11 hits, no base on balls and one unearned run. The Tennessee native always managed to outdo himself against Nashville. But Hub's dominant performance did not satisfy his chief detractor. Between the contests, the bench jockey boldly came onto the field, walked toward Hub in a provocative manner and threatened to have him arrested for some undisclosed charge. Steamboat Johnson, the verbose umpire, was unable to control the situation. Hub had had enough.

Hub demanded that President Heinemann remedy the situation and immediately remove the man from the park or else he would quit the team. Once ejected from the grounds, the "old man who has launched a campaign of bitter slander" continued his abusive tirade on the street outside the stadium after the game. Hub confided that he had never been "ridden" so unmercifully or been the recipient of such virulent "attacks and threats" in all of his years in baseball. "Baseball is my pride and heart's desire," confided the Gallatin Squash.[57] But Hub's honor was brought into question and he was coming to the end of his tether.

Despite Hub's general ineffectiveness on the road (3–7–1) he remained unbeaten at home (12–0) with an important series looming ahead with the red-hot Little Rock Travelers. Pelicans fans were beginning to worry even as passion toward Hub escalated in the stands. In this climate, Hub tasted defeat at home for the first time on August 9. He had weathered a shaky start — two runs on four hits in the top of the first — and cat-callers and boo-birds cried loudly for Dobbs to remove him.[58] Hub settled down and allowed only one hit the rest of the way, but the damage had already been done on the scoreboard (2–1) and to Hub's ego.

During the second week of August the Pelicans struggled to regain their composure and the league lead, so Dobbs inserted Hub in eight straight contests, including four as a starter over a ten-day period. On August 17, the manager signaled Hub to begin warming up for his eighth stint in the box. When Dobbs called for Hub to enter the game, Red Torkelson, a hurler known for his on-field baffoonary and equal to Hub's sense of humor in almost every way, hung a rope around Hub's neck and dragged him from the bullpen to the box like a forlorn cow. The fans in Sulphur Dell were absolutely delighted by the showmanship. Hub not only stifled the Vols rally, he became the winning pitcher.[59] This is a popular anecdote in Hublore, but it is erroneously placed in Boston and not Nashville.

Hiding behind his impish smile, comic personality and propensity for practical jokes, Hub was also a pitcher who put forward a surprising amount of mental preparation for each game. Sitting with reporter W. M. Keefe in a Birmingham hotel lobby, Hub evaluated the Barons lineup and explained how he intended to pitch to each batter. Prior to the game he threw a simulated three innings in warmups. "All I got to do now is get mahse'f good and warm," drawled the Gallatin Squash. His mental and physical rehearsal did no good this day as the men from Rickwood won a closely contested affair, 4–2.[60] But the story illustrated that Hub was far from the empty-headed clown he projected to the public or someone who relied solely on his brute strength and cunning use of saliva.

At the end of August, the Pelicans traveled to Atlanta to square off against the league leaders in a series that promised to test the level of animosity that had been building all summer between both teams. The Pelicans spotted Hub a five-run lead in game one but it evaporated in the fifth when his fielders committed four errors which resulted in six unearned runs. The Pels rallied to win, however. Then Hub begged Dobbs to hurl the second game of a key doubleheader two days later. He left the tilt with the score tied, but the Crackers went on to win the game, sweep the twin bill, and practically lock up first place.[61]

With New Orleans all but eliminated, the crowd of 12,500 at Poncey went into celebration mode. They slapped each other with seat cushions and showered the field with empty bottles. All seemed quite harmless until a mob of several hundred "deadheads" surged onto the field and began taunting the losers. The New Orleans players were wrapped up in their own foul mood, however. Torkelson had argued with Dobbs to stick with the regularly scheduled pitcher for game two, Roy Walker. When Hub failed to hold the Crackers in check, Torkelson challenged the Gallatin Squash to a fight. While fisticuffs were averted, the Pelicans were especially sore about losing to Charlie Frank.[62]

With only two weeks left in the season, Hub faced the despised Crackers at Heinemann Park for the third time in six days. For the fourth time that season, Hub took on a familiar adversary on the slab, Tom Sheehan. Both hurlers were liberally touched for hits — Hub 13 and Sheehan 15 — but surprisingly the damage was minimized as each team scored only one run going into the 11th frame. A playoff intensity permeated the contest as Crackers first baseman Ivy Griffith "ragged" on Hub all afternoon. The game passed the two-hour mark in the 11th when the Crackers loaded the bases and, with one swing of the bat, the Atlanta contingent struck for three runs. But more serious damage was done after Sheehan bowled over Hub as he covered home plate on a passed ball. Spiked on the foot and complaining of a sore back, the Gallatin Squash left the meaningless game. The Pelicans not only lost the game, the series and the pennant; they also lost Hub for the remainder of the campaign. Too bad! Until recently, Hub had had a legitimate shot at a 20-win season. Not now.[63] The slugfest was also a harbinger — the Deadball Era was silently slipping away along with Hub's lengthy career.

The humid climes of New Orleans must have agreed with 37-year-old Hub as his second season figures testify. He started out by extending the previous year's successes, and he posted some eye-catching results — second in team wins (17) and games started (34). But the most amazing achievements included Hub's 260 innings pitched, his most since Vincennes, a staggering WHIP (.904), and an unfathomable 1.56 ERA, a league record that stands to this very day.[64] Hub's pitching accomplishments were all the more amazing considering the return of better hitters who had been serving in the military, and the manufacture of a new, more tightly wound baseball that gave an advantage to the hitters. These accolades were all the more impressive because they occurred in the final year of the Deadball Era. (Most baseball historians recognize 1920 as the beginning of the Modern Era.)

Despite his late-season injury, Hub had reason for optimism going into 1920. After all, he had etched his name in the minor league record books and was widely regarded as one of the top hurlers in the South. Furthermore, he complemented a pitching staff boosted by Roy Walker, Tom Phillips and Red Torkelson. The team's roster also listed two individuals destined for significant roles in Hub's future — Hugh Bradley (first baseman) and Henry "Cotton" Knaupp (second baseman).[65]

Dobbs was cautious with Hub in the preseason. The Gallatin native complained about back stiffness so Dobbs used him only once in a five-inning stint against an amateur team from the Algiers Naval Station. Hub's two-hitter was encouraging but newspapers reported that Hub "may not be ready to go [owing to] a setback."[66] Dobbs slid Hub back to the #3 spot in the rotation but in his debut he lasted only two innings after allowing five runs on six hits to Mobile.[67] One week later, Dobbs called upon Hub to relieve Torkelson in the bottom of the first at Ponce de Leon Park. The Atlanta fans gave the reliever a warm (mocking) reception, and the Gallatin Squash "doffed his cap and bowed politely to the crowd."[68] He lost the game as well as a follow-up contest to the defending league champs a week later. Clearly, something was wrong.

As the team pushed into Birmingham, a humorous incident occurred at Rickwood Field while Hub coached first base and Steamboat Johnson was umpiring the bases. "An urchin occupying a front row of seat ... hurled his cushion playfully at the Arbiter [who], becoming indignant, appealed to a policeman nearby," reported the *Times-Picayune*. "This indiscreet action drew forth drastic action from the fans in that part of the bleachers. For the next five minutes or so it literally rained cushions. Johnson stood up under the shower in fine fashion ... and when the bombardment was over the field was literally covered with cushions."[69] Hub could barely contain himself.

The next two weeks were less amusing to the Gallatin Squash. Hub's futility peaked on May 2 when he recorded only one out against Elberfeld's Little Rock sluggers. Several days later, Dobbs picked up rookie hurler Clyde Barfoot from San Antonio in the Texas League and veteran Tim Murchison from Cleveland.[70] Dobbs now housed seven pitchers in the Pelicans stable and roster-trimming day rapidly approached. In hindsight, the acquisitions of Barfoot and Murchison signaled the end of Hub's tenure in the Crescent City. His days as a New Orleans Pelican were numbered.

Hub managed a nifty five-hit shutout in Chattanooga on May 10, but his first victory was marred by a confrontation with an arbiter named Al Gifford.[71] In the fifth, Gifford awarded the Lookouts' Henry Demoe first base after Hub "rubbed the ball in the dirt and then expectorated in his glove."[72] The umpire had tendered Hub a warning earlier in the game and with the second offense he enforced the league's new policy against the spitball. Writing in the *Times-Picayune,* Cliff Abbo asserted that Hub had gotten off easy because the umpire could have invoked a ten-game suspension. This dispute laid the groundwork for another altercation between Hub and Gifford in the near future.

One month into the season, the Pelicans and Vols were bumping each other in the middle of the standings, and fans in Heinemann Park were becoming restless. Hub's frustration mounted as he tossed three consecutive no-decisions, two of them against a powerful Memphis lineup and its rising pitching star, Dazzy Vance. In one affair, Hub shocked his teammates when he removed his trademark red flannel undershirt in mid-inning in a superstitious effort to break his current cycle of mediocrity. It didn't work. Boisterous Pelicans rooters relentlessly hooted at Dobbs to remove Hub at the first sign of trouble.[73] And the local press supported their dissatisfaction. A pivotal sports page editorial on May 25 posited the question, "Is Old Hub Slipping?" The writer opined that Hub's salary, among the highest in the Southern, should be put to better use in purchasing two quality hitters. Indeed, the team was struggling at the plate, and some observers coveted University of Alabama shortstop Joe Sewell. "Thus far the aged hurler [Hub] has been nothing more than a liability to the club," concluded the damaging article.[74] Some speculated that Dobbs might trade or release Hub during the team's upcoming road swing through Tennessee.

The Nashville Vols were suffering their own version of futility — an alarming defection in which four key players jumped to the outlaw leagues for "vampire money." Their departure left manager Roy Ellam's team desperate for starting pitchers. While the Vols grappled with the "kangarooing" issue, Hub limped through his third straight no-decision at Andrews Field. When the Pels arrived in Sulphur Dell for the Memorial Day twin bill, Hub owned an uninspiring 1–4–3 record. The Gallatin Squash did not appear in the holiday classic, but he was at the center of brewing speculation. When the Birds flew out of town, Dobbs reluctantly left his faltering ace on the Nashville perch, having quietly released Hub to the struggling seventh-place Vols.[75] Before tendering a contract, however, the Vols required Hub to obtain a physical clearance from Dr. Earl Collier, a back specialist. Without question, Hub's impending return sparked a lot of excitement in Middle Tennessee. The young sports editor at the *Tennessean*, Claude "Blinky" Horn, declared, "When he [Hub] is right there is no foxier and more cunning curver in Dixie."[76] Hub Perdue had come home.

The news of Hub's release was not met with universal approval in New Orleans. Writing in the *New Orleans Item* on June 2, Bill Hamilton worried that Hub's departure might come back to haunt the Pelicans. "Very probably ... [Hub] will win a big majority of games ... especially as the ban on paraffin and ground glass has been removed. It was quite true," confided the scribe, "that Hub had to resort to a few artificialities to get the ball to do tricks for him."[77] Hamilton acknowledged that everyone in the league was aware of Hub's arm and back problems, and Dobbs had "nursed" him along accordingly.[78] How many tricks did the crafty old veteran still have tucked up his long, red sleeves?

Two days before his 38th birthday, Hurling Hub Perdue made his triumphant return to the slab at Sulphur Dell. Facing a weakened Chattanooga team, Hub did not disappoint his faithful supporters; he twirled a 7–0 gem and allowed only four Lookouts base runners.[79] "The Gallatin Gunner looked like Walter Johnson and Christy Mathewson all rolled into one," observed Horn.[80] Hub's first outing had provided Nashville rooters with an infusion of optimism for a franchise deeply mired in disappointment. His mere presence reminded many old-timers about the fabled 1908 season. Could Hub weave his magic one more time and restore the club to its glory days?

Hub dropped his next four decisions in disturbing fashion. He lost a three-hitter in Chattanooga on a triple and a suicide squeeze, and he surrendered a game-tying, two-run homer to Gilbert in the bottom of the tenth in New Orleans.[81] But the news stopper occurred at home against Mobile on June 27 when Hub ran afoul of his umpire nemesis again. Gifford had a notoriously short temper and a long history of inciting violence on the field and in the stands.[82] With Bears base runners at the corners in the top of the sixth, an incident was touched off when Hub, in blatant disregard of the Southern's recent policy against the spitball, deposited a significant amount of tobacco spittle into the pocket of his glove. Seeing the indiscretion, Gifford halted play immediately and allowed the base runner at first base to advance to second.

In actuality, the Nashville nine had developed "a history" of its own with Gifford while Hub was still playing for the Pelicans. Writing in his seminal reminiscence about umpiring in the Southern Association during the Deadball Era, Steamboat Johnson described an embarrassing incident in Nashville involving Gifford. "After finishing his talk with the managers about ground rules in Nashville," began Johnson in *Standing the Gaff,* "[Gifford] took out his whiskbroom and began brushing the dirt off home plate. [Al] brushed and brushed, but no plate appeared. A ball player ... watched him a minute, then pointed with his bat and said, 'Here is the plate over here.' Gifford then saw he was several feet away from where the plate really was." [83] Forever after, Nashville players always teased him with a nickname, "Home Plate." Surely, Gifford had marked his calendar for the day he would settle the score with the Vols.

Hub was incensed by Gifford's decision to award the Bears runner second base. He argued that he had not rubbed the ball with an illegal substance "and thereby incurred no violation of the spitball ruling." Gifford was not persuaded and, when the discussion escalated, he tossed Hub from the game and fined him $50. Hub's battery mate, Clarence "Bubber" Jonnard, came to the defense of his beleaguered partner, and Gifford fined him $10 and gave him the boot as well. The crowd became unruly, and one "bug" launched an empty bottle at the official which set off a massive fusillade from the stands.

Gifford had lost control of the game and the crowd, but there were no police to be found. The Bears bench contributed to the confusion, complaining that their base runner on third base should also be allowed to advance. The appeal sent the arbiter into a rant. He disallowed the visitors' objection and when decorum was finally reestablished, Gifford forgot the count.[84]

Hub cried foul after the game. He claimed that the official had "cursed him," reminding everyone that Gifford had fined him two weeks earlier for throwing a spitter in his heartbreaking one-run loss to the Lookouts. Hub threatened not to pitch in future games officiated by Gifford. Horn admitted in his *Touching the Bases* column that the Gallatin Squash had been "in a continual snarl with arbiters lately," and suggested that "Hub really should cure himself of the trick of slobbering on his glove."[85] The Sulphur Dell fans were more sympathetic; at the next game they took up "a collection of nickels, dimes, quarters and halves" and completely paid off Hub's tab. The masses supported their homegrown hero, and Ellam joined in some tongue-in-cheek mischief, purchasing a pack of chewing gum for his suspended ace.[86]

Reflecting on his clashes with Gifford a year later, Hub had a more humorous outlook. Hub posed a question in the *Shreveport Journal*: "Ever hear of a player being fined for spittin'? Spittin' cost me $90 last summer in the Southern. Every time I spit the umpire fined me five, and I wasn't spittin' on the ball either. When the fine got up to $90, I called a halt. 'Ninety's my roll,' I told the ump, 'and if you go any higher, you'll have to wire Gallatin and tell 'em to sell another hog.'"[87]

On the road, Hub was involved in a near-riot in Birmingham. Two days after successfully handling the Barons (5–3), Hub threw two innings of relief in "one of the most complete massacres of the national pastime ever witnessed at Rickwood."[88] Both teams had used four pitchers, who served up 26 hits altogether. The Vols struck for six runs in the top of the seventh, but Hub, "the Moses of the baseball world," promptly returned equal sums in the bottom of the next two innings. Disappointed fans showered the field with "cushions, goober hulls and pop bottles" as the home faithful demonstrated their displeasure with the low quality of baseball. The poor deportment, a repeat of events witnessed a week earlier, was a throwback to more undisciplined times in the early history of the league when rowdyism and drunken behavior were commonplace. Clearly, a public backlash was building in the Southern cities as umpires in the postwar age seemed unable to control either the players on the field or the crowd in the stands. Ironically, a Nashville headline the following day proclaimed "BASEBALL ... THE CLEANEST OF ALL SPORTS."[89]

It was increasingly apparent that Hub had lost his effectiveness on the slab as evidenced by his first month back in Nashville (1–4–1). Surrendering 13 hits to a weak Chattanooga squad and enduring a 13–4 pasting at the hands of Little Rock punctuated the level of his incapacity. Ellam was handcuffed, however, with a growing list of injured pitchers, so he was forced to use Hub eight times in July. Far from restoring the Vols to the glory days, Hub's return had been a disappointment.[90]

J. L. Ray, the new sports editor at the *Banner,* did not see Hub lasting much longer in Nashville. His *Looking Over the Dope* column also reported that clubhouse dissension was beginning to flare up. Indeed, there had been three locker room dust-ups since the Travelers had drubbed Hub back on July 10. As frustration mounted with the decline of on-field performances, the Vols made a surprising move and traded their most successful hurler, Claude Jonnard, the twin brother of catcher Clarence "Bubber" Jonnard, to the first-place Little Rock Travelers for a couple of position players. "We could afford to swap one of them Jonnards," quipped Hub with typical jocularity, "being as we got two of 'em just [look] alike."[91] The deplorable condition of the Vols pitching staff was less amusing, and one week later Claude Jonnard took a no-hitter into the ninth against his former teammates.

Hub produced a pair of highlights during July when he defeated Memphis twice in Russwood, including a 2–0 victory over Vance.[92] But these triumphs over the Chicks were sprinkled amongst six losses. Although no one realized it at the time, Hub closed out his 1920 season in a 9–0 blowout loss at Rickwood in Birmingham on July 31. His final stats, a combined 5–13 record with the Pelicans and Vols, was his worst in 16 years, and his WHIP jumped to 1.25. In a highly unusual contest matching professionals and amateurs, Hub twirled an exhibition against the Springfield (TN) town team on September 1. The narrow 3–1 victory etched by the Vols was a further indication of how much the Gallatin Squash had deteriorated.[93]

League President Martin saved Hub the humiliation of being released when he suspended him for five games stemming from the set of spitball incidents with Gifford. While the timing of the decision was questionable (Martin ran the Memphis club), it gave Nashville management a window of opportunity in which to act. In Hub's absence, the club signed promising rookies Bill Statham from Augusta (SALLY) and George Payne from Des Moines (Western League). They also divulged that Hub had been reassigned to "beat the bushes for young talent" instead of reinstating him on the active roster.[94] The club owners knew it was unthinkable to release Hub outright since he was so immensely popular with Nashville rooters. Horn opined cynically that Hub's new scouting assignment was evidence that the seventh-place club was "merely playing out the [1920] schedule" and rebuilding for next season.

Hub took his new responsibility seriously. Traveling through western Arkansas, he watched a young prospect named Dealis Wade strike out 16 batters for Fort Smith (Western Association). Excited about Wade's potential,

8. Second Tour in the Southern Association

Hub received permission "from springhouse headquarters" to tender the Native American a contract for next season. "I will personally supervise the development of his curve ball," boasted Hub.[95] Nashvillians were thrilled that Hub had scooped Little Rock's Elberfeld on the talented Arkansas hurler.

Hub's second tour in the Southern was punctuated by the greatest personal achievement as well as the lowest performances of his baseball career. As the 1920 season came to a close, no one realistically expected the Gallatin Squash to don his spikes again. Elberfeld, Dobbs and Ellam had stuck with him as long as they possibly could, and each manager had exacted every ounce out of Hub's aging body.

Hub's final four years with Chattanooga, New Orleans, and Nashville also corresponded with the demise of the Deadball Era. In one stretch between August 10, 1917, and July 16, 1919, Hub was arguably the most dominating pitcher in the circuit with a 34–9–2 record. Moreover, Hub established several personal marks which appear on the surface almost inconceivable in light of his corresponding decade of arm trouble. The introduction of a new measurement in the Southern Association for analyzing a pitcher's effectiveness in 1917 — the Earned Run Average (ERA) — would have an unfathomable impact on Hub's baseball legacy.[96] Indeed, years later the Gallatin Squash disclosed that his ERA record stood as the single greatest accomplishment of his entire career.[97] It was amazing that a man of Hub's age and extensive medical resumé was capable of such a feat.

Was there an explanation? There was no question that Hub was forced to adapt to the ban on the spitball. While pitchers in the majors were grandfathered, the same courtesy did not extend to hurlers in the minors. Thus, a veteran like Hub, despite five years of service in the Big Show, carried no weight in the Southern, and he struggled to make the adjustment. Perhaps the warm weather of New Orleans really did soothe his aching arm. Maybe the "cunning pitcher" had learned other deft techniques by which to load, sand, scuff, paraffin, cut and otherwise deface the cover of the horsehide. Or could it have been as simple as Hub experimenting with new grips or throwing the latest craze? Indeed, his improvisation of the forkball might explain the rash of commentary during the second tour regarding his new-found ability to change speeds radically. There is also a smattering of evidence that Hub had altered his speed of delivery in an effort to confuse batters. Taken together — the forkball and a deceptive/unorthodox windup — might have been sufficient to create a substantial drop in ERA. The simplest answer may lie in the huge dimensions of the New Orleans ball yard which allowed outfielders to track down many fly balls.[98] The absolute cause behind his latent success may never be known. Perhaps the Gallatin Squash was merely an anomaly, a freak occurrence that defies any rational explanation. This makes the non–Hublore story of the ERA record all the more intriguing because of its inexplicable nature. But there is no denying his fantastic improvement in the second tour or disputing the remarkable ERA record he set in 1919.

In 1920, the Southern produced four 26-game winners — Dixie Walker (New Orleans), John Morrison (Birmingham), Rube Robinson (Little Rock) and Tom Sheehan (Atlanta), but Hub's decline in overall record plus the games started (23), WHIP (1.24), and IP (147) were the lowest of his entire career.[99] There is little doubt that the back injury precipitated his rapid and irreversible condition. Old Man Hubbard had reached the end of the road.

Hub's poor start in 1920 (1–4–3) had left Dobbs no choice but to trade his broken ace to Nashville. There, Hub could play out his remaining days among Tennessee fans who adored him. Ellam welcomed the Gallatin Squash largely as a drawing card and overused Hub from the start — six games in June and eight more in July before turning him loose in August.

In the post-season, Little Rock went on to play the Fort Worth Panthers, arguably one of the greatest teams in minor league history, in the first ever Dixie Series. This playoff arrangement between the Southern Association and Texas League champions remained a fixture until 1959. For many baseball fans living below the Mason-Dixon Line, the best-of-seven face-off became known as "the World Series of the South."[100] Baseball in Dixie was entering a new and modern age at precisely the moment Hub's Deadball Era stardom was fading. The Gallatin Squash had become an anachronism in a younger man's game.

One of the major cornerstones in the Hublore saga which appeared during the second tour requires clarification. In June 1919, an anonymous letter-to-the-editor was printed in *The Sporting News* claiming that Hub had never stolen a base in all of his years in organized baseball. In a follow-up interview published on June 19, Hub stated emphatically (with tears welling in his eyes and a husky crackle in his voice) that he did, indeed, hold the dubious record of 15-seasons without a stolen base.[101] In the article entitled "ATHLETE NEVER STOLE BASE!," Hub yucked, "The only way I could ever ... steal a base was to get a lantern and go out at night." Determined to steal a base eventually, Hub promised *TSN* "to stay in the game another ten years or else break his leg in the attempt."[102] The unbelievable story streaked across the nation's news wire and created a national stir in the baseball world.[103]

Three weeks later, on July 12, Hub bested the Bears on the slab thanks to some late-inning heroics by Gilbert, who hit his second ninth inning walk-off home run in less than a week. But it wasn't Gilbert's dramatic blast that fans remember. Rather, it was the base running exploits of the bulbous Gallatin Squash. In the fifth, Hub surprised everyone, perhaps even himself, when he stole second base. He rehashed his *TSN* story to the Mobile news media and the account sped across the national news wire a second time. "After ... repining and enviously measuring with a practiced eye the distance between first and second bases, Hubbard Perdue, Pelican pitching ace, has gone and pilfered himself a pillow," joked the *Times-Picayune*. "Now Hub can look Tyrus Cobb in the eye and unflinchingly proclaim that he is a thief in organized baseball." One account chuckled that Bob Coleman, the Bears' catcher, had fallen asleep at the helm. Another rendition stated, "Perdue stole second while Catcher Coleman had gone for a drink of water." [104] Certainly, Hub had the element of surprise working in his favor.

Did Hub draft the original letter to *The Sporting News* himself in a feat of self-promotion? Had the Gallatin Squash set the stage for a designed plan to swipe a base to gain some measure of publicity? Had Coleman been in on the alleged scheme? All is speculation, but the timing of the letter's publication, the follow-up interview and the swiped pillow are awfully coincidental, and the entire episode reeks of self-aggrandizement and collusion. Just as important, was it really Hub's first stolen base ever? A careful examination of box scores indicates that he had pilfered pillows in the past — on three separate occasions to be exact. He swiped base No. 1 as a member of the Vincennes Alices on September 14, 1906, against Cairo; No. 2 as a member of the Boston Braves on September 26, 1912, against the New York Giants; and No. 3 as a member of the Chattanooga Lookouts on September 14, 1917, against the Little Rock Travelers.[105] This factual accounting of four stolen bases (eventually over 19 years) was amazing in itself. But in the annals of Hublore, the eye-popping prospect of nabbing only ONE base not only increased the shock value, it added a taste of expectant humor which is a vital component of Hublore.

The stolen base embellishment brings up an important question regarding where and how baseball scholars obtain their data. While daily box scores supply timely evidence that Hub had actually stolen four bases, the annual league reports and season summaries published in *Spalding's Guide to Base Ball* and the *Reach Guide* left out these thefts. These *Guides* are the foundation for larger statistical baseball data bases today. Since discrepancies exist between local reporting and official league summaries in the Deadball Era, which source is more valid? If baseball scholars side with the daily newspaper accounts this would suggest that the accuracy of larger data bases are flawed. If scholars side with official league releases it would suggest that local information was arbitrarily disregarded. No one should lose any sleep pondering whether the Gallatin Squash stole one or four bases in 19 seasons, but the case raises the specter of discrepancies in a statistical discipline that prides itself in numerical objectivity and precision. If mistakes have been made in the career of a little-known player like Hub Perdue (i.e., the lost season of 1905), what can be said about the validity of statistics for more famous players? This is a troubling problem.

One more clarification regarding Hublore. The most well-known story in Hublore is his alleged base running gaffe in Boston where he missed third base and was called out, and his mistake set off manager Stallings. The episode is appealing because it happened in the major leagues and involves a hot-headed manager and a comic player. The details of this version especially endeared Hub to his Sumner County audience. The actual rendition of the event is less grandiose. The real stage was Sulphur Dell and the date was June 5, 1920. Here is the true story.

The Vols were playing the Lookouts when Hub failed to tag third base while running the bases on a double hit by Pel Ballenger. After he was called out, Hub quipped to Ellam that "he was so shocked at getting that far on the base paths that he neglected the formality of tagging the pillow."[106] Ellam replied that he would personally escort Hub onto the field and show him exactly where third base was located. Sometime in retirement, Hub decided that the actual time and setting lacked dramatic emphasis; it had occurred in a minor league ball yard with a laid-back manager. To Hub, the story had more entertainment value in angering Stallings than amusing Ellam. To its author, the incorrect version also offered more bang to have occurred in the majors and not in the minors. The Gallatin Squash was always on the slab, even in retirement.

As the 1920 season drew to a close, Hub weighed his fleeting baseball options based on the brutal and stark realities of Father Time; he knew that his effectiveness as a pitcher in the Southern was over. Three straight losses to Mobile, a franchise Hub normally dominated for over a decade, was a sure sign that he had nothing left in the tank.[107] Retired life loomed ahead for the Gallatin Squash, that is, unless an unexpected opportunity presented itself in a different avenue other than playing. He did not have to wait long for a new and exciting offer.

Chapter 9

The Mogul

Roy Ellam had just completed his fifth season as manager of the Vols in 1920, and it was arguably his most disappointing campaign. "Whitey's" teams had declined steadily since his inaugural season when Nashville copped the league championship on the abilities of Hub's Gallatin chum, Tom Rogers, and his 24 wins in the box. During Ellam's tenure, the Vols had dropped steadily into the second division where they averaged seventh-place finishes and 26 games off the pace. The 1920 season was no different; Nashville languished at or near the bottom of the Southern in every category — pitching, fielding, and batting. Change was in the air, however, and not only for the leadership of the club but for the Deadball style of play as well. Both situations greatly impacted Hub Perdue.

On October 6, Horn broke a story in the *Tennessean* that the Nashville Board of Directors had voted to dismiss Ellam. The announcement stunned the baseball community. After all, Ellam had a quiet temperament and balanced managerial style not unlike Bernhard, and he was popular with players and the press. The Pennsylvania product was "one of the cleanest and best sportsmen ever to grace a diamond," commented Horn.[1] President J. A. G. Sloan reasoned, however, that Ellam was simply too lenient in his handling of the team.[2] Was it mere coincidence that this overused logic had caused the termination of Dobbs (1907), Bernhard (1910), and Schwartz (1915)? And would the pattern hold true for Ellam's successor?

The question now turned to Ellam's replacement. Who would it be? Horn speculated that Hub was the most qualified (and available) for the position. Sloan ended the speculation several days later. "We have decided to give Mr. Perdue a trial as manager," the club's leader announced.[3] Sloan's wording was hardly a ringing endorsement of the new skipper. The Board confirmed the appointment and Hub made his first public statement as manager in early January: "I hope the boys left us an open date to play the Gallatin Butchers."[4] He always kept an eye on his Sumner County roots.

There was a flutter of reaction in the baseball world to Hub's promotion as manager of the Vols. *The Sporting News* reported on the event beneath a heading, "THIS IS NO JOKE WITH SQUASH." A longtime beat reporter for *TSN* in the Southern Association, Hamilton Love, wrote that choosing Hub was not a random act of stupidity. "Perdue, the famous Gallatin Squash, known to baseball fans ... from coast-to-coast as one of the game's greatest fun-makers, has a job he is going to take seriously," concluded Love. Some people treated his appointment as a joke, but Hub issued a reasoned statement "marked with sound observations that indicate beneath the Squash's happy-go-lucky exterior there is a lot of shrewdness and common sense."[5] Instead of butting heads with the manager, which was Hub's natural inclination (and reputation), he was now the manager himself.

Middle Tennessee fans received word of Hub's new duties with enthusiasm. For many folks, his presence in Sulphur Dell harkened back to the glory days when Nashville baseball echoed success in the Southern. In Gallatin, Hub had long been the recipient of celebrity status in no small measure due to his ongoing connection with professional baseball and the widespread sharing of Hublore tales. Indeed, Hub was a recognizable figure on public streets since his earliest days in balldom. In more recent times, he frequented horse racing tracks in Gallatin and Hartsville, and he rubbed shoulders with powerful local business leaders and municipal politicos. Hub associated with so many notable community figures that he was regularly seen driving around town in the latest model of automobile — like a fancy Buick touring car — and accompanied by friends and one of his beloved dogs. Once, a photographer captured his whereabouts at the Laurel Farms entrance (previously known as Guildwood), a prestigious 220-acre wooded estate surrounded by a hand-cut stone wall.[6]

Some historians believe the man in the back seat was Dr. William Nicholas "Pops" Lackey, and others claim it was Lackey's son. The elder Lackey was born in 1875, attended Vanderbilt, and practiced medicine in Gallatin from 1899–1948. Walter T. Durham, the State Historian for Tennessee, remembers Pops as a progressive individual. Lackey advocated public health reform and called for the creation of a county health inspector many years before such an office was established. He recognized the wisdom of providing clean drinking water and waste disposal facilities for the public when water collection from nearby creeks and outhouses was still in vogue. In terms of social liberality, whites and blacks shared the same waiting room in his office at a time when strict racial segregation ruled the Southern landscape.[7] Whether Hub had befriended Dr. Lackey or his son, either way he was flying in prominent social circles.[8]

As the newly crowned manager of the Vols, Hub enjoyed daily access to

Hub and unidentified man at the gate to Laurel Farms, Gallatin, Tennessee (circa 1915) (Jimmy Perdue Family Papers, Gallatin, Tennessee).

his Sumner County home. The Nashville and Gallatin Interurban Company had connected both town squares with a 27-mile "single track" since 1913. Known as "the Bluegrass Line," the one-hour trip on the electric trolley offered Hub an efficient and more convenient commute than the regular rail service from Bethpage and/or Gallatin to Union Station.[9] Once again, Hub repeated his promise to bring the Vols to Gallatin for an exhibition against the storied Butchers.[10]

Hub embraced his new position with gusto, and he accompanied Sloan to baseball's annual winter meeting in Chicago. There, the major and minor league owners and managers haggled over talent, and Nashville did not return empty-handed. Oftentimes, a transaction between clubs owed to past relationships and friendships established by the men in attendance. Engaging in this system of barter, Hub cornered Johnny Evers, now in his second stint as manager of the Chicago Cubs, and secured the contract of Wallace "Cy" Warmoth. The southpaw had pitched for Evansville (Three-I League) the previous season, and he routinely tossed over 200 innings per year. The 28-year-old workhorse was destined for stardom and became the foundation of Hub's pitching staff.[11]

Aside from his acquisition of Warmoth, Hub had mixed feelings about the gathering in the Windy City. On one hand, John McGraw stroked his ego after congratulating him on his new post, and recollected Hub's playing days in Boston and St. Louis. On the other hand, Hub felt sheepishly out of place; he was rubbing shoulders with the power brokers and magnates of baseball. Furthermore, the devastating details surrounding the Black Sox scandal were slowly emerging, and the episode hung like a dark cloud over the national pastime for the better part of 1921.[12] Upon his return to Nashville, Hub admitted that he tired quickly from the mundane business sessions and felt overwhelmed by the tall skyscrapers in downtown Chicago. Hub pined to return soon to Gallatin, he told a scribe, where he felt more comfortable rolling up his sleeves and taking a walk down a dirt road.[13]

Hub faced an overwhelming task in rebuilding a team that had finished in seventh place last season. The entire left side of the infield required attention with the departures of shortstop Ellam and third baseman Pel Ballenger. The catching assignment, filled by Jonnard in 1920, begged for a replacement especially with Bubber currently slated for the White Sox training camp. Most important, the mound duties were completely up in the air. The top hurlers— Clarence Hodge and Ed Tomlin—were also gone, and the effectiveness of the returning third starter, Molly Meis, was questionable. Only the outfield offered any stability with the return of Mike Burke and Guy "Sal" Dunning. But Hub was also pursuing a Texas Leaguer from Houston (William Jennings Stellbauer) and a castoff from Little Rock (Johnny Frierson). Both prospects had played together for two seasons with the Buffaloes in Texas.

More than 30 players reported to Nashville for the opening session of spring training on March 14. Multiple candidates for catcher, shortstop, and third base joined 16 hurlers who vied for five pitching slots.[14] Many of the invitees hailed from the Texas League, and two-thirds of them were rookies. Still, Hub was charged with building a competitive roster around a limited veteran talent pool. "Perdue goes on the old theory," noted Love, "that large oaks from little acorns grow."[15] The experienced players were shortstop Joe Pepe (16 seasons), catcher Charlie "Tony" Tonneman (11 seasons) and first baseman Hugh "Corns" Bradley (12 seasons). This trio was in the twilight of their careers and Tonneman had come out of a six-year retirement to assist his former battery mate with the crisis at catcher.

Hub evaluated the players and wisely decided to build his team around Burke, a quality individual and veteran of five seasons in the Southern. Burke, no stranger to hard work, had been the first to arrive in February. In 1920, he had split duty between the outer and inner gardens and led the Vols with a .315 batting average. Showing leadership potential, Hub chose him to serve as team captain. Burke balked at the honor, however, believing that the captaincy should be filled by an infielder. Hub reluctantly agreed and selected second baseman Knaupp.[16] This was only the first rebuff of the Gallatin Squash.

Others followed Burke into camp, and after several workouts the team took the field against Vanderbilt. Hub entertained the crowd in the third base coach's box with his well-known mockingbird whistle. He also "swore quite a little at some of his toilers."[17] Dealing with his first disciplinary issue several days later, Hub permanently suspended outfield prospect Tod Miller from the team for public drunkenness.[18] Another problem surfaced when several key pieces to the outfield puzzle held out. Stellbauer visited Nashville and signed a contract but mysteriously returned to Texas the next day. One report said that he was "homesick," and another stated that he didn't like the city.[19] And Frierson was trying to catch on with Memphis. A third outfield prospect, Alexander Aloysius "Duke" Reilly, refused outright to report from Indianapolis. These contract issues remained a thorny issue for some time.

As Horn and Ray eagerly awaited the 1921 exhibition tilts with big league opponents, they conducted a newspaper poll reminiscent of the Rice-Yancey-Ewing referendum in 1908 to change the cogomen of the Nashville club. The scribes amassed a list of proposed names including Confederates, Old Hickories, Tigers, Rebels and Eagles. Hub joined in the fun and suggested Cyclones (a veiled reference to one of his earlier nicknames?) and Whang-doodles. Obviously, the Gallatin Squash did not take the election too seriously. Neither did Nashville citizens — the original moniker stuck.[20]

A plentiful amount of rainfall inhibited most of the practice sessions, and several major league clubs cancelled dates with the Vols, forcing Hub to schedule more games with Vanderbilt in late March. In one encounter with the collegians, both teams utilized so many players that "the box score looked like a census report."[21] The professionals won these meetings handily, and Hub experimented with some of his unproven rookies, including a popular Tennessee slab man, Charles "Red" Lucas.

Nashville squared off against its first professional opponent when the St. Paul Saints visited Sulphur Dell for six games. Although it was early in the preseason, several glaring weaknesses surfaced in the Vols' defensive setup at third and first base. Hub was displeased with the lack of effort of Frank Kane at the hot corner, and Bradley had not yet reported which interfered with plans to convert Bill "Buster" Brown into a twirler. On a brighter note, the outfield situation improved with the late arrivals of Frierson and Stellbauer, and the signing of Eddie Bogart, a utility man who played third base and outfield, from Los Angeles in the PCL.[22]

The Vols' personnel dilemma cleared up slightly when the White Sox released Bubber Jonnard to Nashville.[23] Hub was unconvinced that 39-year-old Tonneman could hold up to the rigors of a full slate, and he held similar worries about a rookie catching prospect, Boyce Morrow. In one of the games versus the Saints, Morrow went 3-for-4 with four RBI and a solo home run.[24] Besides Burke and Brown, Morrow was the only other Vol to demonstrate any pop in the batter's box.

As promised, Hub took the Vols to Gallatin to face the Butchers, where a most embarrassing situation occurred. The amateurs were unavailable to meet the professionals. Moving quickly, Hub organized an exhibition with Williams School. With Hub and Lucas sharing the slab duties, the professionals pounded the prep school, 41–8.[25] The public relations snafu likely did not sit well with Nashville's Board of Directors. Hub had incurred his second snub, albeit accidental, before the regular season had even begun.

Hub's Vols ended the exhibition season against the Columbus Senators and their exciting young second baseman, Buck Herzog. Unfortunately, the ante-season list of opponents had not included a single visit from a major league club, owing to inclement weather. As Nashville prepared to break camp and open league play in Birmingham, Bradley finally arrived to shore up the infield at first base.[26] Hub made his final cuts and he included himself on the 15-man roster, promising to enter the fray at the earliest possible moment.

Prognosticators around the circuit generally agreed that Nashville was doomed to repeat in the second division, but the team boasted a potentially lethal pitching staff—a statement undoubtedly made in deference to the presence of the legendary Gallatin Squash. The last players Hub released were Morrow, who was farmed out to Rome in the Class D Georgia State League, and Lucas, to Jackson. In hindsight, the decision to release the two most promising players from spring training was a huge mistake.

The 1921 Nashville Vols boarded a train at Union Station and bound for Birmingham with the following rostered players:

Infielders

Hugh "Corns" Bradley, 1st base
William "Chick" Knaupp, 2nd base
Joe Pepe, shortstop
Frank Kane, 3rd base

Pitchers

Bill "Buster" Brown
Molly Meis
Wallace "Cy" Warmoth
George Washington Payne
Bill Statham

Outfielders

Johnny Frierson LF
Mike Burke CF
Guy "Sal" Dunning RF
Bill Stellbauer, utility

Catchers

Clarence "Bubber" Jonnard
Charles "Tony" Tonneman

Over 11,000 excited fans jammed into Rickwood Field for Opening Day, 1921. Captain Knaupp submitted Hub's first lineup card, a list that would undergo many changes over the next two months.

1. Knaupp 2nd
2. Pepe ss
3. Bradley 1st
4. Burke CF
5. Stellbauer RF
6. Dunning LF
7. Kane 3rd
8. Jonnard c
9. Statham p

Statham was a wise choice to start the season on the mound. He began the 1920 season with Augusta (SALLY), but graduated to Nashville at midseason. A reliable righty, Statham threw a lot of innings and rarely missed a scheduled appearance. The unanswered question centered on his control.

Carlton Molesworth's hard-hitting Birmingham Barons, supported by the addition of a new shortstop, Pie Traynor, were prepared to battle the Vols in the inaugural contest. The score swung back and forth, but it remained knotted at 2–2 going into extra innings. Hub's incessant whistling echoed off the Rickwood Field enclosure as several Vols posted multiple hits — Pepe, Bradley, and Burke. In the fourteenth frame, however, Birmingham pushed across the winning run in the "grueling and thrilling" three-hour affair.[27]

Bradley emerged as the most prolific hitter on the Vols roster in the first month, but his tardiness and absences were a matter of growing concern. He had begun his baseball career in 1906 and saw limited action with the Boston Red Sox (84 games) in 1910–1912. Corns jumped to the Federal League where he starred for the Pittsburgh Rebels in 1914 and the Brooklyn Tip-Tops and Newark Peppers in 1915. The veteran first baseman spent 12 years in the minors where he put up a respectable .272 career batting average.[28]

Hub was forced to make several lineup changes in the first weeks of the campaign. First, Burke was sent home to deal with the sudden death of his brother. Then Hub released the 19-year-old Lucas to the Jackson Red Sox (Mississippi State League) for further development. The decision was justifiable — the inexperienced youngster grooved too many pitches down the middle of the plate. But Lucas' departure placed the depleted Vols pitching staff in a bind. When Bradley succumbed to a cold and required bed rest, it forced Hub to shift Brown from the pitching rotation back to first base. Warmoth was the reluctant beneficiary of these changes when he faced the ferocious Barons lineup twice over the next three days.[29] By the time the Barons-Vols completed their home-and-home season opening series, the Nashville bunch had a firm lock on last place.

Manager Hub Perdue, 1921 (Jimmy Perdue Family Papers, Gallatin, Tennessee).

The schedule did not get any easier for Nashville as Memphis, reported to soggy Sulphur Dell for a series. Statham, Payne, and Meis failed to control the Chicks' lumbering swatters, however. "Something is wrong in the Vol stable," noted Ray in the *Banner*.[30] Neither did the Vols look sharp defensively; the infielders performed in shoddy fashion, displaying a total lack of teamwork.

Matters flew out of hand in the third and final game when the Chicks pasted the hapless Vols, 14–0. Nashville fielders committed seven errors in "the worst farce seen in the Dell in many a day," wrote a downcast Ray. "The spirit of the team is shattered [by the poor start to the season]" confided the scribe, and had led to "a haphazard atmosphere" on the bench.[31] The Vols reached a crisis point as their frustrations soared. It only took an incident in the slugfest against Memphis to bring it seething to the surface.

The Vols' feelings unraveled in the third when Brown plunked Rinaldo Williams during a Chicks rally. The irate batsman threw his cudgel at the hurler, who responded by walking briskly toward home plate in an aggressive manner. Both men clenched their fists and rolled on the ground throwing punches as the benches emptied. Eventually, the umpire restored order, and he ejected Brown for throwing the outlawed spitter.[32]

The downward spiral continued when Kid Elberfeld brought his Little Rock squad to Nashville. The Travelers picked up where the Chicks left off. The Vols had no answer for the hitting prowess of the visitors. Trailing 10–1 in the sixth, several fist fights broke out in the grandstands, and one heckler so agitated Jonnard after he caught a foul ball near the stands that the burly catcher leaped into the crowd and pummeled the "knocker." Players and bugs alike joined in the melee, and a scanty police detachment restored order with considerable difficulty. The Nashville backstopper was "kicked" from the contest and there was little doubt that President Martin would mete out a fine and suspension shortly. When the game mercifully ended, Little Rock had amassed a lopsided 14–5 victory. The wheels were spinning out of control on Hub's club.[33] And the season was only two weeks old.

The tailspin did not end any time soon. The club wasted a good pitching outing from Payne in the final Little Rock meeting because of recurring defensive lapses. Kane was singled out at third base for sloppy fielding along with Stellbauer, who found it difficult to negotiate the right field incline in Sulphur Dell's dump. The worst-kept secret in town was Hub's search to sign another utility player to complement Bogart. Perhaps the Vols could turn things around with a change of scenery. The upcoming road trip began in hostile territory, however, Russwood Field.[34]

The Vols greeted a rookie Memphis pitcher in a most uncharacteristic fashion — they leaped on him for four runs in the first. A smattering of confidence grew on the Vols sideline, but it was quickly erased in the third frame when the home team exploded for six runs. From this point the contest was never in doubt. The Chicks were about as hot at the Vols were cold, and Hub's club sank to 1–9.[35] There was nowhere to go but up.

To this point it would be generous to say that the Vols pitching had been erratic. Statham and Payne were *bona fide* starters, but Meis was terrible in relief and Brown was mechanically unsound and wild. The arrival of Dealis "Chief" Wade on April 29 offered some hope that a change was in the offing. Hub wasted no time and inserted the ex–Ft. Smith product into the lineup when the Vols traveled to Kavanaugh Field. Perhaps Hub wanted to gloat to Elberfeld in Little Rock for missing out on Wade. The Vols extended their mini-offensive surge and jumped to an 8–0 lead in the third following a successful suicide squeeze and two double steals to bury Elberfeld's club. But Hub's smug triumph was bittersweet as Wade faltered in the bottom of the frame, and he yanked his protégé after he threw ten straight balls. The final result, a 10–5 win, indicated that the Vols might be snapping out of their funk.[36]

Hub took this fleeting moment of success to vent to the press about his concern over vocal fan criticism in Sulphur Dell. The skipper claimed that disenchanted rooters were adversely affecting some of his more sensitive players. He understood their frustrations in the Vols' slow start and the contrasting fast pace set by in-state rivals Memphis and Chattanooga, which held down the top two spots in the standings on May 1. But Hub had no adequate explanation for his languishing pitchers. Nor could he shed light on why the Vols were losing games despite the fact that the lineup boasted four men who were hitting over .300. Indeed, Frierson led the entire circuit at .420.[37] Hub did not comprehend, nor did his detractors, that his team (and league) were in the invisible grip of the new Lively Ball, or Modern Era.

On May 1, the Vols were scheduled to host Birmingham in a doubleheader. This particular twin bill was special in the Southern; very rarely were such features a part of the regular schedule — traditionally, they fell either on holidays or as part of a make-up for cancelled games. The game was rained out, a fortunate situation for the Vols, who had arrived late from Arkansas. The next day, the Vols played snappy defense (for once), and Warmoth twirled a 6–3 gem. "The Vols looked like a team," cheered Ray, "and not like a flock of blundering boobs."[38] Perhaps less sleep was the answer to the Vols' diamond doldrums.

A second oddity introduced in 1921 followed on the heels of the non-holiday doubleheader when the Vols traveled to Chattanooga to open a five-game series. Normally, the only time clubs met for four or five games in the course of a season was to make up contests previously rained out. In the first meeting, Meis combated unseasonably cold weather as well as Lookouts batsmen when he surrendered six runs in the first on the way to a 13–8 defeat. Both teams amassed 33 hits. The following day, the Lookouts outlasted the Vols by one run and, again, both lineups struck for 23 hits. Meis, pitching in relief in the second meeting, was given his release following the consecutive debacles. Generously, Chattanooga manager Strang Nicklin offered the ineffective former Vol a tryout.[39]

The final three contests at Andrews Field were marked by sensational base running exploits and one unexpected sweep of a doubleheader. In the first matter, the Lookouts' fleet infielder, Marty Fiedler, stole home plate primarily off of the inattentive Vols catcher. The spectacular athletic feat excited the local fans, but it also laid bare the Vols' woeful predicament with its ineffective backstopper, Tonneman. But Statham rebounded and held Chattanooga in check to notch a much-needed victory. In the opening game of the twin bill the next day, the Vols greeted their former teammate, Meis, with a constant barrage of grounders that his infielders could not defend. Moreover, Wade tossed a complete game, and Payne followed suit in the second contest. Perhaps the Vols had turned a corner with their three-game winning streak.[40]

Returning to Sulphur Dell, the Vols prepared to host Atlanta. In the first tilt, the hosts appeared ready to hand a victory over to the visitors when the Crackers scored twice in the ninth to even the score. But the Vols executed an exciting cut-off and relay to drop the go-ahead runner at the plate to end Atlanta's threat. Then the Vols roared back in the bottom of the frame on Burke's long sacrifice fly to deep left field to score Bogart. Warmoth, who had recently overcome a bout with scarlet fever, twirled his most impressive slab work of the spring in the second game, and Nashville held on to record its fourth consecutive win. They ultimately extended their streak to six games.[41]

As the league deadline for roster limits approached — May 15 — Hub announced his intention to "take a turn in the box soon."[42] It is not altogether clear why he made such an outlandish statement. After all, he talked freely about his chronic backache in the press. Perhaps Hub was caught up in the euphoria of the Vols' recent successes on the field. Or maybe he felt pressure from President Sloan to make an appearance. He boasted, unrealistically, that he was prepared to insert himself into 20 contests before the end of the season. In order to open a roster spot for himself, Hub loaned Brown to Chattanooga. This was a huge mistake. While Brown had struggled on the slab, he was doing a commendable job filling in at first base for Bradley, who was missing in action on numerous occasions. And Buster's bat was coming to life. Moreover, Hub's ill-advised declaration planted an assumption with the public and team directors that he would compete on the diamond sometime soon.[43]

Although the Vols were showing improvement, the league leaders were playing at an equally torrid pace. In fact, Memphis matched Nashville's victories and the Vols could make no headway, bouncing back and forth between fifth and sixth place. After the team had left town on a two-city road trip to Mobile and New Orleans, President Sloan publicly called out Hub. "You are in a warm climate now," he challenged the Gallatin Squash. "What is your alibi?"[44] Clearly, Sloan was frustrated by the Pelicans' domineering sweep of the Vols (10–3, 12–1) on May 15 as the Birds pummeled Hub's pitchers for 28 hits. Although the team had clawed its way back to respectability in the standings (10–13), the Director clearly wanted to see Hub on the mound, preferably during the upcoming home stand on May 20–31. Hub's participation on the field, rationalized Sloan, would fill the stands with his enthusiastic followers, a principal reason for his hiring of Hub in the first place. Furthermore, Sloan fretted over a published report that four Southern franchises were losing money—Chattanooga, Mobile, Little Rock and Nashville.[45] On the other hand, the Nashville Elite Giants, the local entrant in the Negro Southern League, was playing in front of large, integrated crowds at Sulphur Dell while the Vols were on the road.[46]

The Vols limped home from New Orleans after dropping three out of four games to host a 13-game home stand against the Lookouts, Pelicans, and Bears. In hindsight, one senses that the outcome of these games would determine Hub's future as manager of the Vols. Chattanooga arrived first to begin its five-game series. Much had changed for Nicklin's Lookouts since the two teams had first met; the East Tennessee club had fallen on hard times and slipped into the league cellar. Rumors filled the Nashville sports pages about impending roster moves on both teams. Indeed, Hub had brought in two shortstop prospects supposedly to replace Old Man Pepe, but neither infielder panned out. Both teams pounded out 14 hits in the opener but the 8–6 score went in favor of the visitors, and in the second encounter the Lookouts' third sacker, Fiedler, pilfered home plate for the second time against the Vols. After the game, Tonneman dejectedly hung up his spikes (after only 12 appearances) and told reporters that he was heading home to Prescott, Arizona, to play in an independent league. Tony's sudden departure shocked Hub. Now his team was left without a backup catcher, and Rome refused to release Morrow until the end of its season. Hub was in a real pickle; if Jonnard went down the Vols had no catcher at all.[47]

Nashville and Chattanooga were evenly matched adversaries; they were both inept. In one of the Vols' three victories, Fiedler tried to swipe the dish for an unprecedented third time, but this time Nashville's defense was not caught napping. Even as Hub's team battled multiple personnel issues, the skipper made a bold decision regarding Bradley. The first sacker had been an erratic performer and his irregular attendance often left the team in the lurch. Hub had had enough. He suspended the former big leaguer indefinitely citing a multitude of dissipation infractions in violation of team rules. Bradley joined Miller as the second Volunteer to be released by Hub for repeated public drunkenness. In the meantime, Hub pleaded with Nicklin to return Brown since he now had serious vacancies to fill at first base and pitcher. On May 23, Buster crossed the infield from one dugout to the other. Pleased to be back with Nashville, Brown responded by scoring the winning run in a wild ninth inning where both teams scored a pair of runs and had traded the lead. Brown was a welcome addition.[48]

To this point in the season only Warmoth had showed any consistency on the mound. In other contests, Hub was forced to split time between two or three hurlers — usually Statham, Wade, Payne and sometimes Brown — in an attempt to subdue opposing teams whose batters routinely thumped these pitchers for double-digit base hits. Hub had no one who fit the modern definition of a closer or long reliever. His pitching staff operated by committee, and each hurler needed to be available on a daily basis. It must have tortured Hub not to take the spheroid himself.

The Vols showed signs of offensive reawakening when the Pelicans arrived on May 25. Burke played particularly well, clobbering a home run and tracking down two long fly balls in deep center field. The Vols scored 21 runs in the first two attractions, and lost only the last affair despite lashing 13 base hits.[49] In the finale, the thin ranks of the Vols catching corps was exposed when Jonnard hit safely and Hub asked John Dobbs for a favor — could he use a pinch-runner for his leg-weary backstopper but keep him in the game? Hub knew he was asking Dobbs to break the rules of the game. The Pelican mogul understood Hub's dilemma, however, and he wholeheartedly agreed, a friendly gesture.[50] In trouncing the Birds, the Vols improved to 17–18.

In retrospect, the Bears' arrival at Sulphur Dell signaled the end of the Deadball Era in Nashville. The squads split four contests played between May 29–31, and they combined to score 61 runs on more than 70 base hits. Brown was particularly awesome for the local nines, slugging five safeties in one game, and drove in the winning run with a clutch base hit in the bottom of the final frame in another. Since his return, Brown was hitting at a robust .487 clip. Both managers went through multiple hurlers in each game.[51] Nashville sports writers, who were unaware of this transformational moment in local baseball history, were practically speechless. Horn and Ray found it impossible to explain to their readers why so many hits and runs were going for naught and ending in losses. The owners picked up on the reporters' frustration. The offensive phenomenon seemed unexplainable but someone must be held accountable.

As the team departed for a brief four-game visit to Atlanta in the first week of June, the Vols were celebrating their highly successful and recently completed home stand. Not only did Nashville win all three series, the club had posted a neat 8–5 record and raised its season mark to 19–21. And the manner in which they achieved this success — solid offense and adequate pitching — offered Hub a brief reprieve from his critics. Indeed, the Vols looked forward to another extended home stand when they returned from the Georgia capitol. The only blemish on the hopeful resurgence was a report that Payne had contracted tonsillitis and would see only limited mound duty in the foreseeable future.[52] Meanwhile, Hub received the temporary loan of a pitcher named Rose from Minneapolis to fill Payne's spot in the rotation.

The Crackers were inhospitable guests and mauled the pitcher-thin Vols. Statham retired only one batter and gave up six runs before Wade entered in long relief. Hub was struck in the knee by a sharp line drive during batting practice, and his pain extended to the Vols' stable as well where illness and injury were rife. The time had come for Hub to pitch.[53]

The Tennessee holiday marking the birth of Jefferson Davis (the former president of the Confederacy) was June 3, and Hub climbed the mound for the first time in ten months. The Vols spotted him five runs in the first frame and he took a ten-run lead and nine strikeouts into the seventh. The outcome was never in doubt. Shocking everyone in Poncey, Hub stroked a single and a double that rolled all the way to the wall in left-center field. One observer commented that it would've been "a circuit drive for [most] batters," but the husky Hub walked between first and second base. Clearly, the Gallatin Squash was not in baseball shape, but this was a fine performance for a man turning 39 years of age in four days. The Vols salvaged a split with Atlanta on a two-run home run by Brown, a blast that cleared the Beaudry Motor Company sign in right field, a feat that had been accomplished only once before.[54]

The Vols returned to Nashville for an attractive nine-game home stand (that swelled to 13 owing to four makeup doubleheaders) against powerful opponents — Little Rock, Memphis and Birmingham. Indeed, once the three-team stand ended, the Vols would have played 26 of 30 games at home. The "Hubmen" were confident when they welcomed the Travelers and administered the most one-sided victory of the season at Sulphur Dell (17–2). The Vols had been bolstered by the return of Frank Lankenau, the teacher-minister from Louisiana who made extra money in the summer by twirling in the Southern. The southpaw was welcome relief to Hub, who now dropped Rose from the roster after four ineffective starts.[55]

As fate would have it, Hub's demise as manager of the Vols began on his 39th birthday, ironically on a date that witnessed his Dellians reach their high-water mark at 22–23. Then the long slide over the precipice began. The next day, Little Rock unleashed a 19-hit attack on three defenseless hurlers — Wade, Statham and Brown — while their own ace, Jim Robinson, twirled a commanding 12–4 victory. The Vols looked listless, and Jonnard was noticeably beat up. Both of his legs were sore from overwork, a nasty boil appeared on his neck, and his fingers were gnarled from numerous foul tips. Bubber desperately needed a rest. Sensing an emergency, Hub contacted Dobbs for another favor, and the Pelicans skipper complied by sending Herb "Doc" Smith, a utility player with experience at catcher, outfield and first base.[56]

Hub snapped following a third straight one-sided loss to Little Rock (14–3) on June 8, and he blamed the poor showing on skulkers and slackers. He told Horn that there were simply too many "rule breakers" in the clubhouse, and Sloan had given his consent to "clean house" and find suitable replacements. Indeed, the owner was committed to stripping and rebuilding the team right away in order to produce a new, winning attitude. "Nobody knows any better than I do that something must be done," Hub admitted.[57]

Manager Perdue (right) and unidentified man outside the players' entrance at Sulphur Dell, 1921 (Jimmy Perdue Family Papers, Gallatin, Tennessee).

Horn observed that some of the players "had [intentionally] slowed up" over the past few weeks, and it was becoming obvious to the fans, too.

The next day, Memphis brought their unheralded ten-game lead in the standings to Sulphur Dell. Conversely, the Chicks faced a Vols squad that was plummeting in spirit as well as performance. Hub realized that his tailspinners had reached a crucial crossroads after dropping the opening tilt, so he took the mound for the second time this season in game two. The ancient Squash tossed six strong innings and put his team in position to win, but he earned a no-decision in another losing affair. The skid had grown to five games.[58] His players had failed to respond to his public admonishment in the newspaper or his appearance on the mound. So Hub tried a different approach.

After Memphis manhandled the Vols for their sixth straight loss (12–3), an irate Hub called a closed door meeting in the clubhouse immediately following the game. Horn described the gathering as "a showdown." Hub chastised the team for lack of effort and called out specific players [unidentified in the press] who "subsist on a liquid diet"; the skipper threatened to banish them like Miller and Bradley for their failure to comply with team rules. "Hub is presented with a real problem and one that will take all of his baseball lore and ability [to resolve]," concluded Ray.[59] On the other hand, how could the Vols continually lose, pondered the scribe in disbelief, with so many players batting over .300? Hub introduced Harry "Hap" Morse, a utility player who had just arrived from Vernon in the PCL, and the mogul promised his malingerers that more fresh talent was on the way.

Hub's tirade had only a momentary effect. The next day Memphis completed its four game sweep in a 14–8 offensive parade. Burke and Brown did their usual part for the Vols by stroking four hits apiece, and the locals actually took a rare lead into the seventh.[60] But the malingering effort resurfaced unabated when Birmingham arrived for a four-game set.

The Vols ended their seven-game losing streak on June 12 with a much-needed victory over the Barons in the first game of a twin tilt, but they fell into old habits in the finale. Filling in for Ray, newspaperman E. E. McGill noted, "Never before in the history of balldom have the bats rung with such smashing as they have for the present year."[61] While there had been suspicions among Nashville's sports journalists about the possibility of a livelier ball for over a month, no one understood its cause or significance to the game. They chose, instead, to assign blame for the unexplainable changes that were taking place. The Barons edged the Vols in a doubleheader (3–2 and 10–6) on June 13, and the summer of Nashville's baseball discontent overflowed. "Hub took the men off on a [12-game] road trip last night before the fans got dangerous," chuckled J. L. Ray. "Already there is wailing and gnashing of teeth."[62] A headline in the *Tennessean* read: "Vols gone Long enough to Let Fan Flock Forget."[63]

As storm clouds gathered over Hub, the Vols traveled to Birmingham but without their leading hitter. Burke remained in Nashville nursing a sore foot. Sloan made the journey with the team, a rare occurrence that certainly signaled trouble for Hub since the president had scheduled a conference with the franchise's majority stockholder, Thomas Goodall. The exact subject of their conversation was never released, but one can conjecture that it centered on the future of Hub Perdue.[64]

Hub must have sensed the dire nature of his situation when he elected to take the mound for the third time in the first game of the Birmingham series. The Barons were unsympathetic hosts on the afternoon of June 14. They jumped on the Gallatin Squash for four runs on four hits in the first frame in his farewell appearance in the Southern. Hub removed himself from action but Lankenau and Brown were unable to derail the Barons, who coasted to victory, 14–2. The next day Hub called his second clubhouse meeting, a pre-game gathering, in the bowels of Rickwood. He opened up to the players that their dissension and quarreling was unproductive. "I told them that I wanted them to fight the other team and not each other," explained the besieged manager.[65] But Hub's understanding tone fell upon deaf ears and the Vols proceeded to sustain their 11th loss in 12 tries. Horn criticized outfielders Frierson and Stellbauer for playing with minimum effort and maximum indifference. As the Vols departed for Mobile, Hub sent Stellbauer back to Nashville, forcing him to juggle an already shaky lineup. He inserted his two most recent additions, Harry Morse and Doc Smith, a smart move that paid long-term dividends to the Vols, but too late to save Hub's job.[66]

The Oyster City club was coached by Herman Bronkie, Hub's former Nashville teammate in 1910. The Bears hosted a six-game slate, and their deplorable play was the only reason the Vols had escaped the conference basement. Still, these struggling clubs hoped to seize an opportunity and improve in the standings. Winning every other game, the visitors dropped the finale (13–3), which led the disappointed Horn to estimate that Vols pitchers had surrendered the most runs in the entire South. "No clan in the Martin loop has shown better control than Hub's heavers," chortled Horn. "They are the best in Dixie when it comes to hitting bats."[67]

The pressure on Hub was clearly mounting when Nashville boarded a train for the short trip to New Orleans. The Pelicans were firmly entrenched in second place and were pulling out all of the stops in their desperation to catch the high-flying Chicks. Thus, the Pelicans were in no mood to show any mercy to Hub or his floundering club. The testy tenor of the series was set in the first game when Joe Pepe, a former Pelican with deep roots in the Crescent City, was plunked on the head. With his own frustration boiling over, Hub was tossed in the fourth for arguing balls and strikes. The game seesawed back and forth, but the Birds prevailed, 10–8.[68]

A critical incident cast a dark shadow over Hub's future the next day, June 21. Ironically, it was during a contest reminiscent of the Deadball style. The game witnessed many managerial moves by Dobbs and Perdue, solid pitching, aggressive base running and clutch base hits. Exemplary teamwork ruled the day on both sides of the diamond. The Vols took a 2–1 lead into the bottom of the tenth when the Pelicans mounted a ferocious rally and Hub ordered an intentional walk to set up a force out at any base. The strategy seemed to work, but with two outs the dangerous Gilbert stepped to the plate, and Hub called for another free pass to load the bases. The risky plan backfired when Bert Griffith slashed a single to drive in the tying and winning runs. The Vols were crestfallen by the outfielder's walk-off safety. Hub's decisions had cost him what little respect still existed on his team; indeed, the incident illustrated the hollowness of Hub's command. Back home, one quibbler called it "really dumb baseball."[69]

Great expectations had been placed upon Hub to restore the Vols to prominence despite the lukewarm level of commitment tendered by the Board of Directors. As the Vols replaced the Bears in the league cellar with a 27–34 record, speculation mounted that the Gallatin Squash would soon be deposed. After all, no one was able to explain the Vols' lowly station despite being near the top of the league in offensive output. Some faultfinders dusted off a previously overused excuse to terminate former moguls in Nashville — that the jovial Hub lacked discipline over his players. This time they were correct, but the hammer did not fall just yet.

The Vols dropped the finale in New Orleans and the introduction in Atlanta by identical scores, 9–5. Disturbing headers appeared above both box scores in Nashville: "Ho, Hum!" and "SAME OLD TALE."[70] The Hubmen wrapped up the contests in Poncey with a pair of losses, and the train trip back to Nashville must have been suspenseful. The Vols had dropped 19 of 24 games with the only success coming in Mobile. Before play on June 6 the Vols were 22–23. On that day, they won the first game of a doubleheader to reach the .500 mark. After play on June 25, the Vols were 28–42. On June 26, Hub purchased a morning edition of the *Banner* and he flipped to the sports section. There, the mogul's eyes were greeted by a shocking headline: "New Manager Coming to Vols."[71] The Board of Directors had voted to dismiss Hub while the Vols were *en route* from Georgia. And someone had leaked the decision to the press prior to speaking to Hub face-to-face.[72]

Hurt and angered by the perceived underhandedness of his termination being made in public, Hub phoned Sloan for verification of the report and learned that the story was, indeed, true. Sloan brazenly asked Hub to manage the afternoon game since club owners had not yet agreed on his replacement. Doubly offended, Hub blurted out that no self-respecting individual would accept such an insensitive offer. The next evening, Horn's headline proclaimed to Nashvillians: "'I Am Done with Ball Forever,' Says Perdue."[73] There was no question that Sloan's release of the Board's decision in print had deeply offended Hub. In a parting shot, the Gallatin Squash made a prophetic statement about the future of Nashville baseball (and the minor leagues in general) that was years ahead of its time. Said Hub, the Vols would *never* win until they established a working relationship with some major league club.[74] Always quotable, Hub dropped another one-liner: "That team of mine couldn't beat an egg."[75] Then the Gallatin Squash returned to his Bethpage farm to lick his wounds and raise hogs and tobacco. His nine-year affiliation with the Southern Association had come to an unceremonious end.

Still smarting from the Board's decision, Hub admitted that the news had hit him like "a lightning bolt." "When I returned from a road trip on June 26th," he stated in a letter of complaint to Commissioner Kenesaw Landis, "I noticed in a morning paper that I had been relieved as manager of the club. This was the first I knew of it." Love wrote cryptically in *TSN* that "everybody else in Nashville" seemed aware of the move, however.[76] Hub informed the commissioner that he had requested his immediate release so that he might catch on with another team. Normally, it took 72 hours for a player to clear waivers. For some unknown reason, Hub complained, the club had delayed the process for ten days and had neglected to tender his outright release until July 6. In the meantime, Hub was forced to turn down managing positions in Jackson (MS) and Cleveland (TN) because Nashville still officially held the rights to his contract. Hub petitioned Landis to receive compensation for the remainder of his Nashville salary.[77] The baseball czar eventually awarded Hub $166.66 to cover lost earnings between his termination until the date he cleared waivers. But he was denied compensation for the remainder of the season — $1086.20.[78] Landis did not address Hub's claim of lost employment opportunities. The affable Gallatin Squash was uncharacteristically miffed by the manner in which the baseball moguls had turned on him.[79]

In the final analysis, was Hub a poor manager or were his Vols underperformers? Probably a combination of both, but a complex set of tangible and intangible factors combined to contribute to Hub's ultimate demise. A statistical examination of tangible categories (offense, defense, pitching) as well as an analysis of intangibles (attitudes/performances) reveals that there was plenty of blame (and a few kudos) to go around.

First, the tangibles. Major challenges to Hub's leadership centered on Bradley, Stellbauer and Frierson. Bradley had brought impressive credentials to Nashville — a keen batting eye and major league experience. Stellbauer, too, amassed solid defensive and offensive numbers as a career minor leaguer. In 1921, he led the Vols in triples (15) and was second in batting average (.340). And Frierson hit for high average in the first two months of the season before entering a steady decline. On paper, these three were statistically solid and dependable on offense. But this was where their positive contributions to the team ended. Sniping became their watch-word and intemperance definitely affected Bradley's poor attendance and possibly explained Frierson's remarkable slump in the batter's box from .420 on May 1 to .291 on September 1. Throughout Hub's reign, all three players were in and out of the lineup on multiple occasions for unspecified reasons, and each one eventually became the focus of intense newspaper scrutiny. A Houston teammate of Stellbauer and Frierson in 1918, new manager Chick Knaupp wasted little time and shipped out these two disgruntled players. Knaupp's proactive transfers dramatically improved the attitude in the Vols clubhouse in the twilight of the 1921 campaign.[80]

The indirect role of Knaupp in Hub's downfall also bears scrutiny. Prior to his arrival in Nashville, Knaupp had played almost his entire career in his home state of Texas. A dependable fielder and batter, he led the Vols in base hits (158), runs scored (87), and RBI (82) in 1921. Hub rewarded his dependability with the team captaincy. On the other hand, Knaupp did replace Hub, and one wonders whether there was any politicking involved in his promotion. In an interesting twist of fate, Knaupp and Hub would reunite two years later on a baseball diamond. Any sparks?

Pepe and Eddie Bogart flew under the radar for most of the season, but did they contribute to Hub's woes? The diminutive shortstop had been associated with professional baseball since age 15, and he was now finishing his 16th, and final, year. Under Hub, the Cuban hit 30 percentage points higher (.268) than his lifetime average (.245), not a great surprise since most batting averages improved in 1921. But his trademark foot speed was gone and his range in the field suffered; the shortstop fielded only .930 and committed 58 errors. It was clear from the beginning of the season that Pepe was no longer able to keep "fast company." Hub shifted him to third base, a familiar position over his previous three years before landing in Nashville. But the manager couldn't locate a dependable replacement either through trade or the waiver wire, so he was forced to settle for Pepe's erratic defense. It is safe to assume that the aging middle infielder did not cause undue dissension on the squad owing to his quiet demeanor, and while he underperformed in the field he did not fit in with the team's grousers. Bogart did a nice job as Kane's replacement at third base, but he also filled in whenever needed in the outfield, usually for Frierson. He started slowly at the plate but at the time of Hub's departure he was batting a robust .355. In September, Knaupp traded Bogart to New Orleans, perhaps as compensation for Smith and earlier courtesies extended by Dobbs to Hub. Neither Pepe nor Bogart had challenged Hub's command of the team.

For the most part, the entire pitching corps earned mixed reviews. On the positive side, Warmoth (18–20), Statham (12–22) and Payne (10–19) flung a lot of innings — 285, 265, and 254 respectively. They came within an eyelash of an ignominious accomplishment — three 20-game losers on the same staff. The trio also accounted for 306, 341, and 346 hits allowed respectively. Warmoth led the league in bases on balls (151), and the high ERAs of Statham (5.40) and Payne (5.32) likely did not cast fear into the hearts of opposing batters. Hub's signee, Wade, had been a major fizzle and, by mid-season, he rarely got beyond the fourth inning. Likewise, Brown lacked control but his emergence as a power hitter contributed to his successful readjustment at first base. Only Lankenau pitched with any consistency, finishing the campaign at 10–5.[81]

Looking at the accomplishments of these hurlers beyond 1921 suggests that Hub failed to bring out the best in them. Warmoth spent two seasons with the Washington Senators on the staff with an aging Walter Johnson. Later he was a member of one of the greatest minor league clubs of all time — the 1924 Memphis Chicks — who tied their own 1921 record of 104 victories. He led the team with 20 victories and the league in strike outs (133), and dropped his ERA to 3.20. Payne went on to a most impressive career in the minors. A real baseball gypsy, he hurled the pill for 26 years and notched 348 career wins in the Western League, Southern Association, American Association, PCL, Texas League and SALLY. In the mid–1930s, Payne managed four different teams in the St. Louis Cardinals' farm organization, and in his final year (1940), he appeared nine times on the mound for the Worthington Cardinals (Western League) where he tossed 28 innings at 51 years of age. Statham was the least accomplished of the three principal starters. Throughout his limited six years, mostly in Class C and D, he routinely threw more than 200 innings, but he produced a pedestrian minor league record (66–77). Hub had clearly overworked Statham, and by mid-season he was incapable of pitching complete games. Without a doubt, Hub's mound mainstays — Warmoth, Payne and Statham — found greater success after 1921.

The other pitchers — Wade and Lankenau — deserve special reviews. Both men arrived in Nashville with high expectations, but delivered different results. Wade was Hub's special project. The Gallatin Squash had wrapped his own reputation as a pitching expert around the success of the ex–Ft. Smith product. Hub threw his rookie protégé into the fray immediately but, as the season wore on, young Dealis wore down. He tired quickly, and by mid-season he rarely pitched beyond the middle innings. When his ERA ballooned to over

5.00, Hub relegated him to the bullpen. Wade dropped out of baseball, but he resurfaced three years later for a final hurrah with Petersburg (Virginia State League). In 41 appearances, Wade led the Goobers with 21 losses before hanging up his spikes for good.

Lankenau, on the other hand, reported to the team at an opportune moment. Although the teacher-minister played baseball largely for recreational purposes, he finished the season with a impressive 10–5 record and led the Vols in winning percentage (.667). He turned into a welcome mid-season relief to Hub's beleaguered staff. Lankenau possessed the skills of an effective pitcher, but his long-term prospects never materialized. He appeared briefly for the Vols the following season and then, like Wade, retired from the game forever.

So, exactly whom could Hub rely upon? One need look no further than Jonnard, Burke and Brown to find solid performers on both sides of the ball. Burke, an eventual nine-year veteran in the Southern, led the team in batting average (.348) and covered center field while the other outfield positions were filled by a wide assortment of players. The outfielder quickly earned Hub's confidence, and his choice as team captain might have saved Hub's job. Burke's hustling style and personal demeanor was reminiscent of another popular Volunteer from a bygone era, Doc Wiseman. Jonnard, one of Nashville's heralded baseball twins, was extremely popular with the Sulphur Dell crowd. Despite his youthfulness in 1921 (23), Bubber displayed all of the physical and mental tools required of a solid defender behind the dish. When Hub had no one else to spell Jonnard, the backstopper rose to the challenge despite suffering from a variety of ailments common to his station. Ultimately, Bubber served three short major league stints totaling 103 games with the Pirates (1922), Phillies (1926–1927) and Cardinals (1929). Like Knaupp, Jonnard would cross paths again with Hub in the twilight of his career.

Brown deserves special recognition because of his valuable versatility. A stellar glove man at first base, he willingly accepted Hub's plan to turn him into a pitcher. Although the mound experiment failed, Brown's work around the bag (117 games) and in the batter's box (.314) was exemplary. His 13 home runs led the Vols and established his credentials as a *bona fide* power hitter. Buster tagged three round-trippers on August 5 against Mobile, a Nashville single-game record at the time.[82] In 1922, Buster would pitch one game for Chattanooga and then transfer to the Hopkinsville Hoppers (probably with a recommendation from Hub) in the Class D KITTY. Then Buster followed the example of Wade and Lankenau and disappeared from the professional baseball landscape.

Although Morse and Smith joined Nashville very late in Hub's tenure as field general, both men supplied a much-needed boost at key positions.

Morse held down third base for the remaining 93 games of the season. A product of the Northwestern League and PCL, Hap boasted an illustrious minor league career. Departing from Nashville following the 1922 campaign, he had lengthy stays in St. Paul (American Association, four years) and Dallas (Texas League, seven years). He spent a total of 20 years in the minors and managed the Dallas Steers for four seasons. He was a quality addition to Hub's roster. Smith, acquired in Hub's last days, was an asset to the team as a utility man. He spotted Jonnard (20 games) and played left field (51 games) and first base (13 games) while posting a respectable .276 batting average. Smith amassed an impressive 16-year career in the minors which included six years as manager in the 1930s. Doc's statistics improved with age and when he retired following the 1939 season, he possessed a lifetime .314 batting average and .969 fielding percentage. Like Morse, Smith eventually helped the Vols, but neither player was in the lineup long enough to offer Hub much assistance.

An overview of the Vols' total team offense and defense lends evidence of Hub's abilities as manager. The team started strong ranking third in team offense but slipped to fifth despite the strong batting averages of Burke (fourth), Bogart (fifth) and Stellbauer (sixth). Having three sluggers in the top ten sprinkled in a lineup that finished in the second division did not make sense at the time. Defensively, the Vols floundered in seventh place for most of the year. As noted earlier, the pitchers were overworked, battled illnesses and served up plenty of base hits and runs allowed. Finally, the streaky nature of the 1921 Vols was eerily reminiscent of Hub's former pitching days when he tallied multiple victories followed by agonizing losing stretches. This was Hub's team and he was partially responsible for their shortcomings.

So, in the final analysis, was Hub a poor manager? One point of comparison worth examining is the record of the Vols during the mogulships of Perdue and Knaupp. After all, both managers had dealt with approximately the same talent pool. Consider the chart below:

Managers Perdue and Knaupp in 1921

	W-L	Pct.	Standings/GB
Perdue	28–42	.394	7th/-18
Knaupp	34–48	.414	6th/-41.5
Season	62–90	.408	

The chart illustrates that Knaupp managed 12 more games than Hub, raised the Vols' standing by one spot (seventh to sixth place), and slightly improved the winning percentage (.020). But Nashville rapidly lost ground to Memphis (23.5 games) under Knaupp. These figures bear out that Knaupp's Vols fared no better than Perdue's Vols. In the end, Hub's termination probably had as much to do with intangibles such as the rise of the modern era and personality differences as it did with on-field performance. Let's examine these factors.

The unforeseen demise of the Deadball Era hugely impacted Hub's one and only season as manager of the Vols. The invisible grip, one that no one understood at the time, led to an offensive explosion that was sweeping through the Southern in 1921, and most managers were ill-equipped to adapt to the new situation. Men of Hub's era were steeped in the strategies of "scientific baseball"; he was truly unaware of the monstrous offensive changes engulfing the sport. "Nineteen twenty-one was a remarkable baseball season," note Spatz and Steinberg in *1921*, "one that signaled that a seismic shift in how the game was played was underway."[83] The transition from the Deadball to the Modern Era began (almost imperceptibly) in the South in 1919 but it did not reach full fruition until 1921.[84]

The transfer from "small ball" to "power ball" moved silently through the Southern Association. Consider the number of batters who hit over .300 (minimum of 100 at-bats) between 1919–1921.

Team	*1919*	*1920*	*1921*
Little Rock	0	2	5
New Orleans	2	1	5
Atlanta	1	1	3
Birmingham	2	4	5
Memphis	1	2	7
Mobile	0	0	2
Nashville	1	1	3
Chattanooga	1	0	3
League Ave.	**1.0**	**1.38**	**4.13**

This chart illustrates that the number of .300-plus hitters tripled between 1920 and 1921.[85]

An examination of franchise batting averages and home runs (in parentheses) is further evidence that the Modern Era did not arrive in the Southern until 1921:

Team	*1919*	*1920*	*1921*
Little Rock	.254 (26)	.266 (51)*	.288 (36)
New Orleans	.252 (23)	.248 (29)	.305 (35)
Atlanta	.258 (24)*	.245 (23)	.267 (36)
Birmingham	.262 (19)	.267 (19)	.289 (65)
Memphis	.259 (27)	.259 (43)	.303 (53)*
Mobile	.242 (27)	.223 (37)	.258 (26)
Nashville	.241 (28)	.241 (32)	.286 (41)
Chattanooga	.240 (19)	.237 (24)	.266 (61)
League Ave.	**.251 (24)**	**.248 (32)**	**.282 (44)**

championship season

This chart affirms that the Deadball Era passed away in the 1921 Southern, and the transition between eras was not gradual but sudden. Atlanta (1919), Little Rock (1920) and Memphis (1921) showed a significant jump in offense during their championship runs, but all of the other clubs remained relatively consistent in 1919 and 1920. And the placement of the also-ran teams did not fluctuate much in the standings. Indeed, the three-year sample shows negligible improvement in overall team batting averages until 1921. These charts illustrate that Hub's last full year as an active player in the Southern (1920) was played under conditions more typical of the Deadball Era. On the other hand, his managerial season (1921) witnessed a significant increase in offensive firepower which introduced the Modern Era.

A product of Deadball times, Hub was one of the first casualties of the Modern Era. It is no exaggeration. Hub was an innocent victim in the swirling vortex of change; no one — fans, owners, players, managers — was quick to understand the phenomenon embracing this new age of baseball. Needless to say, Sloan understood one time-worn principle followed by previous Nashville owners — someone would have to be sacrificed for the unexplainable shortcomings of the Vols. And that person was Hub Perdue.

Hub was not so innocent on another intangible that contributed to his own downfall, his jovial personality. It was ironic that Hub, an undisciplined player himself, faced several major disciplinary crises in his brief tenure as skipper of the Vols. How paradoxical that Hub found himself the enforcer of team policy and not joking and breaking team rules himself.[86] Under Hub's watch, the Vols lacked bench decorum and on-field teamwork, and the situation became apparent to everyone. And Hub's light-heartedness was scrutinized even more closely once the team began to lose. Finally, the Gallatin Squash alienated his most ardent supporters when he appeared only three times in the box. No one realized that Hub was no longer physically able to pitch competitively in the Southern.

While Hub did not possess the temperament or self-discipline to become a successful field general, he might have served as a decent pitching coach in a later generation. His years of experience and craftiness in covering up injuries might have fit in somewhere as a pitching or bullpen coach. Of course, this is hindsight. Despite his clownish exterior, Hub was no cream puff; he was a fierce competitor who hated losing and pitched through the pain for many of his 19 campaigns. Hub's fortitude was overshadowed by his humorous side, and this is why we can learn from his ordinariness in the box during an age of newspaper superstars.

Hub tossed his last pitch in the Southern on June 14, 1921, and he brought closure to a respectable nine-year career with the Vols spanning three decades. His cumulative record (111–92), encompassing two separate tours of duty, was quite respectable. Over time, Hub came to terms with his rejection by the Vols, but not his desire to secure another mogulship somewhere else. Commenting in the *Shreveport Journal* the following year, Hub revealed that his sudden termination had not come as a complete surprise. "A couple of friends of mine came into town, and I wanted them to see the game as my guests," Hub recalled. "I had one pass but I needed another. I went to the president of the club, asked him for another pass, expecting of course that I would get it. But he turned me down COLD, and me the manager of the club. I ought to have quit right there. I ought to have known I wasn't in very strong."[87] So, was the age of this Southern iron man over?

Hub's prospect of retirement from baseball seemed imminent and he looked to the future with grave uncertainty. Perhaps he might reinvent himself in a different league, one that still allowed the spitball. Yes, a change of scenery might do Hub Perdue some good. Perhaps in Texas.

Chapter 10

Twilight on the Diamond

After the Vols released Hub in 1921, he worked briefly in Ferd Kuhn's shoe store on 5th Avenue in downtown Nashville. Still, as he approached 40 years of age, Hub felt drawn to the baseball diamond. He lobbied, without success, for several managerial vacancies in the Southern, KITTY and SALLY. When fellow Tennessean and former Atlanta manager "Tobacco Billy" Smith[1] offered him a contract with Shreveport in the Texas League, Hub jumped at the opportunity. Smith remembered Hub's domination of the Southern during his first tour, and it is possible that the fiery mogul planned to use him to work specifically with young pitchers, coach the bases and serve as *de facto* assistant coach. Whatever Smith's motivation might have been to bring Hub out of retirement, he put the rest of the Class A circuit on notice that his nine no longer intended to roll over for the league's powerhouses.[2] The mere presence of the Gallatin Squash on the Gassers' roster provided the Louisiana club with a newfound level of respectability.

It is quite surprising that Hub chose to re-enter the baseball fray, but at least the Texas League offered a change of scenery. Although many of the batters were nearly 20 years his junior, they did not know much about his arm difficulties, control and endurance issues, or inclination to throw an assortment of "cunning" pitches. Furthermore, the Texas climate offered Hub a warm environment (humid subtropical and continental), an important factor to him. The oil refinery business of Shreveport was foreign territory to his Tennessee background, a definite change from the agri-industrial economies of cities in the Southern. But Hub was free to throw the spitter; the Texas League had not enforced the ban and it was a destination for pitchers who still moistened their pitches. Hub faced only a handful of former acquaintances in Stellbauer (Ft. Worth), Torkelson (Beaumont), and Kitchens and Bescher (Wichita Falls).

The *Shreveport Journal* was optimistic about the upcoming campaign. Writing in his *As We Were Saying* column, sports editor Otis Harris placed great faith in Smith's revamped pitching staff. While many of the key hurlers were young rookies — John "Slim" Slappey, Walter "Slim" McGrew and Dennis Burns — the acknowledged mound leader was the not-too-slender Hub. When pitchers reported for their first workout in early March, Smith voiced complete confidence in the Gallatin Squash.[3] The community was encouraged after successful exhibitions against the Chicago White Sox and minor league foes from Little Rock and New Orleans. In the latter case, the Gassers dominated the Pelicans and marched off with the Louisiana Cup, an unofficial award given to the squad with the most victories in the annual six-game, home-and away set. "It is hard to recall a season already gone when the Gassers were so well 'set' to go as is the case this year," concluded Harris. "It is usually the case that the Gassers announce themselves as 'ready' when they aren't ready at all."[4] The local fans eagerly awaited opening day, but the schedule did not favor a fast start because Shreveport hit the road for a trio of series with the top contenders — Ft. Worth, Dallas and Wichita Falls.

Hub made his TL debut against John "Jake" Atz and his champion Ft. Worth club on April 16. Harris noted that Smith had given Atz his first coaching job.[5] Hub surprised everyone, and perhaps himself, when he handcuffed the powerful Panthers sluggers in an impressive six-hit shutout to notch the Gassers' first win of the season.[6] "Hub Perdue, who has more pitching skill from the neck up than most of his younger rivals have from the shoulders down [ended] the Gassers losing streak," reported Harris.[7] Expectations soared in the city on the banks of the Red River for their rejuvenated team, but these were unfounded hopes.

Hub's gem against Ft. Worth was the only bright spot in the first two weeks of the season for Shreveport, and temperamental Tobacco Billy was tossed frequently. Writing in his *Sports Shots* column in the *Wichita Daily Times,* sports editor Paul W. Larkin commented that "there won't be enough chewing tobacco in Wichita Falls to satisfy" the contentious Gassers manager.[8] Larkin's prediction came true when the visiting Gassers sustained their sixth straight lopsided defeat (13–4). The manager reportedly went through numerous plugs of tobacco before the umpire "parked" him for excessive arguing.

Hub's second mound appearance a week later was more typical of his early-season performances — he lasted less than two innings in Dallas and left trailing, 3–0. His Gassers teammates battled back to tie the score but ultimately dropped a one-run decision, though not before their hot-headed manager had been booted yet again for confronting the umpire. The Gasmen were off to a miserable start and quickly descended into the Texas League cellar.[9]

Hub's record stood at 1–1 when Smith mysteriously sat his ancient star for the next three weeks. Recurring arm trouble? Had Smith discovered that the Gallatin Squash was a shadow of his former self? During Hub's absence,

Smith overused his young southpaw, Slappey, whose name suggests how opponents freely swatted his pitches. The Gassers continued to lose by one-sided scores (14–2, 13–2, 10–4), and Harris noted sardonically, "No chronic tailender in the recent history of the [Texas] league has done quite so badly as the Shreveport team. It's the league's welcome mat — its springboard. The fix the Gassers are in is nothing new. They've been in the same fix since the day the season opened."[10] The scribe predicted that the axe would fall shortly on members of the underperforming club.

League rooters were scheduled to be trimmed on May 3 while the Gassers were mired in a seven-game losing streak. Home attendance lagged, and the team's 3–15 record and bottom-feeder status screamed for some kind of change. It was probable that Hub's successful debut against Ft. Worth and his equally impressive ERA (3.40) had caught the attention of Walter Salm, the skipper of the Wichita Falls Spudders. Salm tired of trailing the Ft. Worth Panthers in the standings for the past two seasons and complained about a shortage of quality pitchers. He was prepared to take a risk on the aging Squash. Anything to cop a championship for his North Texas oil town fans, but currently the Spudders occupied third place. Smith agreed to ship Hub to Wichita Falls.[11] The trade reacquainted the Tennessean with his former battery mate in New Orleans, Kitchens. One evaluator of the trade chuckled that the duo of Hub and Kitchens pushed the age meter to the century mark.[12]

Hub was annoyed at the trade at first. Claiming that the decision blindsided him, he also anticipated Smith's short-term future as manager of the Gassers and thought of himself as the logical heir apparent. "It is said when Hub left Shreveport he was so incensed at Billy Smith that he offered to bet the Gasser manager a suit of clothes that he could win 25 games in Texas if given a ball club behind him," reported the *Wichita Daily Times*.[13] Hub's transfer to Wichita Falls also pushed him farther westward and near the limit of his geographic comfort zone. When Hub arrived in North Texas, the region was gripped by political turmoil sparked by the intimidating presence of the Ku Klux Klan. In a revolting sign of the times, the area was ravaged with a number of lynchings that even reached the environs of Wichita Falls.[14]

Hub made an uneventful debut in Wichita Falls flannels on May 8 — three innings of middle relief against Galveston. His first start occurred a week later in Houston, where he flung a complete-game victory after the Spudders bounced back from a four-run deficit to snatch a come-from-behind, 5–4 victory despite Hub's issuance of five bases on balls and seven hits to the Buffaloes.[15] Meanwhile, Salm continued to wheel and deal. He picked up outfielder Bescher, a former teammate of Hub's with the Cardinals.[16] The Salmites also acquired a promising young pitcher, Floyd "Rip" Wheeler, and veteran hurler Bill Fincher from Shreveport in a fire sale.

As time would bear out, Salm rarely used Hub more than once a week. He threw a crisp seven-hit victory in his first home appearance against the San Antonio Bears on May 18,[17] but he frequently deferred a scheduled start to Wheeler and Fincher for middle inning relief assignments. Was the lack of work the result of a sore arm? Was Hub, in reality, the unofficial pitching coach? Was Salm saving Hub for major encounters with top competition like Ft. Worth and Dallas? Or was Hub's lack of work a combination of all three?

Hub's managerial urges spiked at the end of May when Charlie Frank, one of the founding fathers of the Southern Association, passed away at the age of 51 while on sick leave from Atlanta. And Shreveport fired Smith, bringing to an end his 25 years in professional baseball.[18] Now there were two appealing managerial vacancies in locations where Hub had personal connections. It was no secret that the Gallatin Squash was "angling for the job of pilot" with these franchises.[19] Within a week, however, both teams had hired from within their respective organizations. Hub would have to content himself with hurling for the Spudders for the remainder of the season. Clearly, as his on-field abilities continued to deteriorate, Hub ached for an opportunity to direct another club.

In the meantime, Wichita Falls was embarking on a 14-game road trip to Galveston, Beaumont, and Houston where they put together an offensive display reminiscent of Nashville's streak in September 1908. Setting the tone on May 28, the Spudders set a TL record with 25 base hits in a 15–4 route of the Beaumont Exporters. Three days later they roared back from a four-run deficit to plate ten runs in the eighth to hand Houston a stunning 11–5 loss and rescue Perdue from absorbing a loss. In their swing along the Texas Gulf Coast, the Spudders scored 39 runs in a four-game sweep of the Buffaloes. That extended their road record to 10–4 as they outscored all opponents 109–70 and averaged over 12 hits per contest. Moreover, the Spudders had climbed to within one game of the league-leading Panthers.[20] Salm's troops returned in early June for an 18-game home stand against every team in the league beginning with last-place Shreveport. Optimism ran high in the Wichita Falls clubhouse and community.

Hub opened the long home stand in "a snappy contest," claimed Larkin, with "fielding thrills galore." Hub socked a Texas League single to right field with two outs and drove in a run to help his own cause. So surprised was Salm at Hub's bingle that he raced out of the dugout and shook Hub's hand at first base in mock congratulations for his first hit of the season. Infused with bravado, "Hub figured that the opposition had not yet gotten over the shock of his blow and he lit out for second." The problem was that the pitcher had not committed to delivering the ball to home. He simply stepped off the rubber and fired the ball to the second baseman, who tagged Hub out to end the rally. Still, the Spudders won their fifth consecutive game and Hub extended his overall mark to 4–2.[21]

The next day disaster struck when the grandstands at Athletic Park in Wichita Falls caught fire and most of the wood structure burned down. The conflagration in the ball yard interrupted the game in the bottom of the first (on June 3) when a lighted cigarette ignited a seat cushion, and panicked patrons shoved the smoldering fabric through slats in the grandstand floor. The embers landed on a refreshment stand directly below, and flames rapidly engulfed the entire area. The main entrance to the stadium was consumed with flames so the crowd hurriedly exited through a makeshift hole in the chain link fence provided by players who used their bats to create an opening. The "negro bleacher" on the right field line was untouched, but the grandstand was gutted along with the home team's clubhouse (which served as housing for several of the players). Sixty automobiles were destroyed and three people were injured in the melee to escape the blaze.[22]

Plans were put into place to rebuild the stadium as quickly as possible. Temporary stands were erected almost overnight with seating for 2,000 spectators, but a full remodel would not take place until after the season ended. In terms of the fire's impact on the Spudders, they walloped Shreveport the next day (17–1) even as smoldering smoke hung in the air. Hub's team closed the gap on the league leader and owned a six-game winning streak.[23]

In what had already turned into a tradition for Hub, he pitched on his 40th birthday (the newspaper incorrectly reported the event as his 39th). The Spudders took a 7–0 lead into the bottom of the fifth in Beaumont when a thunderstorm interrupted play. When the action resumed, Hub lost his control and was victimized for six runs before Salm summoned relief. The Spudders held on to register their eighth straight win and Hub's fifth overall.[24] But it was about time for the up-and-down nature of Hub's slab work to recur. Three days later, he took the mound against San Antonio in a contest truly representative of the Modern Era. The visiting Bears eked out a 14–13 victory as both clubs combined for 32 hits. The Gallatin Squash lasted only three innings in the seesaw affair and left with the score tied. Four days later he seemed untouchable in a complete game over the guests from Galveston. "The old master ... is apparently in his second childhood these days," chuckled Larkin in the *Wichita Daily Times*.[25] Then Hub promptly turned around and blew a short relief opportunity.[26] Four appearances in ten days was pushing Hub's endurance to the limit.

The favorable home stand drew to a close on June 19 and "Salm's boys" packed their bags for a three-week road trip in which Wichita Falls would visit every TL city. At the moment, the Panthers held a slender two-game lead over the Spudders, a reality that reflected how Ft. Worth had kept pace with Wichita Falls in recent weeks. Time was running out on the Spudders as the first half champion would be crowned on the Fourth of July.

Salm was getting the most out of his players, but recent injuries to two outfielders and an illness to Kitchens were cause for concern. The backstopper duties were turned over to a prospect, John "Smiley" Bischoff, who was also an accomplished hitter. Later, Kitchens had nine teeth extracted in a folk remedy to overcome "the dengue."[27] Larkin also lobbied in the newspaper for the acquisition of two new pitchers.

On June 20, Hub opened the road trip in Galveston with his best stuff to date. He tossed seven complete innings but dropped a heartbreaking 2–1 encounter, and the Sand Crabs nipped the Spudders in all three remaining contests. Likewise, Hub dropped the opening tilt in San Antonio when he surrendered four runs on five singles in the "seventh chapter." Not a good start to a prolonged road trip; Wichita Falls had won only once in its first two stops and dropped six games behind the leaders.[28]

In a managerial decision reminiscent of Bernhard in Nashville, Salm decided to employ Hub to open every road series. In Houston, Hub evened his overall record with a convincing complete game in which he scattered seven hits (three of them triples by Roy Blades) in an 8–4 victory. The toothless Kitchens supported his battery mate with a pair of base hits and four RBI. Beneath a sports page headline reading "Perdue and Kitchens Show Youngsters How to Win Ball Games," Larkin announced the arrival of four new pitchers in Salm's stable. One of them, Vic Keen, turned into quite a productive workhorse.[29]

The Spudders were in Ft. Worth to open the "second season" on the Fourth of July. Hub assumed his new station in the opening salvo of the holiday classic, but he departed after the seventh, trailing by one run. Wichita Falls dropped the traditional twin bill and they joined Shreveport, Houston and San Antonio in that ignominious feat. The Panthers swept the series and the Spudders took a five-game losing streak into Shreveport, the last stop in the abysmal road trip.[30]

Salm's squad had jumped out to an atrocious start to the second half of the season. They had begun the current trip only two games out of first place, but after losing their first two games in Shreveport they were winless in seven tries. Larkin examined the collapse with mounting concern. The scribe pointed out that the Spudders led the circuit throughout the first half in offense (.314) and defense (.967), and he concluded that the main culprit was ineffective pitching.[31] To date, Hub had posted an average record (6–7) but a high ERA (4.65). And he had been yanked from more games than any other Spudder hurler—12 times.

The Spudders returned from their horrendous journey around the circuit with only one win in their pocket. But Salm did not come back from Louisiana empty-handed. The Gassers sold Edmund "Patsy" Flaherty to him.[32] Like Keen, the latest youth in the stable promised to gobble up lots of innings the remainder of the way. Conversely, Hub's role diminished markedly as a starter.[33] Having slid into last place, the Spudders awaited the longest home stand of the season between July 16 and August 12 (with one short road series in Dallas). Every team in the circuit was slated to visit Athletic Park.

No one could have foreseen the stunning turnaround made by Wichita Falls during their mid summer home stand, opening with a doubleheader sweep of the front-running Panthers. After taking a lopsided 14–3 victory in game one, Salm put Hub on the mound for the second contest. He proved his worth in a game reminiscent of Deadball Era "scientific baseball" with plenty of bunts, steal attempts, suicide squeezes and several base runners thrown out at home plate by sensational throws from the outfield. The Spudders proceeded to sweep the three-game series and climb out of the league basement.[34]

Then a pattern of mediocrity on the slab all too familiar to Hub reappeared when he went 2–2 in his next six starts. In the Dallas road opener, the Gallatin Squash was pummeled and lasted only one inning in an eventual 16–5 route. In the finale against the Steers two days later, he squandered a 3–0 lead that began with an errant pickoff throw from Kitchens to first baseman Fred Beck which allowed the base runner to advance into scoring position. Hub, lost his concentration and surrendered three consecutive singles and steals of the keystone sack which produced four runs. Undoubtedly, Hub was irritated by Kitchens' mistake and failed to refocus himself mentally on the next batters or properly hold the runners on base. Larkin was kind in his summary of the game when he concluded, "Hub has been the hard luck hurler of the Spudders this season."[35] In reality, Hub was running out of gas.

The surprise team of the second half of the TL season was Galveston. Indeed, the pesky Sand Crabs had emerged as the Spudders' principal nemesis in both halves of the current campaign. But Hub rose to the challenge in the opening meeting of the two teams despite pitching out of jams in almost every frame. The crustaceans left 13-men stranded on base, including second baseman Tom "Blackie" Connolly, who went 4-for-5. Hub's strategy, to throw at such a deliberately slow pace, infuriated his impatient opponents at the plate and he cruised to a 4–1 victory. Wichita Falls climbed another rung in the league ladder to third place.[36]

At the end of July, Dallas made a blockbuster trade with Beaumont that upset Spudder rooters. In an effort to improve its position in the race, the Steers traded two lesser players and a large sum of cash to the Exporters for three top prospects — Nick DaMaggio, Ed "Slim" Love, and Don Rader.

"Some rule should be made," lobbied the incensed Larkin, "to prevent the 'moneyed' clubs from annexing a championship when another club has risen to the top solely on merit. The almighty dollar gave the boxing game a black eye ... and baseball is headed in the same direction. When baseball ceases to be a sport and the dollar, rather than the game, is the goal, there won't be any attendance records shattered."[37] The multi-player trade involving large sums of cash mirrored future business practices in professional baseball when wealthy owners bolstered their team rosters (and payroll) by purchasing talented players (and pennants). Larkin had railed on the Steers all season, and now his disdain reached new levels of contempt, calling them "the million dollar ball club."[38]

Hub's spotty pattern of performances continued. He lasted only four outs in the opener versus Houston, but the Spudders battled back from a 10–4 deficit to win "an old-fashioned slugfest" in the bottom of the ninth. Three days later, Hub appeared "invincible" in shutting down Beaumont, 3–0, on a three-hitter. It was, unquestionably, his best outing of the season. At the plate, the Gallatin Squash smashed a hard line drive into the left field corner, and Larkin later opined that the blast was a sure double (and perhaps a triple). But the portly Hub loafed to first base and stopped; this lack of hustle incurred the wrath of the journalist. Still, he had helped the Spudders sweep the Exporters and extend the team's victory streak to 12 games.[39] In fact, the Salmites dispatched their first four opponents without a blemish, pushed their streak to 18 games, and climbed into first place for the first time all season on August 6.

Hub, on the other hand, was a non-factor in the final six weeks of the season, going 1–3. His seesaw pattern in the box was concerning Salm. As the team continued its successful ways, Hub was unable to hurl more than three innings at a time. Meanwhile, Keen, Flaherty and Wheeler were piling up win after win. For all practical purposes, Salm shut down Hub as a starter beginning the first week of August in a decision similar to Ellam's in 1920.[40] Indeed, between July 31 and August 22, Hub tossed only three innings.

Meanwhile, the Spudders were on a tear. By the last game of the home stand, Wichita Falls had entered the TL record books. They won 25 straight, they clubbed five home runs in one inning, Wheeler threw 12 straight victories, and outfielder Tex McDonald smashed 11 consecutive base hits. The Spudders had sliced through the opposition and beaten every team in the process until the home finale versus Dallas. As fate would have it, the Steers ended the Spudders' miraculous string at 25 games. In mid–August, the league-leading Spudders prepared for their last major out-of-town trip of the season.[41] Before they left, however, a scandalous event rocked the Wichita Falls club.

In the middle game of the final series, perhaps in a move to disrupt the

Spudders' momentum, Dallas manager Jim "Bad News" Galloway complained to the umpire that someone on the home team had "doctored" the game ball. Indeed, the Steers' spitballer, James "Snipe" Conley, had developed a badly blistered tongue and throat early in the game after "coming in contact with a foreign substance on the ball." Suffering from a "swollen and burned mouth," the hurler was immediately removed from the game. Galloway charged that someone on the Spudders had dipped the spheroid into creosote to intentionally cause injury to Conley.[42]

Galloway's allegation made front page headlines in the *Wichita Daily Times*. Salm defended his players and claimed that the odor on the ball came from tar used by players on their bats (á la George Brett). The conspiracy thickened when an unidentified Spudder allegedly approached Conley after the game and said that he had nothing to do with the episode. Galloway protested the game (a Steers loss), and the umpire collected the game balls and sent them to TL President Doak Roberts for inspection. Larkin jumped into the debate and claimed that, if a Wichita Falls player had soaked the balls, he should "be banned from baseball for life." Roberts had the questionable pills inspected at the University of Texas for chemical residue, and he assembled the Board of Directors to an emergency session after receiving the test results. The balls had, indeed, been soaked in creosote, and the moguls voted unanimously to penalize Wichita Falls by taking away their victory.[43]

The Salmites were dumbfounded. The Board's rebuke cast a suspicious shadow over the Wichita Falls club, giving the franchise a black eye. And the incident raised two follow-up questions: first, had the team cheated before? Clearly, the event tainted the Spudders' recent accomplishments. Second, it raised the paramount question: "who dunnit?" Perhaps the perpetrator(s) would never be identified, although Larkin surmised (without providing evidence) that the mystery man who had spoken to Conley was first baseman Beck. Ultimately, Salm petitioned Commissioner Landis for a reversal of President Roberts' decision (which was not granted).[44] Would the punishment have any effect on the outcome of the TL race? Only time would tell.

One of the more intriguing questions from Hub's Wichita Falls days remains unanswered: was Hub the player responsible for lacing the "creosote ball"? A spitballer himself, the Gallatin Squash understood the consequences of prepping a game ball with such a toxic substance. Certainly, Hub possessed a sense of humor and might try to pull off such a joke. However, the skullduggery was far from amusing, and throughout the serious rhubarb Hub remained silent along with his teammates.

The scandal did not dampen the Spudders' brilliant play on the field. They copped six straight road wins to open a three-game gap over the Panthers. In his first appearance in over two weeks, Hub threw eight strong innings in Beaumont in front of a sparse crowd estimated at less than 200. At one point, he retired five Exporters batters on seven pitches, earning a 6–3 victory to even his record at 9–9. It was Hub's last mound success of the season.[45] He faltered four days later in Galveston after only two innings, and it prompted Larkin to comment, "It has been so long since Hub has finished a contest which he started. Hub tries hard enough. There can be no doubt about that [but] ... there's nothing in baseball sadder than the passing of a veteran. It looks very much as if the 'Gallatin Squash' has passed."[46] Larkin's devastating editorial read like a baseball obituary.

The fortunes of Wichita Falls hung on a four-game tilt beginning in Ft. Worth over the Labor Day weekend as both teams were knotted atop the standings. The importance of the first game was not lost on the Ft. Worth community either. A new radio station, WBAP, sent a reporter to the opener to relay play-by-play details via telephone back to the station, where the staged commentary was distributed over the air waves. The historic first radio broadcast of a TL contest took place with Salm's "Panther-killer" on the mound — Hub Perdue. Despite Hub's handling of Fort Worth in two of three prior meetings, Salm's choice was surprising in light of Hub's checkered results and relative inactivity over the past month. Perhaps the manager believed his veteran of many campaigns was best equipped mentally to handle the bally-hoo (pressure) surrounding the contest — its importance to the standings, radio coverage, boisterous fans, etc. It was shaping into the biggest game of the year on a number of levels.

As the Spudders emerged from their dugout, the Panthers Park faithful started chanting "creosote, creosote, creosote." Hub, amused by the spectacle, thrived on this kind of a stage. The Tennessean was in rare form that afternoon, allowing only one earned run on four base hits, but he trailed 4–2 when Salm pulled him in the seventh. Larkin called Perdue "Steamboat," a metaphor of unexplained meaning, but perhaps a tongue-in-cheek reference to either Hub's propensity to overheat and blow up in the early innings, his plodding efforts on the base paths or his deliberate (labored) slowness in the box.[47] Maybe all three. Several days later, Hub imploded in Shreveport where he blew a lead in relief in his last mound appearance of the season.[48] The head-to-head confrontation with Ft. Worth had not gone well for the Salmites, and by the time Wichita Falls returned home for its final series of the season the Spudders had a firm grip on second place. The second half championship was out of reach; there would be no post-season playoff between the Spudders and Panthers.

As the last innings were playing out in Athletic Park, Larkin cornered several players and inquired about their off-season plans. Some of the Spudders had already left town on "the rattler," no doubt disappointed at missing an extra championship payday. Hub confided to the scribe that he had donned a baseball uniform for the last time. Said the 40-year-old hurler, "the ol' whip ain't what she used to be."[49] Concerning his immediate plans, Hub thought he might head to the Ansonia Hotel on the Upper West Side of Manhattan, and from there he hoped to attend the upcoming World Series between the Yankees and Giants. The elegant hotel of Beaux Arts design was home to several baseball celebrities including Babe Ruth and John McGraw. Many baseball reporters like Grantland Rice had made it an unofficial headquarters for World Series activities, too. Was Hub really bound for New York to socialize with old friends or was his story simply more braggadocio? More importantly, was the Gallatin Squash sincere about the end of his playing days?

Hub's Wichita Falls Spudders had spent both halves of the 1922 season chasing the Ft. Worth Panthers. The North Texas team won a remarkable 94 games, good enough to win the title in most years. But Atz's 1922 Panthers posted 109 victories and ran away with the TL pennant, their third consecutive championship.[50] The ancient Spud, Hub, was not completely ineffective, however. He posted a 10–11 record in 30 appearances with a 4.32 ERA. But opposing batters averaged 11 hits per nine innings off of him. The acquisitions of young hurlers like Wheeler (22–9), Keen (13–1) and Flaherty (11–14) signaled Hub's declining importance in the Spudders stable. As a result, Salm increasingly used Hub as a middle reliever (who usually required relief himself) especially in the second half of the season. And 18 of Hub's decisions took place on the road. Was Salm protecting the inconsistent Hub from hometown criticism? His batting remained horrendous, only three singles (.067).[51] Sadly, the 1922 version of the Gallatin Squash was a shadow of his former self. He was an old man (by baseball standards) playing a young man's game. Wichita Falls carried him on the roster as a formality, but released him in February 1923.

During the winter of 1922, Hub explored another managerial prospect with his former Nashville battery mate, J. Warren "Doc" Seabough. Since his retirement from professional baseball in 1914, Doc had returned to Springfield, Missouri, to clerk in the mechanical department of the St. Louis and San Francisco Railroad. Doc's keen interest in baseball never waned, however, and in 1921 he accepted a major role in rebuilding the Springfield Midgets program. Seabough also agreed to preside over the reconstituted Western Association, a position he held for seven years. In 1923, the Midgets advertised for a new manager, and Hub's name was one of several bantered about for the position. The job went to Clifton "Runt" Marr, a 5'5" minor league third baseman.[52]

So what could possibly have possessed the 40-year-old Gallatin Squash to sign a 1923 player's contract with Charlotte (SALLY)?[53] Perhaps he rationalized that, by dropping down two classifications, he might regain some of his former competitive edge. One thing was certain — the Hornets did not need a new manager. Dick Hoblitzell had ably filled that role since 1922. "Hobby," as he was called in Charlotte, was well qualified to lead a minor league club. A first baseman with 11 years of major league service, his resumé included team captain, clean-up hitter and three world championships with the Boston Red Sox. Hoblitzell maintained a keen batting eye throughout his eventual five years with the Hornets. Hub had competed against Hobby over a decade earlier while Hobby was a member of the Cincinnati Reds.[54]

In Charlotte, Hub rejoined his former second baseman and managerial successor in Nashville, Knaupp. This reunion might have been cause for tension on the bench although nothing of the kind was ever reported. Hoblitzell also picked up power-hitting Ben Paschal, a left fielder destined for a productive .351 season and ultimately a five-year job as back-up to Ruth in New York.[55] The nucleus of Knaupp, Hoblitzell and Paschal transformed the Hornets into an offensive juggernaut, and if the pitchers performed as expected it was not unreasonable to project Charlotte as a leading contender for the 1923 SALLY crown.

The Hornets opened the season strongly and copped six road victories from Augusta and Charleston. On May 2, Hub had matters under control in the final game against the Charleston Pals when trouble erupted. Disagreeing with a call by umpire Charlie Doak in the fourth frame, Hub was "banished to the bench." Charlotte preserved the victory, but the rhubarb exposed his argumentative and temperamental side.[56] As the roster-trimming deadline approached in early May, Hub dropped to the bottom of the staff with a 2–3 record despite the fact that the Hornets sat atop the league. Writing in his sports column, *One Man's Opinion,* Bailey Groome noted that several players were about to be "ditched." Without mentioning specific names, Hub was a likely candidate for dismissal.[57]

Hub's ability to sprinkle an outstanding outing in the midst of disappointing performances was his trademark, and his Charlotte experience was no exception. For instance, on May 8, he threw eight solid innings in Spartanburg but left the contest with no-decision. The Hornets won the game in extra innings on a two-run homer by Paschal.[58] Then, in the last complete game he ever pitched, less than a week later, Hub mastered Columbia in a rout (18–3) to contribute to the Hornets' 13th straight victory.[59] Finally, Hub placed the capstone on his career on May 19 with four innings of relief in both games of a home doubleheader against Augusta. The Gallatin Squash left the diamond with two victories on the same day, the fifth time he had accomplished such a feat in his 19 years of slab work.[60] Without question, this 11-day span was one of the most gratifying stretches in his twilight years. Hub bragged to Groome that he was equally proud of his recent spate of base hits. After swatting three recent safeties and raising his batting average to .150, Hub snickered, "Been trying to hit my stride for 19 years now."[61] Always the comedian right down to the end!

The end came swiftly for Herbert Rodney Perdue in the first week of June. Clinging to a 6–4 lead in the seventh against visiting Spartanburg, Hub surrendered a grand slam to Spinners shortstop Howard Burkett, chasing him from the game.[62] A few days later, Hub lasted for only four outs against the Comers in Columbia, but he miraculously left the game with a 5–3 lead.[63] The next day, Hoblitzell activated Knaupp from the injured list and released Hub on an important date — Hub's 41st birthday. Ironically, Knaupp had been the principal in two of Hub's most devastating personal defeats — his terminations in Nashville and Charlotte. The Hornets eventually won 94 games and easily captured the SALLY crown. But there were no laurels for the Gallatin Squash in 1923, although it marked the seventh time he had competed on a championship roster.

During Hub's two months in Charlotte, he performed adequately — his 4–6 record and 4.08 ERA in 64 innings pitched were journeyman numbers for a slab man. Later, the Hornets defeated Wilson (Virginia State League) in the Class B playoff, but Hub's affiliation with the lower classification illustrates just how far Hub had slid down the baseball ladder. Fifteen years earlier, at the dawn of Hub's professional career, Ewing penned an interesting comment in the *American* that aptly fit Hub's situation in 1923: "As bone-yards for battered, blighted, crumbling, deteriorated, faded, weather-beaten and otherwise retrograde base ball players, the [lower minor] leagues shine."[64] The sun had set on the baseball career of the Gallatin Squash.[65]

In analyzing the twilight of Hub's career, some remarkable similarities surface when comparing his last full season of active service (1920) and intermittent campaign (1922). First, Hub had demonstrated great difficulty in both years getting beyond the fourth inning by early July, and he barely made it into August before his arm was completely shot, which forced his managers to relegate him to the bullpen. On the verge of extinction in both seasons, Hub pitched a great game in late July immediately prior to a long absence in August. Several more statistical similarities leap off the page — the number of innings pitched in 1920 (147) and 1922 (156) remained constant but his suddenly inflated ERA (4.38) and WHIP (1.51) had grown at an alarming rate.

A subjective observation regarding Hub's questionable base running instincts is also in order; his lack of hustle on the base paths turned triples into singles, his lack of attention while taking a lead from first base led to several embarrassing pickoffs, and his aggressive decisions as a base coach sometimes ran his team out of rallies. Being lazy, out of shape and inattentive are bad combinations for base runners from any era. Hub reveled in these base running follies, but it is one of the least amusing aspects of Hublore. Finally, Hub's announced retirement in 1922 mirrored earlier statements in 1915, 1920 and 1921. Was he serious this time?

When a person lives long enough there are often unforeseen events in life that place things like baseball in its proper perspective. Such an incident occurred in 1923 that forever changed the Perdue household and forced the fun-loving Hub to re-evaluate what was really important to him. On September 17, the beloved 14-year-old daughter of Hub and Mable suddenly died from a ruptured appendix.[66]

Kathryn, or "Pud" as the family had nicknamed her, had done well in school and she was particularly gifted in piano.[67] Hub and Mable doted on her, and their daughter's untimely death devastated both of them. Jimmy Perdue claims that neither his grandfather nor grandmother fully recovered emotionally from their loss.[68] Certainly, some of life's comic veneer had been stripped from Hub's jolly demeanor.

Now Hub faced the realization that he would probably manage the family's farm full time for the rest of his life. How would the daily routine of an ordinary citizen feel to him? Perhaps, he might explore a second avenue of employment in the public's eye. After all, Perdue had been captivated by the cheers of the stadium crowds and he still craved the limelight. Would baseball, the game he loved so deeply, fit into his future plans? Although Citizen Hub was retired, he welcomed new challenges as well as the opportunity to polish and add to the annals of Hublore.

Chapter 11

Citizen Hub

Hub had carefully crafted the public persona of the Gallatin Squash as a happy-go-lucky individual, but it is ironic that his private life sometimes reflected a different temperament. Life in the Perdue household was hardly uneventful from the 1920s through the 1950s. Hub's adjustment to civilian life was sometimes bumpy as he dealt with family relationship issues. But his response to a call to public service allowed Hub to work center stage in county politics in a manner well suited to his gregarious nature. His passion for baseball remained strong in these years as evidenced in his efforts to become a professional scout for several National League clubs, and his membership and participation in the Old Timers Baseball Association (OTBA) of Nashville. He frequented public gatherings that paid homage to Tennessee's living baseball legends, which kept the Gallatin Squash in the public eye well into the Golden Era of baseball. Whether he addressed formal or impromptu groups of baseball enthusiasts, Hub regaled audiences with his humorous stories from a colorful and nostalgic bygone era. Time has a way of easing heroes from public memory, however, and by the early 1960s only diehard baseballists even knew who he was.

The year 1924 challenged Hub on a number of fronts. First, he was officially washed up in baseball. Nineteen years of hurling the pill had finally caught up with the 42-year-old. In the meantime, the Grim Reaper paid another visit to the Perdue household. Marion, the 78-year-old patriarch of the Perdue clan, passed away on May 18, 1924. His death, owing to advanced age, surprised no one in the family. His memorial service was held in the same Bethpage Methodist Church he had faithfully served for so many decades. Along with his second wife, Emma, three of Marion's children were in attendance — Cot, who still worked at the Bethpage Farmers and Merchants Bank, Erma, who had married a successful entrepreneur (Rufus Reese), and Hub. Marion was survived by four siblings.[1]

Marion's estate offers a glimpse into the expanse of the Perdue family's holdings in and around Bethpage. Specifically, Marion bequeathed property and cash totaling more than $40,000. He left household furnishings plus $3,000 to his wife. Cot received the farmhouse itself. Hub was given a farm known as the Hibbett Place on the northeast side of Dry Fork Creek and adjacent to the Scottsville Pike, about midway between Bethpage and Gallatin in an unincorporated area known as Sideview. Erma was granted a smaller parcel of land, the Aldred Tract, and an additional $7,000 in cash. Finally, Marion left one of his granddaughters the Webb Place, a substantial property. Marion was meticulous in dividing his assets so that each of the principal beneficiaries received an equal value of approximately $10,000,[2] an impressive endowment for the times. The manner in which Marion divided his estate complied with Tennessee's entailment law which required land holdings to be held by direct descendants for a minimum of two generations.

At first, Hub played a minor role in the day-to-day operation of his new holdings. Over the next two decades he deeded small parcels to his sister, Erma, whose family by marriage had operated the productive Reese Brothers Mule Company on South Dry Fork Road.[3]

Following his retirement from baseball, Hub ached for a more active public role than his farming occupation allowed, so he turned to politics. Certainly his surname was recognizable in Sumner County, and he had extensive marriage and ancestral ties with other prominent families like the Reeses and Durhams. These connections translated into political clout. Hub's fame as a former major league player also provided him with a large degree of name recognition and generated some public awe. So it came as no surprise when Hub decided to run for County Clerk of Sumner County in 1934 at the depths of the Great Depression.

In the 1930s, the offices of County Clerk, County Judge and County Sheriff were the three most powerful administrative positions in Sumner County. Taken as a whole, these offices were the nearest thing in county government to a legislative body. The Clerk set tax rates, kept records of all county financial transactions, and prepared a quarterly balance sheet of the county's expenditures. Beside these revenue concerns, the Clerk preserved accurate court records of every case — recording all suits, motions, actions and decisions. The power of the office even extended to probate matters as they related to registering deeds, wills and marriages.[4] Subjective duties of the office demanded personal integrity, honesty and intelligence in fiscal matters.

Asked why he filed to run for public office, Hub quipped in typical down-home fashion, "I want to build me a new tobacco barn."[5] Apparently, this was the only political platform Hub needed to secure victory at the polls. On August 2, 1934, Herbert Rodney Perdue was elected on the Democratic ticket to succeed Harvey L. Brown as Sumner County Clerk. He was sworn into the office one month later.[6]

Elmer T. Hinton had known Hub for a long time. Born in northern Sumner County near Mitchellville in 1905, Hinton had founded *The Upper Sumner Press* in Portland and covered much of Hub's 12-year tenure in office. In the early 1940s, Hinton's newspaper merged with the *Sumner News-Examiner,* and he accepted an appointment to write for the *Tennessean.* The writer's folksy style and marvelous sense of humor in his "Down to Earth" column attracted a large audience. Indeed, Hinton's fictional characters like Cousin Nud, Uncle Gabe and a hound dog named Old Bluestreak made for entertaining reading.[7] There is no doubt that Hinton was responsible for preserving and perhaps increasing the distribution of many Hublore stories in his column. A barrel-chested man with a deep understanding of human nature, Elmer befriended Hub. And Hinton's service as vice chairman of the Sumner County Court for 18 years brought the two administrators into closer contact at the courthouse.

Hinton and Hub were congenial personalities. The scribe respected Hub's easy-going way of communicating with people, and especially Hub's sensitive treatment of the destitute farmers who visited his office regularly during the economic hard times to unload their burdens, if only temporarily, on a sympathetic ear. According to the newspaperman, Hub's strength as a public servant was his accessibility to everyone and his generosity and empathetic nature toward human suffering and the downtrodden. But Hub's strongest attribute was his humorous streak which Hinton later said rivaled the best performers on *Hee Haw,* a popular variety show on television hosted by country singers Roy Clark and Buck Owens, and co-starring Grand Ole Opry comics Minnie Pearl and Grandpa Jones.[8] Such stories about Hub's friendliness and noted story-telling skills endeared him to his constituents. "There is every evidence that he is a shrewder businessman now [1945]," claimed Hinton, "than during those happy-go-lucky days [as a ballplayer] when his generosity many times outran his judgment." Some critics lampooned that Hub behaved like "a big overgrown boy," and their assertions greatly pleased the "natural showman."[9]

Hinton provided many other insightful comments into Hub's character. "He was not interested in making money," said the scribe. "It was the fun he liked. His conception of wealth is not measured in material things."[10] During the Great Depression, Hub was known to carry a pocketful of coins on his daily walk around Public Square where he would give a penny or nickel to impoverished children. When asked why he behaved in this way, Hub replied with political calculation, "I will still be running [for public office] when they will be old enough to vote for me."[11]

The public's perception of Hub's service to the people of Sumner County was sufficiently chronicled in the local press, and many articles emphasized his honesty. In one letter to the editor at the height of Hub's first bid for reelection, one citizen observed:

> The character of a business is a mirrored reflection of the character of a man or men at its head. The man who is unscrupulous in character will be likewise in the operation of his business or profession.... Hub Perdue, the Clerk of the County Court in Sumner County, bears a high and unimpeachable reputation. As an office holder he has proven the fact that a man of upright honest character, maintaining a strict policy in work or out will go far."[12]

Walter T. Durham, a lifelong resident of Gallatin, confirms Hinton's observations about Hub. The late State Historian of Tennessee, likewise, knew Hub through the eyes of a cub reporter with a funny twist. In the mid–1930s, the *Banner* had been advertising for a county correspondent and Durham, still in high school, applied for the position on stationery stamped with the letterhead of his grandfather, a former state legislator. The *Banner* mistook the originator of the application as the senior Durham, and they excitedly hired him. After Walter had been working for several weeks on the job the error came to light, but the Nashville newspaper was so pleased with his thorough reporting skills that they left him in the position.

Durham frequented Hub's office after he went to work for the *Sumner County Examiner,* and he observed firsthand the actions of the county's highest elected official. Durham affirms that Hub was a good listener and a boisterous storyteller. The door to his office, located in the front right corner of the courthouse, was always open, recalls Durham, and it soon became a clearinghouse for poor folks seeking advice, unemployed citizens looking for a job, and powerful politicos conducting campaign strategy. Durham concludes that Hub earned a positive reputation as "a conscientious and efficient official" who took "an active interest in all civil affairs."[13]

Being the people's choice for Sumner County Clerk illustrated Hub's broad public appeal, but a shrewd political mind existed behind his broad smile.[14] Indeed, Hub's political prowess extended beyond the county as well. In 1938, when the federal government granted Middle Tennessee an additional seat on the regional Court of Appeals, Hub drafted a letter of recommendation to secure the appointment for R. B. C. Howell. Howell was a successful Davidson County businessman and lawyer, as well as the long-standing vice president of the Tennessee Historical Society. Hub sent missives to John B. Cobb (Davidson County Clerk) and Senator Kenneth D. McKellar promoting Howell's candidacy. "Thanking you for any favor you may show him [Howell]," Hub wrote McKellar, "and assuring you that if at any time I can return the favor, my services are at your command."[15] Hub's missive was persuasive and articulate; it also showed a significant amount of political savvy on the part of the Gallatin Squash. In the world of politics, Hub cultivated a mature image to balance his clownish reputation in baseball. The Gallatin Squash had finally grown up.

Hub's election to public office coincided with a significant shift in Sumner County economics. Prior to 1920, the surrounding environs had been largely rural (excluding Gallatin) with small town businesses supplying goods and services to local farmers. But, the industrial age was creeping into the lives of Sumner's 6,000 residents. Beginning in the "Roaring '20s," the county underwent an economic transformation initiated by economic forces far beyond its borders. The lumber mills, along with satellite industries such as furniture manufacture, had begun to play out, and by the early 1930s more diversified conglomerates had arrived — the Jarmen (Genesco) shoe factory, a creamery to produce Bluegrass Butter, and Kraft Foods, which made Philadelphia Cream Cheese. These companies offered non-traditional employment to a Middle Tennessee work force that had heretofore been attached to agriculture or processing plants that depended on farm products such as tobacco and cotton.[16]

At the time of Hub's election another interesting readjustment was taking place in county politics. Until the Great War, a network of Old Guard families — who were tied to the land by postbellum social traditions and politics — had dominated Gallatin and Sumner County affairs, a phenomenon typical of most Southern counties and small towns. In Sumner County, commoners referred to this patrician class as "the Blue Bloods." But a new entrepreneurial power base was born with the arrival of the new factories. This prospering commercial class represented middle class values, a movement which had been under way in large metropolitan areas like Nashville, Chattanooga and Memphis since the early twentieth century. In Gallatin, the newcomers caused considerable social tension and resentment from people whose families had lived in, and ran, the county for generations. The resulting backlash in the polls took place in the early 1930s and resulted in the election of many new faces, including Hub. It was not surprising that his office became known as the gathering place for officialdom driven by a fresh spirit of egalitarianism. Indeed, Hub was one of those figures whom Dewey Grantham describes as a reconciler of tradition and progress, a transitional figure indispensable to Southern modernization.[17] As a result, it is not too outrageous to consider the Gallatin Squash among the most influential figures in Sumner County politics between the onset of the Great Depression and the end of World War II. Hub used the power of personality to establish a populist base not unlike his contemporary, Huey Long of Louisiana, but was nowhere near as ruthless or demagogic. Hub exemplified the "good ol' boy" style of Southern politics.

The mid–1930s were tough years for Sumner County citizens as unemployment remained high. During the height of Hub's campaign and subsequent election, dark clouds generated from the Dust Bowl sprinkled light amounts of midwestern soil on Gallatin, a reminder that hardships existed everywhere in America.[18] Still, Hub passed an uneventful first term and managed to satisfy a majority of the electorate. In 1938, he ran unopposed for reelection and he received more than 3,900 votes or 71 percent of the total number of ballots cast."[19]

In 1940, during Hub's second term, the 100-year-old county courthouse on Public Square was rebuilt as part of a WPA project.[20] The efficiency of the County Clerk surprised his adversaries who had erroneously labeled him a huckster and a short-timer. Hub intuitively understood politics and he honed his skills as a power broker, negotiator, and decision-maker to silence most

Dedication of Sumner County Courthouse, May 1, 1940. County Clerk Hub Perdue is in back row, far right on end (Jimmy Perdue Family Papers, Gallatin, Tennessee).

of his critics. The completion of the new courthouse was one of the crowning achievements of Hub's administration.

Despite the economic adversity that the Great Depression wrought on Sumner County, a major improvement came to the region through one of President Franklin D. Roosevelt's most successful (and controversial) projects—the Tennessee Valley Authority. In Gallatin, the TVA not only built a new power plant which provided a better and more reliable source of energy, its presence also led indirectly to better housing and an overall improvement in the standard of living for the residents of Sumner County. During Hub's watch as County Clerk, Gallatin and the surrounding countryside was emerging from its traditional agricultural base and slowly entering the modern industrial age.[21]

As the county began to recover in the late 1930s, Hub's personal situation improved too. The clearest evidence was provided in the extensive remodeling of his family's residence, an old farmhouse in drastic need of repair. The dwelling he had inherited from his father 15 years earlier was a two-story structure without indoor plumbing, bathroom facilities or electricity. Two wells supplied water for the family and livestock on the 100-acre site. The place looked rather drab in those days, recalled Hub's grandson, Jimmy. These spartan living conditions spoke to the lingering poverty in rural Middle Tennessee communities even in the waning days of the Great Depression. Hub desired to rebuild the home to fit his family's needs as well as match his growing stature as a public official in Sumner County.[22]

The contractor tore down the original frame to its foundation and construction began on a new two-story brick home. While the work progressed, Hub and Mable lived in a converted smoke house located in the back yard. Hub's ten-year-old grandson frolicked at the work site in the massive sand piles left by the masons. A large stand of cedars lined the property along its north side, and Hub had the trees cut down and sawed into tongue-and-groove planks to cover the walls in the living room, dining room and den. The interior of the new abode was quite impressive, and the finished domicile included modern conveniences such as indoor plumbing and electricity.[23] Strangely enough, Hub did not erect the new barn he had campaigned to build.

Hub's tenure in office also overlapped the greatest event of the twentieth century, World War II, and American military preparations touched Sumnerians in a most direct manner. Beginning in September 1942, the Second Army started conducting extensive field maneuvers in Sumner County and staged several mock battles over the ensuing 18 months. It seems the county's terrain closely resembled that of western Europe. In these pre–Normandy invasion days, it was common to see large numbers of infantry, tanks and artillery units moving around the county. Marylin B. Hughes, retired Manuscript Archivist at the Tennessee State Library and Archives, recalls her father's stories about military personnel camping in great numbers in farmers' fields and pastures throughout the Bethpage environs.[24]

The U.S. Army brought an economic boom to Gallatin during the war years. Restaurants and boarding rooms spilled beyond Public Square as the town's population swelled with military and non-military administrative personnel. The Trousdale Home, a local historic landmark, was temporarily transformed into a USO Center. The need for services and products expanded as did the need for necessities like food and clothing. As a result, the greater Sumner County economy thrived like never before.[25]

Despite the county's resurgent prosperity in the early years of World War II, Hub's future success at the polls was not automatic. In 1942, while seeking his third term, he faced a serious challenge for the Democratic Party's nomination when H. F. "Doc" Gambill filed for the office of County Clerk.[26] Despite a lack of newspaper coverage, both candidates waged an aggressive campaign with a heavy schedule of stump speeches from the tiniest hamlets to the largest towns. On Election Day, the *Sumner County News* manned a tabulation board outside its office to inform the electorate of up-to-the-minute results, a Gallatin tradition. Most of the county and state races had been decided by early evening, but such was not the case of Gambill versus Perdue. Thousands of people jammed Public Square in a festive holiday mood to await the announced winner, but the race was not made official until well after midnight when most of the revelers had gone home. Hub defeated Gambill by 124 votes out of over 4,500 ballots cast. The slender margin of victory (51 percent) was largely preserved with a large outpouring for Hub in Sumner County's two largest urban precincts — City Hall and Courthouse in Gallatin. Hub also carried his own rural district, Sideview, by a comfortable margin.[27] Numerically, Hub's support appeared to be eroding from his two earlier victories. In an unexplained twist, Gambill's precinct-by-precinct results were excluded from the unofficial tabulation published a week later. In hindsight, Hub's narrow 1942 victory was a harbinger as far as his political future was concerned.

"I ain't built my barn yet," announced Hub as he prepared for his third re-election bid in 1946."[28] But postwar society was changing rapidly as veterans were returning home to Sumner County in droves, and their worldview was much different from Hub's generation. The world had become a more dangerous and serious place, and Hub's "good ol' boy" demeanor might have come across as antiquated and irrelevant. Layon Brown filed to challenge Hub for his office. Born and raised near Portland, Tennessee, in the northern reaches of the county, Brown came from an illustrious family whose members had served the public as judges, trustees and state legislators. More important, Brown was a war veteran with nearly five years of service in the Third Armored Division of the First Army.[29] Nicknamed "Spearhead" or "Third Herd," his unit saw extensive action from the Normandy invasion to the Battle of the Bulge. Brown had spent the final year of the war in the European theatre with his comrades in Germany.

Brown mounted the stiffest opposition Hub had ever faced politically. Both men shared a common connection with Bowling Green Business University, but this was where the similarity ended. Brown attracted a much younger constituency and he appealed to rural voters. Hub, on the other hand, held onto his traditional urban base in and around Gallatin. The race would be won in the hustings where the stump-speaking skills of candidate and incumbent would be put to the test. The campaign turned into an old-fashioned political dog fight somewhat reminiscent of Jacksonian Tennessee. One week before the election, the *Sumner County News* reported, "an interest in this race is reaching fever heat. Both men are making active campaigns all over the county."[30]

Hub knew that he was in an uphill battle. The American Legion in Gallatin, a large and active chapter, was drumming up support for every candidate with a military background. Although non-partisan in its decision-making, the county, too, was doing everything in its power to encourage a big voter turnout by eliminating the county's portion of the poll tax. The combination of veteran solidarity and a sense that change was in the air was a difficult equation for non-veteran candidates like Hub to overcome.[31] On Election Day, 1946, the *Sumner County News* accurately captured the nature of this campaign, saying that "Old-time politicians are up against it."[32]

Hub possessed solid political instincts and he shared private concerns with family and friends that he doubted his ability to defeat Brown. Speaking to the local newspaper on condition of anonymity, Hub told the reporter that he was worried about the deep coffers of his well-financed opponent as well as the great unknown — "the soldier vote." The reporter was not as pessimistic. In a shocking statement suggestive of election fraud, the scribe concluded, "With plenty of booze said to be on hand, trouble may occur at several polling places during the day."[33] In Hub's case, there was not enough moonshine in the entire county to insure his re-election.

When the ballots were counted, Hub had been resoundingly defeated by 667 votes. He carried his traditional urban strongholds (Gallatin and Hendersonville) where voters accounted for over one-fourth of his overall support. He also carried the Sideview and Bethpage precincts owing to his lifetime residency in these unincorporated communities. One district initially reported a clean sweep of 163–0 going to Hub, raising the suspicion of stuffing or tampering with the ballot box. But in the hinterland beyond the reaches of the Scottsville Pike (Highway 31E) corridor, Hub's support had evaporated. He was pounded unmercifully from between two-to-one to four-to-one in rural communities such as Millersville (58–16), Salem (80–36), Bledsoe (196–48), Westmoreland (260–125), Sulphura (245–72), Fountain Head (237–80), Oakland (266–96), Mitchellville (100–37), and Fairfield (131–44). In Hub's unsuccessful bid for a fourth consecutive term he had amassed only 46 percent of the popular vote. By almost every measure the Gallatin Squash had been trounced.[34] Still, Citizen Hub had led Sumner County through two of its most trying experiences — the Great Depression and World War II. No small accomplishment.

The results of the 1946 Sumner County election were similar to the national election held 14 years later when President-elect John F. Kennedy stated in his inaugural address that the "torch of political power" had shifted

Map of Sumner County, Tennessee (designed by Andrew Green).

to a younger generation of Americans. It was not so much that Perdue's policies as county clerk had been repudiated as it was the result of a seismic shift in grassroots politics where the "greatest generation" was beginning to assert its right to political power. Just as Manager Hub had fallen victim to an unforeseen set of baseball circumstances in 1921 so too did County Clerk Hub fall prey to an unanticipated political realignment in 1946. In each case, Perdue was surprised and disappointed by the outcome.

Hub, now 64 years old and unemployed, cleaned out his corner office in the Sumner County Courthouse. Bitter over his electoral defeat, he sat on his back porch brooding for weeks and filling a brass kettle with an endless trail of cigarette butts. No one could console him. "His defeat," said his grandson, "changed Hub's life and attitude considerably as well as the lives of his kin folks."[35] For one thing, Hub departed to Nashville on a drinking binge in an effort to soften his loss at the polls. He was arrested and a newspaper reporter's photograph showed the deposed Gallatin Squash in his jail cell peering sheepishly behind its bars. After he had sobered up, Hub felt humiliated and ashamed. The episode marked a low point in his life. He spent many secluded days on his Sideview estate where he sometimes wandered next door to visit his sister. Feeling lonely and rejected, Perdue's transition into full retirement from public life mirrored his earlier adjustment to life without baseball. It would not be easy.

To stay busy, Hub remained active in local fraternal, religious and social organizations that had given him a lifetime of satisfaction. He attended monthly meetings of the Bethpage Masonic Lodge #521, and he put aside his bruised feelings to stump for Democratic Party candidates whenever possible. Of course, he was a fixture at the Bethpage Methodist Church as well as Old Timers Baseball Association (OTBA) meetings in Nashville.[36]

Hub and Mable were thunderstruck when their daughter had passed away at such a young age, but their son lived a long and productive life. As a youngster, Polk attended Hawkins Training School in Gallatin and boarded at the Columbia Military Academy in Maury County, despite his complete lack of interest in the martial life. Instead, he developed a keen curiosity in the new field of electronics, and he graduated from the Capital Engineering Institute and National Radio Institute in Washington, D.C.[37] Returning to Gallatin, he obtained the highest classification of commercial license and his ham operator moniker, W4FI, or "Four Fighting Indians on the banks of the Cumberland River in Gallatin, Tennessee" was well known.[38] He was soon recognized locally as "a genius" in the electrical field. Indeed, Polk's passion for his work as a radio engineer (with a specialty in circuitry) was pointing him in a promising direction. Shortly thereafter, Polk married Elizabeth Baber and the couple had one son, Jimmy, who was born on June 2, 1931, in Birmingham, Alabama.

Prior to the outbreak of World War II, Polk logged successful stints with several radio stations — WLAC and WSM in Nashville, WAPI in Birmingham, and WHAS in Louisville. When war broke out, Polk offered his services to the U.S. Navy, but he failed the medical exam. Consequently, he found employment as a civilian with the U.S. Army Signal Corps at Ft. McPherson

Polk Perdue in his radio repair shop, circa 1950s (Jimmy Perdue Family Papers, Gallatin, Tennessee).

near Atlanta. Later, he was assigned to operate the airport radio tower for Bell Aircraft in Marietta, Georgia, where a B-29 plant was located.

As Hub dealt poorly with his electoral defeat in the aftermath of war, Polk invited him to join in a new enterprise — Perdue Radio and Electric Company located on the east side of Public Square in Gallatin. Polk was convinced that Hub's jovial personality, gift of gab and notoriety would be an asset to selling small electronics like radios as well as larger home appliances from his store's Norge line. Soon, the business thrived and it expanded into residential and commercial electrical work. Polk installed the wiring for radio stations WHIN (AM) and WHUB (FM) in Gallatin, and he received the contract to maintain the two-way radio stations for the Gallatin Police Department and the city's electrical department. Polk also offered small electronics and appliance repair in his shop, where his young son received his first lessons in the electrical field.[39] Polk's wife worked as the firm's accountant. Perdue Radio and Electric was a family affair.[40] Unfortunately, Hub rejected Polk's generous offer to join the sales staff, and his decision might have contributed to father-son disagreements which were becoming increasingly more frequent.[41] Instead, Hub formed a company that specialized in painting barn roofs. He hired a crew, lined up jobs and supervised the projects. Hub did not believe in manual labor for himself, and he rarely handled a paint brush or sprayer.

Considerable tension had been building between Hub and Polk beginning in the early 1940s. Hub was well known as a jovial and generous person, but he developed an argumentative attitude toward his son. Whenever Hub did not get his way he resorted to badgering Polk. Hub was a drinker who sometimes indulged too much, and Polk responded to his father's intermittent flair-ups by drinking heavily himself. As a result, Polk's wife and son received the brunt of his misplaced anger and frustration. This darker side of Hub's character in the treatment of his son was seldom, if ever, seen in public, but it caused serious friction within the family.[42]

Why was Hub so overbearing toward Polk? Perhaps we will never know the cause of his outbursts as father-son relationships can be tricky to unravel. There are two theories, however. First, Hub had had a peculiar relationship with his own father. Only once was Marion, the straight-laced entrepreneur, ever seen at one of Hub's games. It could be possible that the family patriarch had disapproved of his son's choice to become a baseball player. Did Hub feel that he did not quite measure up to his father's high expectations as a man of business? If so, the realization could have produced suppressed feelings of failure which Hub then transferred to Polk. Hub also may have used excessive humor to hide deep-seated feelings of disappointment. Second, Hub's outgoing personality contrasted greatly with Polk — who was more introverted, reserved and introspective. Whatever caused this friction between Hub and Polk, they were mired in a rocky relationship.

Unlike the treatment he received from his own father, Polk showed tremendous kindness and generosity toward his own son. When Jimmy, enrolled in the electrical engineering program at Tennessee Polytechnic Institute (now Tennessee Tech University), Polk gave him a 1931 roadster complete with a fold-down rumble seat. The youngest Perdue recalled many exciting trips through the back roads to Cookeville in the green and yellow jalopy, painted in the colors of his beloved Gallatin High School.[43]

During his tenure as county clerk, Perdue began to gradually reconnect with baseball. In the winter of 1938, Harry "War Horse" Rogers suggested the creation of a social organization comprised of baseball enthusiasts in Nashville, and sports editor Raymond Johnson promoted the idea in the Tennessean. The first meeting of the Old Timers Baseball Association of Nashville was held on December 1, 1938 at Shacklett's Restaurant with 82 people in attendance. Distinguished guests included active players Red Lucas and Clydell "Slick" Castleman, two of Hub's former players and now friends.[44] The following year over 125 former ball players and fans attended the hot stove style banquet, and the beerfest turned into an annual event.[45] Hub was a card-carrying member as early as 1945 (# 11).[46] Rarely missing an OTBA session, the Gallatin Squash entertained the attendees into the 1950s with humorous baseball yarns. In Gallatin, Hub particularly delighted in relating stories about his carefree barnstorming days with the Butchers prior to his years in professional baseball. As usual, he was guilty of embellishing past events at all of these gatherings which added to the scope of Hublore. Perhaps, Hub's celebrity status at the national level shined brightest in 1938 and 1939 after he received one vote for induction into the National Baseball Hall of Fame.[47]

Without formalizing an arrangement to work for a major league club, Hub freelanced as a scout in the greater Sumner County amateur leagues. In 1942, he signed his first protégé to a Yankee contract, 17-year-old John William Terry. The young hurler had made a name for himself while pitching for the semi-pro Portland Premiers the previous summer. In his first appearance against Hartsville, Terry had tossed a four-hitter and struck out sixteen batsmen.[48] Another one of Hub's discoveries was Frank Rogan who signed with the New York Giants in the early 1950s. Rogan's career was brief—just three appearances (and a record of 0–2) with the Olean Giants in the Pennnsylvania-Ontario-New York League.[49]

It was not uncommon for former ball players to offer their services to scout for major league clubs, and Hub was no exception. He contacted the Reds, Pirates, Dodgers and Cardinals to inquire into the possibility of scouring the Middle Tennessee region in search of young talent.[50] His solicitation suggests that the septuagenarian yearned to reconnect with his boyhood roots and the profession that had brought him so much pleasure and notoriety. After all, the diamond had defined Hub's *raison d'être* and, in retirement, he nostalgically resurrected fond memories of yesteryear. Polk later claimed that up to the day of his father's death "he never lost his interest in or his love for the game of baseball."[51] Hub made it a point never to miss a baseball broadcast on television or radio. The big league clubs denied Hub a salaried position but several organizations encouraged him to operate on a commission basis.[52]

Two weeks prior to the opening of the 1943 Southern Association season, Russell conducted a fan survey in the *Banner* to select the greatest Vols team of all time as a means to hype the upcoming campaign. The players to be chosen were slated for induction into a non-existent "Vols Hall of Fame," reported Hub's scribe-friend, Hinton. To no one's surprise, the electorate chose the Gallatin Squash as one of seven pitchers along with another Deadball contemporary and onetime Gallatin resident, Shotgun Rogers. Russell's feature recounted Hub's 17-inning, no-decision performance in 1908 (the second longest affair in Vols history) and his brief managerial stint in 1921— two events engrained in the memories of elderly Nashvillians.[53]

Hub maintained a reasonably high profile at Sulphur Dell throughout the 1940s. The Vols generously provided him with a lifetime pass to all home games, a gift from current manager and former teammate, Larry Gilbert. In appreciation, Hub attended several old timers games. In 1947, the OTBA laid plans to sponsor an annual Old Timers Junior All-Star game slated for Sulphur Dell in early August, and it required the active involvement of its members. Under the watchful eye of Johnson, the Tennessean agreed to co-sponsor the event.[54]

On September 8, 1948, Hub returned to the forefront of the Nashville sports scene as a special guest at the Larry Gilbert Silver Jubilee celebration held at one of Nashville's elegant hotels, the Maxwell House. The banquet was the brainchild of Russell to honor the retiring Gilbert and his 31 years as a player, player manager, field manager and general manager mostly in the Southern Association. "Larry Gilbert — here is a name virtually synonymous with Southern Association baseball," boasted Russell.[55]

Gilbert was born in New Orleans in 1891, and as a youth he operated the scoreboard at Athletic Park and later became a standout southpaw hurler across the street at Jesuit High School. The Pelicans manager acknowledged Gilbert's pitching skills and he permitted him to throw batting practice while still a prepster. Bob Tarlton signed Gilbert to a professional contract in 1910 and he played for the Victoria Rosebuds in the Class D Southwest Texas League, where he led the pitching staff with 18 wins. He moved up a classification the following year when he posted another successful season with the Battle Creek Crickets in the Southern Michigan League. Gilbert advanced to the San Antonio Broncos (Texas League) and ended up with the Milwaukee Brewers (American Association). His consistent march through the minors resulted in his ticket being punched by the Boston Braves in 1914. Gilbert played outfield sparingly (72 games) in the year of the "Miracle," but he batted once in the World Series when Philadelphia Athletics pitcher Joe Bush intentionally walked him in the bottom of the twelfth inning of Game 3, part of a sequence of events that led to Boston scoring the winning run.

Gilbert had trouble with major league pitching, however. Midway through the 1915 season, Stallings demoted him to the bush leagues following a loss to Hub's St. Louis Cardinals. Gilbert never wore big league flannels again. He bounced from the Toronto Maple Leafs (International League) to the Kansas City Blues (American Association). Then, the owner of the New Orleans Pelicans, A. J. Heinemann, purchased his contract and Gilbert returned home in 1917 to play under the guidance of Dobbs.

Gilbert paid immediate dividends to the Pelicans. In 1919, he led the Southern Association in batting average (.349), hits (171), total bases (237), and stolen bases (42). He was popularized in the southern press as "the Tris Speaker of the minors." In 1923, Gilbert succeeded Dobbs as manager. Under Gilbert, the Pelicans won five Southern Association crowns over the next 16 years before he jumped to Nashville in 1939, accepting an offer which included partial ownership in the club. There, he tacked on an additional three championships, including the 1940 squad which MLB lists as the # 47 best minor league team of all time.[56] In his illustrious 25 years as a field general in the Southern Association, Gilbert won 2,128 games and .567 winning percentage — all league records.[57] Russell, a Nashville legend in his own right, singled out Gilbert as the man most instrumental in reenergizing Nashville baseball in the 1940s. "Come the year 2000," Russell stated, "(won't that numeral seem odd to the first letter-writers after midnight, December 31, 1999), I'm certain that some researchers will be going to the newspaper files seeking information about an almost legendary baseball character named Larry Gilbert."[58]

Russell invited Julius August Wiseman, "the hero of the Dell," to the Gilbert Silver Jubilee, the architect of so many tricky catches in the right field Dump at Sulphur Dell and owner of the lone RBI in the "08 championship game. Doc politely declined to attend, but he expressed to Russell his heartfelt memories about his playing days with the Vols. "The old town [Nashville] always brings back many pleasant memories and makes me wish I could live over again the gay nineties and the early 1900s," Wiseman wrote. "Those were the days." The former right fielder finished with a glowing tribute to the people of Nashville: "I know something of the hospitality and warm-heartedness of the old South and I wouldn't trade memories with anyone."[59]

Two members of the Vols class of '08 did attend the Gilbert — the team's two Tennesseans, Perdue and McElveen. Perdue entertained the audience with his own rendition of the 1908 championship game. The Gallatin Squash claimed that Mac's sensational tag of Tarleton occurred in the ninth inning, and "Johnny" Rickert had struck a ball that was cleanly fielded by McElveen and turned into a game-ending double play — all erroneous information. The passage of 40 years had blurred Perdue's recollection of details surrounding the big game along with a temptation to enlarge another tale from Hublore. Could the memories of other Nashvillians been any more accurate? Who still living could dispute Hub's version? By 1948, the specific details surrounding "the greatest game ever played in Dixie" had slipped from public memory despite two reprints of Yancey's original play-by-play account in the mid-1930s.[60]

Perdue's description of the offensive side of the sensational seventh inning in the '08 championship game was accurate, however. And McElveen added that Bay's surprising bunt single in that frame was the crucial (and unsung) turning point in the entire game; it had kept the Nashville rally alive and paved the way for Wiseman's clutch base hit with two outs. The audience listened in awe as these two relics from Deadball Era Tennessee reminisced about one of the greatest moments in Nashville's baseball history. A good time was had by all.

The 1952 OTBA assemblage proved to be an important turning point in the history of the organization as well as Hub's role in it. A year earlier, the founder and president, Rogers, had passed away. The reigns of power were turned over to Johnson, a natural choice since his column in the *Tennessean* provided free advertising for the group's annual activities. In 1952, the featured speaker was new Vols manager, Hugh Poland. But, Hub had his opportunity at the dais too, where he kept "the audience [of over 200 people] in stitches" with his charm and good humor.[61] Two notable guests included the current Vols second baseman, Harold "Buster" Boguskie, and retired major league catcher Johnny Gooch from Smyrna, Tennessee. The legendary "Milkman" Jim Turner, currently the pitching coach of the New York Yankees and a local Nashville celebrity, was also present.[62]

No explanation was given for the new meeting location at Speedy's Grill, but this was only one of the minor changes in the group's format. Johnson had much more significant reforms in mind. Some of his proposals did not stick, like scheduling bi-annual meetings to coincide with the end of the World Series in October and the annual Winter Meetings of organized baseball in mid–February. While Johnson sought to preserve the hot stove atmosphere of the body he also tried to limit the time allotted to local speakers to one minute and, instead, schedule a national or regional headliner to deliver a keynote address. In this way, Johnson altered the format of the OTBA forever. The first invitee under the new system was Eddie Glennon, the popular general manager of the Birmingham Barons since 1946.[63] It is conceivable that Hub had been, at least, partially responsible for the gag order on local speakers. After all, he was never at a loss for words in front of a captive baseball audience. Under Johnson's direction, the group shifted its meeting place once again to the Maxwell House.[64] Hub attended the Glennon meeting in 1953, which also honored Johnson for his 35 years of service as sports editor of the *Tennessean*. Noted celebrities in attendance included Charlie Hurth (president of the Southern Association), Larry Gilbert, Earl Mann, heavyweight boxing champion Rocky Marciano, and General Bob Neyland.[65] Thereafter, Hub's attendance at OTBA gatherings was more spotty.

In the mid–1950s, Mable Perdue started to experience health issues that affected her aging husband. Known for her gentle spirit, Yankee orderliness in the household, and collector of antique furniture, she began to experience perception difficulties. After one unnerving episode where Mable was disoriented and behaved erratically, Hub had her committed to a care-giving facility in Murfreesboro. The appropriateness of Hub's decision to institutionalize his wife is subject to debate, but the treatment of psychological ailments better known today as dementia or Alzheimer's was in its infancy at the time. And it was not likely that Hub could physically tend to his ailing wife's needs. Given these circumstances, Hub's decision was probably the most humane and practical way to safeguard Mable. His final decision was stressful and fraught with emotion, and Mable's condition brought Hub face-to-face with his own mortality.

Mable Polk Perdue passed away on May 24, 1960, and her death made the front page in both of Gallatin's weekly newspapers.[66] She had been married to Hub for 59 years. Afterwards, Hub gave away many of Mable's prized antiques to relatives. It appears he was "cleaning house." Mable is buried beneath a flat stone marker in the Perdue family section in Lower Bethpage Cemetery next to three of her children and in-laws.

Two weeks after Mable's death, Hub turned 78 years of age. Although he moved slower, he still possessed strong mental faculties. One of his primary diversions from old age and loneliness was listening to Larry Munson's broadcasts of Vols games on WKDA. Gone were the carefree days when he hopped into his automobile and drove over to Donnie's Sweet Shop in Hartsville or took in the horse races. Gone were the days when he strolled around Public Square and fed off the public's adoration kindled by his baseball and political notoriety as well as the days when enthusiastic fans shouted his name from the grandstands in Boston and Wichita Falls and other destinations in between. Gone were the days when friends and neighbors accompanied him on the Inter-Urban trolley to and from Nashville on game day to see him on the slab or in the manager's seat. Hub Perdue, the Gallatin Squash, was now alone.

Chapter 12

Clown Prince of the Mound

It had been a long time since the days of Rub, Dub, Hub and the Tennessee Cyclone, and as Hub's health began to deteriorate in the mid–1960s he found himself in a nostalgic mood. He reminisced about bygone championships and battling Deadball Era legends. A highly publicized gathering of close baseball associates and an award from the OTBA briefly picked up his spirits, as did the opinions of two close journalists. In his last days, two mysteries of Hublore persisted and the truth about them still plagues modern researchers. Hub was luckier than most — he had been able to pander a child's game into a meaningful playing career that lasted almost 20 years, and after his death he remained a cultural figure in literature, stage and song.

There are two ways to wrap up a biography of Hub Perdue; one direction is through an objective analysis of the cold, hard, statistical facts, and the other avenue is a more subjective, or narrative, approach in dealing with his personal accomplishments (sometimes relying upon statistical evidence as well).

The material compiled in the next few pages will appeal to baseballists who want to know how Hub fared against specific opponents and how he compared to other pitchers through sabermetric instruments. These statistics are generated from www.baseball-reference.com as well as contemporary newspapers accounts (box scores). A brief concluding note is provided for each category.

Cumulative Pitching Record versus Southern Association Foes

	1st Tour	*2nd Tour*	*Total*
Atlanta	9–7	4–8	13–15
New Orleans	4–8	1–3	5–11
Memphis	10–9	8–4	18–13
Birmingham	13–9	4–6	17–15

Little Rock	7–4	6–7	13–11
Chattanooga	1–2	7–4	8–6
Mobile	8–5	10–3	18–8
Nashville	X	9–2	9–2
Montgomery	10–11	X	10–11
Shreveport	0–2	X	0–2
Total	**62–55**	**49–37**	**111–92**

Conclusion: Hub pitched well in Alabama, and he posted a winning record against most Southern Association opponents. He struggled against New Orleans despite many close scores.

Neither Perdue's lost season of 1905 in Hopkinsville/Vincennes nor his brief (and final) mound appearances in the 1921 Southern Association are included in the following statistical analysis.

Minor Leagues (1905–1910/1916–1922)

	Years	W-L	IP
in Southern Assoc.	8	111–92	746*
in other circuits	4	57–37	798
Totals	**12**	**168–129**	**1,544**

*Baseball-reference.com has no account of Perdue's statistics for innings pitched in the Southern Association between 1907–1910.

Conclusion: Sheer perseverance alone qualifies Hub, a 14-year veteran of the minors, as an unmistakable Southern iron man.

Cumulative Pitching Record versus National League Foes (1911–1915)

Philadelphia Phillies	6–14
New York Giants	9–8
Brooklyn Superbas	11–5
Chicago Cubs	3–11
Boston Braves	2–3
St. Louis Cardinals	8–6
Cincinnati Reds	7–10
Pittsburgh Pirates	5–7
Total	**51–64**

Conclusion: Hub pitched best in the Big Apple versus New York and Brooklyn, where his 20 victories represents almost 40 percent of his total, but he struggled against two other high-profile squads — the Cubs and Phillies. And he was mediocre against two of the least successful teams — the Reds and Pirates.

Hub posted a winning record versus St. Louis and Cincinnati in 1912 and 1913, New York and Pittsburgh in 1913, and Brooklyn in 1914 and 1915. He dominated the pennant-winning Giants in 1913 with a 5–1 mark in his best single season mark over an individual team in his five years in the majors. Finally, he was unspectacular in confrontations with the greatest National League legends — Grover Cleveland Alexander (1–2), Christy Mathewson (1–3), and Rube Marquard (1–3). Most of these head-to-head encounters were hard fought, and they include several no-decisions. Hub held a slender edge over one respectable Deadball Era opponent, Jeff Tesreau (3–2). The best single month of his National League career (4–0 in April 1912) and worst single month (0–5 in May 1912 and 1915) sent a mixed message. For the most part, Hub's monthly performances were pedestrian and hovered around the .500 mark. His cumulative Major League accomplishments are charted below:

	Years	W-L	GS	IP	ERA
Major Leagues	5	51–64	161	918	3.85

WAR

Within the Society for American Baseball Research (SABR) there are statisticians who have developed a system of numerical analysis to determine the relative worth of an individual player as compared to other players at the same position. The system is called WAR and it calculates the number of victories an individual adds to his team over the course of a season by comparing his output to that of a replacement player — an average AAA player. The sabermetricians interpret the results with the following scale:

8 +	MVP
5 +	All-Star quality
2 +	Major League starter
0 +	reserve (substitute) quality
< 0	replacement

Using the WAR formula it is possible to compute Hub's value to the Braves and Cardinals. Hub's WAR looks something like this:

1911	-.5
1912	2.8
1913	1.1
1914	-1.0 with Boston/ + 1.6 with St. Louis
1915	-1.2
overall	1.9

Conclusion: These figures reveal that Hub's best year in the majors was 1912, and he declined markedly in his final two seasons. Yet, in his most productive year (1913) he registered more victories, posted a lower ERA and surrendered almost one-third fewer hits than in the previous season. Depending on which statistic is valued more, Hub was in his prime in 1912 and/or 1913. Fuel for a good argument! Unfortunately, there are no WAR statistics for the minors to evaluate his comparable worth.

WHIP

There is another statistic to assist sabermaticians in assessing the value of a pitcher — WHIP — or Walks plus Hits per Innings Pitched. Many baseball researchers consider WHIP a more accurate indicator of a pitcher's worth than the traditional ERA. WHIP measurements between 1.0 to 1.25 are considered very good. WHIP below 1.0 is outstanding, and anything above 1.5 is poor. Examine the data for Perdue below:

1906	.75
1911	1.61
1912	1.40
1913	1.13
1914	1.30
1915	1.39
1916	1.10
1917	1.07
1918	1.14
1919	.90
1920	1.24
1922	1.51
1923	1.41

Conclusion: Hub's WHIP confirms what less scientific indicators like subjective sports reports and impressions of managers and players had already surmised: he was a dominant force in 1906 and 1919. He also showed remarkable consistency between 1916 and 1918 as a very good pitcher. In terms of his National League seasons, Hub's cumulative WHIP (1.35) was slightly below average. The pivotal year, 1920, records a sudden drop-off, and by 1922 he is no longer effective on the slab.

Hub's Warm Weather Excuse: Does It Hold Up Statistically?

One of the most oft-repeated aspects of Hublore was Hub's self-scripted excuse that he did not perform well early in the season owing to cold weather. Do the statistics support his allegation? Consider the graphs below:

Graph 1

Month-by-Month in the Minors

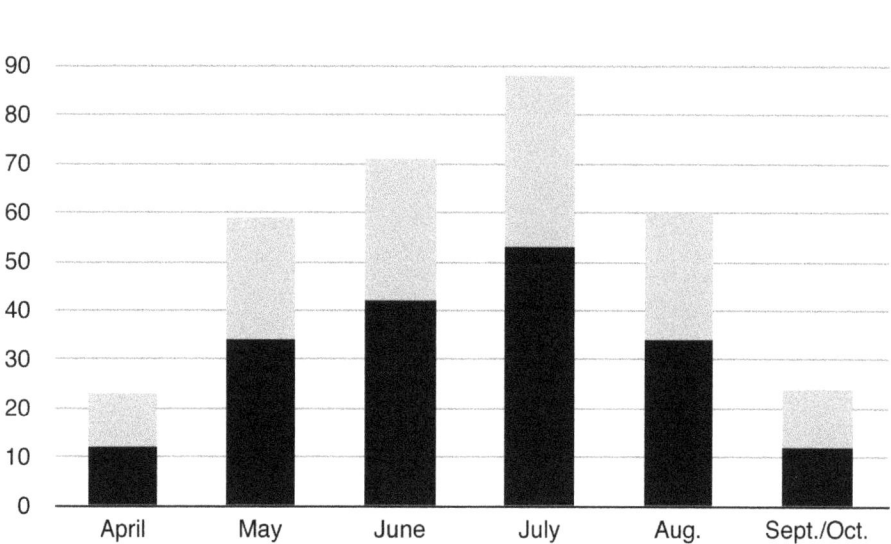

Conclusion: In the minors, Perdue was most effective in the hot summer months when his pitcher-of-record frequency was greatest. As expected, his opportunities in April and May were fewer. But, the startling feature is the similarity between the total number of decisions in the cool springtime of April and May (83) and the hot summertime of August and September (85). Furthermore, Perdue posted the same number of wins in April and September (14), and May and August (34). The total number of losses is practically identical too — April (11) and September (12), and May (24) and August (25). The conclusion to be drawn from this pyramid-shaped graph is that Perdue started and finished slowly in the minors. Do major league statistics confirm these results? Consider the next graph:

Graph 2

Month-by-Month in the Majors

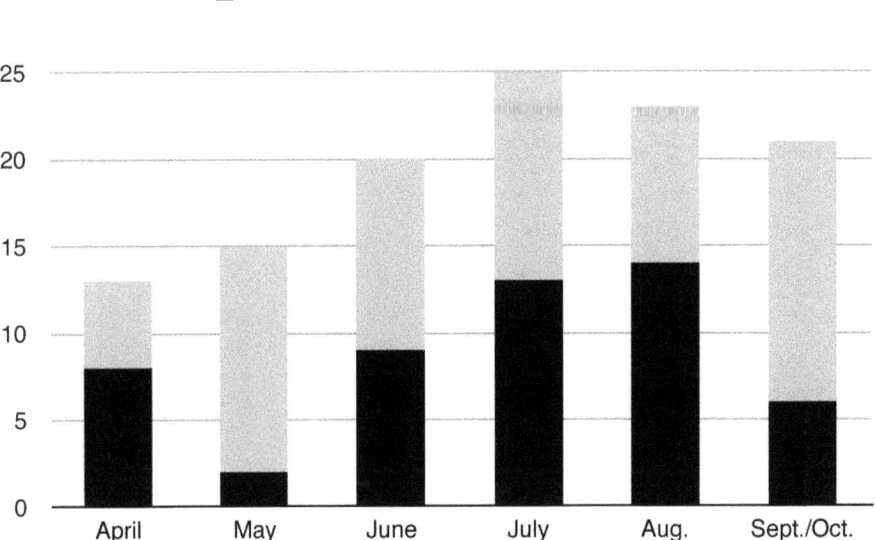

Conclusion: In the majors, Perdue started even slower than in the minors. Similar to his minor league record, Hub's month of May (2–13) practically mirrored September (6–15) in futility. This graph also corroborates Hub's claim that June-July-August were his most successful months, when a majority of his big league victories took place. Combining his major and minor league record over seventeen seasons offers additional insight into his "warm weather" claim. Consider the next graph:

Graph 3

Cumulative Major/Minor Record Month-by-Month

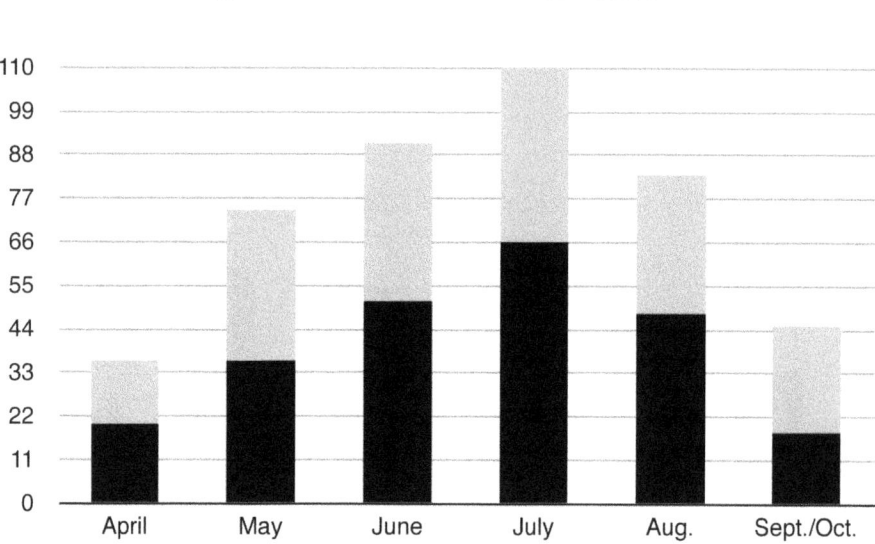

Conclusion: This graph produces a number of unexpected irregularities. First, Perdue actually posted a winning record and percentage in the cool weather month of April (22–16, .578), and nearly so in May (36–37, .493). Second, his winning percentage and mound decisions in the warm weather months of June (50–39, .562) and August (48–34, .585) were practically identical. Third, the Tennessean was at his absolute worst in September (20–27, .425). Fourth, his drop-off in wins during August and September is revealing. These figures do not support Hub's claim that he performed better in warm weather, only that he was involved in more decisions in July (66–44, .600). This combined graph absolutely confirms that Perdue finished his seasons more poorly than he started. An examination of Hub's no-decisions adds a final piece of evidence to this argument. Consider the last graph:

Graph 4

Cumulative Major/Minor Record of "No Decisions" Month-by-Month

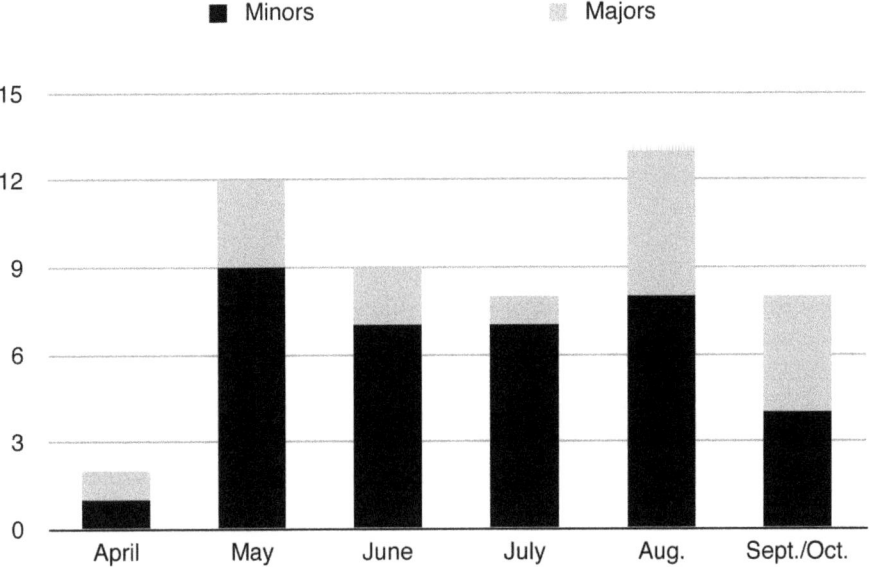

Conclusion: Sometimes the number of wins and losses can be misleading, but not when combined with the non-pitcher-of-record data. First, Perdue was inactive in April, glaringly ineffective in May when afternoon temperatures were beginning to rise, and in August when he probably succumbed to arm weariness. Doesn't Hub's large number of no-decisions in August also challenge his argument that he performed best in the summer heat? Nevertheless, the "warm weather pitcher" myth persists in Hublore, despite the existence of overwhelming statistical evidence to the contrary.

Now, for the subjective (narrative) analysis of Hub's baseball career (with a sprinkling of statistics). Writing in *How Bill James Changed Our View of Baseball*, baseball historian John Thorn concludes, "For a whole generation of fans and fantasy players, stats have begun to outstrip story and that is a sad thing."[1] The rage to analyze baseball through statistics has mushroomed since the mid–1980s, and sabermetricians such as James have assisted many researchers in rethinking traditional views and reshaping our current understanding of the national pastime. That being said, if the numbers overpower other forms of analysis in interpreting careers like the Gallatin Squash's, then Hub's exploits are hardly worthy of our attention. Other than his longevity in the game and his fantastic ERA record in 1919, Hub's overall career was numerically blasé. However, if we scratch beneath the surface of the figures and examine his life, we find that then the baseball world of Hub Perdue is filled with wonderful stories, humorous anecdotes, tall tales, and life lessons.

There is a strong case to be made for Hub's contribution to seven championship teams: Vincennes (1905, 1906), Nashville (1908), Boston (1914), Louisville (1916), New Orleans (1918) and Charlotte (1923). He led championship pitching staffs in victories in Vincennes (25 in 1906) and New Orleans (12 in 1918) and took second place honors in Nashville (16 in 1908). On non-title rosters, he led staffs in Nashville (23 in 1909) and Boston (13 in 1912 and 16 in 1913). In addition, he was the second most effective pitcher in Nashville (11 in 1907), Chattanooga (15 in 1917), and New Orleans (17 in 1919). This illustrates that Hub was an integral member of the pitching staffs on championship and non-championship teams alike, and he usually filled the number one or number two spot in the rotation. In other words, Hub made positive contributions to most of the rosters on which he served up to 1920.

Another argument in support of Hub's value centers on his slab battles against Deadball Era legends as well as personal marks he established. In Perdue's own words, there were three specific baseball events that stand out as personal highlights. First, Hub's greatest memory — the 3–0 win over Mathewson and New York in the Boston home opener in 1912 which established his reputation in the press as a giant killer. The second was his marathon 17-inning performance in Mobile in July 1908. Not only did the no-decision contest earn him a reputation as a southern iron man with grit and perseverance; it also launched his career as a fan favorite in Nashville. Hub's third highlight was the one aspect of his career that requires no embellishment, his miraculous 1.56 ERA record in 1919. According to Hub, the mark stood out as his proudest accomplishment in baseball. It is remarkable how he was able to establish such a feat given his advancing age and long history of arm trouble. The unexplained aspect of the ERA deed makes it all the more intriguing. How did he do it? Perhaps, there will never be a satisfactory answer to this query, thus qualifying it as the biggest unsolved mystery in Hublore.

Several aspects of Hub's five years in the National League will never appear on a stat sheet. First, Hub was absent on 15 occasions for ten days or longer. Today he would be placed on the disabled list. On three separate occasions he missed two months and three times he missed at least one month, the equivalent of more than an entire season. Second, if Hub had been a pitcher under today's pitcher-of-record rules, it would be necessary to make a slight correction to his overall record: + .002 in winning percentages involving over 20 games. Third, if his managers employed modern pitching strategies, Perdue probably would have been converted into a middle reliever no later than 1914 when he still had "good stuff" but rarely exhibited the endurance necessary to complete an entire game.

There is no doubt that Hub contributed to the baseball legacy in upper Middle Tennessee. In Sumner County lore, he is joined on the stage with other pitchers from Gallatin like Bill Chenault and Tom Rogers. Throughout the greater Nashville metropolitan area, Hub also shared the limelight with Jim Turner, George "Noodles" Hahn, Red Lucas and Johnny Gooch. But, every ex-ballplayer living in the area recognized that there was something unique about the Hub.

Shortly after the Southern Association shut down in 1961, the OTBA met in the decaying Sulphur Dell clubhouse to reminisce about "old time baseball." There, emcee Russell entertained the audience with quick-witted anecdotes from Hub's life on the diamond.[2] But, there is no denying that, just as the once great ballyard was falling into disrepair (and would eventually disappear), the 79-year-old Hub Perdue was also fading from Nashville's memory.

Hub began to experience serious health issues in the early 1960s, possibly related to his lifetime habits of smoking, drinking and chewing tobacco as well as being overweight. Of course, those were different times when tobacco use was deeply ingrained in the culture of the South. Once, Hub was admitted to a hospital and his good friend, Hinton, paid him a visit. In a gesture of goodwill that would outrage modern physicians, the newspaperman gifted Perdue a carton of Phillip Morris cigarettes.

Hub resided in the Beene Nursing Home in Hartsville in the mid–1960s. When the octogenarian was too ill to attend the annual OTBA in early 1967, Hub welcomed four very special guests to his bedside. Raymond Johnson recounted the visit in his "One Man's Opinion" column in the Tennessean. Longtime New York Yankees great Jim Turner accompanied former Hub protégé, Red Lucas as well as Clydell "Slick" Castleman, a Tennessean and former pitcher for the Vols and New York Giants in the 1930s. The ex-players reminisced about old-time baseball in light-hearted banter which clearly cheered Hub. Lucas told one humorous story about his former mentor; "Did Hub ever tell you about the time they were having a big celebration in a town near Boston and he thought they were honoring him? And when Hub found out that the name [of the town] was Marblehead, he knew he belonged there."[3] Everyone laughed.

Lucas had turned into a legitimate big leaguer. After spending three years in the minors, he appeared briefly with the New York Giants (three games) before being sent to the Boston Braves in a rule 5 draft in 1924. Two years later he received his big break with Cincinnati. Nicknamed "the Nashville Narcissus," Lucas played eight seasons with the Reds and five more with the

Pirates. His best season was in 1929 when he led the National League in WHIP (1.20), hits per 9 innings (8.9) and complete games (28). He finished second in wins (19), walks per 9 innings (1.9) and WAR (5.4). Lucas received six votes for MVP of the National League. When his career ended, Red boasted fifteen years in the majors with a 157–135 record and 3.72 ERA. By every measure, the former protégé had had a better career than his mentor.[4]

Hub offered several stories of his own at the bedside gathering. "I never did throw no spitter," grinned Hub mischievously with a cigarette pressed firmly between his lips. "I didn't know how."[5] Hub had cleverly forgotten his 1959 admission in the *Nashville Tennessean Magazine* about the finer qualities of the Burnley twist or his run-ins with umpires or the many accounts in newspapers from his playing days that contradicted his assertion. Hub also revealed that Mathewson had refused to show him how to throw his famous fadeaway. "Matty would tell you nothin'," said Hub cagily.

Hub also entertained the party with an argument designed to dispel the belief that he was a terrible batter. Hub retold a story he once shared with Hinton about his alleged weakness in the batter's box. Perdue used a mathematical equation to make his case, and he lampooned that the results of his calculation would prove himself a lifetime .380 hitter. Perdue simply multiplied the number of years he played (19) by his yearly batting average (.020); or, $19 \times .020 = .380$.[6] He concluded, tongue-in-cheek, that he was also a fearsome swatter owing to his famous extra-long bat.

Despite all of the levity, there was a serious undertone to the bedside gathering, which was marred by Hub's obvious physical deterioration. "It was one of those heartwarming affairs," concluded Johnson. As the guests prepared to leave for home Hub's tearstained eyes were clearly visible for all to see. Who knew if they would ever meet again?

Returning to Nashville, Johnson spearheaded a collection drive to purchase a plaque to honor Perdue's service to Nashville baseball with plans to present it to him at the OTBA banquet three weeks later. On February 9, 1967, Russell accepted the award in Hub's behalf—inscribed to "Hubbard" Perdue.[7] The next day, the sportswriter recounted the familiar story of Torkelson dragging Hub to the mound by a rope tied around his neck in New Orleans in his *Sidelines* column in the *Banner*. Unfortunately, the feats of the ballplayer who had plied his trade on the slab at Sulphur Dell almost half a century earlier were fading from the memories of many Nashvillians. Always ones to appreciate a good joke, Russell and Perdue were kindred spirits when it came to sharing humorous anecdotes in front of a crowd. This time, however, it was gallows humor because Hub was dying.

Herbert Rodney Perdue, the ex-ballplayer with "a million dollar arm and a two cent head," passed away on October 31, 1968, on a date set aside for youthful hijinks.⁸ How appropriate for the huckster, Hub! The "Pride of Sumner County," as Rice had once called him, was 86 years old. His funeral attracted a large number of family and friends, and featured one of Hub's favorite hymns, "The Old Rugged Cross." Hub is buried beneath a flat gravestone in the family section of Lower Bethpage Cemetery alongside his wife and infant children. His parents and other family members rest nearby.⁹

Following Hub's death, a second loose end survived in Hublore. Specifically, who had coined one of the most colorful nicknames in baseball history, the Gallatin Squash? The honor historically has gone to Grantland Rice. Remember, the Nashville sportswriter had called Perdue "the Sage of Squashville" in the Tennessean late in the 1910 season just prior to their respective departures to New York City and Boston. But "the Sage of Squashville" is not "the Gallatin Squash." Rice briefly referenced "the Gallatin Squash" in *The Evening Mail* on April 30, 1912, but he did not use the phrase again for the rest of the season. Then, there are the January 2–5, 1913, interviews with Hub in the *Boston Daily Globe* and *Nashville Banner* where the nickname was presented as common knowledge. So, the moniker's origin lay sometime between Rice's departure from Nashville and his passing comment in April 1912. Was Rice the genuine author or was the invention of the Gallatin Squash really steeped in Tennessee's oral tradition? Had Gallatians taken Rice's "Squashville" remark and localized it? Was the catchy nickname a product of the colloquial language of Middle Tennessee but not found in print until 1912? Could Hub have manufactured it himself?

Seven years after Hub's death, E. L. Doctorow published *Ragtime, A Novel*. The award-winning book captured daily life in New York City at the dawn of the twentieth century through the lenses of an African American jazz performer, an affluent middle class family and Jewish immigrants. The classic novel was a wonderful collection of vignettes that successfully captured the social complexities of an emerging modern America. Of course, Doctorow could not ignore the role of baseball and its importance to the bourgeoning new society, and this is where Hub entered his story. In Chapter 30, a father and son trek to the Polo Grounds via trolley to attend a Giants game where Marquard squared off with the blue-flanneled ace of the Boston Braves, Hub Perdue. Doctorow captured the vivid sensations of the afternoon, complete with clouds of cigar smoke drifting into the air, and McGraw's "vile epitaphs" directed toward Perdue. The highlight of the entertaining six-page narrative was a description of two bench-clearing brawls brought about after a spiking incident and a retaliatory beaning.¹⁰

Doctorow added several Braves players into the narrative — Rabbit Maranville, Dick Rudolph, Gene Cocreham, Otto Hess, Butch Schmidt and Herbie Moran. The mentioning of these names allows for a bit of detective work to determine whether the author was referencing a specific game. Perdue had faced Marquard six times throughout his career (1-3-2) but only four times as a member of the Braves. Two of the head-to-head matches had taken place in Boston and St. Louis, and only one of the face-offs in the Polo Grounds contained similarities to Doctorow's account. On September 2, 1912, Labor Day, the two pitchers in question were locked in a 2–2 tie through eight innings in front of 15,000 fans. Mathewson entered in the ninth and he threw four innings of relief. Doyle's three-run home run in the twelfth inning spoiled Hub's spectacular outing. The problem is that only one of the players mentioned by Doctorow was on Boston's 1912 roster—Hess. Maranville debuted with the Braves over one week later (September 10), and Moran did not even join Boston until August 1914, two months after Hub had been traded to St. Louis. From this information, it is safe to say that Doctorow did not use a specific Perdue–Marquard encounter to set the scene in *Ragtime*; instead, he used literary license to create a composite from several Braves–Giants during the years 1912–1914. As Doctorow's novel spawned a Hollywood movie (1981) and a Broadway musical (1996), Perdue was immortalized in popular culture through literature, film, stage and song.

Perdue's longevity as a pitcher of 19 years is impressive. Until his final two seasons when he had turned 40 years of age, Perdue's performance in the minors was at the highest level. But there is little doubt that Perdue failed to live up to his raw talent on the national stage as his eight years in the Southern Association greatly overshadowed his much shorter tenure in the National League. In the end, Hub's happy-go-lucky nature affected a promising career in the Big Show. It has been suggested, however, that his name could have been remembered today in the same breath with some of the great pitchers of the Deadball Era. Said *The Sporting News*: "Baseball experts of Perdue's period said he might have been a great pitcher if he had taken himself and his work more seriously."[11] Writing the *Banner*, Russell later described the Gallatin Squash as "one of the game's gifted comics" who tragically "clowned his way right out of the major leagues."[12] Hinton hit the nail on the head when he called his good friend "a clown prince of the diamond."[13]

In one case, Hub's reputation as a team jester was interpreted differently by a famous contemporary ballplayer. When Honus Wagner wrote a syndicated newspaper piece in the winter of 1915–16, he acknowledged the importance of funny men and their use of humor in the game of baseball. He posited that such humor was an absolute necessity to break up the monotony, tension and stress of a competitive six-month-long season. The Bucs shortstop credited a short list of men who provided this valuable service—Nick Altcock and Germany Schaefer in the American League, and Steve Evans, Rabbit Maranville and Hub Perdue in the National League.[14]

12. Clown Prince of the Mound

In the end, it is impossible to discredit the mischievous nature of Hub Perdue's character. To him, the sport of baseball was an activity to be enjoyed, and if someone wanted to pay him to play it, then so be it. In this sense, Hub was a throwback to a bygone period before the Deadball Era when the game was not a science and it had not yet turned it into a big business. Even in old age, Hub played baseball with a youthful enthusiasm, and he remained unaware of (or disregarded) the monumental changes taking place around him. Whether he plied his craft on the bumpy cow pastures of Sumner County or in the noisy surroundings of Sulphur Dell or in the majestic setting of the Polo Grounds, Perdue conducted himself with a carefree spirit. His lack of self-discipline did not mean that he willfully sought to disrespect the game; rather, it simply indicated that the he played for one primary reason — to have fun. And so he did.

Postscript

Changes to Perdue's record in Baseball-reference.com

While errors in huge statistical databases such as Baseball-reference.com are not uncommon, corrections must take place once new information is uncovered, and such is the case of Perdue's pitching and stolen base record. Consider the following data which is currently missing from Perdue's body of work:

1. **Perdue's 1905 season:**

	W-L	IP	R	H	SO
1905 Hopkinsville (Kitty-D)	11–5	137	22	23	2
1905 Vincennes (Kitty-D)	8–4	116	16	73	50
Adjusted grand totals:	19–9	253	38	96	52

2. **Perdue's 1921 season:**

	GS	W-L	IP	R	H	SO
1921 Nashville (Southern-A)	3	1–1	16.3	12	22	10

3. **Stolen bases:**

Hub stated publicly as late as 1919 that he had never stolen a base. Yet, the record indicates that he swiped one sack in the 1906, 1912, 1917, and 1919 seasons.

A Fitting Tribute

The city of Gallatin, Tennessee is a beautiful community blessed with many fine parks. One large recreation complex contains a cluster of finely manicured baseball fields, and they address the importance of the game to local residents. Wouldn't it be appropriate if one of the diamonds was dedicated to the memory of the home-grown product who pitched in the major leagues a century ago: the pitcher with a quirky nickname who put the city on the baseball map? Perhaps a bronze likeness depicting Perdue's confident air on Opening Day, 1912, with a plaque on a brick base listing his baseball chronology? Such a tribute is befitting of Hub Perdue, the Gallatin Squash.

Chapter Notes

Preface

1. David Maraniss, *When Pride Still Mattered: Lombardi* (New York: Simon & Schuster, 2010 reprint), 295.

Chapter 1

1. For a statistical overview of Hub Perdue's pitching career, see Hub Perdue file, A. Bartlett Giamatti Research Center, National Baseball Hall of Fame Library, Cooperstown, NY; Hubbard Perdue, Player Career Index, *The Sporting News* Archive, St. Louis, MO; *The Baseball Encyclopedia: The Complete and Definitive Record of Major League Baseball*, 9th ed (New York: Macmillan, 1993), 174–75, 178, 182, 1181, 2155; Marshall D. Wright, *The Southern Association in Baseball, 1885–1961* (Jefferson, NC: McFarland, 2002), 122, 124, 132, 140, 187, 191, 197, 199, 208, 214. Useful narrative information can be found in John A. Simpson, *"The Greatest Game Ever Played in Dixie": The Nashville Vols, Their 1908 Season, and the Championship Game* (Jefferson, NC: McFarland, 2007).

2. *Goodspeed's History of Sumner, Smith, Macon and Trousdale Counties* (Nashville: Goodspeed Publishing, 1887), 818.

3. Jay Guy Cisco, *Historic Sumner County, Tennessee with Genealogies of the Bledsoe, Cage and Douglass Families and Genealogical Notes of Other Sumner County Families* (Nashville: Clearfield, 2002 reprint), 34–35; *Goodspeed's History of Sumner County*, 797; Walter T. Durham, *Old Sumner: A History of Sumner County, Tennessee From 1805 to 1861* (Nashville: Parthenon Press, 1972), xi; Dee Gee Lester and Kenneth Calvin Thomson, Jr., *Around Gallatin and Sumner County* (Dover, NH: Chalford, 1998), 6–7.

4. Walter T. Durham and James W. Thomas, *A Pictorial History of Sumner County, Tennessee, 1786–1986* (Nashville: Williams Printing Co., 1986), 7. Durham, was a resident of Gallatin, the Tennessee state historian, and a prolific writer on Sumner County history since the 1970s.

5. Durham and Thomas, *A Pictorial History of Sumner County*, frontmatter, 1–2; *Goodspeed's History of Sumner County*, 800–2; Cisco, *Historic Sumner County*, 4, 12, 15, 37.

6. Walter T. Durham and Glenda Millikan, eds., *Gallatin 200: A Time Line History Celebrating the Bicentennial of Gallatin, Tennessee* (Franklin, TN: Hillsboro Press, 2002), 3–4; Durham and Thomas, *A Pictorial History of Sumner County*, 18–19; *Goodspeed's History of Sumner County*.

7. See L. A. Absher article on Perdue family in *Gallatin News-Examiner*, March 14, 1988.

8. Lee Alton Absher, *Some Early Settlers of Upper Sumner County, Tennessee* (Knoxville: 1966), 30, 37; Durham, *Old Sumner:* ix; Shirley Wilson, *Sumner County, Tennessee: Index to the Loose Records, 1786–1930* (Hendersonville, TN: Richley Enterprises, 1988), 16; Margaret Cummings Snider and Joan Hollis Yorgason, *Sumner County, Tennessee: Cemetery Records* (Owensboro, KY: McDowell, 1981), 11–63; Lester Thomson, Jr., *Around Gallatin*, 7; Byron Sistler, *Sumner County, Tennessee: Bible, Family, and Tombstone Records* (Nashville: Sistler and Associates, 2004), 88–92; Durham and Millikan, eds., *Gallatin 200*, 28; Doug Drake, Jack Masters, and Bill Puryear, *Founding of the Cumberland Settlements: The First Atlas, 1779–1804* (Gallatin, TN: Warioto, 2009), map B-12; *9th U.S. Census, 1870, Sumner County, Tennessee; 1870 U.S. Census: Sumner County, Tennessee (abstract)* (Gallatin, TN: Sumner County Archives, 1995), 120, 122, 126, 133.

9. *Non-Population Census Schedules for Tennessee (1860); 8th Census (1860) for Agriculture; Slave Schedules of the 8th Census (1860), Sumner*

County, Tennessee. For more on the economic and psychological implications connected with loyalty to the Southern Confederacy, see Gavin Wright, *The Political Economy of the Cotton South: Households, Markets, and Wealth in the Nineteenth Century* (New York: Norton, 1978), 144–57; Reid Mitchell, *Civil War Soldiers: Their Expectations and Their Experiences* (New York: Touchstone Books, 1988), 7–8; James M. McPherson, *For Cause and Comrades: Why Men Fought in the Civil War* (New York: Oxford University Press, 1998), 101, 114. Also see Blanche Henry Clark, *The Tennessee Yeoman, 1840–1860* (Nashville: Vanderbilt University Press, 1942); Chase C. Mooney, *Slavery in Tennessee* (Bloomington: Indiana University Press, 1957), 122.

10. Lester and Thomson, *Around Gallatin and Sumner County*, 7–8; *Goodspeed's History of Sumner County*, 801; Walter T. Durham, *Josephus Conn Guild and Rose Mont: Politics and Plantation in Nineteenth Century Tennessee* (Nashville: Hillsboro Press, 2003).

11. Durham and Thomas, *A Pictorial History of Sumner County*, 18–19.

12. Durham, *Old Sumner*, 169.

13. See *Goodspeed's History of Tennessee*, 861.

14. *Goodspeed's History of Sumner County*, 814–15; Durham and Millikan, eds., *Gallatin 200*, 39–42; Lester and Thomson, *Around Gallatin and Sumner County*, 8; Walter T. Durham, *Rebellion Revisited; A History of Sumner County, Tennessee from 1861 to 1870* (Nashville: Parthenon Press, 1982), 152. Eventually, Sumner County produced more than 3,000 soldiers for Confederate service.

15. Durham, *Rebellion Revisited*, 152, 174. Afterwards, McAdams was caught attempting to steal a neighbor's horse, and local ex–Confederates eked out their revenge when the "traitor" was tried, convicted and sentenced to the state penitentiary.

16. *Ibid; 12th U.S. Census (1880);* Era W. Stinson and Elizabeth Sue Spurlock, *Sumner County, Tennessee; Sumner County, Tennessee Marriages, 1839–1875* (Bowling Green, KY: 1985), 101.

17. Snider and Yorgason, *Sumner County Cemetery Records*, 27; *Goodspeed's History of Sumner County*, 911; *12th U.S. Census, 1900, Sumner County, Tennessee; Nashville Banner*, May 20, 1924; Michael Denning, *Death Certificates of Sumner County, Tennessee, 1921–1925* (Nashville: 2000), 8; Lester and Thomson, *Around Gallatin and Sumner County*, 8; Durham and Thomas, *A Pictorial History of Sumner County*, 115–17; Durham, *Old Sumner*, 16.

18. *Goodspeed's History of Sumner County*, 806; Durham and Millikan, eds., *Gallatin 200*, 7, 36, 45; Lester and Thomson, *Around Gallatin and Sumner County*, 81.

19. John David Collier, "Herbert Rodney 'Hub' Perdue," in *Precious Memories* (1999), 41.

20. Durham and Millikan, eds., *Gallatin 200*, 45; Lester and Thomson, *Around Gallatin and Sumner County*, 12, 35, 66.

21. *Prominent Tennesseans, 1796–1938* (Lewisburg, TN: Who's Who, 1940), 84.

22. *Sumner County, Tennessee, Marriage Records, County Clerk's Office*, 1899.

23. At 89 years of age, Horace died on September 25, 1932, and is buried in Oaktown Cemetery. See *Vincennes Sun-Commercial*, September 26, 1932; *Vincennes Post*, September 27, 1932; Knox County, Indiana, Death Indexes, book H-18; W. H. H. Terrell, *Indiana Volunteers, Fifty-first Regiment; Report of the Adjutant General of the State of Indiana*, vol. 5 (1866), 526. U.S. Census, 1910, Indiana.

24. *Gallatin Examiner and Sumner County Tennessean*, May 26, 1960; *Sumner County News*, May 26, 1960.

25. The concept of "cow pasture games" first appeared in Elmer Hinton, "Gallatin Squash," in *Nashville Tennessean Magazine*, October 7, 1945. It was revisited in Collier, "Herbert Rodney 'Hub' Perdue," in *Precious Memories*, 41.

26. Elmer Hinton, *Let's Do Away with August* (Nashville: Impact Books, 1970), 83. In another variation to this story, a hickory limb had been fashioned into a crude bat, and Hub's pitch broke it. See John David Collier, *Tell Me a Story* (1990), 26; Collier, *Precious Memories*, 41–43; Elmer Hinton, "Gallatin Squash"; *NTM*; Jimmy Perdue Interviews, October 11, 17, 2010.

27. For samples of amateur baseball contests in Nashville, see stories throughout the *American* in the summers of 1900–1901. For the remainder of this study, all three Nashville dailies — the *American*, *Banner* and *Tennessean* — will be footnoted in short form.

28. *Banner*, July 3, 1900.

29. *American*, June 2, 1901.

30. *Banner*, July 10, 1900.

31. *Banner*, August 4, 1900, August 25, 1900, August 31, 1900.

32. Don H. Doyle, *Nashville in the New South, 1880–1930* (Knoxville: University of Tennessee, 1985), 43.

33. See John Bibb, "It's All in the Juice," in *Nashville Tennessean Magazine*, August 9, 1959.

34. *American*, June 22, 1901.

35. *Gallatin Examiner*, August 29, 1903.

36. Durham and Millikan, eds., *Gallatin 200*, 45.

37. See Rice's biographical clip of Guild in

Tennessean, May 5, 1909. Later, Guild established a successful law practice and judicial career in Gallatin and Nashville. He died in 1948. See *Banner*, March 15, 1948.
38. *Gallatin Examiner*, September 13, 1902.
39. *Gallatin Examiner*, August 16, 1902.
40. *Gallatin Examiner*, September 13, 1902.
41. *The Tennessean* (Gallatin), May 30, 1903.
42. *Gallatin Examiner*, June 20, 1903.
43. *Gallatin Examiner*, August 29, 1903.
44. See Wright, *The Southern Association in Baseball*, 5–76; Bill O'Neil, *The Southern League: Baseball in Dixie, 1885–1994* (Austin, TX: Eakin, 1994), 1–21; Neil J. Sullivan, *The Minors: The Struggles and the Triumphs of Baseball's Poor Relation from 1876 to the Present* (New York: St. Martin's, 1990), 9.
45. *American*, June 10, 1900; *Banner*, June 12, 1900.
46. Powell, a Pennsylvanian who started his professional career in 1884 and played as far away as Seattle, was known affectionately as "the grand old man" of the Southern Association. He realigned with Atlanta in 1903, but lived in New Orleans. He died there on August 7, 1953 at the age of 92. See Tim Darnell, *Southern Yankees: The Story of the Atlanta Crackers* (1995).
47. *American*, June 14, 17, 1900; *Banner*, June 14, 1900.
48. Wright, *The Southern Association in Baseball*, 77.
49. *Memphis Commercial-Appeal*, October 1, 4, 7, 10, 11, 1900.
50. *Memphis Commercial-Appeal*, October 7, 1900.
51. *American*, October 7, 1900.
52. *American*, October 8, 1900.
53. *American*, October 8, 1900.
54. See S. Derby Gisclair, "The Early Southern Association, 1901–1926." Paper delivered at Third Annual Southern Association of Baseball Conference, Birmingham, AL, April 2006.
55. *Banner*, October 20, 25, 1900; *Memphis Commercial-Appeal*, October 21, 1900; O'Neal, *The Southern League*, 21.
56. *Banner*, November 5, 1900.
57. *Banner*, March 1, 4, 1901. In contemporary literature, Kavanaugh is usually misidentified as "William."
58. For more on Cunningham and the Underwood lawsuit, see John A. Simpson, *S. A. Cunningham and the Confederate Heritage* (Athens: University of Georgia, 1994), 131–45.
59. *American*, April 6, 1901.
60. *Banner*, April 1, 8–12, 22, 23, 30, 1901; *American*, April 1, 1901; Dan Levitt, "Frank 'Noodles' Hahn," in Tom Simon, ed, *Deadball Stars of the National League* (Washington, DC: Brassey's, 2004), 233–34.
61. *American*, May 2, 3, 5–7, 1901; See Doyle, *Nashville in the New South*, 143.
62. *American*, July 24, August 1, 8, 11, September 4, 1901. Head and his successor, Hilary House, were two of the most progressive civic leaders in the state.
63. *Chattanooga Daily Times*, July 16, 30, 1901; *American*, August 10, 1901; O'Neal, *The Southern League*, 14, 21.
64. *American*, September 3, 1901.
65. *American*, September 19, 21, 1901.
66. For a closer look at Nashville's near collapse and Little Rock's desperation drive at the end of the season, see *American*, September 21–26, 1901.
67. *American*, October 4–6, 1901.
68. *American*, August 19, 1901. Successful entrepreneurs of the industrial revolution in the South have been called "New Men," a distinction to separate them from old moneyed families of the antebellum era. See Don H. Doyle, *New Men, New Cities, New South: Atlanta, Nashville, Charleston, Mobile, 1860–1910* (Chapel Hill: University of North Carolina, 1990); Don H. Doyle, *Nashville in the New South*.
69. *American*, October 4–6, 1901.
70. See Snider and Yorgason, *Sumner County Cemetery Records*, 11–27; *Sumner County, County Clerk's Office, Marriage Records*; Byron Sistler, *Sumner County, Tennessee: Bible, Family, and Tombstone Records* (Nashville: Sistler and Associates, 2004 reprint of WPA document), 88–92; *Gallatin News*, April 8, 1905; *14th U.S. Census (1920), Sumner County, Tennessee*.
71. For an introduction to the strengths of the Lost Cause ideology on postwar white Southerners, see Simpson, *S. A. Cunningham and the Confederate Heritage*; John A. Simpson, *Edith D. Pope and Her Nashville Friends: Guardians of the Lost Cause in the Confederate Veteran Magazine* (Knoxville: University of Tennessee, 2003).
72. Hinton, "Gallatin Squash"; Collier, *Precious Memories*, 41.

Chapter 2

1. The KITTY started in 1903 with four entrants from Kentucky (Paducah, Owensboro, Henderson and Hopkinsville), two teams from Tennessee (Clarksville and Jackson), and one team apiece from Indiana and Illinois (Vincennes and Cairo respectively). By 1906, the Kentucky contingent had been reduced to one team (Paducah), and there were Illinois fran-

chises in Jacksonville, Danville and Mattoon-Charleston. After the inaugural season, Tennessee did not boast a team again until 1910.

2. For more on the history and peculiarities of Deadball Era baseball, see Benjamin G. Rader, *Baseball: A History of America's Game* (Urbana: University of Illinois, 1992); Steven A. Riess, *City Games: The Evolution of American Urban Society and the Rise of Sports* (Urbana: University of Illinois, 1989); Steven A. Riess, *Touching Base: Professional Baseball and American Culture in the Progressive Era* (Westport, CT: Greenwood, 1980); Sullivan, *The Minors*; Harold Seymour and Dorothy Seymour Mills, *Baseball: The Early Years* (New York: Oxford University, 1960); David Q. Voigt, *American Baseball*, 3 vols. (Norman: University of Oklahoma, 1966–1983); O'Neal, *The Southern League*; Wright, *The Southern Association*; Marc Okkonen, *Baseball Memories, 1900–1909: An Illustrated Chronicle of the Big Leagues' First Decade* (New York: Sterling, 1992); Lawrence S. Ritter, *The Glory of Their Times: The Story of the Early Days of Baseball Told by the Men Who Played It* (New York: Morrow, 1984 reprint); Tom Simon, ed, *Deadball Stars of the National League* (Washington, DC: Brassey's, 2004); David Jones, ed, *Deadball Stars of the American League* (Dulles, VA.: Potomac, 2006).

3. For more on the colorful sports vernacular of the Deadball Era and its meaning, see Paul Dickson, *The New Dickson Baseball Dictionary* (New York: W.W. Norton, 2009). For background information on early baseball in Nashville during the Southern League (1885–1898), see Skip Nipper, *Baseball in Nashville* (Chicago: Arcadia, 2007), 9, 11; Bill Traughber, *Nashville Sports History: Stories from the Stands* (Charleston: The History Press, 2010), 25–30; Bill Traughber, "The Nashville Seraphs, 1895," in *The National Pastime; A Review of Baseball History* 23 (2003): 57–59.

4. *Paducah Sun*, 6, January 30, 1905.

5. *Paducah Evening Sun*, May 9, 1905. South Kentucky College was founded in 1849 and built on Belmont Hill in Hopkinsville. The institution burned down three times and was renamed McLean College in its later years. It closed in 1914. It is not known whether Hub enrolled in the school as a student.

6. *Gallatin News*, May 6, 1905. Also see *The Reach Official Guide (1906)*, 345; *Spalding's Official Base Ball Guide (1907)*, 252–53.

7. *Hopkinsville Kentuckian*, May 16, 1905.

8. See *Gallatin News*, May 27, June 10, 1905; Bibb, "It's All in the Juice"; Collier, *Precious Memories*, 41.

9. *Hopkinsville Kentuckian*, June 1, 6, 10, 13, 24, 1905.

10. *Hopkinsville Kentuckian*, June 20, 1905.

11. *Hopkinsville Kentuckian*, June 15, July 1, 1905.

12. *Gallatin News*, 1, July 8, 1905.

13. *Hopkinsville Kentuckian*, July 20, 1905. Also see *Vincennes Sun*, July 21, 1905; *Vincennes Capital*, July 20, 1905; *Vincennes Morning Commercial*, July 21, 1905.

14. Gosnell's proposal was ludicrous in that the league had played 50 games prior to dismemberment in late July, and only 20 games in the final five weeks. The "halves" were hardly equal in importance.

15. *Hopkinsville Kentuckian*, July 22, 1905.

16. *Vincennes Capital*, July 20, 1905. Bomar signed with Decatur in the Three-I League. See *Paducah Sun*, July 26, 1905.

17. *Vincennes Morning Commercial*, July 21, 1905.

18. *Vincennes Sun*, June 10, 1906; *Vincennes Capital*, June 10, 1906; *Vincennes Morning Commercial*, June 10, 1906; Peter Morris, "Eddie Kolb," in SABR BioProject.

19. *Paducah Sun*, July 26, 1905. League Park in Vincennes was located on the trolley line down Washington Avenue. The wooden stadium burned down three times and by the 1920s it was known as Fairgrounds Park. It has long since disappeared from the Vincennes landscape but the original site is adjacent to Gregg Park today. See *Vincennes Sun-Commercial*, April ,18 2010.

20. *Vincennes Sun*, July 26, 1905; *Vincennes Capital*, July 26, 1905; *Vincennes Morning Commercial*, July 26, 1905.

21. *Vincennes Sun*, July 29, 1905; *Vincennes Capital*, July 29, 1905; *Vincennes Morning Commercial*, July 29, 1905.

22. *Vincennes Sun*, July 29, 1905; *Vincennes Capital*, July 29, 1905; *Vincennes Morning Commercial*, July 29, 1905.

23. *Vincennes Sun*, August 4, 7, 1905; *Vincennes Capital*, August 4, 7, 9, 1905; *Vincennes Morning Commercial*, August 4, 7, 1905.

24. Quoted in *Vincennes Sun*, August 1, 1905.

25. *Vincennes Sun*, August 4, 1905; *Vincennes Capital*, August 4, 1905; *Vincennes Morning Commercial*, August 4, 1905; *Paducah Sun*, August 4, 17, 1905.

26. *Vincennes Sun*, August 17, 1905; *Vincennes Capital*, August 17, 1905; *Vincennes Morning Commercial*, August 17, 1905.

27. *Vincennes Capital*, August 17, 1905.

28. *Paducah Sun*, August 26, 1905.

29. *Vincennes Capital*, August 17, 1905.

30. *Vincennes Sun*, August 21, 1905; *Vincennes Capital*, August 21, 1905; *Vincennes Morning Commercial*, August 21, 1905.

31. *Vincennes Sun,* August 21, 1905; *Vincennes Capital,* August 21, 1905; *Vincennes Morning Commercial,* August 21, 1905.
32. *Gallatin News,* August 26, 1905.
33. *Vincennes Sun,* August 25, 1905; *Vincennes Capital,* August 25, 1905; *Vincennes Morning Commercial,* August 25, 1905.
34. *Vincennes Sun,* August 28, 1905; *Vincennes Capital,* August 28, 1905; *Vincennes Morning Commercial,* August 27, 1905.
35. *Vincennes Sun,* August 28, 1905; *Vincennes Capital,* August 28, 1905. Both teams disbanded after its conclusion.
36. See Brian Spangle, "A Kitty League Pennant," in *Vincennes Sun-Commercial,* August 31, 2003. Gosnell was the owner of a liquor and cigar shop on Fairgrounds Avenue. See *Elks Bazaar Souvenir* [pamphlet], *Vincennes Lodge No. 291, BPOE* (Vincennes, 1907) in Byron R. Lewis Historical Library, Vincennes University, Vincennes, IN.
37. *Gallatin News,* September 23, 1905.
38. See Hub Perdue, Player Contract Card, A. Bartlett Giamatti Research Center, National Baseball Hall of Fame Library, Cooperstown, NY; Lloyd Johnson and Miles Wolff, eds, *The Encyclopedia of Minor League Baseball,* 1st ed (Durham, NC: Baseball America, 1993), 110; *The Reach Official Guide (1906),* 345; *Spalding's Official Base Ball Guide (1907),* 252–53; *Paducah Sun,* September 13, 1905.
39. The reference to "Igerrotes" is puzzling. Perhaps it is a reference to the native population of Luzon in the Philippines (igorotes) who were in a guerrilla-style insurrection with occupying American forces which continued to rage sporadically in 1906. Or it might have been the closest the newspaper could come to a more defamatory term with a similar pronunciation — idiot.
40. See *Vincennes Daily Sun,* April 14, 23, 27, 1906.
41. *Paducah Evening Sun,* July 13, 1906.
42. *Vincennes Daily Sun,* May 4, 1906.
43. *Vincennes Daily Sun,* May 2, 3, 4, 1906; *Vincennes Capital,* May 2, 3, 4, 1906; *Vincennes Commercial,* May 2, 3, 4, 1906.
44. *Vincennes Daily Sun,* May 4, 1906.
45. *Vincennes Daily Sun,* May 4, 1906; *Vincennes Capital,* May 4, 1906; *Vincennes Morning Commercial,* May 4, 1906; *Paducah Evening Sun,* May 4, 1906.
46. *Vincennes Daily Sun,* May 4, 8, 10, 14, 16, 19, 23, 28, 31, 1906; *Vincennes Capital,* May 4, 8, 10, 14, 16, 19, 23, 28, 31, 1906; *Vincennes Morning Commercial,* May 4, 8, 10, 13, 16, 19, 23, 28, 31, 1906; *Paducah Evening Sun,* May 4, 8, 14, 16, 28, 31, 1906.
47. *Paducah Evening Sun,* May 31, 1906.

48. *Vincennes Capital,* May 21, 1906; *Vincennes Morning Commercial,* May 20, 1906.
49. *Vincennes Daily Sun,* June 30, 1906; *Vincennes Capital,* May 29, June 30, 1906; *Vincennes Morning Commercial,* May 29, June 30, 1906.
50. See *Vincennes Daily Sun,* June 6, 28, 1906; *Vincennes Capital,* June 6, 28, 1906; *Vincennes Morning Commercial,* June 6, 9, 28, 1906; *Paducah Evening Sun,* June 28, 1906.
51. During the streak, Hub mastered Cairo (3–1), swept Paducah and Mattoon twice, split games with Danville, and beat Jacksonville once. See *Vincennes Daily Sun,* May 31, June 6, 11, 13, 20, 21, 23, 25, 28, July 3, 6, 10, 1906; *Vincennes Capital,* May 31, June 6, 11, 13, 20, 21, 23, 25, 28, July 3, 6, 10, 1906; *Vincennes Morning Commercial,* May 31, June 6, 10, 13, 20, 23, 26, 28, 1906; July 3, 6, 10, 1906; *Paducah Evening Sun,* May 31, June 13, 23, 25, 28, July 3, 6, 1906.
52. See *Vincennes Capital,* June 18, 19, July 14, 26, 1906;
53. *Vincennes Capital,* May 10, 1906 reprint from the *Danville Commercial News.* Veatch played baseball professionally from 1884 to 1897. See www.baseball-reference.com.
54. See *Vincennes Daily Sun,* June 21, 1906; *Vincennes Capital,* May 12, 1906; *Vincennes Morning Commercial,* June 20, 1906; *Paducah Evening Sun,* May 4, 1906.
55. See *Vincennes Morning Commercial,* July 6–7, 15, 1906.
56. *Paducah Evening Sun,* July 13, 1906. Also see *Vincennes Daily Sun,* July 13, 1906; *Vincennes Capital,* July 13, 1906; *Vincennes Morning Commercial,* July 13, 1906; *Banner,* April 7, 1907.
57. *Vincennes Daily Sun,* July 18, 1906; *Vincennes Capital,* July 18, 1906; *Vincennes Morning Commercial,* July 18, 20, 1906.
58. See *Cairo Bulletin,* August 4, 1906.
59. See *Paducah Evening Sun,* August 3, 1906; *Vincennes Daily Sun,* August 3, 1906; *Vincennes Capital,* August 3, 1906; *Vincennes Morning Commercial,* August 3, 1906; *Cairo Bulletin,* August 4, 1906.
60. *Paducah Evening Sun,* August 9, 1906; *Vincennes Daily Sun,* August 9, 1906; *Vincennes Capital,* August 9, 1906; *Vincennes Morning Commercial,* August 9, 1906.
61. *Paducah Evening Sun,* August 17, 1906; *Vincennes Daily Sun,* August 17, 1906; *Vincennes Capital,* August 17, 1906; *Vincennes Morning Commercial,* August 17, 1906.
62. See *Paducah Evening Sun,* August 17, 18, 1906; *Vincennes Daily Sun,* August 18, 1906; *Vincennes Capital,* August 18, 1906; *Vincennes Morning Commercial,* August 18, 1906.
63. *Paducah Evening Sun,* August 24, 1906; *Vincennes Daily Sun,* August 25, 1906; *Vincennes*

Capital, August 21, 1906; *Vincennes Morning Commercial,* August 25, 30, 1906.

64. Hub Perdue, Player Contract Card, A. Bartlett Giamatti Research Center, National Baseball Hall of Fame Library, Cooperstown, NY; *Spalding's Official Base Ball Guide (1907),* 252–53; Johnson and Wolff, eds, *The Encyclopedia of Minor League Baseball,* 110–112; *Sporting Life* January 23, February 2, March 2, 9, 1907; *Sumner Examiner-Press,* January 26, 1961; *Paducah Sun,* August 24, September 14, 1906. For more on Chance's successful rebuilding of the 1906–1908 Chicago Cubs, see John Lund, *1908: A Look at the World Champion 1908 Chicago Cubs* (2008); Cait N. Murphy, *Crazy '08: How A Cast of Cranks, Rogues, Boneheads and Magnates Created the Greatest Year in Baseball History* (N.Y.: Collins, 2008). For a novel approach, see Alan Alop and Doc Noel, *The Best Team Ever.*

65. *Vincennes Morning Commercial,* August 25, 1906.

66. *Paducah Evening Sun,* September 2, 1906; *Vincennes Daily Sun,* September 2, 1906; *Vincennes Capital,* September 1, 1906; *Vincennes Morning Commercial,* September 2, 1906.

67. *Paducah Evening Sun,* September 10, 1906; *Vincennes Daily Sun,* September 10, 1906; *Vincennes Capital,* September 10, 1906; *Vincennes Morning Commercial,* September 1,1 1906.

68. *Paducah Evening Sun,* August 24, 1906; *Vincennes Daily Sun,* August 25, 1906; *Vincennes Capital,* August 21, 1906; *Vincennes Morning* Commercial, August 25, 30, 1906.

69. *Spalding's Guide, 1907,* 252. For season statistics presented by league president Gosnell, see *Vincennes Capital,* September 15, 1906; www.baseball-reference.com.

70. *Illinois State Register* [Springfield], September 8, 1906. See *Vincennes Daily Sun,* September 8, 1906.

71. For coverage of the ill-fated barnstorming tour, see *Vincennes Daily Sun,* September 10–20, 1906.

72. *Chicago Daily Tribune,* March 6, 1907. Also see Cindy Thomson, *Three Finger Brown: The Mordecai Brown Story* (New York: Bison, 2009), 100.

73. *Chicago Daily Tribune,* March 9, 20, 22, May 7, 1907.

74. Frank made several unsuccessful bids to purchase Hub's contract from Chance. Perdue balked at the New Orleans trade offer and told Chance that he would rather play closer to home if sent to the minors.

75. *Chicago Daily Tribune,* March 11, 1907.

76. Story reprinted from *Chicago Tribune* in the *Paducah Evening Sun,* March 14, 1907.

77. For more on the trade, see *American* March 28, 1907; *Banner* March 28, 1907; Hub Perdue, Player Contract Card, A. Bartlett Giamatti Library, National Baseball Hall of Fame Library, Cooperstown, NY; *Sporting Life,* April 13, 20, 1907 (hereafter referred to as *SL*). Hub wore the red undershirt throughout his career, a flamboyant fashion statement that matched his colorful personality and style. See *New Orleans Times-Picayune,* May 23, 1920.

78. *Chicago Daily Tribune,* March 28, 1907. Chance shipped Chenault to Louisville.

79. See Wright, *The Southern Association in Baseball,* 117–122.

80. Dobbs went on to establish remarkable managerial numbers in the Southern Association. His careeer spanned 23years with seven different teams. He is second only to Larry Gilbert in all-time wins (1,841), losses (1,453), and winning percentage (. 559). See www.southernassociationbaseball.com/managers; Wright, *The Southern Association in Baseball, 1885–1961,* 121–22; Simpson, "*The Greatest Game Ever Played in Dixie,*" 27.

81. For the complete 1907 roster, see Wright, *The Southern Association in Baseball,* 121–122.

82. Rice emerged as the most recognizable sports writer in the country by the 1920s when his work entered national syndication. He is credited with writing more than 7,000 poems, 22,000 columns, and 1,000 magazine articles by the time of his death in 1954. For more detailed biographical information on Rice's early life and career in Nashville, see Charles Fountain, *Sportswriter: The Life and Times of Grantland Rice* (New York: Oxford University, 1993), 3–7, 33–57, 62–86, 90.

83. *Banner,* March 27, 1907; *American,* March 28–April 17, 1907.

84. *Chicago Daily Tribune,* March 28, 1907.

85. *Banner* April 13, 1907.

86. *Banner* May 4, 1907.

87. *American,* April 23, 1907.

88. *American,* May 9, 1907.

89. *Banner,* May 11, 1907.

90. *American,* May 10, 1907. Also see *SL* May 25, 1907.

91. *American,* May 16, 1907.

92. *American,* May 17, 25, 1907; *Banner,* May 17, 21, 24, 25, 1907.

93. *Banner,* May 25, 1907; *American,* June 11, 1907.

94. *Banner,* June 11, 19, 1907; *American,* June 11, 1907; *SL,* June 29, July 7, 1907.

95. *Tennessean,* June 30, 1907. Also see *SL,* July 20, 1907.

96. *American,* July 13, 1907.

97. *Tennessean,* July 13, 1907.

98. *American,* July 13, 1907; *SL,* July 20, 1907.

99. *Tennessean,* August 1, 2, 3, 1907; *SL,* August 17, 1907; *American,* August 4, 1907.

100. Red Elm Park was originally build in 1896 on rich river bottoms near the Mississippi River. The infield surface rose to a point at the pitcher's slab to improve drainage during heavy rainfall and annual floods, giving the field a turtle shell shape. Located between Jefferson and Madison Avenues and Edgeway and Dunlap streets, the cozy park seated 3,000 patrons. The left field wall rose 424 feet from home plate. The park was rebuilt in 1915 (renamed Russwood) and remodeled in 1921. It burned down in 1960, and today the former location is a medical center. See Simpson, *"The Greatest Game Ever Played in Dixie,"* 76, 261; Benson, *Ballparks of North America,* 224; O'Neal, *The Southern League,* 38, 268; John Guinozzo, *Memphis Baseball* (Memphis: Commercial-Appeal, 1980), 1–4.

101. *Banner,* May 28, 1908.

102. *American,* September 2, 1907; *Banner,* 4 September 1907.

103. *American,* August 7, 1907; *Banner,* August 8, September 2, 4, 1907; *SL,* 24 August 14, September 21, 1907.

104. *Tennessean,* August 31, 1907.

105. *Tennessean,* September 15, 1907. Also see *Banner,* September 16, 1907; *American,* September 16, 1907.

106. *Tennessean,* August 21, 1907.

107. *Tennessean,* September 14, 1907.

Chapter 3

1. *American,* December 29, 1907; *Tennessean,* December 31, 1907; *Banner,* January 1, 1908; *SL,* January 4, 1908; *The Sporting News,* January 9, 1908 (hereafter referred to in short form as *TSN*).

2. See *Tennessean,* September 9, 1908.

3. Simpson, *"The Greatest Game Ever Played in Dixie,"* 65, 68.

4. Nashville Base-ball Association, State of Tennessee, Secretary of State, Charter of Incorporation, Book U-7, 108–109; *Nashville City Directory, 1907;* Doyle, *Nashville in the New South,* 200; Waller, *Nashville, 1900–1910,* 165, 316.

5. Waller, *Nashville, 1900–1910,* 89, 114; *American,* January 25, 1908; *Nashville City Directory, 1908,* 190, 199, 442, 583, 693, 731; *Nashville City Directory, 1909,* 325, 473, 620, 738; *Who's Who in Tennessee: A Biographical Reference Book of Notable Tennesseans of Today* (Memphis: Paul and Douglass, 1911), 408, 450; Ilene J. Cornwell, *Biographical Directory of the Tennessee General Assembly.* 3 vols. (Nashville: Tennessee Historical Commission, 1988), 3: 678–679; Will T. Hale and Dixon L. Merritt, *A History of Tennessee and Tennesseans: The Leaders and Representative Men of Commerce, Industry and Modern Activity,* 4 vols (Chicago: Lewis, 1913), 4: 889–890, 1044; Austin P. Foster and Albert H. Roberts, *Tennessee Democracy: A History of the Party and Its Representative Members— Past and Present,* 4 vols (Nashville: Democratic Historical Association, 1940), 3: 806–811; J. T. Moore, *The Volunteer State, 1769–1923,* 2 vols (Nashville: S. J. Clarke,1923), 2: 778–779.

6. Riess, *Touching Base,* 51, 92–93. Also see Riess, *City Games,* 214; Rader, *Baseball: A History of America's Game,* 85. For more on the important connection between the location of trolley routes and urban expansion in Nashville, Doyle, see *New Men, New Cities, New South,* 190. Also see Michael Benson, *Ballparks of North America: A Comprehensive Historical Reference to Baseball Grounds, Yards, and Stadiums, 1845 to Present* (Jefferson, NC: McFarland, 1989), 14; O'Neal, *The Southern Association,* 37; Darnell, *Southern Yankees,* 14, 47.

7. Philip J. Lowry, *Green Cathedrals: The Ultimate Celebration of all 273 Major League and Negro League Ballparks* (New York: Addison-Wesley, 1992), 184–85

8 . Lowry, *Green Cathedrals,* 184–85; Benson, *Ballparks of North America,* 245; O'Neal, *The Southern League,* 37–39; *The Encyclopedia of Tennessee History and Culture* (Nashville: Rutledge, 1998), 896; Sulphur Dell, Vertical File, William Waller Collection, Special Collections, Jean and Alexander Heard Library, Vanderbilt University, Nashville, TN; Jennifer M. Bartlett and Charles P. Stripling, and Fred. M. Prouty, *Historical and Archaeological Investigations of the Site of the Tennessee Bicentennial Mall, 40DV469, Davidson County* (Nashville: Tennessee Department of Environment and Conservation, Division of Archaeology, 1995), 35–38; Edward Michael Ashenback, *Humor Among the Minors: True Tales from the Baseball Brush* (Chicago: M. A. Donohue, 1911), 148.

9. A tremendous amount of information on Julius Augustus Wiseman was obtained from an eight-hour interview with his three children in 2004. The interviews with Dr. James A. Wiseman, Dr. Donald E. Wiseman, and Mrs. Jeanne Wiseman Groenke were held in Cincinnati, OH, on April 4–5, 2004. Also see Donald E. Wiseman, "Julius Augustus 'Doc' Wiseman (1877–1953): The Hero of the Dell," (unpublished family genealogy). Also consult Darl L. Stephenson, *Headquarters in the Brush: Blazer's Independent Union Scouts* (Athens, OH: Ohio University, 2001); Patricia L. Faust, ed, *Historical*

Times Illustrated Encyclopedia of the Civil War (New York: Harper & Row, 1986), 510–511; Certificate of Death, Julius Augustus Wiseman, Ohio Department of Health; Wright, *The Southern Association*, 63, 70, 78, 84, 96, 101, 109, 115, 121, 124, 131, 140, 145; *The Burnet Woods Echo*, May 10, 24, June 14, 1897, Blegin Library Archives, University of Cincinnati, Cincinnati, OH; James A. Wiseman to John A. Simpson, January 27, February 2, 9, 2004, in possession of the author; Simon, ed, *Deadball Stars of the National League*, 355–357; *Nashville Tennessean and the Nashville American*, July 10, 11, 1912; *Banner*, July 8–11, 1912; Russell, *Vols Feats*, 18; *Cincinnati City Directory, 1909–1927*; J. A. Wiseman to Jim Wiseman, November 12, 1949, and Larry Gilbert to M. C. Saunders, April 15, 1953, in possession of Dr. James A. Wiseman, Cincinnati, OH; *Banner*, April 9, 10, 1953; *TSN*, April 22, 1953.

10. *Tennessean*, April 19, 1908.

11. Ashenback, *Humor Among the Minors*, 148.

12. *Tennessean*, January 14, 1908. For other accounts, see J. D. Brown, "The Name Stuck," *Nashville Tennessean Magazine*, April 12, 1947; Russell, "Grantland Rice Gave It a Name ... Sulphur Dell," *Nashville Magazine* (February 1957); Fountain, *Sportswriter*, 39.

13. *Tennessean*, January 14, 1908

14. *Tennessean*, February 14, 1908.

15. *Banner*, February 15, 1908.

16. Yancey's plea was acknowledged as teams went by standard nicknames beginning in 1908—Atlanta Crackers, Birmingham Barons, Little Rock Travelers, Memphis Turtles (Chicks in 1911), Mobile Sea Gulls, Montgomery Senators, New Orleans Pelicans, and Nashville Vols. O'Neal, *The Southern League*, 85; Wright, *The Southern Association in Baseball*, 123–29.

17. See *Banner*, February 18, 1908; *Tennessean*, February 17, 1908; *American*, February 21, 1908.

18. *Banner*, February 18, 1908.

19. *Tennessean*, February 29, 1908; *Banner*, February 29, 1908; *American*, February 29, 1908.

20. See reprinted version in Fred Russell's "*Sidelines*" column, *Banner*, July 4, 1968.

21. *Tennessean*, April 24, 30, 1908; *Banner*, 24, 30 April 1908; *American*, April 24, 30, 1908.

22. *Tennessean*, June 5, 1908; *Banner*, 5 June 1908; *American*, June 5, 1908.

23. *Tennessean*, July 3, 1908.

24. *TSN*, July 16, 1908.

25. *Tennessean*, July 10, 1908.

26. *Banner*, July 10, 1908.

27. See Fred Russell and George Leonard, *Vols Feats: Records, History, and Tales of the Nashville Baseball Club in the Southern Association, 1901–1950* (Nashville: Banner Press), 40; Simpson, "*The Greatest Game Ever Played in Dixie*," 88, 112.

28. *Tennessean*, July 14, 1908; *Banner*, July 14, 1908; *American*, July 14, 1908; *TSN*, July 23, 1908; *SL*, July 25, 1908.

29. *Tennessean*, July 16, 1908; January 17, 1945.

30. *Tennessean*, August 2, 1908; Simpson, "*The Greatest Game Ever Played in Dixie*," 127–28.

31. *Banner*, August 4, 1908.

32. *Tennessean*, August 4, 1908.

33. Sitton, a Clemson product, had taken spring training with the Vols but returned to Jacksonville. There, the spitballer helped the Jays win the SALLY championship. See Carl Vedder Sitton file, Player Career Index, *The Sporting News Archive*, St. Louis, MO.

34. *American*, August 19, 1908.

35. *Tennessean*, August 24, 1908; *Banner*, 24 August 1908; *American*, August 24, 1908; *TSN*, August 27, 1908; *SL*, August 29, 1908; Simpson, "*The Greatest Game Ever Played in Dixie*," 135–36.

36. *Ibid*.

37. *Tennessean*, August 31, 1908; *Banner*, August 31, 1908; *American*, August 31, 1908; *SL*, September 12, 1908.

38. *Tennessean*, September 1, 1908; *TSN*, 3 September 1908.

39. *Tennessean*, September 4, 1908; *Banner*, September 4, 1908; *American*, September 4, 1908.

40. *Tennessean*, September 4, 1908; *Banner*, September 4, 1908; *American*, September 4, 1908; Simpson, "*The Greatest Game Ever Played in Dixie*," 147.

41. James Warren "Doc" Seabough began his 11-year professional catching career in 1904 with Pittsburg of the Missouri Valley League. A steady backstop, Seabough remained Perdue's battery mate for the duration of his first tour in Nashville. Upon his retirement from baseball, Seabough worked for the St. Louis and San Francisco Railway, organized the Springfield Midgets, and briefly served as president of the Western Association in the 1920s. For more on Seabough, see Simpson, *The Greatest Game Ever Played in Dixie*," 211–12; Harold C. Evans, "Baseball in Kansas, 1867–1940," *Kansas Historical Quarterly* 9 (1940): 175–192; J. Warren Seabough, Player Career Index, *The Sporting News Archive*, St. Louis, MO; Wright, *The Southern Association*, 121, 124, 131, 140, 145, 154, 159; *TSN*, October 23, 1924; Johnson and Wolff, eds., *Encyclopedia of Minor League Baseball*, 163, 165; [Springfield] *Leader and Press*, May 10, 1960; 14th U.S. Census, 1930; *The Frisco Employees' Magazine*, 1925–1935.

42. *Tennessean,* September 6, 1908; *Banner,* September 7, 1908; *American,* September 6, 1908; *TSN,* September 10, 1908; *SL,* September 19, 1908.
43. *American,* September 6, 1908.
44. *American,* September 9, 1908; *Tennessean,* 9 September 1908.
45. *Tennessean,* September 11, 1908.
46. *Tennessean,* September 11, 1908.
47. *Tennessean,* September 17, 1908. For other results, see *Banner,* September 17, 1908; *American,* September 17, 1908; *TSN,* September 24, 1908; *SL,* September 26, 1908.
48. For detailed summation of team statistics, see Simpson, "*The Greatest Game Ever Played in Dixie,*" 156–158. Duggan's contribution included a no-hitter against Little Rock on September 10, 1908.
49. *Banner,* September 17, 1908.
50. *Tennessean,* September 21, 1908.
51. *Banner,* September 17, 1908.
52. *Tennessean,* September 18, 1908; *Banner,* September 18, 1908; *American,* September 18, 1908.
53. *Tennessean,* September 18, 1908.
54. *Tennessean,* September 19, 1908; *Banner,* September 19, 1908; *American,* September 19, 1908.
55. *Tennessean,* September 19, 1908; *American,* September 19, 1908.
56. *Tennessean,* September 1,9 1908.
57. *Memphis Commercial-Appeal,* September 1,9 1908.
58. *Tennessean,* September 20, 21, 1908; *American* September 19, 20, 1908; *Banner,* September 20, 21, 1908.
59. *Tennessean,* September 20, 1908; *American* September 19, 20, 1908; *Banner,* September 20, 21, 1908.
60. *Tennessean,* September 20, 21, 1908. Alf Williams, the president of the Harris-Davis Company, was the most visible booster in the Sulphur Dell grandstands throughout the summer. See *Nashville City Directory, 1909* (Nashville: Marshall, Bruce and Polk, 1909), 1215.
61. *Banner,* September 20, 1908.
62. *Banner,* September 20, 1908; Simpson, "*The Greatest Game Ever Played in Dixie,*" 167. Larry Gilbert, a friend of Tarlton, confides that the first baseman never forgot his costly base running mistake that potentially cost the Pelicans the pennant. See *Banner,* September 9, 1948. On the other hand, Daubert claims that McElveen's effort was the best defensive play he ever witnessed. See Jake Daubert, "The Greatest Play I Ever Saw," *Baseball Magazine* (August 1911), 15.

63. *Banner,* September 20, 1908; *Tennessean,* September 21, 1908; *American,* September 20, 1908.
64. *Banner,* September 21, 1908.
65. *Peoria Journal,* March 21, 1952.
66. *Banner,* September 20, 1908; *Tennessean,* September 20, 1908; *American,* September 20, 1908.
67. *Banner,* September 20, 1908; *Tennessean,* September 20, 1908; *American,* September 20, 1908.
68. See Wright, *The Southern Association in Baseball,* 339–40. For detailed play-by-play of the championship game prepared by the team's official scorekeeper (Yancey), see *Banner,* September 21, 1908.
69. *Banner,* September 21, 1908.
70. *American,* September 20, 1908.
71. *Tennessean,* September 20, 1908.
72. *Tennessean,* September 22, 1908.
73. See Simpson, "*The Greatest Game Ever Played in Dixie,*" 189–191.
74. *Tennessean,* May 13, 1962.

Chapter 4

1. *Tennessean,* March 1, 1909.
2. Doyle, *Nashville in the New South, 1880–1930,* 165. For more information on House, see Moore, *Tennessee,* vol. 3, 866–69; Hale and Merritt, *A History of Tennessee and Tennesseans,* vol. 4, 992; *Who's Who in Tennessee: A Biographical Reference Book of Notable Tennesseans of Today.*
3. Doyle, *Nashville in the New South,* 165–71.
4. *Tennessean,* March 12–14, 1909. Also see *Banner,* March 12–13, 1909; *American,* March 12–15, 1909.
5. *American,* March 14, 1909.
6. *Banner,* March 18, 1909. Yancey had resigned to take a similar position in Chattanooga. Jones started his career in journalism as a cub reporter for the *American.* He moved to the *Banner* to accept the new position of sports editor, but assumed other department duties shortly thereafter. Jones left the newspaper after 25 years of service and launched the Tennessee Legislative Service, a daily summation of the activities of the General Assembly. He died in 1937. See *Banner,* January 6, 1937.
7. *American,* March 14, 1909.
8. *American,* March 25, 1909.
9. *Tennessean,* March 19, 1909; *Banner,* March 19, 1909; *American,* March 19, 1909.
10. *Banner,* April 1, 1909.
11. *Tennessean,* March 27, 31, 1909; *American,* March 27, 31, 1909; *Banner,* March 27, 31, 1909.

12. *Tennessean,* April 5, 1909.
13. *American,* March 25, 1909.
14. *Tennessean,* April 9, 1909; *American,* April 9, 1909; *Banner,* April 9, 1909.
15. *Tennessean,* April 14, 1909.
16. *Tennessean,* April 11, 1909; *American,* April 15, 1909; *Banner,* April 13–14, 1909.
17. *American,* April 16, 1909.
18. *American,* April 10, 1909; *Banner,* April 10, 1909.
19. *Tennessean,* April 16, 1909; *American,* April 16, 1909; *Banner,* April 16, 1909.
20. *Tennessean,* April 17, 1909. Also see *Tennessean,* April 17, 1909; *American,* April 17, 1909; *Banner,* April 17, 1909; *SL,* April 24, 1909.
21. *Banner,* April 27, 1909.
22. *Tennessean,* April 22, 1909; *American,* April 22, 1909; *Banner,* April 22, 1909; *SL,* May 1, 1909.
23. For more on these events, see Simpson, "The Greatest Game Ever Played in Dixie," 179; James Summerville, *The Carmack-Cooper Shooting: Tennessee Politics Turned Violent* (Jefferson, NC: McFarland, 1993); Simpson, *S. A. Cunningham and the Confederate Heritage,* 146–49.
24. *Tennessean,* April 26, 1909. For other accounts of Hub's recent success, see *American,* April 27, 1909; *Banner,* April 27, 1909; *SL,* May 8, 1909.
25. *Tennessean,* April 28, 1909.
26. *Tennessean,* May 5, 1909.
27. *Tennessean,* May 9, 1909.
28. *Tennessean,* May 9, 1909.
29. *American,* May 7, 1909. For the leaked story, see *Banner,* May 5, 1909.
30. See Hinton, "Gallatin Squash."
31. *Tennessean,* May 11, 1909; *American,* 11 May 1909; *Banner,* May 11, 1909; *SL,* May 15, 1909.
32. *Banner,* May 11, 1909.
33. *Tennessean,* May 11, 1909.
34. *Banner,* May 25, 1909. For details of the game, see *Tennessean,* May 25, 1909; *American,* May 25, 1909; *SL,* June 6, 1909.
35. *Banner,* May 28, 1909.
36. Wright, *The Southern Association in Baseball,* 132, 136.
37. *Tennessean,* June 14, 1909; *American,* June 14, 1909; *Banner,* June 14, 1909; *SL,* June 26, 1909.
38. *Tennessean,* July 4, 1909.
39. *Tennessean,* July 8, 1909.
40. *Banner,* July 24, 1909.
41. *American,* June 27, 1909.
42. *Banner,* June 1, 1909.
43. *American,* July 18, 1909.
44. *Tennessean,* August 18, 1909. Also see *American,* August 18, 1909; *Banner,* August 18, 1909. "Vinegar Dan" or "Old Dan" Pfenninger began his Southern Association career calling balls and strikes in 1903. He remained with the league for over 20 years, and was later named one of the league's best arbiters of all time. See *TSN,* November 6, 1924, April 6, 1935.
45. *Tennessean,* July 18, 1909. For other reports of the game, see *American,* July 18, 1909; *Banner,* July 18, 1909; *SL,* July 3,1 1909.
46. *Tennessean,* August 11, 1909; *American,* 11 August 1909; *Banner,* August 11, 1909; *SL,* July 31, 1909.
47. See *Tennessean,* July 22, 29, 1909; *American,* July 22, 29, August 10, 1909; *Banner,* July 22, 29, 1909; *SL,* August 7, 1909.
48. *Tennessean,* August 13, 1909; *American,* August 13, 1909; *Banner,* August 13, 1909; *SL,* August 21, 1909.
49. *Tennessean,* August 15, 1909; *American,* August 15, 1909; *Banner,* August 16, 1909; *SL,* August 28, 1909.
50. *Banner,* August 20, 1909.
51. *Tennessean,* September 1, 1909; *American,* September 1, 1909; *Banner,* September 1, 1909; *SL,* September 18, 1909
52. *Tennessean,* September 10, 1909; *American,* September 10, 1909; *Banner,* September 10, 1909; *SL,* September 18, 1909.
53. *Tennessean,* September 14, 1909; *American,* September 14, 1909; *Banner,* September 10, 1909; *SL,* September 18, 1909.
54. *American,* September 20, 25, 1909.
55. See *American,* July 22, 1909.
56. *Tennessean,* February 22, 23, 1910.
57. See Harry "Steamboat" Johnson, *Standing the Gaff: The Life and Hard Times of a Minor League Umpire* (New York: Bison, 1994 reprint), 129. Goldsmith's Sons frequently advertised in *Baseball Magazine.*
58. *Tennessean,* February 24, 1910; *Banner,* February 8, 17, 24, 1910.
59. *Tennessean,* March 2–6, 1910; *Banner,* 17 March 1910.
60. *Tennessean,* March 15, 1910; *Banner,* 15–16 March 1910.
61. *Banner,* March 18, 23, 1910.
62. See *Tennessean,* March 24–25, 1910; *Banner,* March 19, 1910.
63. *Tennessean,* March 29, April 2, 6, 10, 1910; *Banner,* March 29, April 2, 6, 11, 1910; *American,* March 29, April 2, 6, 10, 1910.
64. *American,* April 25, 1910.
65. *Tennessean,* April 18, 22, 1910; *Banner,* April 18, 22, 1910; *American,* April 18, 22, 1910; *SL,* April 30, 1910.
66. *Tennessean,* May 27, 1910.
67. *American,* April 21, 1910.
68. *Tennessean,* April 26, 29, 1910; *Banner,*

April 26, 1910; *American,* April 29, 1910; *SL,* May 7, August 13, 1910. For more on Doc White, see *Tennessean,* July 7, 1910.

69. *Tennessean,* May 3, 1910. Also see *Banner,* 3 May 1910; *American,* May 3, 1910; *SL,* May 14, 1910.
70. *Banner,* May 5, 1910.
71. *Tennessean,* May 27, 1910; *Banner,* May 27, 1910; *American,* May 27, 1910.
72. *Tennessean,* May 28, 1910; *American,* July 2, 1910; *SL,* June 25, 1910.
73. *Tennessean,* June 22, 1910; *Banner,* June 22, 1910; *American,* June 22, 1910; *SL,* July 10, 1910.
74. *Tennessean,* July 1, 1910. Also see *Banner,* July 1, 1910; *American,* July 1, 1910; *SL,* July 10, 1910.
75. Game results for the period between May 19–July 19 were as follows: @ Mobile 1–0/@ Montgomery 0–2/Mobile 2–1/Chattanooga 0–2/Atlanta 0–1/Birmingham 1–0/Montgomery 1–0/Mobile 6–0/@ Birmingham 2–0.
76. *Tennessean,* July 7, 10, 1910; *Banner,* July 7, 11, 1910; *American,* July 7, 10, 1910; *SL,* July 16, 23, 1910.
77. *Banner,* July 11, 1910.
78. *Tennessean,* July 16, 1910; *Banner,* July 16, 1910; *American,* July 16, 1910; *SL,* July 23, 1910.
79. *Banner,* July 20, 1910. The Vols stacked their equipment and prepared for a five-city road swing while an African American women's baseball team arrived at Union Station from St. Louis. The Broncho Bloomer Girls were scheduled to play in Sulphur Dell against the Nashville Giants—a men's squad of the same race—in "the first [transgender] game of its kind," according to Johnson. See *American,* July 20, 1910.
80. *Tennessean,* July 24–26, 1910; *Banner,* July 25, 1910; *American,* July 24–25, 1910; *SL,* August 6, 1910.
81. *Tennessean,* August 11, 1910; *Banner,* August 1, 1 1910; *American,* August 11, 1910; *SL,* August 20, 1910.
82. *Tennessean,* August 14, 1910.
83. *Tennessean,* August 18, 22, 1910; *Banner,* August 18, 22, 1910; *American,* August 18, 22, 1910; *SL,* August 27, September 3, 1910.
84. *American,* September 1, 1910.
85. *Tennessean,* September 2, 1910.
86. *Tennessean,* September 2, 3, 1910; *Banner,* September 2, 3, 1910; *American,* September 2, 3, 1910; *SL,* September 10, 1910.
87. *Tennessean,* September 11, 1910; *Banner,* September 11, 1910; *American,* September 11, 1910; *SL,* September 24, 1910.
88. Wright, *The Southern Association in Baseball,* 137–142.
89. *Tennessean,* September 19, 1910; *Banner,* September 19, 1910; *American,* September 18, 1910.
90. *Tennessean,* September 24, 1910.
91. *Tennessean,* September 24, 1910.
92. *Tennessean,* September 25, 1910. Bernhard made Memphis his official residence for most of the decade.
93. *Tennessean and American,* September 29, 1910; *Banner,* September 29, 1910.
94. *Banner,* June 6, 1910.
95. *Banner,* September 23, 1910.
96. See ex-president Kuhn's open letter to the public in *Tennessean and American,* March 8, 1911. For national coverage of the confusing episode, see *SL,* October 22, 29, November 5, 1910. Hub Perdue, Player Contract Card, National Baseball Hall of Fame Library, Cooperstown, NY.
97. See the first edition of the *Nashville Tennessean and American,* September 26, 1910. Also see *American,* September 25, 1910.
98. See James K. Skipper, Jr., *Baseball Nicknames: A Dictionary of Origins and Meanings* (Jefferson, NC: McFarland, 1992), 216.
99. *Tennessean and American,* December 14, 1910.
100. See Wright, *The Southern Association in Baseball,* 132.
101. Nashville played its first doubleheader on April 21, 1909. Rice called the games "a historic double decker." See *Tennessean,* April 22, 1909.
102. *Tennessean,* May 13, 1962.
103. See *SL,* July 2, 1910.
104. See last chapter for breakdown of Hub's overall career in the Southern Association.

Chapter 5

1. *SL,* October 22, 1910, January 14, 1911; *Boston Daily Globe,* January 3, 1911; www.retrosheet.org.
2. Philip J. Lowry, *Green Cathedrals: The Ultimate Celebration of Major League and Negro League Ballparks* (New York: Walker & Company, 2006), 26. Today, the field's location is occupied by the Orange Line of the MBTA.
3. See Harold Kaese, *The Boston Braves, 1871–1953* (Boston: Northeastern University, 2004 reprint), 115. Kaese, a sportswriter and columnist in Boston for over 40 years, originally wrote the book in 1948 to commemorate the Braves' first World Series in 34 years. Ironically, the Braves played the Indians.
4. Kaese, *The Boston Braves, 1871–1953,* 122–24.
5. Mark Sternman, "Fred Tenney," in Tom Simon, ed, *Deadball Stars of the National League* (Washington, DC: Brassey's, 2004), 309–310.

6. In 1920, McTigue passed away in Nashville at age 29. See www.baseball-reference.com; www.retrosheet.org.
7. *Boston Daily Globe,* March 14, 1911.
8. *Boston Daily Globe,* March 16, 1911.
9. For a useful treatment of Alexander, see John C. Skipper, *Wicked Curve: The Life and Troubled Times of Grover Cleveland Alexander* (Jefferson, NC: McFarland, 2006).
10. *Boston Daily Globe,* April 22, 1911. Throughout Perdue's career in the National League, Daubert had great success against him not only at bat but also in the stolen base department. Daubert joined Joe Tinker of the Cubs and Fred Snodgrass of the Giants as the most successful hitters against Perdue in 1911, all going 4–10. See www.retrosheet.org.
11. *Boston Daily Globe,* May 12, 1911.
12. *Boston Daily Globe,* May 20, 1911.
13. *Boston Daily Globe,* June 24, July 8, 1911.
14. *Boston Daily Globe,* July 13, 16, 1911.
15. See www.retrosheet.org.
16. See *Boston Daily Globe,* May 20, 1911; Tom Ruane, "The Deadball Era's Worst Pitching Staff," *The Baseball Journal* (Fall 2009): 131–36.
17. See *Boston Daily Globe,* August 13, 18, 22, 24, 1911.
18. *Boston Daily Globe,* July 1, 1911.
19. *Boston Daily Globe,* September 13, 1911.
20. *Boston Daily Globe,* October 3, 1911; www.retrosheet.org.
21. *Boston Daily Globe,* October 15, 1911.
22. www.baseball-reference.com.
23. Kaese, *The Boston Braves, 1871–1953,* 128–29.
24. Kaese, *The Boston Braves, 1871–1953,* 129
25. See www.baseball-reference.com; www.retrosheet.org.
26. *Boston Daily Globe,* February 18, 1912.
27. See Charles Cutter, *Cutter's Guide to the Hot Springs of Arkansas* (Charleston: Nabu Press, 2010 reprint); Dee A. Brown, *The American Spa: Hot Springs Arkansas* (Little Rock: Rose, 1982); *Boston Daily Globe,* February 28, March 1, 1912.
28. *Boston Daily Globe,* March 1, 1912.
29. *Boston Daily Globe,* April 7, 1912.
30. David Anderson, "Johnny Kling," in Tom Simon, ed, *Deadball Stars of the National League,* 95. Also see Gil Bogen, *Johnny Kling: A Baseball Biography* (Jefferson, NC: McFarland, 2006).
31. *Boston Daily Globe,* April 12, 1912.
32. *Boston Daily Globe,* April 16, 1912. Hub's exciting victory over the Giants coincided with front page headlines announcing the tragic sinking of the *Titanic.*
33. *Boston Daily Globe,* Apri l21, 1912.
34. See *Boston Daily Globe,* May 8, 11, 17, 22, 26, 29, 1912.
35. *Boston Daily Globe,* June 12, 1912.
36. www.retrosheet.org; Baseball Encyclopedia, 2155.
37. See *SL,* July 6, 1912.
38. *Boston Daily Globe,* June 22, 1912; Marquard went on to win 19 straight games, a modern record. He earned four victories against the Braves. See Kaese, *The Boston Braves, 1871–1953,* 130.
39. Hinton, "Gallatin Squash"; *Gallatin News-Examiner,* October 25, 1991.
40. *Boston Daily Globe,* June 26–28, 1912; *SL,* July 6, 1912. Also see *Tennessean,* January 20, 1913.
41. *Boston Daily Globe,* July 6, 1912.
42. *Boston Daily Globe,* August 18, 20, 1912. Also see Hub Perdue, Player Contract Card, National Baseball Hall of Fame Library, Cooperstown, NY. In the immediate aftermath of his signing the new contract, Hub defeated Cincinnati to even his record at 11–11, the first time he had reached the .500 mark since May 22. See *Boston Daily Globe,* August 22, 1912.
43. *Boston Daily Globe,* July 9, 1912; *SL,* July 6, 1912, September 7, 1912.
44. *SL,* September 7, 1912. Also see Kaese, *The Boston Braves, 1871–1953,* 131.
45. *Boston Daily Globe,* July 28, 1912.
46. See *New York Times,* September 8, 1912; David L. Fultz, "The Baseball Players Fraternity," in *Baseball Magazine* (May 1913): 69–72; Brian McKenna, "David L. Fultz," in SABR BioProject. The Fraternity was an early version of the current Major League Baseball Players Association.
47. *Boston Daily Globe,* September 3, 1912.
48. *Banner,* October 17, 1912.
49. *Boston Daily Globe,* January 3, 21, 1913.
50. *Boston Daily Globe,* January 13, 1913.
51. *Banner,* January 3, 1913. Spick Hall mirrored Nye's mention of the new moniker in his *Maelstrom of Sports* column in the *Nashville Tennessean and Nashville American.*
52. *Boston Daily Globe,* January 13, 1913. On the newspaper front, T. H. Murnane turned over the Boston Braves beat to James C. O'Leary, Jr.
53. As a player, Stallings put in time with the Toronto Canucks and Birmingham Ironmakers (1887), Stockton and Galveston Giants (1888), Oakland Colonels and Toledo Black Pirates (1889), Hartford and Brooklyn Bridegrooms (1890), and San Jose Dukes (1891–1892). See www.baseball-reference.com.
54. *TSN,* November 15, 1961.
55. See Martin Kohout, "George Stallings," in Simon, ed, *Deadball Stars of the National League,* 323–24; Kaese, *The Boston Braves, 1871–1953,* 136–38.
56. *Tennessean,* January 20, 1913.

57. Dennis Auger, "Joseph Connolly," in Simon, ed, *Deadball Stars of the National League*, 329–30; Dick Leyden, "Walter 'Rabbit' Maranville," Simon, ed, *Deadball Stars of the National League*, 320–22.
58. See Kohout, "Stallings," in Simon, ed, *Deadball Stars of the National League*, 324.
59. *Boston Daily Globe*, February 16, 1913.
60. See Walter "Rabbit" Maranville, *Run, Rabbit, Run; The Hilarious and Mostly True Tales of Rabbit Maranville* (Phoenix: SABR, 2012 reprint), 13
61. See *Boston Daily Globe*, March 15, 1913.
62. See *Boston Daily Globe*, March 22, 27, April 1, 6, 1913.
63. *Boston Daily Globe*, April 11, 1913.
64. *New York Times*, April 11, 1913.
65. *Boston Daily Globe*, April 18, 1913.
66. *Philadelphia Evening Star*, April 14, 1913.
67. *Philadelphia Evening Star*, April 14, 1913.
68. *Boston Daily Globe*, April 20, 1913.
69. *Boston Daily Globe*, June 15, 1913.
70. *The Upper Sumner Press*, April 30, 1943.
71. *Boston Daily Globe*, June 18, 1913.
72. *Boston Daily Globe*, June 26, 1913. Harry Coveleski is generally considered the first of the "Giant-Killers" for defeating New York three times in five days in 1908. See Ed Rose, "Pop Kelchner, Gentleman Jake, The Giant-Killer, and the Kane Mountaineers," in *The Baseball Research Journal* 41 (Spring 2012): 47–48.
73. *Boston Daily Globe*, July 8, 1913.
74. *Boston Daily Globe*, July 15, 1913.
75. *Boston Daily Globe*, July 9, 1913. Hub batted only .104 and ranked 175 out of 183 pitchers in 1913 with only seven base hits. See *Boston Daily Globe*, December 1, 1913.
76. *St. Louis Daily Globe-Democrat*, September 12, 1914.
77. The story first appeared in *St. Louis Daily Globe-Democrat*, September 12, 1914. Also see *Baseball Magazine* (August 1945): 308; Simpson, "The Greatest Game Ever Played in Dixie," 220–21. Hub Perdue file, A. Bartlett Giamatti Research Center, Cooperstown, NY; Hubbard Perdue, Player Career Index, *The Sporting News Archive*, St. Louis, MO; *TSN*, November 16, 1968; *Banner*, November ,1 1968. Moving from one side of the plate to the other side was not exactly foreign to the National League. In fact, Pat Ragan, a pitcher for Brooklyn employed the same batting strategy against the Braves in April 1914. Did manager Wilbert Robinson flip out? See *New York Tribune*, April 19, 1914.
78. Thirty years later, Hub offered a variation to the story claiming that the event took place not against Pittsburgh but rather on a larger stage versus Jeff Tesreau and the New York Giants in the Polo Grounds. See *TSN*, November 11, 1944; *Banner*, November 2, 1944.
79. www.retrosheet.org; *Baseball Encyclopedia*, 2155.
80. *Boston Daily Globe*, August 9, 1913.
81. *Boston Daily Globe*, August 15, 24, 29, September 11, 20, 1913.
82. *Boston Daily Globe*, September 20, 1913.
83. *Boston Daily Globe*, August 19, 1913.
84. *Boston Daily Globe*, September 7, 1913.
85. *Boston Daily Globe*, September 25, 1913.
86. *Boston Daily Globe*, September 30, 1913.
87. www.retrosheet.org; *Baseball Encyclopedia*, 2155.
88. www.retrosheet.org; *Baseball Encyclopedia*, 2155.
89. Hub claimed to have received overtures from the Chicago and Pittsburgh franchises in the Federal League. See *SL*, February 7, 1914.
90. Kaese, *The Boston Braves, 1871–1953*, 143.
91. *SL*, February 7, 1914. The tour visited 27 American cities where a combined 100,000 fans were treated to 31 games. The 34-day tour also went overseas to 13 countries. In all, the party traveled over 30,000 miles. See, James E. Elfers, *The Tour to End All Tours: The Story of Major League Baseball's 1913–1914 World Tour* (Lincoln: University of Nebraska, 2003). Also see Charles C. Alexander, *John McGraw* (Lincoln: University of Nebraska, 1995).
92. Bibb, "It's All in the Juice"; *NTM*; Miscellaneous clipping by John Oliver, Trousdale Historical Society, Hartsville, TN, in Jimmy Perdue Family Collection; Collier, *Tell Me a Story*, 42.
93. *Boston Daily Globe*, September 30, 1913.
94. *Boston Daily Globe*, January 21, 1914; *SL*, February 21, 1914. Evidence on the back of Hub's 1912 baseball card indicates that Marion Perdue managed the bank office.
95. *SL*, February 7, 1914.
96. *Boston Daily Globe*, February 15, 1914.
97. *Boston Daily Globe*, February 12, 1914.
98. See *New York Tribune*, February 12, 14, 1914.
99. Photographs, *Baseball Magazine* (May 1914): front matter.
100. *SL*, March 5, 1914.
101. *Boston Daily Globe*, February 13, 1914; *Tennessean*, 12 February 1914.
102. *Boston Daily Globe*, February 16, 1914.
103. *Boston Daily Globe*, March 13, 1914.
104. *New York Tribune*, February 13, March 7, 12, 1914.
105. Gessler (1880–1924) lasted only 11 games at the helm of Pittsburgh. He returned home to

establish a successful medical practice. See Bill Nowlin, "Doc Gessler," in SABR BioProject.
106. *Boston Daily Globe,* March 19, 1914.
107. *Boston Daily Globe,* March 21, 22, 1914; *Atlanta Constitution,* March 21, 1914.
108. *Boston Daily Globe,* March 21, 22, 1914; *Atlanta Constitution,* March 21, 1914.
109. *Baseball Encyclopedia,* 2425; David Shiner, "John Joseph Evers," in Simon, ed, *Deadball Stars of the National League,* 102. In 1914, Evers was reportedly the highest paid ball player in baseball. Also see Kaese, *The Boston Braves, 1871–1953,* 139, 145.
110. *SL,* March 5, 14, 1914.
111. At the time of the story-telling, Mitchell was the manager of the Chicago Cubs. See *Chicago Evening Post,* April 16, 1919. For accounts of both preseason games in the nation's capitol, see *Boston Daily Globe,* April 6, 1913; April 11, 1914.
112. Chicago and Philadelphia teams were snubbed by the "blanket series" altogether. See Jeffrey Obermeyer, "B 18 Felt Blankets — A Closer Look," *The Vintage and Classic Baseball Collector,* May/June 1996.
113. *New York Tribune,* April 19, 1914.
114. *Boston Daily Globe,* April 19, 1914.
115. *Boston Daily Globe,* May 12, 1914. Boston scored four runs in the top of the sixth inning to tie the score, 4–4, but Hub surrendered four runs on six hits in the bottom of the frame to seal the New York victory.
116. Kaese, *The Boston Braves, 1871–1953,* 152–53.
117. See *New York Tribune,* June 12, 13, 1914; *Boston Daily Globe,* June 11, 12, 1914.
118. *Boston Daily Globe,* June 11, 1914.
119. *New York Tribune,* June 14, 1914; *Atlanta Constitution,* June 14, 1914; *Washington Post,* June 14, 1914.
120. *Boston Daily Globe,* June 30, 1914; www.retrosheet.org; *Baseball Encyclopedia,* 2515; *New York Tribune,* June 25, 30, 1914.
121. Russell, *Vols Feats,* 32; Russell, *Bury Me in an Old Press Box,* 100; *SL,* November 14, 1914; *Banner,* November 1, 1968; *Tennessean,* April 2, 1998.
122. *TSN,* November 11, 1920.
123. Kaese, *The Boston Braves, 1871–1953,* 152.
124. *TSN,* September 17, 1914.
125. See *Boston Daily Globe,* December 6, 13, 20, 1914.
126. *Boston Daily Globe,* December 20, 1914.
127. Fred Russell, *I'll Try Anything Twice* (Nashville: McQuiddy, 1945), 53.
128. See 1914 Boston Braves roster information in www.baseball-reference.com.
129. *St. Louis Post-Dispatch,* August 15, 1914.
130. *St. Louis Daily Globe-Democrat,* September 12, 1914.
131. *St. Louis Post-Dispatch,* August 15, 1914; *St. Louis Times,* October 1, 1914.
132. *Banner,* November 1, 1968. Also see, *TSN,* November 16, 1963, in Hubbard Perdue file, *The Sporting News Archive,* St. Louis, MO; Author's interview with Fred Russell, April 7, 1999, Nashville, TN.

Chapter 6

1. Stuart Schimler, "Miller Huggins," in Simon, ed, *Deadball Stars of the National League,* 355. Huggins left in 1918 and managed the legendary New York Yankees squads of the 1920s. He was elected to the Baseball Hall of Fame as a manager by the Veterans Committee in 1964. Also see *Baseball Encyclopedia,* 177, 1043; www.baseball-reference.com.
2. For more on the Robison family connection with the St. Louis Cardinals, see Peter Golenbock, *The Spirit of St. Louis: A History of the St. Louis Cardinals and Browns* (New York: Avon Books, 2000), 82.
3. Joan Thomas, "Helene Robison Britton," in *Deadball Stars of the National League,* 361.
4. Lowry, *Green Cathedrals,* 199; Ritter, *Lost Ballparks: A Celebration of Baseball's Legendary Fields* (New York: Penguin, 1994), 188. Today, Beaumont High School is at the original site of Robison Field.
5. *St. Louis Post-Dispatch,* June 30, 1914; *St. Louis Daily Globe-Democrat,* June 30, 1914; *St. Louis Times,* June 30, 1914.
6. *St. Louis Daily Globe-Democrat,* September 12, 1914; *TSN,* September 17, 1914.
7. *St. Louis Times,* June 30, 1914.
8. *St. Louis Daily Globe-Democrat,* July 1, 1914.
9. *St. Louis Star,* April 1, 1915.
10. *St. Louis Post-Dispatch,* July 10, 1914.
11. *New York Tribune,* July 10, 1914; *St. Louis Post-Dispatch,* July 10, 1914; *St. Louis Daily Globe-Democrat,* July 10, 1914; *St. Louis Times,* July 10, 14, 1914.
12. *New York Tribune,* July 15, 1914; *St. Louis Post-Dispatch,* July 15, 1914; *St. Louis Daily Globe-Democrat,* July 15, 1914; *St. Louis Times,* July 15, 1914.
13. Lawrence S. Ritter, *Lost Ballparks,* 19–21.
14. See *St. Louis Post-Dispatch,* July 17, 22, 1914; *St. Louis Daily Globe-Democrat,* July 18, 22, 1914. Normally, Daubert, Zack Wheat, and

Casey Stengel fared best against Hub for Brooklyn.
15. *St. Louis Post-Dispatch,* Jul y26, 1914; *St. Louis Daily Globe-Democrat,* July 26, 1914.
16. *St. Louis Post-Dispatch,* August 1, 1914; *St. Louis Daily Globe-Democrat,* August 1, 1914; *St. Louis Times,* August 1, 1914.
17. See *St. Louis Times,* July 14, 16, August 12, 1914.
18. *St. Louis Post-Dispatch,* August 11, 1914; *St. Louis Daily Globe-Democrat,* August 11, 1914; *St. Louis Times,* August 11, 1914.
19. *St. Louis Post-Dispatch,* August 11, 1914.
20. *St. Louis Post-Dispatch,* August 23, 1914. Also see *St. Louis Daily Globe-Democrat,* August 23, 1914; *St. Louis Times,* August 23, 1914.
21. *St. Louis Post-Dispatch,* August 31, 1914; *St. Louis Daily Globe-Democrat,* August 31, 1914; *St. Louis Times,* August 31, 1914.
22. *St. Louis Post-Dispatch,* September 6, 1914; *St. Louis Daily Globe-Democrat,* September 6, 1914.
23. *Washington Post,* September 20, 1914.
24. See *St. Louis Post-Dispatch,* September 20, 25, 1914; *St. Louis Daily Globe-Democrat,* September 20, 25, 1914; *New York Tribune,* September 20, 25, 1914; *St. Louis Times,* September 25, 1914.
25. *New York Tribune,* September 25, 1914.
26. *St. Louis Daily Globe-Democrat,* September 25, 1914.
27. See article by Jimmy Trodglen in *Gallatin News-Examiner,* October 15, 1991.
28. *The Baseball Encyclopedia,* 184; www.baseball-reference.com.
29. *St. Louis Daily Globe-Democrat,* September 14, 25, 1914.
30. For an overview of the city championship games, see *St. Louis Times,* October 7–13, 1914. Niehaus compiled a 4–5 record in the majors, largely as a reliever. His greatest impact took place in the minors where he compiled a 201–163 record from 1911 through 1929. See www.baseball-reference.com.
31. J. C. McMurtry, *Humor in Tennessee Justice* (Tompkinsville, KY: Monroe County Press, 1979), 96; *Banner,* November 1, 1968; *Tennessean,* April 2, 1998.
32. *St. Louis Post-Dispatch,* May 1, 1915. Also see *St. Louis Times,* May 27, 1915.
33. The Cardinals defeated the Browns in four out of six games. See *St. Louis Times,* March 28–April 12, 1915; *St. Louis Globe-Democrat,* March 28–April 12, 1915; *St. Louis Post-Dispatch,* March28–April 12, 1915.
34. *St. Louis Star,* April 1, 1915.
35. Paul Sallee and Eric Sallee, "Harry Franklin 'Slim' Sallee," in Simon, ed, *Deadball Stars of the National League,* 344–47. Sallee saved six games to lead the National League in 1914 while adding 18 victories.
36. Steve Steinberg, "William Leopold Doak," in Simon, ed, *Deadball Stars of the National League,* 358–60.
37. *St. Louis Globe-Democrat,* July 1,3 1915.
38. *St. Louis Globe-Democrat,* April 27, 1915. Also see *St. Louis Post-Dispatch,* April 27, 1915; *St. Louis Times,* April 2,7 1915.
39. *St. Louis Globe-Democrat,* April 25, 1915.
40. See *TSN,* November 25, 1920.
41. *St. Louis Post-Dispatch,* May 13, 1915; *St. Louis Globe-Democrat,* May 13, 1915; *St. Louis Times,* May 13, 1915.
42. *St. Louis Post-Dispatch,* May 18, 1915; *St. Louis Globe-Democrat,* May 18, 1915; *St. Louis Times,* May 18, 1915.
43. *St. Louis Globe-Democrat,* May 18, 1915.
44. *St. Louis Post-Dispatch,* May 28, 1915; *St. Louis Globe-Democrat,* May 28, 1915; *St. Louis Times,* May 28, 1915.
45. *New York Tribune,* May 29, 1915.
46. *St. Louis Globe-Democrat,* June 10, 1915. Also see *St. Louis Times,* June 10, 1915; *St. Louis Post-Dispatch,* June 10, 1915.
47. *St. Louis Globe-Democrat,* June 25, 1915; *St. Louis Times,* June 25, 1915; *St. Louis Post-Dispatch,* June 25, 1915; *St. Louis Star,* June 25, 1915.
48. *St. Louis Times,* June 29, 1915.
49. *St. Louis Star,* June 25, 1915.
50. *Ibid.;* www.retrosheet.org; www.baseball-reference.com.
51. *St. Louis Post-Dispatch,* June 29, 1915.
52. Lyle Spatz and Steve Steinberg, *1921. The Yankees, the Giants and the Battle for Baseball Supremacy in New York* (Lincoln: University of Nebraska, 2010), 24, 344, 347, 365. Huggins especially attracted the wrath of New York scribes for his alleged mismanagement of Bob Shawkey in Games 3 and 6 of the 1921 World Series.
53. *St. Louis Times,* June 29, 1915.
54. *SL,* July 10, 1915; *Christian Science Monitor,* June 30, 1915.
55. *St. Louis Globe-Democrat,* July 14–17, 1915; *St. Louis Times,* July 14–17, 1915; *St. Louis Post-Dispatch,* July 14–1,7 1915.
56. *St. Louis Globe-Democrat,* July 18, 1915; *St. Louis Times,* July 18, 1915; *St. Louis Post-Dispatch,* July 18, 1915.
57. *St. Louis Globe-Democrat,* July 23, 1915; *St. Louis Times,* July 23, 1915; *St. Louis Post-Dispatch,* July 23, 1915; *New York Tribune,* July 23, 1915.
58. *St. Louis Globe-Democrat,* August 24, 1915; *New York Tribune,* August 24, 1915; *Christian Science Monitor,* August 2,4 1915.
59. *St. Louis Globe-Democrat,* August 31,

1915; *St. Louis Times,* August 31, 1915; *St. Louis Post-Dispatch,* August 31, 1915; *New York Tribune,* August 28, 31, 1915.

60. *New York Tribune,* September 5, 1915.

61. *St. Louis Globe-Democrat,* September 2, 1915; *St. Louis Times,* September 2, 1915; *St. Louis Post-Dispatch,* September 2, 1915.

62. *St. Louis Globe-Democrat,* September 19, 1915; *St. Louis Times,* September 19, 1915; *St. Louis Post-Dispatch,* September 19, 1915; *New York Tribune,* September 19, 1915.

63. *St. Louis Globe-Democrat,* October 1, 1915; *St. Louis Times,* October 1, 1915; *St. Louis Post-Dispatch,* October 1, 1915.

64. Johnson, *Standing the Gaff,* xix, 37–38. Originally written in 1935, Johnson's memoir covered his 37-year career (1910–1946) as a minor league arbiter, primarily in the Southern Association. He officiated over 5,700 games in his career and received his nickname from Atlanta sports editor Ed Danforth (p. 49–50). He once claimed to have been the target of over 4,000 bottles thrown by irate fans throughout his colorful career. Later, Hub occasionally crossed paths with Johnson in the minors.

65. For game summaries of the 1915 city championship, see *St. Louis Globe-Democrat,* October 5–10, 1915; *St. Louis Times,* October 5–10, 1915; *St. Louis Post-Dispatch,* October 5–10, 1915.

66. *Baseball Encyclopedia,* 2155; www.retrosheet.org.

67. McMurtry, *Humor in Tennessee Justice,* 96.

68. *Banner,* November 1, 1968; *Tennessean,* April 2, 1998.

69. *Chicago Daily Tribune,* March 28, 1907.

70. *SL,* November 27, 1915.

71. *New York Tribune,* November 23, 1915; *SL,* November 27, 1915.

72. *St. Louis Globe-Democrat,* December 3, 1915; *New York Tribune,* November 23, 1915.

73. *St. Louis Star,* December 28, 1915.

Chapter 7

1. *New York Tribune,* March 26, 1916. In addition to the Louisville Colonels, the AA was comprised of the Columbus Senators, Indianapolis Indians, Kansas City Blues, Milwaukee Brewers, Minneapolis Millers, St. Paul Saints, and Toledo Iron Men. See www.baseball-reference.com; Johnson and Wolff, eds, *Encyclopedia of Minor League Baseball.*

2. *Louisville Courier-Journal,* April 19, 1916. For a summary of Clymer's career, see www.baseball-reference.com; www.retrosheet.org.

3. See David Nemec, *The Beer and Whiskey League: The Illustrated History of the American Association—Baseball's Renegade Major League* (New York: Lyons and Burford, 1994).

4. John Bernard Wathen inherited his father's distillery business during the Civil War. In 1875, J. B. and his brother, Nick, expanded and built a large facility in Lebanon, Kentucky, and expanded again in 1899 with the purchase of the Old Grand-Dad label. J. B. died in 1919 just months before prohibition went into effect. Otho H. Wathen, educated at Notre Dame, was a major stockholder in the family's company. See "Otho H. Wathen," in Ben LaBree, *Press Reference Book of Prominent Kentuckians* (Louisville: Standard Printing Co., 1916): 133; www.straightbourbon.com.

5. See *Louisville Courier-Journal,* June 10, 1916.

6. *Louisville Courier-Journal,* April 1, 3, 1916.

7. *Louisville Courier-Journal,* April 17–18, 1916.

8. *Louisville Courier-Journal,* April 20, 1916.

9. *Louisville Courier-Journal,* April 29, 1916.

10. *Louisville Courier-Journal,* May 1, 1916.

11. *Louisville Courier-Journal,* May 4, 1916.

12. Toledo remained the Iron Men for three years. See *Cleveland Plain Dealer,* April 16, 1916; *Toledo News Bee,* April 15, 1916.

13. *Louisville Courier-Journal,* June 4, 1916. Also see box scores for Hub's other three games against Toledo in *Louisville Courier-Journal,* May 26, August 5, September 29, 1916.

14. *Louisville Courier-Journal,* June 13, 15, 1916.

15. *Louisville Courier-Journal,* June 16, 1916.

16. Lester and Thomson, *Around Gallatin and Sumner County,* 50.

17. Wright, *The Southern Association in Baseball,* 176–77; O'Neal, *The Southern League,* 33–34.

18. See Wright, *The Southern Association in Baseball,* 176–77; O'Neal, *The Southern League,* 33–34; Russell and Leonard, *Vols Feats,* 19. Rogers played in the majors until 1921, but he was forever haunted by Dodge's death. In a testament to his grief, he married four times. He passed away in 1936 from an alcohol-related illness at the age of 44. For a Rogers family reminiscence, see John P. Lopez, "Baseball Death Jogs Painful Memory for Longtime Fan," *Houston Chronicle,* August 19, 2007.

19. *Louisville Courier-Journal,* July 15, 1916.

20. For game summaries of the "doctoring" controversy, see *Louisville Courier-Journal,* July 17, 24, 1916.

21. See remarks of Sam H. McMeekin in *Louisville Courier-Journal,* July 17, 1916.

22. *Louisville Courier-Journal,* July 28, 1916.
23. For game accounts of the crucial series in Kansas City, see *Louisville Courier-Journal,* August 20–23, 1916.
24. *Louisville Courier-Journal,* August 27, 1916.
25. *Louisville Courier-Journal,* August 30–31, September 1, 1916.
26. *Louisville Courier-Journal,* September 6, 1916.
27. *Louisville Courier-Journal,* September 8, 1916.
28. *Louisville Courier-Journal,* September 12, 16, 1916.
29. *Louisville Courier-Journal,* September 30, 1916.
30. www.baseball-reference.com.
31. *Louisville Courier-Journal,* September 30, 1916.
32. Luque, Palmero, Killifer and Daniels also opted out of the extended series. See *Louisville Courier-Journal,* October 1, 2, 1916.
33. *Louisville Courier-Journal,* October 2, 1916. For a complete account of the Omaha series see *Louisville Courier-Journal,* October 5–9, 1916
34. *Louisville Courier-Journal,* April 2, 1917.
35. *Louisville Courier-Journal,* April 7, 1917.
36. See Tom W. Cooke, "Hub Perdue Shows Real Form as a Sorceress," in *Louisville Courier-Journal,* April 2, 1917.
37. *Louisville Courier-Journal,* April 2, 1917.
38. *Louisville Courier-Journal,* April 15, 1917.
39. *Louisville Courier-Journal,* April 15, 1917.
40. *Louisville Courier-Journal,* April 26, 1917.
41. *Louisville Courier-Journal,* May 3, 8, 1917.
42. O'Neal, *The Southern League,* 301; Wright, *The Southern Association in Baseball,* 176–82; *The Baseball Encyclopedia,* 2203; www.baseball-reference.com; www.retrosheet.org; Johnson and Wolff, eds, *The Encyclopedia of Minor League Baseball,* first edition, 144.

Chapter 8

1. *Chattanooga Daily Times,* May 9, 1917; *Chattanooga News,* May 12, 1917.
2. See Kirk's reprinted rhyme in *Chattanooga Daily Times,* May 27, 1917.
3. See Stephen Martini, *The Chattanooga Lookouts & 100 Seasons of Scenic City Baseball* (Cleveland, TN: Dry Ice, 2005), 26–27.
4. Martini, *The Chattanooga Lookouts,* 14; O'Neal, *The Southern League,* 228–30.
5. Martini, *The Chattanooga Lookouts,* 15.
6. Wright, *The Southern Association in Baseball,* 30; Martini, *The Chattanooga Lookouts,* 16–17, 20–21.

7. Martini, *The Chattanooga Lookouts,* 22–23; O'Neal, *The Southern League,* 228.
8. David Jenkins, *Baseball in Chattanooga* (Chicago: Arcadia, 2005), 7, 25. While the Chattanooga franchise historically occupied the second tier in league standings, it won the last championship in Southern Association history in 1961.
9. Zeboim Cartter Patten, Sr., was a well known industrialist and successful capitalist. Among his accomplishments was the purchase of the *Chattanooga Times* from S. A. Cunningham, manufacturer of patent medicines, founder of a bank, and real estate and life insurance companies. Andrews was owner of the Andrews Paper Box Company. See *The Tennessee Encyclopedia of History and Culture,* 724; Simpson, *S. A. Cunningham and the Confederate Heritage,* 57, 67; Martini, *The Chattanooga Lookouts,* 24.
10. Jenkins, *Baseball in Chattanooga,* 127; Martini, *The Chattanooga Lookouts,* 24.
11. O'Neal, *The Southern League,* 229.
12. *Chattanooga Daily Times,* May 12, 14, 1917; *Chattanooga News,* May 12, 14, 1917.
13. *Chattanooga Daily Times,* May 19, 24, 1917; *Chattanooga News,* May 19, 24, 1917.
14. *Chattanooga Daily Times,* June 1, 1917; *Chattanooga News,* 1 June 1917.
15. O'Neal, *The Southern League,* 38, 268.
16. *Chattanooga Daily Times,* June 8, 1917; *Chattanooga News,* June 8, 1917.
17. *Chattanooga Daily Times,* June 28–30, 1917; *Chattanooga News,* June 28–30, 1917.
18. *Chattanooga Daily Times,* June 19, 24, 25, 1917; *Chattanooga News,* June 19, 24, 25, 1917.
19. *Chattanooga Daily Times,* July 5, 1917; *Chattanooga News,* July 5, 1917.
20. *Chattanooga Daily Times,* July 9, 1917; *Chattanooga News,* July 9, 1917.
21. *Chattanooga Daily Times,* July 25, 1917. For game accounts versus Mobile, see *Chattanooga Daily Times,* July 13, 23, 25, 1917; *Chattanooga News,* July 13, 23, 25, 1917.
22. *Chattanooga Daily Times,* August 11–12, 27–28, 31, 1917; *Chattanooga News,* August 11, 13, 28–29, 31, 1917.
23. *Chattanooga Daily Times,* August 11, 1917; *Chattanooga News,* August 11, 1917.
24. *Chattanooga Daily Times,* August 18, 1917; *Chattanooga News,* August 18, 1917. The hurling duo of Long (0–10) and Ching (0–13) set a Southern Association mark for ineptitude, and Mobile finished in the cellar, 62 games behind. It came as no surprise when Mobile, seeking a fresh start, changed its nickname to "Bears" in 1918. See Wright, *The Southern Association in Baseball,* 183, 188–89.
25. *Chattanooga Daily Times,* September 4,

1917; *Chattanooga News,* September 4, 1917; *Banner,* September 4, 1917; *Memphis Commercial-Appeal,* September 4, 1917; *Banner,* September 4, 1917; *Tennessean,* September 4, 1917.

26. Johnson and Wolff, eds, *The Encyclopedia of Minor League Baseball,* 146; Wright, *The Southern Association in Baseball,* 187.

27. Wright, *The Southern Association in Baseball,* 187; www.baseball-reference.com.

28. Elberfeld signed immediately with Little Rock and Mike Finn left Beaumont in the Texas League and signed on with Chattanooga. Finn was coming to the end of an illustrious 20-year career as a manager, all but two of those years in the Southern Association. See *Chattanooga Daily Times,* September 23, 1917; *Chattanooga News,* September 23, 1917; www.baseball-reference.com.

29. *New Orleans Times-Picayune,* March 29, April 15, 1918.

30. In April 1917, the U.S. Congress passed the Selective Service Act, and Secretary of War Baker announced his "work or fight" directive — a statement ordering all men ages 21–30 to file for military service. Baker's order did not affect married men who owned property or were engaged in work deemed essential to the war effort. See Michael J. Lyons, *World War I: A Short History* (Englewood, NJ: Prentice Hall, 1994), 298–307; Gerald Shenk, *Work or Fight!: Race, Gender, and the Draft in World War One* (New York: Palgrave Macmillan, 2005).

31. Lyons, *World War I; A Short History,* 298–307; Shenk, *Work or Fight!: Race, Gender, and the Draft in World War One.* Crowder, an Army lawyer, was given the assignment to implement the Selective Service Act nationwide.

32. *New Orleans Times-Picayune,* April 19, 20 1918. Hub's five-hitter was overshadowed by the successful sale of Liberty Bonds which raised $112,000.

33. *New Orleans Times-Picayune,* April 24, 1918. The Frank-Heinemann conflict began when the New Orleans owner filed a claim with the National Commission to force his former manager to repay a $1,629 loan. When the Commission ordered Frank to pay back Heinemann, the feud was on and it spilled onto the baseball diamond in several ugly, violent incidents. See *SL,* January 27, April 14, 1917.

34. *New Orleans Times-Picayune,* May 5, 1918.

35. *New Orleans Times-Picayune,* May 28, 1918.

36. *New Orleans Times-Picayune,* May 25, 1918.

37. *New Orleans Times-Picayune,* June 1, 1918.

38. *New Orleans Times-Picayune,* June 6, 1918.

39. *New Orleans Times-Picayune,* June 10, 1918.

40. *New Orleans Times-Picayune,* June 11, 1918.

41. *New Orleans Times-Picayune,* June 16, 20, 23, 28, 1918. In a remarkable example of physical endurance, Kitchens caught every inning of every game for New Orleans in 1918.

42. Wright, *The Southern Association in Baseball,* 191; www.baseball-reference.com.

43. For accounts of Hub's five games in Minneapolis, see *Minneapolis Morning Tribune,* July 8, 11, 15, 19, 21, 1918. Also see Wright, *The Southern Association in Baseball,* 190–91; www.baseball-reference.com; Johnson and Wolff, eds, *The Encyclopedia of Minor League Baseball,* first edition, 148.

44. *Grand Rapids Tribune,* November 14, 1918.

45. Martin held the presidency of the Southern Association for 19 years, the longest tenure in league history. See O'Neal, *The Southern League,* 21, 59.

46. *New Orleans Times-Picayune,* March 26, 1919.

47. *New Orleans Times-Picayune,* April 15, 1919. The injury was later reported as a "strained arm." See *New Orleans Times-Picayune,* May 19, 1919.

48. *New Orleans Times-Picayune,* April 21, 1919.

49. *New Orleans Times-Picayune,* May 26, 1919. For game accounts of earlier victories over Little Rock and Chattanooga, see *New Orleans Times-Picayune,* May 19, 23, 1919.

50. See *New Orleans Times-Picayune,* May 30, 31, June 2, 7, 1919.

51. *New Orleans Times-Picayune,* June 12, 1919.

52. *New Orleans Times-Picayune,* June 17, 22, 1919.

53. *New Orleans Times-Picayune,* July 3, 1919.

54. *New Orleans Times-Picayune,* July 9, 1919.

55. *New Orleans Times-Picayune,* July 25, 28, 1919.

56. *New Orleans Times-Picayune,* July 31, 1919. News of the belligerent fan even made it to New York. See *New York Times,* August 26, 1919.

57. *New Orleans Times-Picayune,* August 2, 1919.

58. *New Orleans Times-Picayune,* August 10, 1919.

59. *New Orleans Times-Picayune,* August 18, 1919.

60. *New Orleans Times-Picayune,* August 26, 1919.

61. *New Orleans Times-Picayune,* August 29, 31, 1919.

62. *New Orleans Times-Picayune,* August 31, 1919.

63. *New Orleans Times-Picayune,* September 3, 1919. The collision resulted in a spinal injury that never fully healed. See Bibb, "It's All in the Juice."
64. Wright, *The Southern Association in Baseball,* 199. Wright entitles the chapter on the 1919 season "Hub Perdue." Also see Johnson and Wolff, eds, *The Encyclopedia of Minor League Baseball,* first edition, 149.
65. Wright, *The Southern Association in Baseball,* 204–5; www.baseball-reference.com.
66. *New Orleans Times-Picayune,* April 14, 1920.
67. *Banner,* April 17, 1920; *New Orleans Times-Picayune,* April 17, 1920.
68. *New Orleans Times-Picayune,* April 23, 1920.
69. *New Orleans Times-Picayune,* April 25, 1920.
70. *Banner,* May 2, 11, 1920; *New Orleans Times-Picayune,* May 3, 7, 12, 1920.
71. Al M. Gifford, a minor league shortstop and outfielder, resided in Chattanooga. He played in the Wisconsin State League (1895), Southern League (1896, 1898), Southeastern League (1897), New York State League (1900), Southern Association (1901), Three-I League (1903), and Tennessee-Alabama League (1904). He officiated from 1905 to 1920 in the Southern Association, Eastern League, American Association and SALLY. See www.baseball-reference.com; Wright, *The Southern Association in Baseball,* 64–65, 69, 80.
72. *New Orleans Times-Picayune,* May 11, 1920.
73. *New Orleans Times-Picayune,* May 16, 23, 29, 1920.
74. *New Orleans Times-Picayune,* May 25, 1920.
75. *Banner,* June 1, 1920; *Tennessean,* June 1, 1920; *New Orleans Times-Picayune,* June 2, 1920.
76. *Tennessean,* June 1, 1920. Claude S. "Blinky" Horn had a distinguished career in Nashville journalism. Born in the Edgefield district, Blinky acquired a first-hand knowledge of the city from an early age. He started at the *Tennessean* in 1912, held several positions, and in 1919 he succeeded John H. Nye as sports editor. He was considered an authority on baseball. His longtime friend at the *Banner,* Fred Russell, commented that Blinky was a colorful analyst in his 25 years behind the desk at the *Tennessean.* See *Banner,* May 21, 1937. Also see *Clarksville Leaf-Chronicle,* May 21, 1937; *Bristol News Bulletin,* May 21, 1937.
77. See quote in *Banner,* June 6, 1920; *Tennessean,* June 6, 1920.
78. *New Orleans Item,* June 2, 1920.
79. *Banner,* June 6, 1920; *Tennessean,* June 6, 1920.
80. *Tennessean,* June 6, 1920.
81. See *Banner,* June 10, 14, 19, 24, 1920; *Tennessean,* June 10, 14, 24, 1920.
82. His past problems in the New York State League (1900) and Mississippi State League (1904) were reprinted in *May's Landing Current* (NJ), January 14, 1905.
83. Johnson, *Standing the Gaff,* 84–85.
84. For a complete account of the game, see *Banner,* June 28, 1920; *Tennessean,* 28 June 1920.
85. *Tennessean,* June 29, 1920.
86. *Tennessean,* June 30, July 1, 2, 1920.
87. *Shreveport Journal,* April 3, 1922.
88. *Banner,* July 4, 1920; *Tennessean,* 4 July 1920.
89. *Banner,* July 4, 1920; *Tennessean,* 4 July 1920.
90. *Banner,* July 3, 7, 11, 14, 20, 24, 28, 31, 1920; *Tennessean,* July 3, 7, 11, 14, 20, 24, 28, 31, 1920.
91. *Banner,* 12 July 1920; *Tennessean,* July 12, 1920.
92. *Banner,* July 14, 24, 1920; *Tennessean,* July 14, 24, 1920.
93. *Banner,* September 2, 1920.
94. See *Banner,* July 15, August 4, 12, 1920; *Tennessean,* July 15, 1920.
95. *Banner,* August 26, 1920.
96. Wright, *The Southern Association in Baseball,* 183, 197.
97. Hinton, "The Gallatin Squash."
98. The dimensions of Athletic Park, or Pelican Park, changed in 1914 — 427' to left field, 405' to center field and 418' to right field. See O'Neal, *The Southern League,* 39.
99. Wright, *The Southern Association in Baseball,* 208.
100. Wright, *The Southern Association in Baseball,* 516; O'Neal, *The Southern League,* 43.
101. See *TSN,* June 19, 1919.
102. This story went national as well. See *Grand Rapids Tribune,* August 21, 28, 1919; *Connellsville (PA) Daily Courier,* August 25, 1919.
103. See *La Crosse Tribune and Leader-Press,* July 18, 1919.
104. Miscellaneous newspaper clipping, Jimmy Perdue Family Collection.
105. See *Vincennes Capital,* September 15, 1906; *Boston Daily Globe,* September 27, 1912; *Chattanooga Daily Times,* September 15, 1917; *Chattanooga News,* September 15, 1917; *New Orleans Times-Picayune,* July 13, 1919; *TSN,* July 17, 1919.
106. *Tennessean,* June 6, 1920.
107. Hub posted an 11–0 record versus Mobile from August 30, 1910 to April 16, 1920.

Chapter 9

1. *Tennessean,* October 6, 1920.
2. James Aiken Green Sloan was a Nashville contractor who joined a new investment group headed by Thomas Goodall to purchase the Vols in 1917. While Goodall remained the majority stockholder, Sloan served as president of the Board of Directors until 1926. See *Banner,* April 6, 1946.
3. *Tennessean,* October 10, 1920.
4. *Banner,* January 9, 1921.
5. *TSN,* November 11, 1920. For a local article on Hub's managerial debut, see *Sumner County News,* January 20, March 10, 1921.
6. The centerpiece of the property was a Victorian home of gingerbread design. By the late 1950s, the once impressive home and property fell into disrepair. Following frequent bouts with vandals, the home was demolished in 1977. See *Historic Homes of Sumner County,* Laurel Farms.
7. Interview with Walter T. Durham, October 21, 2010.
8. Dr. Lackey died in 1951. See *Banner,* July 18, 1951.
9. Durham, *A Pictorial History of Sumner County,* 19.
10. *Sumner County News,* March 31, 1921.
11. *Banner,* January 21, 1921. Warmoth played 14 years in the minors (1917, 1919–1931), mostly in the Southern and American Associations. See www.baseball-reference.com.
12. See Spatz and Steinberg, *1921,* 10–16.
13. *Banner,* January 21, 1921.
14. *Banner,* January 23, 1921. Promising pitchers included Dealis Wade (Hub's discovery from Ft. Smith) and converted first baseman Bill "Buster" Brown. Young returnees from the previous season — George Payne and Bill Statham — were joined by newcomers Fred "Red" Lucas and Frank "Parson" Lankenau.
15. *TSN,* March 17, 1921.
16. See *Banner,* April 2, 1921.
17. See *Banner,* March 19, 20, 1921.
18. *Banner,* March 23, 1921.
19. *Banner,* April 8, 1921; *Tennessean,* April 6, 1921.
20. See *Banner,* January 30, February 13, 1921.
21. *Banner,* March 26, 1921.
22. *Banner,* April 10, 11, 13, 1921; *Tennessean,* April 10, 11, 13, 1921.
23. On his first visit to Sulphur Dell from his parents' rural Wartrace farm, a freckle-faced, red-headed lad later remembered carrying Jonnard's shin guards into the stadium. Fred Russell, the iconic sports editor of the *Nashville Banner* from 1929–1998 and later known as the dean of Southern sportswriters, cherished that moment fondly for the rest of his life. Interview with Fred Russell, April 1999.
24. *Banner,* April 4, 1921; www.baseball-reference.com.
25. *Banner,* April 7, 1921.
26. *Banner,* April 13, 1921; *Tennessean,* April 13, 1921.
27. *Banner,* April 14, 1921; *Tennessean,* April 14, 1921.
28. www.baseball-reference.com.
29. *Banner,* April 15–18, 1921; *Tennessean,* April 15–18, 1921.
30. *Banner,* April 19, 20, 1921.
31. *Banner,* April 22, 1921.
32. *Banner,* April 22, 1921.
33. *Banner,* April 24, 1921; *Tennessean,* April 24, 1921.
34. *Banner,* April 25–26, 1921; *Tennessean,* April 25–26, 1921.
35. *Banner,* April 26, 28, 1921; *Tennessean,* April 26, 28, 1921.
36. *Banner,* April 30, 1921; *Tennessean,* April 30, 1921.
37. On May 1, team batting leaders included Frierson (.420), Stellbauer (.354), Burke (.326), Knaupp (.322), Bradley (.281), Bogart (.267), and Jonnard (.250). See *Banner,* May 8, 1921; *Tennessean,* May 8, 1921.
38. *Banner,* May 3, 1921.
39. *Banner,* May 4–6, 1921; *Tennessean,* May 4–6, 1921.
40. *Banner,* May 7, 8, 22, 1921; *Tennessean,* May 7, 8, 22, 1921.
41. *Banner,* May 9, 10, 15, 1921; *Tennessean,* May 9, 10, 15, 1921.
42. *Tennessean,* May 12, 1921.
43. *Banner,* May 10–13, 1921; *Tennessean,* May 10–13, 1921.
44. See *Banner,* May 16, 1921; *Tennessean,* May 16, 1921.
45. *Banner,* May 20, 1921.
46. For more on Nashville's entrant in the Negro Southern League organized by Tom Wilson in 1920, see Nipper, *Baseball in Nashville,* 33–37; Darnell, *Southern Yankees,* 150; O'Neal, *The Southern League,* 83. Other franchises were the Atlanta Black Crackers, Birmingham Black Barons, Jacksonville Red Caps, Memphis Red Sox, Montgomery Grey Socks, New Orleans Crescent Stars and later the Chattanooga Black Lookouts and Choo Choos.
47. *Banner,* May 21, 22, 25, 1921; *Tennessean,* May 21, 22, 25, 1921.
48. *Banner,* May 23, 24, 1921; *Tennessean,* May 23, 24, 1921.
49. *Banner,* May 26–29, 1921; *Tennessean,* May 26–29, 1921.

50. *Banner,* May 28, 1921; *Tennessean,* 28 May 1921.
51. *Banner,* May 30, 31, June 1, 1921; *Tennessean,* May 30, 31, June 1, 1921.
52. *Banner,* June 1, 1921; *Tennessean,* June 1, 1921.
53. *Banner,* June 2, 3, 1921; *Tennessean,* June 2, 3, 1921.
54. *Banner,* June 4, 5, 1921; *Tennessean,* June 4, 5, 1921.
55. *Banner,* June 6, 7, 1921; *Tennessean,* June 6, 7, 1921. Rose went 1–3 in one-sided losses.
56. *Banner,* June 7, 8, 1921; *Tennessean,* June 7, 8, 1921.
57. *Tennessean,* June 9, 1921.
58. *Banner,* June 10, 1921; *Tennessean,* June 10, 1921.
59. *Banner,* June 12, 1921. Also see *Banner,* June 11, 1921; *Tennessean,* June 11, 12, 1921.
60. *Banner,* June 12, 1921; *Tennessean,* June 12, 1921.
61. *Banner,* June 13, 1921.
62. *Banner,* June 14, 1921.
63. *Tennessean,* June 14, 1921.
64. *Tennessean,* June 14, 1921. Atlanta replaced its manager the same day.
65. *Tennessean,* June 14, 1921.
66. *Banner,* June 15, 1921; *Tennessean,* June 15, 1921.
67. *Tennessean,* June 20, 1921.
68. *Banner,* June 21, 1921; *Tennessean,* June 21, 1921.
69. *Banner,* June 22, 27, 1921; *Tennessean,* June 22, 1921.
70. *Banner,* June 24, 25, 1921; *Tennessean,* June 24, 25, 1921.
71. *Banner,* June 26, 1921. The evening newspaper similarly headlined "Hub Perdue Relieved As Skipper of the Vols." See *Tennessean,* June 26, 1921.
72. *Tennessean,* June 26, 1921.
73. *Tennessean,* June 27, 1921. Sloan eventually picked Chick Knaupp to run the team.
74. *Tennessean,* June 27, 1921.
75. *Tennessean,* June 30, 1920.
76. *TSN,* July 7, 1921.
77. See the response of the National Commission to Perdue's claim in Miscellaneous Letter, Jimmy Perdue Family Collection.
78. See Hub Perdue, Player Contract File, National Baseball Hall of Fame Library, Cooperstown, NY; *Wichita Daily Times,* May 14, 1922.
79. *TSN,* April 27, 1922.
80. See www.baseball-reference.com. Stellbauer appeared in 116 games for the Vols and landed in Fort Worth (Texas League). Frierson played fewer than 100 contests in Nashville and ended up with Jackson in the Class D Mississippi State League.
81. Wright, *The Southern Association in Baseball,* 214.
82. *Tennessean,* August 7, 1921.
83. Spatz and Steinberg, *1921,* xv, 37, 143.
84. There was no greater testament to the lingering Deadball Era in the Southern than a game played on June 13, 1919 between Chattanooga and Atlanta. Fans at Andrews Field were treated to a marvelous extra-inning affair that lasted almost four hours. The hurlers—Rube Marshall of the Lookouts and Ray Roberts of the Crackers—tossed the entire game. Only the onset of darkness put an end to the contest knotted at two runs apiece. See O'Neal, *The Southern League,* 37.
85. See Wright, *The Southern Association in Baseball,* 198–216. Statistical information for the charts compiled from data in www.baseball-reference.com.
86. *TSN,* June 2, 1921.
87. *Shreveport Journal,* April 3, 1922.

Chapter 10

1. www.baseball-reference.com. Shreveport was the end of the road in Smith's 24-year managerial career in the minors.
2. The 1922 Texas League included the Shreveport Gassers, Fort Worth Panthers, Dallas Steers, Wichita Falls Spudders, Beaumont Exporters, San Antonio Bears, Galveston Sand Crabs and Houston Buffaloes. See www.baseball-reference.com.
3. *Shreveport Journal,* March 11, 25, 1922.
4. *Shreveport Journal,* March 27, 1922.
5. *Shreveport Journal,* April 12, 1922.
6. *Wichita Daily Times,* April 17, 1922; *Shreveport Journal,* April 17, 1922.
7. *Shreveport Journal,* April 17, 1922. Also see *Shreveport Times,* April 17, 1922.
8. *Wichita Daily Times,* April 18, 19, 1922.
9. *Wichita Daily Times,* April 23, 1922; *Shreveport Times,* April 23, 1922.
10. *Shreveport Journal,* May 23, 1922.
11. *Wichita Daily Times,* May 6, 1922. Also see *Shreveport Journal,* June 3, 1922.
12. Frank "Pop" Kitchens began his 23-year career in the minors in 1907. Predominantly a catcher and outfielder, the Texan plied his trade primarily in the Southern Association and Texas League. See www.baseball-reference.com.
13. See *Wichita Daily Times,* May 13, 1922.
14. See *Wichita Daily Times* throughout the month of May 1922.
15. *Wichita Daily Times,* May 13, 1922.
16. *Wichita Daily Times,* May 14, 17, 1922; www.baseball-reference.com.

17. *Wichita Daily Times,* May 18, 1922.
18. Catcher John Vann replaced Smith, but the Gassers never did recover from their horrendous start. The woeful team eventually trailed the frontrunners by more games than they won (56). See Johnson and Wolff, eds, *The Encyclopedia of Minor League Baseball,* first edition, 157.
19. See *Wichita Daily Times,* May 26, 1922.
20. See *Wichita Daily Times,* May 22–31, 1922.
21. *Wichita Daily Times,* June 3, 1922; *Shreveport Times,* June 3, 1922.
22. *Wichita Daily Times,* June 4, 1922.
23. *Wichita Daily Times,* June 5, 1922.
24. *Wichita Daily Times,* June 8, 1922.
25. *Wichita Daily Times,* June 15, 1922.
26. See *Wichita Daily Times,* June 15–18, 1922.
27. See *Wichita Daily Times,* July 14, 1922.
28. *Wichita Daily Times,* June 21, 25, 1922.
29. *Wichita Daily Times,* June 30, 1922.
30. *Wichita Daily Times,* July 5, 1922.
31. *Wichita Daily Times,* July 9, 1922.
32. Edmund J. Flaherty was the nephew of Patsy Flaherty. He led an interesting life in addition to his brief four years in pro baseball. Born in Washington, DC in 1897, he was signed by Clark Griffith in 1916. During World War I, he served as a pilot in the U. S. Army Air Corps. Afterwards, he pitched in the semi-pro Delaware Shipyards League and several minor league circuits before being called up in late September 1921, by the New York Giants. He was a multi-talented athlete and played pro football in the mid–1920s. Eventually, he turned to acting. He appeared in over 250 movies as a bit actor and worked with such Silver Screen icons as Gary Cooper, Ronald Reagan, the Marx Brothers, Bob Hope, Shirley Temple, Errol Flynn, Clark Gable, Frank Sinatra, Humphrey Bogart, Spencer Tracy, Abbott and Costello, James Stewart, John Wayne, Henry Fonda, and Douglas Fairbanks, Jr. In the 1950s, Flaherty became involved with the new television industry largely as a public relations figure. His colorful life ended in 1970. See Bill Hickman, "Pat J. Flaherty" in SABR BioProject.
33. *Wichita Daily Times,* July 10, 1922.
34. *Wichita Daily Times,* July 16, 17, 1922.
35. *Wichita Daily Times,* July 19, 21, 23, 1922.
36. *Wichita Daily Times,* July 24, 1922.
37. *Wichita Daily Times,* July 26, 1922.
38. *Wichita Daily Times,* August 1, 1922.
39. *Wichita Daily Times,* July 31, 1922.
40. See *Wichita Daily Times,* July 28, 31, August 7, 1922.
41. *Wichita Daily Times,* August 12, 13, 1922.
42. *Wichita Daily Times,* August 13, 1922.
43. *Wichita Daily Times,* August 18, 19, 1922.
44. *Wichita Daily Times,* August 26, 1922.
45. *Wichita Daily Times,* August 23, 1922.
46. *Wichita Daily Times,* August 27, 1922.
47. *Wichita Daily Times,* August 31, 1922.
48. *Wichita Daily Times,* September 8, 1922.
49. *Wichita Daily Times,* September 14, 1922.
50. Atz's 1922 Panthers are ranked #17 on the list of the Top 100 minor league teams of all time. See www.minorleaguebaseballcom.
51. See final season statistics in *Wichita Daily Times,* September 17, 1922.
52. Simpson, "*The Greatest Game Ever Played in Dixie,*" 211; *TSN,* December 2, 1922; www.baseball-reference.com.
53. Besides the Charlotte Hornets, the South Atlantic League (SALLY) in 1923 included the Augusta Tygers, Greenville Spinners, Spartanburg Spartans, Charleston Pals, and Columbia Comers. See www.baseball-reference.com.
54. For more biographical information on Hoblitzell, see Tom Simon, *Dick Hoblitzell,* in SABR BioProject; Tom Simon, Dick Hoblitzell, in Simon, ed, *Deadball Stars of the National League,* 249–50.
55. For more on Paschal's five years of limited service with the Yankees and 13 years in the minors, where he averaged .315 at the plate, see www.baseball-reference.com.
56. *Charlotte Observer,* May 3, 1923; *Charlotte News,* May 3, 1923.
57. *Charlotte Observer,* May 8, 10, 1923.
58. *Charlotte Observer,* May 9, 1923.
59. *Charlotte Observer,* May 13, 1923; *Charlotte News,* May 13, 1923.
60. *Charlotte Observer,* May 20, 1923; *Charlotte News,* May 20, 1923.
61. *Charlotte Observer,* May 20, 1923.
62. *Charlotte Observer,* June 3, 1923; *Charlotte News,* June 3, 1923.
63. *Charlotte Observer,* June 7, 1923.
64. *American,* June 3, 1907.
65. *TSN,* June 21, 1923; Also see Hub Perdue, Player Contract Card, National Baseball Hall of Fame Library, Cooperstown, NY.
66. *Statewide Index to Tennessee Death Records* (1914–1931), vol. 10: 508.
67. See Kathryn's complex sheet music book inscribed by a New York producer in possession of Jimmy Perdue, Gallatin, TN.
68. Author interview with Jimmy Perdue, July 20, 2010; James H. Perdue, "The Adventures of the Boy Lieutenant; A Saga of the Battle of Boredom in the Korean Conflict, staged in the deserts of Arizona" (unpublished autobiography) in Jimmy Perdue Family Papers: 4.

Chapter 11

1. *Banner,* May 20, 1924; Snider and Yorgason, *Sumner County Cemetery Records,* 27; Denning, *Death Certificates of Sumner County,* 8.
2. *Sumner County, Tennessee: Wills, County Clerk's Office,* 1924–1942.
3. Reese Brothers Mule Company is still in operation. For a history of the company, see www.reesemules.com.
4. For more detailed explanation of the duties of the office of county clerks in Tennessee, see *Michie's Tennessee Code of 1938; The General Laws of Tennessee* (Charlottesville, VA: Michie, 1938), 1683–1685.
5. Collier, *Precious Memories,* 42.
6. *Sumner County, Tennessee, Minute Book, County Clerk's Office,* 1933–1936, vol. 29: 226. Unfortunately, there are no surviving newspapers from 1934 to show precinct tabulations, and voting records on file at the Sumner County Courthouse only go back to 1962.
7. See "Elmer Hinton" entry in Van West, ed, *The Tennessee Encyclopedia of History and Culture,* 428; *Tennessean,* December 9, 1979; *Sumner News-Examiner,* December 10, 1979.
8. See Hinton, "Gallatin Squash"; Collier, "Precious Memories"; 41; Bibb, "It's All in the Juice"; McMurtry, *Humor in Tennessee Justice,* 95.
9. Hinton, "Gallatin Squash."
10. Hinton, "Gallatin Squash."
11. McMurtry, *Humor in Tennessee Justice,* 95.
12. Miscellaneous newspaper clipping, Jimmy Perdue Family Collection.
13. *Prominent Tennesseans, 1796–1938,* 84; Author's interview with Walter T. Durham, October 21, 2010; *Gallatin News Examiner,* November 10, 2010.
14. Walter T. Durham to John A. Simpson, April 10, 2010.
15. Hub Perdue to Hon. K. D. McKellar, May 25, 1938, in Robert Boyte Crawford Howell Papers, Manuscript Division, Tennessee State Library and Archives, Nashville, TN.
16. Durham, *A Pictorial History of Sumner County,* 49–51; Durham and Millikan, *Gallatin 200,* 61; Lester and Thomson, *Around Gallatin,* 91.
17. See Dewey W. Grantham, *Southern Progressivism: The Reconciliation of Progress and Tradition* (Knoxville: University of Tennessee, 1983).
18. Durham and Millikan, eds, *Gallatin 200,* 61.
19. *Sumner County News,* August 11, 1938. His first opponent back in 1934, Harvey L. Brown, made a successful bid for a senate seat in the Tennessee General Assembly.
20. Durham and Millikan, eds, *Gallatin 200,* 78; *Sumner County News,* May 3, 1940.
21. James H. Perdue, "Gallatin from Kerosene to Nukes," in Jimmy Perdue Family Papers, 3–4.
22. Perdue, "Gallatin from Kerosene to Nukes," 2; Author's interview with Jimmy Perdue, July 20, 2010.
23. Perdue, "Gallatin from Kerosene to Nukes," 2; Author's interview with Jimmy Perdue, July 20, 2010.
24. Durham and Thomas, *A Pictorial History of Sumner County,* 99; Durham and Millikan, eds, *Gallatin 200,* 64; *Gallatin Examiner,* August 21, 1942; Author's conversation with Marilyn B. Hughes, March 10, 2010, Nashville, TN.
25. Interview with Walter T. Durham, October 21, 2010.
26. *Sumner County News,* July 10, 1942.
27. *Sumner County News,* August 13, 14, 1942.
28. Hinton, "The Gallatin Squash"; *Gallatin Examiner and Sumner County Tennessean,* April 5, 1946; *Sumner County News,* April 4, 1946.
29. *Sumner County News,* March 7, 1946.
30. *Sumner County News,* July 25, 1946.
31. *Sumner County News,* June 6, 1946.
32. *Sumner County News,* August 1, 1946.
33. *Sumner County News,* August 1, 1946.
34. *Sumner County News,* August 8, 1946; *Gallatin Examiner and Sumner County Tennessean,* August 9, 1946.
35. Perdue, "The Adventures of the Boy Lieutenant," 4–6.
36. *Prominent Tennesseans, 1796–1938:* 84.
37. Perdue, "Gallatin from Kerosene to Nukes," 1; *Banner,* January 20, 1971.
38. Perdue, "The Adventures of the Boy Lieutenant," 5.
39. See Perdue, "Gallatin from Kerosene to Nukes," 3.
40. After owning the business for 13 years, Polk sold it in the late 1950s and went to work for the Federal Aviation Agency for 10 years installing airport guidance systems throughout the Southeast. He retired in 1968. Polk Perdue died on January 19, 1971, two days before his sixty-ninth birthday. He outlived his father by only twenty-seven months. He is buried in Crestview Memorial Park, Gallatin, along with his aunt, Erma, who died in 1954 and uncle, Cotton, who died in 1937. See Snider and Yorgason, *Sumner County Cemetery Records,* 14–42, 14–63; *Polk's Gallatin City Directory, 1960* (St. Louis: R.L. Polk and Co., 1961): 138.*Sumner County News,* January 25, 1971; *Gallatin Examiner and Sumner County Tennessean,* January 28, 1971; *Banner,* January 20, 1971.

41. Letter from Jimmy Perdue to the author, September 6, 2012.
42. Perdue, "The Adventures of the Boy Lieutenant," 6–7.
43. Jimmy Perdue eventually earned a degree in electrical engineering from Tennessee Tech. He worked for many years with the TVA nuclear plants at Brown's Ferry and Watts Bar. Today, Jimmy is retired and lives with his wife, JoAnn, in Gallatin. See Perdue, "The Adventures of the Boy Lieutenant, 18.
44. *Tennessean*, December 1, 1939; *Banner*, December 2, 1938.
45. *Tennessean*, December 7, 1939; *Banner*, December 8, 1939.
46. Aside from his 1945 membership card, Hub is pictured with Bain Stewart and New York Giants scout Hank DeBerry at the 7th annual OTBA. See *Tennessean*, January 17, 1945. Hub's grandson, Jimmy Perdue, possesses his 1945 membership card.
47. See Baseball Chronology.com, http://www.baseballchronology.com.
48. See *Gallatin News Examiner*, November 10, 2010.
49. Hub typed a contract whereby Rogan agreed not to sign with any professional team without consulting Hub first since "he [Hub] has coached me." See Jimmy Perdue Family Collection. For details on Rogan's brief career, see Baseball Chronology.com, http://www.baseballchronology.com.
50. See the following letters in the Jimmy Perdue Family Collection, Henry J. Peters [Ass't Director, St. Louis Browns] to H.R. Perdue, February 12, 1953; George Sisler [Pittsburgh] to Hub Perdue, July 15, 1952; Laddie Placek [Director of Scouts, Cleveland Indians] to Hub Perdue March 10, 1953; W. H. "Buddy" Lewis [Regional Scout, St. Louis Cardinals] to Hub Perdue, n.d.
51. Miscellaneous newspaper clippings, Jimmy Perdue Family Collection.
52. See letters in the Jimmy Perdue Family Collection, Henry J. Peters [Ass't Director, St. Louis Browns] to H.R. Perdue, February 12, 1953; George Sisler [Pittsburgh] to Hub Perdue, July 15, 1952; Laddie Placek [Director of Scouts, Cleveland Indians] to Hub Perdue March 10, 1953; W. H. "Buddy" Lewis [Regional Scout, St. Louis Cardinals] to Hub Perdue, n.d.
53. See *The Upper Sumner Press*, April 30, 1943. This newspaper served the northern reaches of Sumner County centered in Portland, TN; *Gallatin News-Examiner*, May 14, 1943. Other teammates from the 1908 championship team receiving honorable mentions in the voting included Daubert, Duggan, Kellum, Bay and Wiseman. See *Banner*, April 22, 1943.

54. *Tennessean*, January 14, 1947. Johnson took a particularly keen interest in the OTBA and he usually participated in their festivities. Indeed, his sports page dwarfed Russell's *Banner* in coverage of the OTBA.
55. Fred Russell and George Leonard. *Vols Feats; Records, History and Tales of the Nashville Baseball Club in the Southern Association, 1901–1950* (Nashville: Banner Press, 1950): 5.
56. "Top 100 Teams," http://www.milb.com/milb/history/top100.
57. See Southern Association Baseball.com, http://www.southernassociationbaseball.com; Russell and Leonard, *Vols Feats,* 4–6. Incidentally, Dobbs' lofty accomplishments in the Southern Association are second only two Gilbert's: 23 years, 1,841 wins, .559 winning percentage.
58. *Banner,* September 9, 1948.
59. J.A. Wiseman to Fred Russell, [n.d.], 1948 in possession of James A. Wiseman, Cincinnati, OH.
60. Russell reprinted the game account twice under the title "THE GAME OF THE CENTURY." See *Banner,* September 18, 1934, April 12, 1936. Johnson referenced the game in one sentence in a 1962 tribute to Doc Wiseman, and Bill Traughber revisited "the greatest game ever played in the South" in *City Paper* (Nashville), August 3, 2001. Also see Simpson, *"The Greatest Game Ever Played in Dixie,"* 192–93. In an interview granted to the author on April 7, 1999, Russell recalled only vague details about Perdue, McElveen and the '08 championship game. It is fair to say that the dean of southern sportswriters had forgotten more about Nashville baseball history than most people had ever known. An American original, whose reputation as a practical joker rivaled Perdue, passed away on January 26, 2003. For a recent treatment of Russell's life, see Andrew Derr, *Life of Dreams; The Good Times of Sportswriter Fred Russell* (Macon: Mercer University Press, 2012).
61. *Tennessean,* January 22, 1952.
62. *Tennessean,* January 18, 1952; *TSN,* January 30, 1952. Gooch had a marvelous eleven-year career the the Major Leagues with Pittsburgh, Brooklyn and Cincinnati. He added ten more years in the minor circuit. See Bill Nowlin, "Johnny Gooch," in SABR BioProject; Baseball Reference.com, www.baseball-reference.com.
63. Glennon, the popular General Manager of the Birmingham Barons from 1946–1961, and Lefty Gomez are the only two speakers to appear twice at OTBA meetings. Other notable headliners include Gabe Paul (1956), Jimmy Dykes (1958), Dixie Walker (1964), Eddie Stanky (1968), Smoky Burgess (1975), George Stein-

brenner (1980), Whitey Ford (1982), Buck Showalter (1992), Tommy Lasorda (1994), Buck O'Neil (2000), Harmon Killebrew (2001), and Doc Gooden (2011). For a complete listing of presenters, see Nashville Baseball Old Timers Association, http://www.otbaseball.com.
    64. See *Tennessean,* January 30, 1958.
    65. *TSN,* October 28, 1953.
    66. *Gallatin Examiner and Sumner County Tennessean,* May 26, 1960; Sumner County News, May 26, 1960.

Chapter 12

    1. John Thorn, "Prove It," in Gregory F. Augustine Pierce, ed, *How Bill James Changed Our View of Baseball* (Skokie, IL: ACTA, 2007), 49.
    2. TSN, February 7, 1962, April 11, 1962.
    3. *Tennessean,* January 22, 1967. Charles "Red" Lucas was a legitimate big league star. See www.baseball-reference.com.
    4. www.baseball-reference.com.
    5. *Tennessean,* January 22, 1967; *Gallatin Examiner,* November 7, 1968.
    6. See Hinton, "Gallatin Squash."
    7. *Banner,* February 10, 1967. The plaque is in the possession of Jimmy Perdue, Gallatin, TN.
    8. Perdue, "Gallatin from Kerosene to Nukes," 1.
    9. Simpson, "*The Greatest Game Ever Played in Dixie,*" 222; *Tennessean,* November 1, 1968; *Gallatin Examiner,* November 7, 1968. Also see the registry book for list of funeral attendees in possession of Jimmy Perdue, Gallatin, TN.
    10. E. L. Doctorow, *Ragtime, A Novel* (New York: Random House, 2007 reprint), 227–232.
    11. *TSN,* November 16, 1968 in Hubbard Perdue, Vertical File, *The Sporting News Library and Archive,* St. Louis, MO.
    12. *Banner,* November 1, 1968.
    13. Hinton, "The Gallatin Squash."
    14. *Boston Daily Globe.* January 30, 1916.

Bibliography

Primary Sources

Public Records

Knox County, Indiana, Death Indexes, County Clerk's Office, 1932.
Statewide Index to Tennessee Death Records (1914–1931), vol. 10. Secretary of State, Tennessee State Library and Archive.
Sumner County, Tennessee, Marriage Records, County Clerk's Office, 1899, 1904.
Sumner County, Tennessee, Minute Book, County Clerk's Office, 1934–1946.
Sumner County, Tennessee, Wills, County Clerk's Office, 1924–1942.
U.S. Census, *Agriculture, Sumner County, Tennessee*, 1860.
U.S. Census, *Non-Population Census Schedules for Tennessee* (1860).
U.S. Census, *Population, Knox County, Indiana*, 1910.
U.S. Census, *Population, Sumner County, Tennessee*, 1870–1930.
U.S. Census, *Slave Abstracts, Sumner County, Tennessee*, 1840–1860.
1870 U.S. Census: Sumner County, Tennessee (abstract). Gallatin, TN: Sumner County Archive, 1995.

Books and Pamphlets

Ashenback, Edward Michael. *Humor Among the Minors: True Tales from the Baseball Brush*. Chicago: M. A. Donohue, 1911.
Beers, D. G. and Company, *Map of Sumner County, Tennessee*. Philadelphia: D. G. Beers, 1878.
Cincinnati City Directory, 1909–1927.
Cisco, Jay Guy. *Historic Sumner County, Tennessee with Genealogies of the Bledsoe, Cage and Douglass Families and Genealogical Notes of Other Sumner County Families*. Nashville: Clearfield, 2002 reprint.
Elks Bazaar Souvenir [pamphlet], *Vincennes Lodge No. 291, BPOE*. Vincennes, 1907.
Goodspeed's History of Sumner, Smith, Macon and Trousdale Counties. Nashville: Goodspeed, 1887.
Foster Austin P. and Albert H. Roberts. *Tennessee Democracy: A History of the Party and Its Representative Members—Past and Present*, 4 vols. Nashville: Democratic Historical Association, 1940.
Hale, Will T. and Dixon L. Merritt. *A History of Tennessee and Tennesseans: The Leaders and Representative Men of Commerce, Industry and Modern Activity*. 4 vols. Chicago: Lewis Publishing, 1913.
Johnson, Harry "Steamboat." *Standing the Gaff: The Life and Hard Times of a Minor League Umpire*. New York: Bison, 1994 reprint.
LaBree, Ben. *Press Reference Book of Prominent Kentuckians*. Louisville: Standard Printing, 1916.
Lane, F. C. *Batting*. Cleveland: Society for American Baseball Research, 2001 reprint.
Maranville, Walter "Rabbit." *Run, Rabbit, Run: The Hilarious and Mostly True Tales of Rabbit Maranville*. Phoenix: Society for American Baseball Research, 2012 reprint.
Moore, John Trotwood. *The Volunteer State, 1769–1923*, 2 vols. Nashville: S. J. Clarke, 1923.
Nashville City Directory, Nashville: Marshall, Bruce and Polk, 1907–1910.
Terrell, W. H. H. *Indiana Volunteers, Fifty-first Regiment: Report of the Adjutant General of the State of Indiana*, vol. 5 (1866).

Who's Who in Tennessee: A Biographical Reference Book of Notable Tennesseans of Today. Memphis: Paul and Douglass, 1911.

Manuscripts and Other Unpublished Material

Bartlett Giamatti Research Center, National Baseball Hall of Fame Library, Cooperstown, NY
    Player Contract Cards and Vertical Files
        Harry Elbert Bay
        Hub Perdue
        William Henry Bernhard
        Theodore P. Breitenstein
        Jacob Ellsworth Daubert
        John Dolittle Hardy
        Pryor Mynatt McElveen
        Carl Vedder Sitton
Blegin Library Archives, University of Cincinnati, Cincinnati, OH
    The Burnet Woods Echo
Jean and Alexander Heard Library, Vanderbilt University, Nashville, TN
    Grantland Rice Collection
    William Waller Collection
The Sporting News
    Player Contract Cards
        Harry Bay
        William H. Bernhard
        Ted Breitenstein
        Jake E. Daubert
        John Dolittle Hardy
        Pryor M. McElveen
        Hubbard Perdue
        James Warren Seabough
        Carl Vedder Sitton
        Julius A. Wiseman
Tennessee State Library and Archive, Nashville
    Vertical Files
        Fred Russell
        Sulphur Dell
Nashville Base-ball Association, State of Tennessee, Secretary of State, Charter of Incorporation, Book U-7.
        Robert Boyte Crawford Howell Papers

Newspapers and Periodicals

Atlanta Constitution
Baseball Magazine
Boston Daily Globe
Bristol News Bulletin
Cairo Bulletin
Charlotte News
Charlotte Observer
Chattanooga Daily Times
Chattanooga News
Chicago Daily Tribune
Chicago Evening Post
Christian Science Monitor
Clarksville Leaf-Chronicle
Cleveland Plain Dealer
Connellsville Daily Courier (PA)
The Frisco Employee's Magazine, 1925–1935.
Gallatin Examiner
Gallatin Examiner and Sumner County Tennessean
Gallatin News
Gallatin News-Examiner
Grand Rapids Tribune
Hopkinsville Kentuckian
Houston Chronicle
La Crosse Tribune and Leader Press
Leader and Press (Springfield, MO)
Louisville Courier-Journal
Mays Landing Current (NJ)
Memphis Commercial-Appeal
Minneapolis Morning Tribune
Nashville American
Nashville Banner
Nashville Tennessean
Nashville Tennessean and Nashville American (merged)
New Orleans Times-Picayune
New York Evening Mail
New York Times
New York Tribune
Paducah Evening Sun
Paducah Sun
Peoria Journal
Philadelphia Evening Star
Reach Official Guide, 1906
St. Louis Daily Globe-Democrat
St. Louis Post-Dispatch
St. Louis Star
St. Louis Times
Shreveport Journal
Shreveport Times
Spalding's Official Baseball Record, 1906–1919
Sporting Life, 1906–1918
The Sporting News, 1902–1968
Sumner County News
Sumner Examiner-Press
The Tennessean (Gallatin edition)
Toledo News Bee
Upper Sumner Press (Portland, TN)
Vincennes Capital
Vincennes Daily Sun

Vincennes Morning Commercial
Vincennes Post
Vincennes Sun-Commercial
Washington Post
Wichita Daily Times (TX)

Private Papers and Collections

Jimmy Perdue Family Papers, Gallatin, TN.
James D. Wiseman Correspondence, Cincinnati, OH.

Secondary Sources

Articles

Bibb, John. "It's All in the Juice." *Nashville Tennessean Magazine,* August 9, 1959.
Brown, J. D. "The Name Stuck." *Nashville Tennessean Magazine,* April 12, 1947.
Evans, Harold C. "Baseball in Kansas, 1867–1940." *Kansas Historical Quarterly* 9 (1940).
Hinton, Elmer. "Gallatin Squash." *Nashville Tennessean Magazine,* October 7, 1945.
Obermeyer, Jeffrey. "B 18 Felt Blankets — A Closer Look." *The Vintage and Classic Baseball Collector,* May/June 1996.
Ruane, Tom. "The Deadball Era's Worst Pitching Staff." *The Baseball Research Journal* (Fall 2009).
Russell, Fred. "Grantland Rice Gave It a Name ... Sulphur Dell." *Nashville Tennessean Magazine,* February 7, 1957.
Spangle, Brian. "A Kitty League Pennant." *Vincennes Sun-Commercial,* August 31, 2003.
Traughber, Bill. "Nashville Hosted Greatest Game Played in South." *The City Paper* (Nashville), August 3, 2001.
_____. "The Nashville Seraphs, 1895." *The National Pastime: A Review of Baseball History* 23 (2003).

Books and Pamphlets

Absher, Lee Alton. *Some Early Settlers of Upper Sumner County, Tennessee.* Knoxville: 1966.
Alexander, Charles C. *John McGraw.* Lincoln: University of Nebraska, 1995.
Bartlett, Jennifer M., Charles P. Stripling, and Fred M. Prouty. *Historical and Archaeological Investigations of the Site of the Tennessee Bicentennial Mall, 40DV469, Davidson County.* Nashville: Tennessee Department of Environment and Conservation, Division of Archaeology, 1995.
The Baseball Encyclopedia: The Complete and Definitive Record of Major League Baseball, 9th edition. New York: Macmillan, 1993.
Benson, Michael. *Ballparks of North America: A Comprehensive Historical Reference to Baseball Grounds, Yards and Stadiums, 1845 to Present.* Jefferson, NC: McFarland, 1989.
Bogen, Gil. *Johnny Kling: A Baseball Biography.* Jefferson, NC: McFarland, 2006.
Brown, Dee A. *The American Spa: Hot Springs Arkansas.* Little Rock: Rose , 1982.
Clark, Blanche Henry. *The Tennessee Yeoman, 1840–1860.* Nashville: Vanderbilt University, 1942.
Collier, John David. *Precious Memories.* 1999.
_____. *Tell Me a Story.* 1990.
Cornwell, Ilene J. *Biographical Directory of the Tennessee General Assembly.* 3 vols. Nashville: Tennessee Historical Commission, 1988.
Cutter, Charles. *Cutter's Guide to the Hot Springs of Arkansas.* Charleston: Nabu, 2010 reprint.
Darnell, Tim. *Southern Yankees: The Story of the Atlanta Crackers.* 1995.
Denning, Michael. *Death Certificates of Sumner County, Tennessee, 1921–1925.* Nashville: 2000.
Derr, Andrew. *Life of Dreams: The Good Times of Sportswriter Fred Russell.* Macon: Mercer University, 2012.
Dickson, Paul. *The New Dickson Baseball Dictionary.* New York: W.W. Norton, 2009.
Doctorow, E. L. *Ragtime, A Novel.* New York: Random House, 2007 reprint.
Doyle, Don H. *Nashville in the New South, 1880–1930.* Knoxville: University of Tennessee, 1985.
_____. *New Men, New Cities, New South: Atlanta, Nashville, Charleston, Mobile, 1860–1910.* Chapel Hill: University of North Carolina, 1990.
Drake, Doug, Jack Masters, and Bill Puryear. *Founding of the Cumberland Settlements: The First Atlas, 1779–1804.* Gallatin, TN: Warioto, 2009.
Durham, Walter T. *Josephus Conn Guild and Rose Mont: Politics and Plantation in Nineteenth Century Tennessee.* Nashville: Hillsboro, 2003.
_____. *Old Sumner; A History of Sumner County, Tennessee from 1805 to 1861.* Nashville: Parthenon, 1972.
_____. *Rebellion Revisited; A History of Sumner County, Tennessee from 1861 to 1870.* Nashville: Parthenon, 1982.

Durham, Walter T. and Glenda Millikan, eds., *Gallatin 200: A Time Line History Celebrating the Bicentennial of Gallatin, Tennessee*. Franklin, TN: Hillsboro, 2002.

Durham, Walter T. and James W. Thomas. *A Pictorial History of Sumner County, Tennessee, 1786–1986*. Nashville: Williams, 1986.

Elfers, James E. *The Tour to End All Tours: The Story of Major League Baseball's 1913–1914 World Tour*. Lincoln: University of Nebraska, 2003.

Faust, Patricia L., ed., *Historical Times Illustrated Encyclopedia of the Civil War*. New York: Harper & Row, 1986.

Fountain, Charles. *Sportswriter: The Life and Times of Grantland Rice*. New York: Oxford University, 1993.

Golenbock, Peter. *The Spirit of St. Louis: A History of the St. Louis Cardinals and Browns*. New York: Avon, 2000.

Grantham, Dewey W. *Southern Progressivism: The Reconciliation of Progress and Tradition*. Knoxville: University of Tennessee, 1983.

Guinozzo, John. *Memphis Baseball*. Memphis: Commercial-Appeal, 1980.

Hinton, Elmer. *Let's Do Away with August*. Nashville: Impact, 1970.

Jenkins, David. *Baseball in Chattanooga*. Chicago: Arcadia, 2005.

Johnson, Lloyd and Miles Wolff, eds., *The Encyclopedia of Minor League Baseball: The Official Record of Minor League Baseball*. Durham, NC: Baseball America, 1993.

Jones, David, ed., *Deadball Stars of the American League*. Dulles, VA: Potomac, 2006.

Kaese, Harold. *The Boston Braves, 1871–1953*. Boston: Northeastern University, 2004 reprint.

Lester, Dee Gee and Kenneth Calvin Thomson, Jr., *Around Gallatin and Sumner County*. Dover, NH: Chalford, 1998.

Lowry, Philip J. *Green Cathedrals: The Ultimate Celebration of All 273 Major League and Negro League Ballparks*. New York: Addison-Wesley, 1992.

Lund, John. *1908: A Look at the World Champion 1908 Chicago Cubs*. 2008.

Lyons, Michael J. *World War I: A Short History*. Englewood, NJ: Prentice Hall, 1994.

Maraniss, David. *When Pride Still Mattered: Lombardi*. New York: Simon & Schuster, 2010 reprint.

Martini, Stephen. *The Chattanooga Lookouts & 100 Seasons of Scenic City Baseball*. Cleveland, TN: Dry Ice, 2005.

McMurtry, J. C. *Humor in Tennessee Justice*. Tompkinsville, KY: Monroe County, 1979.

McPherson, James M. *For Cause and Comrades: Why Men Fought in the Civil War*. New York: Oxford University, 1998.

Michie's Tennessee Code of 1938: The General Laws of Tennessee. Charlottesville, VA: Michie, 1938.

Mitchell, Reid. *Civil War Soldiers: Their Expectations and Their Experiences*. New York: Touchstone, 1988.

Mooney, Chase C. *Slavery in Tennessee*. Bloomington: Indiana University, 1957.

Murphy, Cait N. *Crazy '08: How A Cast of Cranks, Rogues, Boneheads and Magnates Created the Greatest Year in Baseball History*. New York: Collins, 2008.

Nemec, David. *The Beer and Whiskey League: The Illustrated History of the American Association — Baseball's Renegade Major League*. New York: Lyons and Burford, 1994.

Nipper, Skip. *Baseball in Nashville*. Chicago: Arcadia, 2007.

Okkonen, Marc. *Baseball Memories, 1900–1909: An Illustrated Chronicle of the Big Leagues' First Decade*. New York: Sterling, 1992.

O'Neil, Bill. *The Southern League: Baseball in Dixie, 1885–1994*. Austin, TX: Eakin, 1994.

Pierce, Gregory F. Augustine, ed., *How Bill James Changed Our View of Baseball*. Skokie, IL: ACTA, 2007.

Prominent Tennesseans, 1796–1938. Lewisburg, TN: Who's Who, 1940.

Rader, Benjamin G. *Baseball: A History of America's Game*. Urbana: University of Illinois, 1992.

Riess, Steven A. *City Games: The Evolution of American Urban Society and the Rise of Sports*. Urbana: University of Illinois, 1989.

_____. *Touching Base: Professional Baseball and American Culture in the Progressive Era*. Westport, CN: Greenwood, 1980.

Ritter, Lawrence S. *The Glory of Their Times: The Story of the Early Days of Baseball Told by the Men Who Played It*. New York: Morrow, 1984 reprint.

_____. *Lost Ballparks: A Celebration of Baseball's Legendary Fields*. New York: Penguin, 1994.

Russell, Fred. *Bury Me in an Old Press Box*. New York: A. S. Barnes, 1957.

_____. *I'll Try Anything Twice*. Nashville: McQuiddy, 1945.

Russell, Fred, and George Leonard. *Vols Feats:*

Records, History and Tales of the Nashville Baseball Club in the Southern Association, 1901–1950. Nashville: Nashville Banner, 1950.

Seymour, Harold, and Dorothy Seymour Mills. *Baseball: The Early Years.* New York: Oxford University, 1960.

Shenk, Gerald. *Work or Fight!: Race, Gender, and the Draft in World War One.* New York: Palgrave Macmillan, 2005.

Simon, Tom, ed. *Deadball Stars of the National League.* Washington, DC: Brassey's, 2004.

Simpson, John A. *Edith D. Pope and Her Nashville Friends: Guardians of the Lost Cause in the Confederate Veteran Magazine.* Knoxville: University of Tennessee, 2003.

_____. *"The Greatest Game Ever Played in Dixie:" The Nashville Vols, Their 1908 Season, and the Championship Game.* Jefferson, NC: McFarland, 2007.

_____. *S. A. Cunningham and the Confederate Heritage.* Athens: University of Georgia, 1994.

Sistler, Byron. *Sumner County, Tennessee: Bible, Family, and Tombstone Records.* Nashville: Sistler, 2004 reprint.

Skipper, James K., Jr. *Baseball Nicknames: A Dictionary of Origins and Meanings.* Jefferson, NC: McFarland, 1992.

Skipper, John C. *Wicked Curve: The Life and Troubled Times of Grover Cleveland Alexander.* Jefferson, NC: McFarland, 2006.

Snider, Margaret Cummings, and Joan Hollis Yorgason. *Sumner County, Tennessee: Cemetery Records* Owensboro, KY: McDowell, 1981.

Spatz, Lyle, and Steve Steinberg. *1921: The Yankees, the Giants and the Battle for Baseball Supremacy in New York.* Lincoln: University of Nebraska, 2010.

Stephenson, Darl L. *Headquarters in the Brush: Blazer's Independent Union Scouts.* Athens, OH: Ohio University, 2001.

Stinson Era W., and Elizabeth Sue Spurlock. *Sumner County, Tennessee: Sumner County, Tennessee Mariages, 1839–1875.* Bowling Green, KY: 1985.

Sullivan, Neil J. *The Minors: The Struggles and the Triumphs of Baseball's Poor Relation from 1876 to the Present.* New York: St. Martin's, 1990.

Summerville, James. *The Carmack-Cooper Shooting: Tennessee Politics Turned Violent.* Jefferson, NC: McFarland, 1994.

Thomson, Cindy. *Three Finger Brown: The Mordecai Brown Story.* New York: Bison, 2009.

Traughber, Bill. *Nashville Sports History: Stories from the Stands.* Charleston: The History Press, 2010.

Van West, Carroll, ed. *The Encyclopedia of Tennessee History and Culture.* Nashville: Rutledge, 1998.

Voigt, David Q. *American Baseball,* 3 vols. Norman: University of Oklahoma, 1966–1983.

Waller, William. *Nashville, 1900–1910.* Nashville: Vanderbilt University, 1972.

Wilson, Shirley. *Sumner County, Tennessee: Index to the Loose Records, 1786–1930.* Hendersonville, TN: Richley, 1988.

Wright, Gavin. *The Political Economy of the Cotton South: Households, Markets, and Wealth in the Nineteenth Century.* New York: Norton, 1978.

Wright, Marshall D. *The Southern Association in Baseball, 1885–1961.* Jefferson, NC: McFarland, 2002.

Unpublished Material

Gisclair, S. Derby. "The Early Southern Association, 1901–1926." Paper delivered at Third Annual Southern Association of Baseball Conference, Birmingham, AL, April 2006.

Perdue, James H. "The Adventures of the Boy Lieutenant: A Saga of the battle of boredom in the Korean Conflict, staged in the deserts of Arizona" (unpublished autobiography) in Jimmy Perdue Family Papers.

Perdue, James H. "Gallatin from Kerosene to Nukes," in Jimmy Perdue Family Papers.

Wiseman, Donald E. "Julius Augustus 'Doc' Wiseman (1877–1953): The Hero of the Dell" (unpublished family genealogy).

Interviews

Jimmy and JoAnn Perdue, October 2010–October 2012.
Walter T. Durham, April 2011.
James A. Wiseman and family, April 2004.

Internet

www.baseball-reference.com
www.minorleaguebaseball.com
www.retrosheet.org
www.sabr.org/bioproject

Index

Numbers in ***bold italics*** indicate pages with photographs.

Abbaticchio, Ed (Batty) 18
Adams, Charles (Babe) 105, 155
Alexander, Grover Cleveland (Old Pete) 1, 92, 96, 114, 121, 124, ***131***, 132, 137, 230
Altrock, Nick 2, 240
Alvin York Day at Sulphur Dell 156
American Association 155; team affiliations 258*n*1
Ames, Leon (Red) 1, 114, ***131***
Anderson, P.L. (Butch) 13, 15
Andrews, Oliver Burnside 147
Andrews Field (Chattanooga) 82, 148, 161, 179; tornado damage 148–49
Ashenback, Edward Michael 48
Athletic Park (Nashville) 12, 19, 43, 57; modern improvements 39, 46–47
Athletic Park (New Orleans) 47, 223; dimension changes to 261*n*98; renamed 153
Athletic Park (Wichita Falls) 201, 204; fire damage 199
Atz, John (Jake) 196, 205

B-18 blanket series 112
Babb, Charlie 37, 84
Backus, John O. 35
Baker, Newton (Secretary of War) 152
Baker Bowl (Philadelphia) 93, 112
"battle for Tennessee" rivalry 149–50
Baugh, Robert H. (president, Southern Association) 153
Bay, Harry (Deerfoot) 51, 54, 62, 70, 80, 82–83, 86, 225
Becker, Beals 127
Beene Nursing Home (Hartsville) 237
Bernhard, Bill (Berny or Strawberry Bill) 50–51, 53, 55, 57–59, 62, 65, 67–68, 70, 72–78, 80–82, 125, 146, 169, 200; firing 83–85; hired by Memphis 84; hired by Nashville

46; influence on Perdue 65, 86–87, 89; rebuilding the Vols (1910) 87
Bescher, Bob 104, 120, 132, 195
Bethpage (TN) 10; Civil War actions 8–9; founding and business growth 7–8
Bischoff, John (Smiley) 200
Bledsoe Creek (valley) 6, 8–9
Blue Grass Line (interurban trolley) 10, ***171***
Bogart, Eddie 173, 177, 179, 188–89, 191
Boguskie, Harold (Buster) 225, 226
Bomar, Charlie 25
Bowles, W.J. 17
Bowling Green Business University (later Western Kentucky University) 11, 13
Bradley, Hugh (Corns) 159, 172, 174, 187–88; background and concerns 175; dismissal 180–81
Brahic, Dick 28, 32–34
Braves Field (Boston) 120, 130
Breitenstein, Ted (Breit or Red) 41, 59–60, 62; umpire 148, 153
Bresnahan, Roger (The Duke) 119, 137, 144
Britton, Helene Robison 118–19
Bronkie, Herman (Dutch) 77, 80, 185
Broun, Heywood 124
Brown, Charles (Buster) 92
Brown, Bill (Buster) 173, 177–78, 181–***83***, 184–85, 189–90
Brown, James S. 47, 60, 69
Brown, Layon 216–17
Brown, Mordecai (Three Finger) 35–***36***, 114
Brown, Tom (umpire) 54
Buchanan, Jim 76
Burke, Mike 172, 179, 181, 184–85, 190–91
Butler, Willis (Kid) 51, 54, 61–62, 70, 83

Cairo (Giants) 28, 30, 32
Cantillon, Joe (Pongo Joe) 136, 155

273

274 Index

Carmack, Edward Ward: assassination and murder trial 66, 70; debate with Patterson 57
Carpenter, W.B. (umpire) 52, 57–**58**, 62, 75
Carr, James B. 47
Case, Charlie 73–74, 78
Castleman, Clydell (Slick) 222, 237
Castro, Louis (The Cuban) **40**
Cather, Ted 113
Champion, S.A. 47
Chance, Frank 1, 33, 34, 37, 78
Cheek-Neal (amateur team) 13
Chenault, Bill 15, 23–24, **31**, 34–35, 67, 237
Chesapeake and Nashville (railroad) 9–10
Ching, Dick 150, 259n9
Clymer, William (Derby Bill) 102, 136–37, 140, 143–46; background 135; concern over Perdue's unauthorized leave 140, 142
Cobb, Ty 99, 167
Coleman, Bob 167
Conley, James (Snipe) 203
Cooke, Tom W. 136–39
Cooper, Duncan 66, 70
cork-centered baseballs 77
Coveleski, Harry 81
cow pasture games 5, 11, 13, 244n25
Cravath, Clifford (Gavvy) 96, 106, 114, 127
Creosote ball incident 203
Crowder, Enoch (provost marshall general) 152
Cunningham, Sumner A. 18, 47, 70
Curtis, Joe (sports editor, *Chattanooga News*) 146

Daubert, Jake (Gentleman Jake) 1, 51, 53–54, 61–62, 64, 66, 68, 83, 87, 89, 92, 114; player's union affiliation 99; power hitting 56, 59
Davis, L.C. 120, 122
Deadball Era 1, 5; demise 165, 192–93; purple prose 24; style of play 23–24
Decoration (Memorial) Day 25
"Details" (chalk scoreboards) 39, 57–**58**, 60
Dickel, George A. 59
Dickson, Walter (Hickory) 95
Dixie Series 166
Doak, Bill 118, 124, 126–28
Doak, Charlie (umpire) 206
Dobbs, Johnny 18, 37–41, 46, 83–84, 102, 146–47, 150, 153, 158–61, 165–66, 169, 181, **183**, 186, 189, 224; managerial career 248n80
Doctorow, E.L. 239–40
Dodge, Johnny 138
Dolan, Albert (Cozy) 119, 122
Doolan, Mike 96, 99
Dovey, George 90
Dovey, John 90

Doyle, Larry 100, 103, 114, 122, 128, 240
Duggan, Johnny 26–29, 35, 54, 57, 59, 70, 73–74, 76, 78; no-hitter 56
The Dump (right field incline, Sulphur Dell) 18
Duncan Hotel (Nashville) 56
Dundon, Gus 61–62
Dunning, Guy (Sal) 172
Durham, Walter T. 6, 170, 212

Eason, Malcolm (umpire) 128
East, Walter 51, 67, 69–70, 75, 77, 83
Ebbets, Charles 52, 65, 67–68, 83, 85–87, 89–90, 130
Ebbets Field (Brooklyn) 120
Eclipse Park (Louisville) 136, 140, 144
Elberfeld, Norman (Kid) 145–47, 149–50, 160, 165, 177–78; resigns from Chattanooga 152
Ellam, Roy 161, 163, 165–66, 168–69, 172, 202
Engel, Joe 153
Evans, Steve 2, 108, 121, 144, 240
Evers, Johnny 1, 37, **171**; traded to Braves 109–10, 114
Ewing, William James, Jr. 53, 56, 59, 64, 67, 69, 74, 76, 79, 173, 207; sponsors Nashville's team nickname contest (1908) 49–50; sports editor, *Nashville American* 38–40

Federal League 109–10, 118, 125, 137
Fiedler, Marty 179–80
Fincher, Bill 197–98
Finn, Mike (Irish) 19–20, 29, 37
Fisher, Newt (Ike) 15–18
Fisher, Tom 37
Fitzgerald, John F. 95
Flaherty, Edmund (Patsy) 201–2, 205; career 264n32
Flaherty, Patrick (Patsy) 153
Fletcher, Art (umpire) 127
Flood, Tim 77, 80, 82
Frakes, Willie 15, 23–25, 27; death 28; tribute games 29
Frank, Charlie 16–17, 19, 21, 37, 59, 84, 150, 153, 159, 198
Fraternity of Professional Baseball Players 99, 114
Frierson, Johnny 172–74, 178, 185, 187–88
Fultz, Dave 114

Gaffney, James E. 94, 101, 109
Gallatin (TN): Civil War actions in 8; establishment 6; modernization 10
Gallatin Butchers (amateur team) 13–15
Gallatin Pike 7–8, 10
Galloway, Jim (Bad News) 203
Gambill, H.F. 216
Garner, Russell E. 148
Garvin, Lee 56

Gerard, Kitty 27, 142
Gesler, Henry (Doc or Brownie) 109–*11*; background 255*n*105
Gifford, Al (umpire): career 261*n*71; conflicts with Perdue 160, 162–64; run-in with Nashville team 162
Gilbert, Larry 127, 149, 153, 162, 166, 186, 226; background 223–34; manager of Nashville 223–24; managerial record 266*n*57; nickname 224
Gilroy, Tom 70, 72–73
Glennon, Eddie 226
Gooch, Johnny 225, 237; career 267*n*63
Goodall, Thomas 185
Goodspeed's History of Sumner County 9
Gosnell, Clifton C. 25, 27, 29–32, 34; background 247*n*36
Grand Ole Opry 211
Grantham, Dewey W. 213
The Greatest Game Ever Played in Dixie 2, 64
Gremminger, Ed (Battleship) 80
Griner, Dan 126–27
Groh, Henry (Heinie) **123**
Groome, Bailey (sports editor, *Charlotte Observer*) 206
Guild, Willy 13, 15
Guildwood 10, 170

Hahn, George (Noodles) 18, 21, 237
Hall, Spick (sports editor, *Nashville Tennessean*) 85
Hardy, John (Scrappy Jack) 38, 41, 54, **63**, 73; Hardy-Yerkes altercation 43, 54, 98
Harris, Otis (sports editor, *Shreveport Journal*) 195–96
Hartsville (TN) 6
Haury, Chris 15–16
Head, James Marshall 19
Hee Haw 211
Heinemann, A.J. 152, 157, 224
Heinemann Park (New Orleans) 153, 156, 160
Henline, Noah 53
Herzog, Buck 92, 174
Hess, Otto 239–40
Hickman, Gordon (The Featherweight Phenom) 55–56
Hightower, Mims 147
Hinton, Elmer T. 22, 98, 237–38, 240; journalism background 211
Hirsig, William G. 47; president of Nashville's Board of Directors 85–86
Hoblitzel, Dick 92, 206
Hopkinsville (Browns) 24; disbanded 25
Horn, Claude (Blinky): journalism career 261*n*76; sports reporter and editor, *Nashville Tennessean* 72, 161–64, 169, 173, 181, **183**–85, 187
Hornsby, Rogers (Rajah) 1, 114, 132

Hot Springs (AR) 95, 109–10
Hotel Eastman 95
Howell, R.B.C. 212
Howse, Hillary 66
Hoyt, Waite 154
Hublore: defined 2, 167; stories in 10–11, 22, 24, 32, 50, 54, 77, 79, 89, 98, 105, 108, 118, 125, 127, 133–37, 142–44, 146, 158, 163, 166–68, 170, 207–8, 211, 222, 225, 236, 239
Huggins, Miller (Hug) 1, 110, 113–14, 118–19, 122, 124–26, 128–33; career and awards 256*n*1
Humor Among the Minors 48
Hurlburt, Ed 62
Hurth, Charlie 226
Hyatt, Ham 148

In Sulphur Dell (poem) 49

Jackson, Joe (Shoeless Joe) 1, 82
James, William (Seattle Bill) 1, 102, 116
Johnson, Allen 82, 84; poem 79; sports editor, *Nashville American* 79; termination 85
Johnson, Ban 17
Johnson, Harry (Steamboat) (umpire) 77, 132–33, 157, 160, 162; career 258*n*64
Johnson, Raymond 52, 222, 225–26, 237–38; sports editor, *Nashville Tennessean* 223
Johnson, Walter 112
Jones, Fielder 125
Jones, Verner Moore 68–70, 73, 75–76, 78, 81, 84; journalism career 251*n*6; poems 72; sports editor, *Nashville Banner* 67
Jonnard, Clarence (Bubber) 162, 164, 172, 173, 174, 181, **183**, 190; fight and suspension 177
Jonnard, Claude 164
Juul, Herb 53, 74

Kaese, Harold 115; journalism career 253*n*3
Kavanaugh, Williams Marmaduke (president of Southern Association) 18, 20, 49, 54, 59, 61, 69, 77, 86; death 150
Kavanaugh Field (Little Rock) 150, 178
Keen, Vic 200–2, 205
Keener, Sid C. 121; sports editor, *St. Louis Times* 119, 130
Kellum, Winford (Win) 68, 70, 73, 76; Kellum-McElveen altercation 54–55, 98
Kent, Reed W. 17, 19
Kentucky-Illinois-Tennessee League (Kitty) 23, 27–28; formal and informal team nicknames 30, 247*n*39; team affiliations 245*n*1
Keupper, Henry 78, 80
Killifer, Wade 132
Kirke, Jay 142–44
Kitchens, Frank (Pop) 153, 155–56, 195, 197, 200–1

Index

Klem, Bill (umpire) 113, 121
Kling, Johnny (Noisy) 92–93, 101–2, 146; career 95; conflict with Perdue 98–99
Knaupp, Henry (Cotton) 159
Knaupp, William (Chick) 173–75, 191–92, 206–7; team captain/manager of Nashville 188
Kolb, Eddie 26, *31*, 34
Kuhn, Ferdinand E. 59–60, 69, 87, 195; president of Nashville's Board of Directors 47; termination 85

Lackey, William Nicholas (Pops) 170, *171*
Lajoie, Napoleon 46, 84, 86
Lake, Fred 90
Landis, Kenesaw Mountain 187, 203
Lane, F.C. 109
Lankenau, Frank (Parson) 156, 182, 185, 189–90
Larkin, Paul W. 198, 200–4; baseball as big business (editorial) 202; sports editor, *Wichita Daily Times* 196
Larry Gilbert Silver Jubilee 223–25
Lea, Luke 38
League Park (Vincennes) 26, 30, 33; description 246*n*19
Lister, Pete 38
Lloyd, Harry 24
Lobert, Hans 106, 114
Long, Huey 213–*14*
Long, Tom 150, 259*n*9
Lord, Bris 62–*63*, 102
Love, Hamilton 52, 170, 172, 187
Lower Bethpage Cemetery 7, 9, 21
Lucas, Charles (Red, or The Nashville Narcissus) 173–75, 222, background 237–38
Luque, Adolfo (The Cuban) 135, 142
Lynch, Mike 77
Lynch, Tom 104

"Ma Tings" episode 142–44
Mack, Connie 78, 101, 135
Magnolia Park (Beaumont) 155
Mann, Les 102, 121
Manuel, Mark (Moxie) 72
Maranville, Walter (Rabbit) 1–2, 100, 102, 106, 114, 121, 239–40
Marquard, Richard (Rube) 1, 98–99, 104, 113–14, 114, 127, 230, 239–40
Martin, John D. 148; president of Southern Association 155; suspension of Perdue 164
Mathewson, Christy (Big Six) 1, 39, 93, 96, 99, 103, 131, 230, 236, 238, 240
Matthews, Harry 62
Mattison, L.Q. 27, *31*, 34
McCormick, Mike (Dude) 38; poor attitude and first departure from team 41–42; release 51, 83

McElveen, Pryor (Mac) 38, 42, 51, 61, 64, 66, 68, 83, 87; defensive skills 61, 100, 225, 251*n*62; Kellum-McElveen altercation 54–55, 98
McGraw, John (Mugsy, or The Little Napoleon) 1, 39, 85, 93, 96, 100, 102–4, 118, 122, 128, 172, 205, 239; invites Perdue on World Tour (1913) 108–10
McTigue, William Patrick (Rebel) 90–92, 95, 103
Meadows, Lee 126, *131*
Meis, Molly 172, 174, 177–79
Middleton, Jim (Rifle Jim) 126, 135, 139, 142
Miller, Roy (Doc) 98
Miracle Braves 115, 124
"mix 'em up" incident 105, 121
Modern Era 192
Molesworth, Carlton 85, 175
Monroe Park (Mobile) 51
Montgomery, Roy 61
Moran, Herbie 239–40
Morrow, Bryce 174, 180
Morse, Harry (Hap) 184–85, 190–91
Mother Dorn 127
Munson, Larry (Nashville radio sportscaster) 226
Murnane, Tim H. 92–93, 100
Murphy, Billy: criticism of Perdue 129–30
Murphy, Charles W. 109
Murphy, Frederic J. 90

Nashville American: baseball coverage 12; team nickname contest (1908) 49–50
Nashville and baseball: championship game (1908) 61–63, 225; commercial and sports rivalry with Memphis 42, 54; early amateur teams 12–13; early team nicknames 38, 41, 49; establishment of professional team 16; ex–Confederate iconography 70–71; new team owners (1908) 47; opening day ceremony 69
Nashville Athletic Club (NAC) 12
Nashville Banner: baseball coverage 12; team nickname contest (1908) 49–50
Nashville Elite Giants 180
Nashville Tennessean: baseball coverage 12; team nickname contest (1908) 49–50
National Association of Professional Baseball Leagues 21
Negro Southern League entrants 262*n*46
Nicklin, John B. 20
Nicklin, Strang 179, 181
Nicollet Park (Minneapolis) 155
Niehaus, Dick 125, 129
Niehoff, Bert 127
Northrop, George (Jerky Jake) 135, 139, 142
Noyes, Harry 69, 76–77
Nye, Jack H. 101

O'Connor, W.J. 122, 125; sports editor, *St. Louis Post-Dispatch* 120, 129
Old Brother Hubbard (poem) 122
Old Timers Baseball Association of Nashville (OTBA) 52, 209, 223, 237; award to Perdue 238; founding 222; organizational reforms 225–26
O'Leary, James C., Jr. 103–4, 110, 112–13, 254n52
Opening Day ceremonies 30–*31*, 69, 144, 153
O'Toole, Marty 104, 142

Paducah (Indians) 23–24
Page, George 90
Page, Louis 90
Paschal, Ben 206
Paskert, George (Dode) 1, 106, 112, 114, 132
Patten, Zeboim Cartter, Jr. 147
Patterson, Malcolm (governor of Tennessee) 60, 64, 69–70; debate with Carmack 57
Payne, George Washington 164, 174, 177–79, 181–82, 189
Pearsons, Ed 41
Pepe, Joe 80, 172, 174, 180, 185, 188–89
Perdue, Cotton Warren (Cot) 9, 109, 209
Perdue, Daniel: family, landholdings and prosperity 6–7
Perdue, Daniel Green 7
Perdue, Herbert or Hub (The Gallatin Squash): appetite and overweight concerns 36, 39, 68, 78, 88, 109, 120–21, 207; arm therapy, surgeries and x-rays 80, 92–94, 137; baseball idiosyncrasies 32, 44–45; batting weakness 73, 100, 139, 205, 207, 238; birth 9; career pitching summaries 228–36; championship teams 29, 35, *63*–64, 124, 140, 154, 207, 236; childhood 10; claims to National Commission 42, 187; college baseball 10–11, 24; conflict with Kling 98–99; conflict with Stallings 105, 112–13, 115–16; conflict with Ward 96; connection with pool halls 67, 77; contract negotiation strategies 67, 77, 98–99, 114, 125; death 238–39; dismissal as manager of Nashville 186–87; early political interests 67; family tensions 221–22; feature articles in *Boston Daily Globe* 101; final season statistics 30, 35, 43, 64, 77, 87–88, 94, 100, 106, 124, 133, *141*, 150–52, 154–55, 159, 164–65, 205, 207; with Gallatin Butchers 14–15; generosity 211; greatest accomplishments 165, 236; habitual pitching trends 43–44, 87–88, 108, 157, 207; hired to manage Nashville 169, *176*; illegal pitches 113, 157, 160–63, 165; injuries 31, 65, 68–69, 73, 78–78, 80, 87, 89, 92, 102, 114, 125, 133, 137, 155, 161, 236; invitation to join World Tour (1913) 108–9; iron man performances 33, 42, 44, 53, 55–56, 83, *131*, 157–58, 206, 236; lost season (1905) 30; major league drafts 35–37, 54, 76, 83; marriage 11; memberships in fraternal, social and religious organizations 219, 222, 266n51; nicknames 5, 26, 28, 30, 41, 46, 56, 70–71, 82, 88, 100, *107*, 139, 142, 204, 239; off-season employment 50, 109, 134; opinion of Stallings 102, 116–17; Perdue-Torrey pitchers' duel 51–52, 223, 236; physical size 46; pitching mechanics 114–15; pitching records 52, 159, 236; poem 105; political aspirations and career 210–19; pride in Confederate heritage 8–9, 21–22, 118, 127; scouting interests 164–65, 209, 222, 266n46, 48; selection to all–Vols team 223; spitball secrets 108, 237; streak pitching 82, 87, 93, 96, 99, 105, 114, 122, 130, 140, 202, 204, 206; trade rumors and attempts 96, 102, 104, 109–*11*, 119, 126; trade to St. Louis 113, 119; union activity 99, 102, *111*, 114; WAR statistical value of 230; WHIP statistical value 231
Perdue, Jimmy 208, 215, 221 education 222, 266n41
Perdue, Kathryn (Pud): birth 14; death 208
Perdue, Mable Polk 11; death 226
Perdue, Marion Blair 8, 125, 221; death 209; estate 210; marriage and family 9; remarriage 21, 209; successful farmer and businessman 9
Perdue, Polk 219, 223; background 219–21; birth 14; death 266n40
Perdue, Virgil Blair 9, 21
Perdue, Zoritha E. (Durham) 9
Perritt, Pol 118, 126
Pershing, Gen. John (Black Jack) 152
Pfenninger, Dan (Vinegar Dan) (umpire) 74; background 252n44
Phelon, William A. 109
Phillips, William (Silver Bullet or Whoa Bill) 59
Poland, Hugh 225
Polk, Horace Shepherd 11
Polo Grounds (New York) 93, 96, 102, 104, 113, 122, 124, 127, 130–*31*
Ponce de Leon Park (Poncey) (Atlanta) 47–48, 75, 153, 156, 160, 182, 186
Powell, Abner 16, 20–21; background 245n46
Power, John T. 99
Portland (TN) 7, 211
prohibition (in Tennessee) 66, 70

Ragtime (novel, movie and musical) 239–40
Rariden, Bill 102
Ray, J.L. 173, 177–78, 181, 184; sports editor, *Nashville Banner* 164
Red Elm Park (Memphis) 16, 54, 80, 148; description 249n100;

Reese, Erma Perdue 209–10; birth 9
Reese Brothers Mule Company 210
Rice, Grantland 11, 18, 43, 46, 51–52, 56–59, 66, 69–71, 73–74, 76, 78–84, 108, 173, 205, 239; coins "greatest game ever played in Dixie" 64, 225; evaluation of Perdue's major league prospects 83; journalistic resumé 248*n*82; naming of Sulphur Dell 49; *Nashville* sports figure 12–13; poems 64, 72; relocation to New York City 85; sponsors Nashville's team nickname contest (1908) 49–50; sports editor, *Nashville Tennessean* 38
Rickert, Joe (Diamond Joe) 61, 225
Rickwood Field (Birmingham) 83, 160, 163–64, 175, 185
Roberts, Doak 203
Robertson, Jim 69, 76–77
Robinson, Jim *183*
Robinson, Wilbert (Uncle Robbie) 85
Robison Field (St. Louis) 119
Rogan, Frank 222, 266*n*45
Rogers, Harry (War Horse) 222, 225
Rogers, Tom (Shotgun) 138, 169, 237; later life 258*n*18; selection to all–Vols team 223
Rohe, George (Whitey) 61-*63*
Rudolph, Dick (Baldy) 102, 121, 132, 239
Russell, Fred 223–26, 237–38, 240; background 262*n*23; death 266*n*61; sports editor, *Nashville Banner* 113
Russell, William Hepburn 90, 93
Russwood (Memphis) 154, 164, 177; renovation (1915) 148
Rutledge, Lou 24

St. Charles Hotel (New Orleans) *40*, 56
Sallee, Harry (Slim) 1, 114, 118, 124, 126, 128
Salm, Walter 197–98, 200–4
Sample, Guy 20
Savidge, Ralph (The Human Ripcord) 52–53, 55
Schaefer, Herman (Germany) 2, 108, 240
Schwartz, Bill (Blab) 81, 84, 169
Seabough, J. Warren (Doc) 36, 55, 70, 74, 80, 86, 205; background 250*n*41
Sengtown (originally Perdue) (TN) 7
Sewell, Joe 161
Sheehan, Tom 156, 159, 166
Sheridan, J.B. 126
Shields, Charlie 42
Siegle, Johnny 51, 70, 76, 82–83
Sitton, Carl Vedder 53–54, 56, 59–60, 66, 83, 86; 61-*63*; background 250*n*33
Slag Pile (or Crampton Bowl, Birmingham) 42, 48
Slappey, John (Slim) 196–97
Sloan, James Aiken Green (J.A.G.) 47, 169, 171, 179, *183*, 185–87, 193, 262*n*1; challenge to Perdue 180

Smith, Herb (Doc) *183*, 185, 190–91
Smith, William (Tobacco Billy) 37, 41, 74, 77–78, 84, 195, 198
Sorrells, Bill 38, 42, 83; release 51
South Atlantic League (Sally) 264*n*53
South End Grounds III (Boston) 89–90
Southern Association: early shut down (1917) 154; final shut down (1961) 237; founding 15–18; introduction of ERA statistic (1917) 155, 165; Kent embezzlement scandal 19; Perdue's record 228–29; Reserve Clause 20; salary cap 77–78; scheduling irregularities and reforms 54, 77, 86, 178; team nicknames 250*n*16
Southern League 12, 20, 147; founding and financial weakness 17
Spalding's Guide 35, 167
Spatz, Lyle 130, 192
Speaker, Tris (Spoke) 1, 52, 86, 100, 142
Sporting Life 99, 127
The Sporting News 52, 113, 127, 166–67, 187, 240
Stallings, George Tweedy (Gentleman George) 104–13, 115, 119, 124–25, 134, 145–46, 224; career 101–2, 254*n*53; feature articles in *Boston Daily Globe* 115–16; "mix 'em up" incident 105, 121; platoon system 102
Stanton, John C. 147
Stanton Field (Chattanooga) 147
Statham, Bill 164, 174–75, 177–79, 181-*83*, 189
Steinberg, Steve 130, 192
Stellbauer, William Jennings 172–74, 177, 185, 187–88, 191, 195
Stengel, Charles (Casey) 1, 48, 122
Stockard, Sam J. 60
Stockton, Roy 126
Street, Charles (Gabby, or Old Sarge) 148
Sulphur Dell (Nashville) 75, 78, 136, 161, 182, 184; annual floodwaters 67; demolition 237; Dump references 48; improvements (1908) 47, 59–60; Opening Day ceremony 69; unique field layout 47–48
Sumner County (TN): antebellum plantations 7; Civil War actions 8; creation 6; early settlement and growth 6; economic growth (1920s) 213; expansion of transportation 7, 9–10; geographic description 5; impact of TVA 215; native unrest 6; political and social transformation 213, 216–19; restoration of county courthouse building *214*; World War II 215
Sumner County clerk: duties 210; Perdue's tenure as 210–19
Sweeney, Bill 36, 92, 99, 103, 109–10

Take Me Out to the Ball Game (song) 55
Tarlton, Bob 61-*63*, 223, 225

Tener, John K. 110, 113
Tenney, Fred 90, 92–93
Terry, John William 222
Tesreau, Jeff 1, 102, 114, 120, 230
Texas League: entrants 263n1
Thorn, John 235
Thorpe, Jim 1, 138
Tinker, Joe 109, 136
Titus, John 98, 104–5
Tonneman, Charlie 70, 74, 172, 174, 179–80
Torkelson, Chester (Red) 156, 158–59, 195, 238
Torrey, Lucien (Clarence): Perdue-Torrey pitchers' duel 51–52
Traynor, Harold (Pie) 175
Tuero, Oscar (The Cuban) 154
Tullatuckee Normal College 10
Turner, Jim (Milkman) 225, 237
Tyler, George (Lefty) 92, 100, 112, 120, 122

Vance, Clarence (Dazzy) 144, 149, 161, 164
Vaughn, Harry (Dad) 37
Veatch, Bill (Peek-a-boo) 32
Viebahn, Bill 73–74, 78–79
Vincennes (Alices) 24–28; championships 28–29; Ladies Day scandal 33
Vinson, Ted 77, 80, 82

Wade, Dealis (Chief) 164–65, 178–79, 181–83, 189–90
Wagner, Honus (The Flying Dutchman) 1–2, 105, 114, 240
Walker, Roy (Dixie) 159, 166

walks plus hits per innings pitched (WHIP) 231
Ward, John Montgomery 94–95, 98–99, 101; conflict with Perdue 96
Warmoth, Wallace (Cy) *171*-72, 174–75, 178, 181, 189
Wathen, Otho H. 136, 258n4
West Baden (IN) 35, 37
West End Park (Little Rock) 39; renamed 150
Wheat, Zack (Buck) 1, 55, 87, 89, 114, 122
Wheeler, Floyd (Rip) 197–98, 202, 205
Whitted, George (Possum) 101, 113, 132
Wilkerson, George (Wilk) 26, 34
Williams, Alf 60, 69
wins above replacement (WAR) 230
Wiseman, Julius Augustus (Doc) 18, 38, 42, 48, 55, 62, 64, 67, 70, 75, 78, 86, 190, 224; disciplining 76; friend of Huggins 118–19
"work or fight" order 152, 260n30
World Baseball Tour (1913) 108–10, 255n91

Yancey, Richard Hunter, Jr. 39, 42, 52, 57, 64, 173, 225; in Chattanooga (1909) 147; *Chattanooga Times* 147; official scorekeeper (Nashville) 61, 251n68; sponsors name-the-team contest in Nashville (1908) 49–50, 250n16; sports editor, *Nashville Banner* 38
Yerkes, Stanley (Yank) 38, 83; Hardy-Yerkes altercation 43, 54, 98; release 51
Young, Denton (Cy) 1, 93, 114; gift to Perdue 99

Zimmerman, Henry (Heinie) 106, 114, 128

www.ingramcontent.com/pod-product-compliance
Ingram Content Group UK Ltd.
Pitfield, Milton Keynes, MK11 3LW, UK
UKHW041928140426
5217IPUK00014B/368